Meatsplaining

ANIMAL PUBLICS

Melissa Boyde & Fiona Probyn-Rapsey, Series Editors

The Animal Publics series publishes new interdisciplinary research in animal studies. Taking inspiration from the varied and changing ways that humans and non-human animals interact, it investigates how animal life becomes public: attended to, listened to, made visible, included, and transformed.

Animal Death
Ed. Jay Johnston and Fiona Probyn-Rapsey

Animal Welfare in Australia: Politics and Policy
Peter Chen

Animals in the Anthropocene: Critical Perspectives on Non-human Futures
Ed. The Human Animal Research Network Editorial Collective

Cane Toads: A Tale of Sugar, Politics and Flawed Science
Nigel Turvey

Engaging with Animals: Interpretations of a Shared Existence
Ed. Georgette Leah Burns and Mandy Patersonn

Fighting Nature: Travelling Menageries, Animal Acts and War Shows
Peta Tait

The Flight of Birds: A Novel in Twelve Stories
Joshua Lobb

A Life for Animals
Christine Townend

Meatsplaining
Ed. Jason Hannan

Obaysch: A Hippopotamus in Victorian London
John Simons

Meatsplaining

The Animal Agriculture Industry and the Rhetoric of Denial

Edited by Jason Hannan

SYDNEY UNIVERSITY PRESS

First published by Sydney University Press
© Individual contributors 2020
© Sydney University Press 2020

Sydney University Press
Fisher Library F03
University of Sydney NSW 2006
AUSTRALIA
sup.info@sydney.edu.au
sydneyuniversitypress.com.au

A catalogue record for this book is available from the National Library of Australia.

NATIONAL
LIBRARY
OF AUSTRALIA

ISBN 9781743327104 paperback
ISBN 9781743327081 epub
ISBN 9781743327203 mobi
ISBN 9781743327210 pdf

For the Winnipeg vegan community

Contents

Acknowledgements   ix

Foreword   xiii

Introduction: The meat industry explains things to us   1
Jason Hannan

1   Pink slime is good for you? The animal-industrial complex   31
     as neoliberal–neoconservative corporate ventriloquism
     Norie Ross Singer

2   Grieg in the henhouse: 12 seconds at the contested   59
     intersections of human and nonhuman animal interests
     Daniel Lees Fryer

3   Ethical meat from family farms? Transparency and   79
     proximity in a blog marketing campaign on broiler
     production
     Saara Kupsala

4   Whose land? Whose beef? Marketing beef in Canada   103
     Kelsey Speakman

5   Colouring outside the lines: Symbolic legitimacy and the   135
    Dietary Guidelines for Americans
    Barbara Willard

6   Meat taboo: Climate change and the EU meat lobby   163
    Núria Almiron

7   Exporting meat, exporting progress? The Australian meat   187
    export industry and discourses of development and
    modernisation
    Eliza Waters and Gonzalo Villanueva

8   'Stewed in mighty symbolism of wealth, power and   209
    masculinity': The legitimation of 'meat'-eating through
    anti-vegan rhetoric in mainstream US news
    Lisa Barca

9   Veganism and Mi'kmaq legends   237
    Margaret Robinson

10 Nonhuman animal labour and transformative dialogue: 247
    (Re)worlding meat
    C. Vail Fletcher and Alexa M. Dare

11 The Save Movement: Bearing witness to suffering animals   267
    worldwide
    Anita Krajnc

12 Afterword: Meatsplaining in the Pyrocene   299
    Jason Hannan

About the Contributors   314

Index   319

Acknowledgements

This book is the product of a certain frustration, that of confronting the systematic, well-funded, and relentless propaganda of the animal agriculture industry, arguably one of the most powerful forms of modern industrial capitalism on the planet today. Although frustration can sometimes give way to a sense of futility, it can also lead to critique and resistance. One crucial step toward the latter end is to name the devil. That's what this book sets out to do. And so the idea of meatsplaining was born.

My interest in the rhetoric of the animal agriculture industry arose through my teaching and civic engagement. At the University of Winnipeg, I have been very fortunate to be able to teach a fun and rewarding course called The Rhetoric of Animality. I am grateful to my department Chair and dear friend Jaqueline McLeod Rogers for encouraging me to create this course in the first place and for giving me all the departmental support I could possibly ask for. Since introducing the course in 2015, I have had the pleasure of teaching some very bright students, who care deeply about animals and the planet. These students have come from a wide range of disciplines, creating a lively atmosphere for vigorous discussion and debate. This also means that I receive some highly original research papers, which have played a large part in my education about animal exploitation. I am grateful to my students for teaching me as much as I have taught them.

One of my main preoccupations over the last several years has been to work with an incredible committee to organise Winnipeg VegFest, an annual festival that attracts some 4,000 visitors each year. The primary aim of Winnipeg VegFest is to raise awareness about animals and the planet, and to cultivate an ethic and lifestyle of compassion. Each year, we host a remarkable lineup of speakers, who include academics, activists, artists, physicians, and scientists. Among them, I am especially grateful to Carol Adams, Milton Mills, Caldwell Esselstyn, Gary Francione, Anita Krajnc, Margaret Robinson, Camille Labchuk, Dave Nickarz, and Anna Pippus, from whom I have learned so much about the animal agriculture industry.

It also bears mentioning that this volume was designed explicitly with the Winnipeg VegFest community and similar communities across the globe in mind. It further bears mentioning that VegFest would not have been possible without the immense generosity of the University of Winnipeg and the Winnipeg Humane Society. Annette Trimbee, Chris Minaker, and Javier Schwersensky deserve special recognition and gratitude for their financial and institutional support for VegFest since its inception.

I wish to thank my colleagues at the University of Winnipeg and the University of Manitoba for their support for VegFest over the last few years: Fiona Green, Matthew Flisfeder, Robyn Flisfeder, Kimberley Ducey, Naniece Ibrahim, Peter Ives, Paul Lawrie, Rosaria Moretti-Lawrie, Ray Silvius, Jill Bucklaschuk, Arthur Walker-Jones, Sharanpal Ruprai, Dana Medoro, Serenity Joo, Jane Barter, Andrew McGillivray, Angela McGillivray, Delia Gavrus, Christina Fawcett, Alan Joseph McGreevy, and David Navratil.

I owe sincere thanks to Melissa Boyd and Fiona Probyn-Rapsey for taking the initial interest in this volume and for including it in their wonderful Animal Publics series at Sydney University Press. I also cannot speak highly enough of SUP's incredible staff. Sincere thanks are owed to Agata Mrva-Montoya, Denise O'Dea, Nathan Grice, Joanna Butler, Marie-Louise Taylor, and Susan Murray. They deserve high praises for their incredible professionalism and hard work, especially under the challenging conditions of the COVID-19 pandemic. It has been a sincere pleasure working with them.

Acknowledgements

Some of the material in this volume has been published previously. I would like to acknowledge the publishers for their permission to reprint that material here. A portion of the Introduction previously appeared in Hannan, J. (2019). A blind spot in political theory: Justice, deliberation, and animals. *Journal of Animal Ethics* 9(1), 27–38. Chapter Nine previously appeared in Robinson, M. (2013). Veganism and Mi'kmaq legends. *The Canadian Journal of Native Studies* 33(1), 189–196.

Lastly, I wish to thank the contributors to this volume, both for writing excellent chapters and for their patience as we navigated our way through the long and winding road to publication. Their contributions not just met, but far exceeded my expectations. I can only hope that they are as pleased with the final outcome as I am.

Foreword

Considerable social engineering has occurred in the last one hundred years to promote and increase the consumption of the flesh, eggs and milk of other animals, especially among the relatively more affluent throughout the world. In the United States the deadly theft of land from Indigenous peoples and free-living nonhuman animals made possible the profitable expansion of ranching. These economic gains were made even greater by the oppression of slaughterhouse workers – disproportionately people of colour and immigrants – who were economically coerced into killing ever-growing numbers of cows, pigs, chickens and similarly oppressed other animals. Such monstrous oppression was possible due to oppressors' control of the state apparatus, and it was rationalised and normalised through the use of speciesism, racism, sexism, classism and related ideologies spun and disseminated by capitalist elites. Early in the 20th century powerful business entities seized control of nascent mass media technology, including those companies within the animal-industrial complex who sought to convince the public that consumption of slaughterhouse fare was safe, healthy and essential.

For instance, in the 1920s, Edward L. Bernays, considered by some to be the founder of US public relations, created a campaign to promote a 'bacon and egg' breakfast, a morning meal he deviously implied was supported by physicians. Some very popular early 20th-century radio programs in the United States were sponsored by slaughterhouse firms, which included one starring comedians George Burns and Gracie Allen who plugged the George A. Hormel & Company product SPAM; derived from oppressed pigs. One of the first fast food companies, White Castle, campaigned at length to increase consumption of their 'hamburgers' by targeting college students, mothers and children with claims that their product was safe and highly nutritious. In advertisements during World War II the United States government perpetuated the long-standing idea that the consumption of 'meat' was very important for men, especially 'fighting men'.

Other powerful countries also violently expropriated lands for ranching and utilised similar strategies to increase the consumption of slaughterhouse products. In the 1950s, for example, slaughterhouse firms in Canada sought to promote outdoor barbequing by suggesting 'a direct relationship between meat, barbecuing and virile, heterosexual masculinity'. Chris Dummitt writes:

> [C]anadian Packers sought to strengthen the association between meat and barbecuing. In the summer of 1955, the company offered a free portable brazier to consumers who purchased a specific amount of their canned meat products, including beef stew, bologna, beans with wieners, and Klik pork luncheon meat. In the image accompanying the offer, a smiling apron-clad man serves a Fred-Flintstone-size steak to an appreciative female onlooker, suggesting that Canadian Packers could continue its service to the virile, meat-hungry new barbecue owner. (Chris Dummitt, 1998, 'Finding a Place for Father: Selling the Barbecue in Postwar Canada', *Journal of the Canadian Historical Association*, Volume 9, Number 1, 216). [Italics added]

For decades such advertising campaigns and related narratives thoroughly blanketed the cultures of many Western societies. One facet of this indoctrination has been the contention that human animals are natural flesh eaters and that 'meat' consumption is essential for human health. Indeed, for decades the academic establishment not only largely genuflected to the animal-industrial complex, but also promoted the idea that the practice of stalking, killing and eating other animals made possible both human social and brain development. As numerous scholars have observed, much of the established scholarship and theory of the past largely was a reflection of the hegemonic culture and conventions of the times.

Today, when growing numbers of people have instant access to information, it takes considerable ideological manoeuvring to maintain the nefarious belief that most nonhuman inhabitants of the planet are merely 'food' and that their oppression is both natural and necessary. The rapidly growing body of critical work by new generations of scholars is producing a rising public awareness of the awful oppression of other animals and its connection to a myriad of critical global problems, which includes the climate emergency and the growing threat of a deadly global pandemic. And today scholars increasingly are talking about the entangled oppression of humans and other animals, oppression that is entangled economically, politically and ideologically. In response to this growing public consciousness of the harms resulting from the oppression of other animals, the defenders of the slaughterhouse companies and related enterprises are working overtime, and with considerable imagination, to counter truth telling and calls for justice and total liberation.

This powerful volume brings into focus and critically examines the rhetorical devices and arguments used to defend the continued oppression of other animals as food. Professor Hannan has masterfully assembled works from brilliant scholars who expose and challenge some of the spurious and dangerous rationalisations spewed by those industries that profit from unspeakable suffering and global destruction. This powerful, timely and essential work exposes 'meatsplaining' and will no doubt help to facilitate the awareness and resistance necessary for the creation of a truly sustainable global food system and a more just future for all.

David Nibert
Professor of Sociology
Wittenberg University

Introduction: The meat industry explains things to us

Jason Hannan

I live in Winnipeg, Manitoba. My province is celebrated for its vast prairie landscapes, its quiet and peaceful lakes, its rustic lifestyle and its warm and friendly people. In the popular Canadian imagination, Manitoba represents nature at its most innocent and pristine. One thinks of endless beige grasslands, softly blowing in the wind against a backdrop of deep-blue skies and a radiant sun. Culturally, Manitoba represents a folksy pastoralism, exemplified by a social gospel of community, an ethic of humility and the value of modesty. This popular image, poetic and romantic, is a powerful and evocative medium for promoting tourism in the province. It's also a powerful and evocative medium for promoting local industry.

Manitoba happens to be the largest pork-producing province in the country. This status is a point of pride for Manitoba Pork, a massive and powerful lobby group representing the local hog industry. Manitoba Pork exploits the popular image of the province as pristine prairie country, and of Manitobans as good-natured people. They exploit this image to tell a clever and crafty story. Through billboards that blanket local cities, buses and highways, Manitoba Pork disseminates images of an innocent farming community, run exclusively by small, local families who have only the purest of intentions at heart.

These images are also found on their website. In one such image, we see a father standing alongside his son, looking out to the

1

horizon.[1] In another, we see a young woman smiling in a vast green field, her family's farm in the background.[2] In a third, we see a happy couple standing in front of their farm, proudly posing with their two young children.[3] Everyone in these images is white, a deliberate casting choice designed to feed the industry's self-congratulatory image of purity and innocence. The billboards tell a story of hardworking people, a virtuous animal farming industry and the importance of animal farming to the local economy. Perhaps most crucially, they tell a story of community, in which Manitobans work together for the environment, produce nutritious food and uphold animal welfare. With the industry's numerous hog barns located deep in the countryside, conveniently out of the public eye, city dwellers and even country folk can be forgiven for buying into the myth of a benign and bucolic hog industry.

That myth, carefully crafted over a decades-long public relations campaign, occasionally gets punctured and torn asunder. When it does, it reveals a black and hellish nightmare. One such case arose after an undercover investigation in 2012 by the animal advocacy organisation Mercy For Animals. In a video released to CTV's *W5*, a current affairs program featuring investigative and undercover reporting, Mercy For Animals captured horrifying footage of animal abuse that contradicted the popular myth of an ethical and compassionate hog industry.[4] The footage shows filthy living conditions for thousands upon thousands of pigs. It shows pregnant sows imprisoned in gestation crates, barely larger than their bodies and tight enough to prevent the sows from ever turning around. It shows workers trying, but failing, to kill a sow with a bolt gun, eventually resorting to a steel rod to get the job done. It shows workers kicking adult pigs and using electric prods to force them to move from one part of the enclosure to another. It shows tiny piglets getting their tails cut off and male piglets getting castrated. Both procedures are carried out without any anaesthetic. It is impossible to forget the haunting squeals of the tiny piglets. They

---

1   Manitoba Pork, 'Producers'.
2   Manitoba Pork, 'Economy'.
3   Manitoba Pork, 'Sustainability Focus'.
4   Kennedy 2014.

are the stuff of nightmares. But unlike the viewer, who is likely to be traumatised by the footage, the farm workers captured in the video appear to have fallen into the monotony of routine violence. They betray no signs of sympathy for the animals under their care – only impatience, frustration, annoyance and anger.

The most disturbing footage in the video involves the killing of piglets deemed deficient for the purposes of hog production. Some of these piglets are injured. Others are deformed. Others still are sick. The cost of caring for them far outweighs the cost of disposing of them. These tiny animals are picked up by their back legs and forcefully slammed onto a concrete floor. The aim is to inflict blunt trauma to the head, cracking the skull and severely damaging the brain, thereby permanently knocking the tiny animals out of consciousness, though not necessarily killing them. The workers assigned to this uniquely sadistic task go through the motions like workers at an ordinary assembly line. The motions are mindless and repetitive. They're carried out with not even the slightest thought or reflection. From the workers' perspective, the only guiding principle is efficiency. Anything less than unthinking, unreflective and efficient killing would slow down this part of the hog barn operation.

Yet several of the piglets fail to be knocked out after the first swing. They lie on the floor, writhing and twitching on the bloodstained concrete, tortured by what must be the most excruciating and unbearable pain. These piglets, the least fortunate among them, are picked up and slammed again and again until they are finally knocked out. Their bodies are then thrown into a giant pile of their dead brothers and sisters. Even then, several bodies in the pile appear to be moving. For all the priority devoted to efficiency, the hog industry clearly does not prioritise a quick and painless death for the tiny rejected creatures whose lives add zero value to the bottom line.

Yet the most shocking part of this story was not the undercover footage of animal cruelty, but rather the public statements by industry representatives. Almost all of what was captured by the undercover investigation, it turns out, falls under standard industry practices and guidelines. In Canada, it's perfectly legal to confine pregnant sows in small gestation crates. It's perfectly legal to kill them with a bolt gun. It's perfectly legal to cut off a piglet's tail and to castrate male piglets, and to perform both procedures without any anaesthetic. None of these practices violate Canadian law. All of them are sanctioned by the industry. Law and industry are intimate bedfellows. Even the practice of slamming a piglet onto a concrete floor is standard procedure. 'Blunt trauma,' says Dr Robert Friendship, an industry veterinarian, 'is regarded as an acceptable method of euthanasia in that it renders the pig quickly unconscious.' An 'acceptable method', Friendship says, with the voice of decisive moral authority.[5]

Industry standards are a curious thing. Slamming a piglet onto a concrete floor has been euphemised as 'thumping'. While one thump to kill a piglet is considered acceptable, multiple thumps are not. The piglet must be killed in the first thump. And while multiple shocks with an electric prod are considered unacceptable, single shocks are not. Presumably, then, the difference between single and multiple thumps, as between single and multiple shocks, is the difference between ethical and unethical – humane and inhumane – treatment. By this line of reasoning, if farm workers were simply to follow industry standards, they would necessarily be acting ethically and humanely. What the CTV story revealed, then, was not so much another unsettling case of animal cruelty, but rather the surreal nature by which the animal agriculture industry and, by extension, Canadian law manage to transform the most twisted and inhumane forms of behaviour into acceptable conduct through the invocation of 'standards' – a stark example of industry rationality resembling the absurdist bureaucratic universe of a Kafka novel. According to industry rationality, it's ethical if it's legal. It's ethical if it's standard practice. It's ethical if an industry veterinarian says so. By implication, anyone who protests to the contrary is naive and ignorant. But how could such atrocious logic have ever become normalised? Under what structure or system could it have achieved such power and authority? Through what analytical framework can we best make sense of the rhetoric of the animal agriculture industry?

---

5   Kennedy 2014.

Animals under capitalism

When Manitoba Pork creates an idyllic fantasy about pig farming, or when an industry spokesperson defends violence against farm animals as 'standard' practice, these are not individual and isolated cases of manipulative rhetoric. Rather, they form a genre of rhetoric that's part of a much larger and deeply entrenched system. That system has a name: capitalism. Shining a light on this system – its main components, its perverse logic, its driving force, its reactionary defence mechanisms – is essential for making sense of the rhetoric of the animal agriculture industry.

That rhetoric is best understood through a political economic lens. Arguably, the most systematic attempt to apply that lens is Bob Torres' *Making a Killing: The Political Economy of Animal Rights*.[6] In keeping with the Marxist roots of political economy, Torres follows Marx in starting with the particular and the concrete to arrive at the general and the abstract. That is, he starts with the commodity form of meat to arrive at a structural understanding of the meat industry. For Marx, the commodity is the secret to understanding the nature of capitalism. As Marx writes in the opening lines of the first volume of *Capital*:

> The wealth of societies in which the capitalist mode of production prevails appears as an 'immense collection of commodities'; the individual commodity appears as its elementary form. Our investigation therefore begins with the analysis of the commodity.[7]

The meat industry serves as a rather pertinent case study for Marx's analysis of capitalism. Torres uses the example of the hamburger, one of the most familiar and ubiquitous commodities in modern consumer culture, to illustrate the nature of meat as a commodity. When we buy a hamburger from a fast food restaurant, we buy a stand-alone product; that is, a product divorced from the sites and chains of production that created it. What we do with that hamburger after the fact is of no concern to the fast food restaurant. Whether we eat it, burn it or toss

---

6   Torres 2007.
7   Marx 1992 [1867], p. 125.

it, the restaurant only cares that it has been paid for. Following Marx, Torres observes that the hamburger thus holds two types of value: use value and exchange value. Use value is the satisfaction that a hamburger typically provides to the consumer. For the most part, people eat hamburgers to satisfy a hunger craving. Satiation is its use value.

Exchange value, on the other hand, is the financial value the hamburger holds in the marketplace, the arena of economic exchange. The hamburger is one commodity among countless commodities in a vast and complex system of production and consumption. For Marx, the central puzzle of the commodity is not its use value, but rather its exchange value. Why is *this* hamburger from *that* fast food restaurant worth so many dollars and cents? What does the price of the hamburger represent? More importantly, what does it conceal?[8]

According to Marx, when we delve deeper into the commodity form, we discover that commodities embody labour – the labour, for example, that went into the production of the meat, the bun and the condiments; into the transportation of each item from different sites of production; and into the preparation of the final product at the fast food restaurant. This labour is secured under a capitalist mode of production, an economic order in which a relative handful of wealthy individuals own the means of production, and a great mass of workers are forced to sell their labour in a competitive labour market for cut-throat wages in order to survive. Commodities are thus products of exploitation. They are the bearers and vessels of oppressive power relationships between capitalists and workers.

But as Marx points out, this relationship is obscured by a market-based society in which exchange value is the predominant form of value. We only see the final product and the price attached to it. We don't see the sites and chains of production, the complex history and exploitative relationships behind it. In a market-based society, all we see, because all we are conditioned to see, is exchange value. This widespread myopia has powerful implications for how we understand the world around us, including the people with whom we share that world. As Marx writes in the preface to *A Contribution to the Critique of Political Economy*:

---

8   Torres 2007, pp. 30–31.

In the social production of their lives, men enter into relations that are specific, necessary, and independent of their will, relations of production which correspond to a specific stage of development of their material productive forces. The totality of these relations of production forms the economic structure of society, the real basis from which arises a legal and political superstructure, and to which correspond specific forms of social consciousness. The mode of production of material life conditions the social, political, and intellectual life-process generally. *It is not the consciousness of men that specifies their being, but on the contrary their social being that specifies their consciousness.*[9]

This is one of the more powerful and enduring, if controversial, of Marx's many insights into the nature of capitalism. Our market-based society forces us, conditions us, into social relationships of market-based exchange. As members of the labour force, we think like commodities. We relate to one another as commodities. We even become commodities on the labour market, commodities in the giant cycle of production and consumption. The logic of the marketplace colonises our thinking, our perceptions, our values, our emotions, our basic structure of expectations. According to Marx, the tragic effect of this social and mental conditioning is the false belief that value inheres in products, rather than being artificially determined by the capitalist mode of production. We therefore treat commodities as isolated and independent objects – stand-alone units of wealth and value. Commodities thus take the form of what Marx calls a 'social hieroglyphic'.[10]

A hieroglyph is a code. It needs to be deciphered. In the case of commodities, the code obscures the nature of the referent. Marx refers to the formation of this 'social hieroglyphic', this process of mystification, as commodity fetishism. Commodities are fetishised when we see them as possessing inherent value and an independent existence. The danger of commodity fetishism is that it blinds us to the social and productive conditions out of which commodities arise. Commodity fetishism creates the fantasy of a commodity synthesised

---

9   Marx 1994, p. 211. Emphasis added.
10   Marx 1992 [1867], p. 167.

out of thin air, abstracted out of its exploitative conditions, cut off from its own history and origins. In the case of meat products, we speak of ' beef', 'pork', ' hamburgers', ' hotdogs', 'sausages', 'drumsticks' and 'paté', all showcased in bright colours, encased in shiny plastic packaging, bearing absolutely no correspondence to the animals from which they originated. Carol Adams calls this the 'absent referent'.[11] For most consumers, the absence of the animal referent, a formerly living, breathing, thinking, feeling being, does not register in their consciousness. These consumers are liable to be shocked when they realise the origins of some of their favourite meat products.

An example can help illustrate the power of commodity fetishism and the universal acid of exchange value. A clever prank on Brazilian TV, available on YouTube, features a fake butcher at the supermarket.[12] The butcher offers samples of pork sausage to passing customers, who try the samples and appear impressed. The butcher then asks the customers if they would like some fresh pork sausage. They agree. The butcher then turns the handle on a hilariously fake sausage-making machine, churning out links of sausage. But when the machine stops after two links, he asks the customers to wait patiently while he reaches behind the counter and picks up an adorable little piglet. To the customers' horror, he places the piglet inside the machine. Little do the customers know that the piglet is safely delivered into the arms of another actor hiding beneath the table. The butcher then proceeds to turn the handle. The machine emits a fake squealing sound and magically churns out more sausage links. The customers are aghast by what they see. One spits out her sample. Another pleads with the butcher to stop. A third physically tries to stop him from loading the piglet into the machine. A fourth looks around in wild disbelief. A fifth shakes her head and walks away in disgust. A sixth gets angry and hits the fake butcher on the arm – twice. They all refuse to buy the sausage. When it was just neatly arranged as samples on a plate, they had no problem with it. It was a stand-alone commodity, a product with no history. But when they were forced to make the connection between the commodity and the animal, they could not endure it. They had been

---

11   Adams 2015, p. 20.
12   Vatafuck 2012.

so conditioned to think in terms of exchange value, so brainwashed by commodity fetishism, that they appeared to think pork sausage somehow fell from the sky or perhaps grew on trees. The prank proved to be an amusing, albeit highly revealing, means of tearing through the illusion of the commodity and exposing the brutal reality behind the production of meat.

For Marx, tearing through the illusions of the commodity not only reveals the social relationships concealed within it, but also answers the puzzle of how the capitalist derives his profit. Just as the hamburger in Torres' example holds both use value and exchange value, the labour power of workers holds both types of value. The use value of labour power corresponds to the exchange value of the products of that labour in the marketplace. But the exchange value of labour power corresponds to the cost of the worker's subsistence, what we call subsistence wages. Marx discovered that the source of profit lies in the difference between the two. The capitalist does not acquire profit through bargaining in the marketplace. Rather, he secures it at the point of production. When the use value of labour exceeds its exchange value, the capitalist keeps the difference. This difference, which Marx calls surplus value, is the secret of the capitalist's profit.

Marx's theory of surplus value was intended to explain the extraction of profit through the exploitation of human workers. But what about animals? What status do they hold, what role do they play, in the business of animal farming? How does the capitalist extract value out of animals? One historian, Jason Hribal, argues that animals are members of the working class.[13] He challenges the idea that animals historically became private property through some natural process of domestication. He proposes a different history composed of three stages: expropriation, exploitation and resistance. Hribal replaces the term 'livestock' with 'living stock' to emphasise the status of farm animals as living commodities. But from the standpoint of the animals themselves, Hribal argues, they are not commodities, but rather slaves. They are forced against their will to perform labour: producing hair, leather, milk, eggs and flesh. Like slaves, animals receive no compensation for their labour. The surplus value goes entirely to the capitalist. In a gesture of solidarity,

---

13   Hribal 2003, pp. 435–453.

Hribal challenges mainstream labour history by acknowledging the role of animals in the history of capitalism. He rejects the anthropocentric conception of labour and expands the circle of the working class to include animals. In his more recent work, Hribal documents the history of animal resistance against capitalist exploitation, making the case for animal agency and political will.[14]

But Torres objects to the idea of farm animals as members of the working class.[15] While farm animals sometimes escape and sometimes fight back, they cannot organise. They cannot unionise. They cannot bring about a revolution. Yes, they have voices, but no *political* voice. Torres thinks of animals as somewhat like slaves and somewhat like workers, exhibiting patterns from each without being fully like either. He therefore invents a new category for the unique status of animals under capitalism: 'superexploited commodities'. Unlike workers, animals cannot freely opt out of their labour. They cannot leave the farm the way a human worker might leave the factory. Unlike human slaves, animals can be rapidly bred to develop more desirable and profitable bodies. They can be multiplied on an incomparably larger scale. Also, unlike human slaves, farm animals are eaten. Their body parts, bodily secretions and eggs become commodities. Torres is therefore right to place animals under an altogether different category.

What unifies the animal and the human slave, however, is their status as private property. Private property is central to capitalism. Those who own the factories have the power to exploit workers. But in the case of animal farms, those who own the animals have the power to exploit animal labour and animal bodies. Treating animals as property obliterates the distinction between animals and machines. Under capitalism, animals become machines.[16] They are treated like mechanical systems, into which the farmer adds inputs and from which he collects outputs. If the goal is money, it makes sense to manipulate the biology of animals and create mutant beings that produce more flesh, milk, eggs, leather, wool and fur. The only limitation to this mad drive to extract every last drop of profit from animal bodies are those

---

14   Hribal 2011.
15   Torres 2007, p. 39.
16   Harrison 2013.

imposed by their biology. At some point, animals will break. They can no longer give birth. They can no longer produce milk. They can no longer lay eggs. At that point, they either get discarded, slaughtered or turned into some new product, like animal feed, in a system eager to find value where value was never before thought to exist.

Although Marx did not concern himself with animals, he did regard private property as the root of all oppression. From a Marxist point of view, violence is encoded into a liberal society through the institution of private property. From an animal rights point of view, speciesism is encoded through that same institution. For all its talk of freedom and liberty, liberalism is a hierarchical worldview in which human subjects are naturally endowed with inalienable rights, including the right to own and exploit animals. To a bourgeois liberal who obsessively clings to the idea of private property, the animal liberation movement thus represents a grave existential threat. Animal liberation challenges the assumptions on which the entire liberal worldview and political economic order are based. Fierce opposition to animal liberation is therefore not just a matter of protecting private profit. It is also a matter of upholding an entire value system predicated upon human superiority over animals. Yet, this fierce opposition to animal liberation is just one reason for the reactionary rhetoric of the meat industry.

The threefold threat

If the meat industry is currently in the midst of a fierce propaganda battle to protect its public image, that's because it now confronts three distinct but extremely powerful threats to its power and legitimacy: moral, environmentalist and biomedical.

The moral threat

The first threat, as indicated above, is the moral critique of animal farming. This critique has grown in severity over time. Animal welfare groups have an old and venerable history dating back to the 19th century. These formative organisations were motivated by the biblical imperative to practise stewardship over divine creation. While these formative organisations initiated some of the first animal protection laws in the Western world, they by no means called for the abolition of animal farming.[17]

The birth of modern industrial animal farming both introduced a new form of systematic violence against animals yet also sparked the animal rights movement as we know it today. The development of large-scale animal farming, the reduction of farm animals to insentient machines, the increasing concentration of large numbers of animals in extremely confined spaces and the impersonal techniques of mass reproduction and mass slaughter effectively redefined the very idea of animal cruelty. The first highly publicised investigation into the horrors of the American meat industry was Upton Sinclair's classic and unforgettable novel *The Jungle*, first published in 1906.[18] A passionate and committed socialist who wished to expose the appalling treatment of migrant workers in Chicago's notorious stockyards, Sinclair's most significant achievement was to have thoroughly horrified the American public through his extremely graphic depiction of the dirty and inhumane conditions in the American meat industry. According to popular lore, Theodore Roosevelt is said to have thrown his breakfast sausages out the window after reading *The Jungle*. The severe public outrage ignited by *The Jungle* prompted Roosevelt in 1906 to sign the *Federal Meat Inspection Act* and the *Pure Food and Drug Act*.[19]

It would take another 60 years, however, before an organised movement against the meat industry would emerge. The 1960s saw the beginnings of this movement. Some of its earliest figures included John Prestige, founder of Hunt Saboteurs Association, a direct action group devoted to abolishing fox hunting in Britain; Ruth Harrison, author of *Animal Machines*[20]; novelist Brigid Brophy, author of the influential 1965 *Sunday Times* article 'The Rights of Animals'[21]; Richard Ryder, who coined the term 'speciesism'[22]; Stanley and Roslind Godlovitch,

---

17   Beers 2006.
18   Sinclair 1988.
19   Sinclair 1988, p. xii.
20   Harrison 2013.
21   Brophy 1965.

who edited the seminal 1974 collection *Animals, Men and Morals*[23]; and Peter Singer, author of the hugely influential *Animal Liberation*.[24] Singer has arguably played the biggest role in setting the terms for contemporary debate about animal ethics. Through his lucid prose and compelling arguments, he has put countless meat-eaters, including popular American writer Michael Pollan, on the defensive.[25] Singer also inspired Ingrid Newkirk to form PETA, the largest animal rights organisation in the world today.[26]

The rise of PETA onto the global stage has revolutionised the fight for animal rights. Although many animal rights activists have objected to PETA's tactics, including their infamous publicity stunts and deliberate, performative sexualisation of women's bodies, there is no question that PETA has effectively pushed the animal rights agenda into the mainstream of public consciousness. Through numerous investigations, PETA has exposed shocking brutality against animals in the meat, dairy, egg, fur, leather, vivisection and circus industries. These investigations have been effective in generating national and even international headlines, making PETA the main prism through which much of the world has learned about the problem of systemic violence against animals.

Other animal rights powerhouses include Mercy For Animals, Compassion Over Killing, Animal Aid UK, Animals Australia, Animal Angels, Animal Equality, Four Paws International, and Canadians for Ethical Treatment of Farm Animals. Together, these organisations have conducted a staggering number of investigations, producing bone-chilling video footage of wide-scale violence against animals – farmed and wild. While this footage sometimes receives coverage from major news organisations, it has more recently found a powerful outlet on social media. Through short, shocking but digestible video clips, which can easily be shared online, this cohort of animal rights organisations has disseminated and reinforced a simple yet compelling

---

22 Ryder 2005.
23 Godlovitch, Godlovitch & Harris 1974.
24 Singer 1995.
25 Pollan 2002.
26 Guither 1998, p. 48.

narrative about the meat industry as inherently abusive, inhumane, amoral and sociopathic. These efforts have since spawned a wave of so-called ag-gag laws, aimed at preserving secrecy and punishing animal activism.[27]

Documentary film has proven to be another potent means of raising awareness and shifting public opinion. Films such as *Earthlings*, *The Cove*, *Blackfish*, *Speciesism*, *Death on a Factory Farm* and *Dominion* have left audiences so shaken to their very core that they have been forced to re-examine their most basic values and practices, in many cases compelling them to go vegan. Animal rights films do more than show graphic footage of animal cruelty in different industries. They also tell a gripping story that places animal cruelty in perspective. They explain the reasons and the conditions behind the cruelty and what can be done to fight animal exploitation. To make the message accessible, animal rights documentaries are now freely available online. They are also shown in many classrooms at various levels, thereby fostering a critical perspective on animal industries in younger audiences. This accessibility explains in part why Millennials are now embracing veganism in larger numbers than any other age group.[28]

The environmentalist threat

In October 2018, the United Nations Intergovernmental Panel on Climate Change released an alarming report about the coming global warming apocalypse.[29] According to the IPCC report, average global temperatures would need to remain within 1.5 degrees Celsius of overall warming, as opposed to the 2 degrees recommended by the 2016 Paris climate agreement. Should we exceed 1.5 degrees, the IPCC report argues, the outcome would be grave: the complete eradication of coral reefs, uncontrollable wildfires, deadly heat waves, permanent droughts and disastrous floods. Beyond 1.5 degrees of warming, the global economy will experience a crushing blow, dropping by at least 20 per cent. Low-lying coastal cities will be wiped off the map. Tropical

---

27   Wilson 2014; Fiber-Ostrow & Lovell 2016.
28   Hancox 2018.
29   Masson-Delmotte et al. 2018.

diseases like dengue fever will claim tens of millions of lives. Hundreds of millions will suffer from water shortages. Grain production will drop by half, leading to severe food shortages. The coming water and food crises are expected to ignite lasting and bloody regional wars.

The very idea of runaway climate change and ecological catastrophe has justifiably created widespread fear about the fate of humanity and has led to increasing pressure on local and federal governments, as well as the United Nations, to take action and ensure a habitable planet for future generations. One sector that has come under intense scrutiny is the fossil fuel industry, which has acknowledged the reality of climate change in private for decades, yet has actively promoted climate denial in public.[30] But a less obvious sector coming under increasing scrutiny for its role in climate change is the animal agriculture industry.

Just two days after the release of the 2018 IPCC report, a landmark study published in *Nature* argued that our modern industrial food system is 'a major driver of climate change, changes in land use, depletion of freshwater resources, and pollution of aquatic and terrestrial ecosystems through excessive nitrogen and phosphorous inputs'.[31] The authors show that meat and dairy consumption is responsible for the highest percentages of phosphorous and nitrogen applications, blue-water use, cropland use and greenhouse gas emissions. The report warns that a failure to change our food system will mean that all of these environmental pressures will worsen dramatically over the next 40 years, with food-related greenhouse gas emissions expected to nearly double. The report also indicates that plant-based diets can help prevent the worsening of climate change. *The Guardian* translated the tame language of the *Nature* report into a blunt headline: 'Huge Reduction in Meat-Eating "Essential" to Avoid Climate Breakdown'.[32]

Yet, the IPCC report was hardly the first study to document the link between the meat industry and climate change. We have known about this link for at least two decades. In 2006, the UN Food and Agriculture

---

30   Washington & Cook 2011.
31   Springmann et al. 2018.
32   Carrington 2018.

Organization published *Livestock's Long Shadow: Environmental Issues and Options*.[33] The FAO report noted that livestock make up 20 per cent of the Earth's terrestrial biomass and that animal agriculture takes up 30 per cent of all arable land on Earth. The report also documents the staggering rate and scale of land degradation, deforestation, desertification and carbon emissions, and the role of livestock production in water depletion and pollution as well as being a threat to biodiversity. It proposes several measures for mitigating livestock-related climate change, including environmental regulations, technological development and suggestions for dietary change. The report notably found 'reasons for optimism' in 'the tendency towards vegetarianism within developed countries'.[34]

The increasing alarm about the meat industry's destructive effects on the environment has sparked a new movement that might be called climate veganism. The philosopher Ray Monk, a notable biographer of Bertrand Russell and Ludwig Wittgenstein, provides an excellent example of the rationale for climate veganism. In an essay for *The New Statesman* entitled 'Why I Became a Vegan – and Why You Should, Too', Monk writes about having shocked his friends and family by announcing that he had become vegan.[35] He admits his longstanding love of sausage, chicken and cheese. He also admits that he has long acknowledged the inherent brutality of animal farming. Yet what finally prompted him to go vegan was the realisation, brought home by recent studies, that animal agriculture is a driver of climate change and mass extinction. After reviewing the evidence from several recent studies, Monk confesses that he misses his sausage and cheese, but that 'for the sake of the planet, for the sake of animals, and for our own sake, veganism is an idea whose time has come'. It turns out that the possibility that we might wipe out the conditions for our own existence, along with that of countless other species, is a powerful reason for Monk and many others like him to change their diet, lifestyle and basic moral outlook on life.

---

33 Steinfeld et al. 2006.
34 Steinfeld et al. 2006, p. 11.
35 Monk 2017.

The biomedical threat

One of the fastest growing dietary movements to emerge over the last 15 years is health-based veganism. Two of the pre-eminent leaders of this movement are Dr T. Colin Campbell and Dr Caldwell Esselstyn. Campbell and Esselstyn have each made critical discoveries about the relationship between diet and disease. Together, they have pioneered a new dietary paradigm that entails the abandonment of animal foods and the embrace of a whole-foods, plant-based diet.

Campbell's principal contribution to biomedical research is a large-scale epidemiological study of rural China.[36] A collaborative project between Cornell University, Oxford University and the Chinese Academy of Preventive Medicine, the famed 'China Study' compared the relationship between diet and health outcomes in rural China. The study found a positive correlation between meat consumption and cancer mortality, but a negative correlation in the case of plant foods. Campbell and his colleagues reached the resounding conclusion that the dietary key to minimising cancer risk was the maximisation of plants in one's diet. Campbell later co-authored *The China Study*, a book inspired by the Cornell-Oxford-China project, exploring the effects of animal-based foods on various aspects of human health.[37] Reviewing hundreds of studies, *The China Study* demonstrates a solid link between the consumption of animal foods and a wide range of degenerative conditions, including different types of cancer, heart disease, diabetes, osteoporosis, rheumatoid arthritis, Alzheimer's and macular degeneration. *The China Study* was a surprising international bestseller.

Whereas Campbell discovered the benefits of a whole-foods, plant-based diet through the scientific route, Esselstyn discovered the same benefits through the clinical route. As a long-time surgeon at the Cleveland Clinic in Ohio, Esselstyn became intimately familiar with the challenges of treating heart disease through drugs and surgery. In the early 1980s, he had casually observed that in those parts of the world where people did not follow a meat-heavy Western diet, the rate of heart disease was dramatically lower. In 1985, Esselstyn therefore

---

36   Chen, Campbell, Junyao & Peto 1990.
37   Campbell & Campbell 2006.

decided to launch a program at the Cleveland Clinic to find out whether a plant-based diet could arrest or even reverse coronary artery disease (CAD). The initial study, which consisted of a modest 22 patients, found that in 17 of the patients, the progression of CAD had been completely arrested, and in four of the patients, it had actually been reversed. (One patient dropped out of the study.)[38] Though the study was small, it had nonetheless demonstrated the power of dietary intervention to tackle heart disease, the number one cause of death in the West.

Campbell and Esselstyn later became the focus of the 2011 documentary Forks Over Knives.[39] A synthesis of Campbell's and Esselstyn's research, *Forks Over Knives* managed to craft a compelling and accessible story about the disastrous effects of a meat-heavy diet on public health and the healing power of a whole foods, plant-based diet. *Forks Over Knives* has played a very big role in promoting health-based veganism. Other prominent names in this movement include Dr Michael Greger, Dr Melanie Joy, Dr Milton Mills and Dr Garth Davis. Through books, articles, public talks and interviews, these proponents of plant-based nutrition have become the icons of a new movement, whose remarkable staying power has defied critics who dismiss veganism as a mere fad diet. Just as the desire to avoid climate catastrophe is a powerful motivator to go vegan, the desire to avoid cancer and heart disease is a similarly powerful motivator.

The aim of this book

This book is about the meat industry's response to the threefold threat: moral, environmentalist and biomedical. In many ways, the predicament in which the industry today finds itself is similar to that of the fossil fuel industry. Scientific and environmental consensus now implicates the fossil fuel industry, threatening its power and profits. In response, the industry has launched a fierce public relations campaign to discredit its critics, control the popular narrative, and protect its public image. It has assembled a massive and powerful ideology

---

38   Esselstyn Jr, Ellis, Medendorp & Crowe 1995.
39   *Forks Over Knives*. 2011. Directed by Lee Fulkerson. New York: Virgil Films.

machine, composed of think-tanks and lobby groups that sow public confusion and doubt about climate change.[40] The primary form of reactionary industry rhetoric is denial – the denial of the empirical reality of climate change and the denial of the validity of climate science.[41] This reactionary rhetoric of denial takes several forms. It masquerades as scepticism. It brands climate change a scientific 'controversy'. It accuses climate scientists of fraud. It dismisses environmentalism as a false religion. It dismisses climate change as a liberal conspiracy. In its most extreme and cynical form, it describes climate change as an ideological tool for the spread of communism.[42]

Like the fossil fuel industry, the animal agriculture industry resorts to a rhetoric of denial. But the substance and machinery of that denial are complicated by the threefold threat. The animal agriculture industry lacks a singular analogue to climate denialism. To be sure, the reactionary rhetoric of the animal agriculture industry *is* denialism, but of multiple and distinct forms: the denial of violence against animals, the denial of environmental pollution and destruction, and the denial of the link between meat consumption and adverse health effects. How then should we conceptualise this denial? Through what overarching term? This book proposes the term *meatsplaining* as an umbrella concept for the multiple forms of denialism perpetuated by the animal agriculture industry. Meatsplaining, of course, is a play on mansplaining, the clever term that entered the digital feminist lexicon following the publication of Rebecca Solnit's now-classic essay, 'Men Explain Things to Me'.[43]

In her essay, Solnit recounts an unfortunate experience she had while attending an upper-crust social gathering at an opulent cabin on the slopes of Aspen, Colorado. Solnit, then in her forties, felt out of place among the crowd of older and distinguished guests. As she and a friend were getting ready to leave, the host insisted they stay for a while. Himself an older man, the host had heard that Solnit had

---

40 Washington & Cook, 2011.
41 I am using the term 'reactionary' here in the sense intended by Hirschman 1991; Robin 2017; and Shorten 2015.
42 McKewon 2012.
43 The original essay is reprinted in Solnit 2014.

recently published 'a couple of books' and wanted to hear what they were about. She had, in fact, published seven books. She began to talk about her most recent book, *River of Shadows: Eadweard Muybridge and the Technological Wild West*. The host then interrupted her and asked, 'And have you heard about the *very important* Muybridge book that came out this year?' Solnit wondered what the odds were of two Muybridge books being published in one year. He began telling her about this 'very important book', which she soon realised was hers. The host had assumed that she had not read it, let alone written it. He further assumed the authority to lecture her about it, even though he himself had not actually read the book but was instead merely going by a review in *The New York Times Book Review*. He had to be told repeatedly that it was her book before it finally sank in, at which point he was left 'stunned speechless'.[44] Incredibly, the host then carried on as before, now knowingly explaining a book to its author.

As Solnit observes, the simple yet forceful and commanding act of a man interrupting and talking down to a woman functions as a silencing mechanism. By assuming the authority to lecture others, men often reduce women to the role of passive students, thereby undermining their standing to speak. In doing so, they delineate certain types of social and intellectual territory as belonging exclusively to men. This subconscious exercise of patriarchal power is ubiquitous. As Solnit says:

> Every woman knows what I'm talking about. It's the presumption that makes it hard, at times, for any woman in any field; that keeps women from speaking up and from being heard when they dare; that crushes young women into silence by indicating, the way harassment on the street does, that this is not their world. It trains us in self-doubt and self-limitation just as it exercises men's unsupported overconfidence.[45]

The cultural norm of men explaining things to women, she says, is part of an 'archipelago of arrogance'.[46]

---

44 Solnit 2014, p. 4.
45 Solnit 2014, p. 4.
46 Solnit 2014, p. 8.

In many ways, the dynamic of obnoxious and overconfident men explaining things to women bears a striking similarity to the animal agriculture industry explaining things to its critics. Meatsplaining functions as a silencing mechanism. The extreme condescension and patronising character of meatsplaining serves to shut down critics of the meat industry, to paint them as and reduce them to petulant and ignorant children, to eliminate them from the sphere of rational discourse. Meatsplaining delineates discursive boundaries. It establishes who possesses and who lacks the credibility to speak about what happens in animal farms and slaughterhouses. It defines what constitutes the normal, the rational and the mainstream, and what constitutes the fringe. Those who are effectively boxed into the latter group by definition lack credibility. If vegans are branded as irrational, violent and extremist, they will perforce lack the moral standing to speak and be taken seriously.

Meatsplaining further rests on certain reductive tropes: that vegans necessarily have poor health; that they are ignorant about animals, ecology and human health; that vegans have some sort of scheming 'agenda', whereas the meat industry is somehow felicitously free of any such agenda; that vegans are too sanctimonious and lack a sense of humour, a popular trope that feeds anti-vegan trolls and even viral marketing campaigns[47]; that vegans are too angry and emotional for civilised gatherings; that vegans are simultaneously hypersensitive victims yet also tyrannical bullies; and that veganism, because it is inherently violent and extremist, is a threat to social order.[48]

Although the concept of meatsplaining intended in this volume refers primarily to a form of industry rhetoric, the phenomenon of meatsplaining also operates on an interpersonal level. Meatsplaining can be understood as an extension of mansplaining. It follows a similar gender dynamic and reproduces many of the same patterns of patriarchal power and domination. It is not a coincidence that vegans and animal rights activists are overwhelmingly women. In the United States, women make up almost 80 per cent of the vegan community.[49]

---

47 Waxman 2015; Todisco 2019.
48 MacInnis & Hodson 2017; Dhont & Hodson 2014.
49 Huffpost 2017.

That men make up only a fraction of the vegan community is a reflection of popular cultural attitudes about meat and masculinity. In many cultures, masculine identity is notoriously bound up with the performative consumption of meat, a phenomenon explored by Carol Adams in her classic study, *The Sexual Politics of Meat*.[50] Masculinity is a fragile and sensitive thing. It's easily threatened by critiques of cherished male myths, not least among them the myth that meat makes the man. It is not surprising, then, that so many men should feel threatened by veganism and become positively hysterical over the very idea of animal rights. Moreover, despite marketing attempts to portray the meat industry as woman-friendly, it remains overwhelmingly male-dominated.[51] There are, then, both cultural and institutional reasons why meatsplainers are, more often than not, men – men who presume the authority to lecture vegans about protein, canine teeth and the caveman diet.

This volume is a first attempt to bring systematic attention to the phenomenon of meatsplaining – an integral part of modern animal agriculture that has long evaded critical analysis. Like other profit-driven industries, the animal agriculture industry aggressively seeks to shield itself from external threats. To that end, it employs a distinct set of rhetorical strategies by which to neutralise public criticism and shield itself from public scrutiny. This volume is an exploration of those strategies. It seeks to answer the following questions: What are the recurring strategies of persuasion by which the meat industry alleviates public outrage over the treatment of animals? What narratives, myths and fantasies does the meat industry employ to sustain its image in the public imagination? How does it respond to concerns about its environmental impact? How does it respond to concerns about its impact on public health? How does it construct vegans and animal rights activists for the popular imagination? By no means a thorough and exhaustive set of analyses, this volume is merely an initial examination of animal agriculture industry rhetoric.

---

50   Adams 2015.
51   Slade 2016.

Chapter breakdown

This volume is divided into four parts. Part I examines the role of meatsplaining as a public relations strategy for specific animal industries: beef, eggs and poultry. Part II examines the role of meatsplaining in the context of government policy and international trade. Part III examines negative representations of vegans. The stereotyping of vegans as a fringe and exclusively white community is one of the most common strategies for discrediting veganism as a lifestyle. Lastly, Part IV explores forms of praxis against meatsplaining. The volume thus ends on a positive note by offering a framework for hope and resistance.

Part I: Farm animals

In 'Pink slime is good for you? The animal-industrial complex as neoliberal–neoconservative corporate ventriloquism', Norie Singer examines the American beef industry's handling of the notorious 'pink slime' scandal. In 2012, *ABC News* provided a shocking look at pink slime, the off-putting meat by-product used as a filler for ground beef and other meat products. The *ABC* exposé created a public relations nightmare for the beef industry. In response, the industry adopted the strategy of corporate ventriloquism: using external figures to speak and act for the industry. In this case, the corporate ventriloquism consisted of three distinct rhetorical techniques: the greenwashing of pink slime, the lateral appropriation of neoliberal talking points about consumer health and safety, and astroturfing on behalf of the industry through organisations such as the Center for Consumer Freedom. As Singer observes, while the pink slime scandal undoubtedly played a huge role in educating the public about the revolting nature of meat production, there is still a long way to go.

In 'Grieg in the henhouse: 12 seconds at the contested intersections of human and nonhuman animal interests', Daniel Lees Fryer analyses a short video ad that appeared on Facebook in 2017. The ad, just 12 seconds long, depicts an organic egg farmer playing Edvard Grieg's 'Morning Mood', a classic melody often used in children's cartoons, as a means of comforting and relaxing his egg-laying hens. Fryer examines the complex layers of meaning encoded into the seemingly simple video: animal welfare and ethical consumerism; the farmer as responsible steward, keeping his working hens happy; a romantic conception of Norwegian nationalism; and the reduction of animal farming to a form of visual entertainment. But the ad, far from being passively accepted by Facebook users, became a critical site of contestation and public deliberation over the ethics of animal farming. As Fryer argues, social media offer vegans and animal rights activists a public forum for critiquing the traditionally one-sided messaging of the animal agriculture industry, and for advocating on behalf of farm animals.

In 'Ethical meat from family farms? Transparency and proximity in a blog marketing campaign on broiler production', Saara Kupsala explores the rhetorical function of 'transparency' in the meat industry. Modern industrial animal agriculture has come under fire for the secrecy of its operations. To combat the popular image of secrecy, one meat industry marketing campaign in Finland invoked transparency and proximity as a way to promote a more humane image. This campaign involved food and lifestyle bloggers touring a Finnish broiler farm and slaughterhouse. The campaign presents a fascinating case study for the negotiation of meaning between the industry and the public. As Kupsala observes, many consumers challenged the marketing campaign, seeing through its strategic attempt at public image management. She rightly draws our attention to the ways in which 'the devices for enhancing transparency serve to conceal, rather than illuminate, key moral issues in meat production'.

In 'Whose land? Whose beef? Marketing beef in Canada', Kelsey Speakman explores the Canadian beef industry's campaign to construct a nationalist myth about Canadian beef. Her study concentrates on the marketing efforts of Canada Beef, an industry umbrella organisation devoted to the promotion of a crafty myth labelled the 'Canadian Beef Advantage', which blends elements of Canadian nationalism, innocent wilderness, frontier landscapes and good-natured family ranches. Speakman deftly deconstructs this myth through a critical discourse analysis. She shows how the industry narrative obscures a dark reality: European settlement of Indigenous land, the near-total extermination of the local buffalo population, and the reliance upon poor and desperate migrant workers. As Speakman demonstrates, the myth of the 'Canadian Beef Advantage' rests upon capitalist and colonial power and domination.

Part II: Policy, trade and development

In 'Colouring inside the lines: Symbolic legitimacy for meatsplaining in the Dietary Guidelines for Americans', Barbara Willard examines the meat industry's response to the proposal for revising the USDA's Dietary Guidelines for Americans (DGA). In light of the recent scientific consensus concerning the link between diet and the environment, the USDA's Dietary Guidelines Advisory Committee proposed incorporating sustainability into the DGA. The American diet, they argued, should be healthy not just for the human body but also for the planet. In response to this proposal, the American Meat Institute and the National Cattlemen's Beef Association immediately launched a critique of the proposal for a sustainable diet. They challenged the science behind the proposal, claiming that expert opinion is divided and that the proposal was therefore not based on 'sound science'. Willard finds a parallel between the meat industry's response to the Advisory Committee's proposal and the rhetoric of climate denial. Her chapter is a heartfelt plea to heed the scientific evidence and revise the DGA 'for the sake of the planet, our health, and most importantly the animals that suffer due to our unsustainable dietary patterns'.

In 'Meat taboo: Climate change and the EU meat lobby', Núria Almiron examines the public relations strategies of the European meat industry to preserve its unsustainable practices and avoid environmental regulations. Almiron documents how the industry shamelessly employs the tactics of the fossil fuel, tobacco and vivisection industries. Confronted by the empirical reality of climate change and the consensus of the scientific community, the European meat industry has sought to downplay the first and create doubts about the second. The industry's response to environmental concerns is to promote technological solutions, which conveniently enable the meat industry to avoid any fundamental change. As Almiron observes, this tactical response dodges moral responsibility for the industry's negative impact on the environment.

In 'Exporting meat, exporting progress? The Australian meat export industry and discourses of development and modernisation', Eliza Waters and Gonzalo Villanueva explore the rhetoric of development in the Australian meat industry. In response to the growing global demand for meat, the Australian meat industry has stepped up its exports to Asia and the Middle East. These exports are bolstered by a rhetoric of development about the importance of meat as a staple of modernity. Australian meat is constructed as a measure of wealth and status, an object of conspicuous consumption, a sustainable product and a necessary component of good health and nutrition. According to the development narrative, it is vital for non-Western countries not just to consume more meat, but to consume Australian meat in particular. As Waters and Villaneuva argue, the development narrative serves as an instrument of capitalism, colonialism and speciesism.

Part III: Representing vegans

In '"Stewed in mighty symbolism of wealth, power and masculinity": The legitimation of "meat"-eating through anti-vegan rhetoric in mainstream US news', Lisa Barca provides an invaluable look at the way veganism is represented in major American newspapers. Veganism, she notes, is fundamentally antithetical to capitalism. By contrast, mainstream news organisations are not just corporate entities; they are also voices of the capitalist political economic order. Barca therefore conducts a critical discourse analysis to uncover the patterns of bias in media coverage of veganism. She finds that positive coverage is limited to vegan recipes, while the ethical core of veganism is entirely overlooked. Veganism is often portrayed as a fad diet, an odd and amusingly eccentric practice set against the self-evident normalcy of eating meat. Worse, vegan activists are typically portrayed as irrational and extremist, while their critics are not. Barca offers some useful suggestions for journalists to provide better reporting on vegans and veganism.

In 'Veganism and Mi'kmaq Legends', Margaret Robinson proposes an eco-feminist and postcolonial reading of legends of the Mi'kmaq First Nations people of Nova Scotia to derive a novel basis for an Indigenous veganism. Against the European settler colonial worldview, which envisions humanity as standing above nature, Robinson's reading of Mi'kmaq legends calls for a radical equality between human and nonhuman animals. The dynamism and responsiveness of Aboriginal traditions, she argues, calls for a shift away from historical practices of hunting and fishing toward a lifestyle respectful of animals and nature. Robinson shows that a vegan lifestyle rooted in Aboriginal traditions challenges the rhetoric of the modern commercial fishing industry, which presents itself as the economic saviour of Aboriginal communities.

Part IV: Resistance

In 'Nonhuman animal labour and transformative dialogue: (Re)worlding meat', C. Vail Fletcher and Alexa Dare examine the terms, tropes and presuppositions of public and private discussions about meat. They find that these discussions are mediated through a logic and worldview shaped by meat industry rhetoric, which upholds human power and domination over nonhuman animals. Drawing from Donna Haraway, they propose a strategy of disruption, of unsettling the implicit humanistic biases that shape public discussions about meat. Instead, they suggest a different model of public communication, one that avoids the lure of meat industry logic.

In 'The Save Movement: Bearing witness to suffering animals worldwide', Anita Krajnc provides a remarkable account of the explosive rise of the global Save Movement. Krajnc achieved international fame after facing a criminal prosecution for feeding water to pigs on their way to slaughter. This simple act of compassion became the Save Movement's iconic gesture of bearing witness to farm animals. Inspired by Krajnc's activism and her victory in court, Save Movement chapters have been established all over the world. In her essay, Krajnc narrates a powerful story of hope and resistance, as thousands of activists make use of social media, as well as the tools of labour organising and strategising, to build a truly global movement devoted to the world's most vulnerable beings.

References

Adams, C. (2015). *The Sexual Politics of Meat: A Feminist-Vegetarian Critical Theory*. New York: Bloomsbury.

Beers, D. (2006). *Of Cruelty: The History and Legacy of Animal Rights Activism in the United States*. Athens, OH: Swallow Press/Ohio University Press.

Brophy, B. (1965). The rights of animals. *The Sunday Times*. 10 October. Reprinted in Brophy, B. (1966). *Don't Ever Forget: Collective Views and Reviews*. London: Jonathan Cape, 5–21.

Campbell, T. C. and T. M. Campbell, II (2006). *The China Study: The Most Comprehensive Study of Nutrition Ever Conducted and the Startling Implications for Diet, Weight Loss, and Long-Term Health*. Dallas, Texas: Benbella Books.

Carrington, D. (2018). Huge reduction in meat-eating 'essential' to avoid climate breakdown. *The Guardian*. 10 October. https://bit.ly/3288202

Chen, J., T. C. Campbell, L. Junyao and R. Peto. (1990). *Diet, Lifestyle, and Mortality in China: A Study of the Characteristics of 65 Chinese Counties*. Ithaca, NY: Cornell University Press.

Dhont, K. and G. Hodson (Eds.) (2019). *Why We Love and Exploit Animals: Bridging Insights from Academia and Advocacy*. London: Routledge.

Esselstyn Jr, C. B., S. G. Ellis, S. V. Medendorp and T. D. Crowe (1995). A strategy to arrest and reverse coronary artery disease: A 5-year longitudinal study of a single physician's practice. *Journal of Family Practice* 41(6), 560–569.

Fiber-Ostrow, P. and J. S. Lovell (2016). Behind a veil of secrecy: Animal abuse, factory farms, and ag-gag legislation. *Contemporary Justice Review* 19(2), 230–249.

Godlovitch, R., S. Godlovitch and J. Harris (Eds.) (1974) *Animals, Men, and Morals*. New York: Grove Press.

Guither, H. D. (1998). *Animal Rights: History and Scope of a Radical Social Movement*. Carbondale, IL: University of Southern Illinois Press.

Hancox, D. (2018). The unstoppable rise of veganism: How a fringe movement went mainstream. *The Guardian*. 1 April. https://bit.ly/2CF3ENe.

Harrison, R. (2013). *Animal Machines*. Oxfordshire, UK: CABI.

Hirschman, A. (1991). *The Rhetoric of Reaction: Perversity, Futility, Jeopardy*. Cambridge, MA: Harvard/Belknap.

Hribal, J. (2003). 'Animals are part of the working class': A challenge to labor history. *Labor History* 44(4), 435–453.

Hribal, J. (2011). *Fear of the Animal Planet: The Hidden History of Animal Resistance*. Chico, CA: AK Press.

Huffpost (2017). Veganism is a woman's lifestyle, according to statistics. *Huffington Post. 6* December. https://bit.ly/3kT54ow

Kennedy, T. (2014). Undercover investigation reveals disturbing and inhumane treatment of factory farm animals. *CTV News.* 20 June. https://bit.ly/2FrbcnE

MacInnis, C. C., and G. Hodson (2017). It ain't easy eating greens: Evidence of bias toward vegetarians and vegans from both source and target. *Group Processes & Intergroup Relations* 20(6), 721–744.

Manitoba Pork (n.d.). Economy. https://bit.ly/2Q4lzzQ

Manitoba Pork (n.d.). Producers. https://www.manitobapork.com/producers

Manitoba Pork (n.d.). Sustainability Focus. https://bit.ly/315MtxL

Marx, K. (1992, [1867]). *Capital: Volume 1.* London: Penguin.

Marx, K. (1994). *Selected Writings* (L. H. Simon, Ed.). Indianapolis, IN: Hackett Publishing.

Masson-Delmotte, V., P. Zhai, H-O Pörtner, D. Roberts, J. Skea, P. R. Shukla, ... T. Waterfield (Eds.) (2018). Global warming of 1.5°C: An IPCC Special Report on the impacts of global warming of 1.5°C above pre-industrial levels and related global greenhouse gas emission pathways, in the context of strengthening the global response to the threat of climate change, sustainable development, and efforts to eradicate poverty. Geneva: Intergovernmental Panel on Climate Change.

McKewon, E. (2012). Talking points ammo: The use of neoliberal think tank fantasy themes to delegitimise scientific knowledge of climate change in Australian newspapers. *Journalism Studies* 13(2), 277–297.

Monk, R. (2017). Why I became a vegan – and why you should, too. *New Statesman.* 1 November. https://bit.ly/ns-vegan

Pollan, M. (2002). An animal's place. *The New York Times Magazine.* 10 November. https://www.nytimes.com/2002/11/10/magazine/an-animal-s-place.html

Robin, C. (2017). *The Reactionary Mind: Conservatism from Edmund Burke to Donald Trump* (2nd ed.). Oxford, UK: Oxford University Press.

Ryder, R. (2005). All beings that feel pain deserve human rights. *The Guardian.* 6 August. https://www.theguardian.com/uk/2005/aug/06/animalwelfare

Shorten, R. (2015). Reactionary rhetoric reconsidered. *Journal of Political Ideologies,* 20(2), 179–200.

Sinclair, U. (1988). *The Jungle.* Champaign, IL: University of Illinois Press.

Singer, P. (1995). *Animal Liberation.* New York: Random House.

Slade, R. (2016). The male-dominated meat industry is in need of skilled labor. Why not women? *The Boston Globe.* 31 October. https://bit.ly/3iRuhxP

Solnit, R. (2014). *Men Explain Things to Me.* Chicago, IL: Haymarket Books.

Springmann, M., M. Clark, D. Mason-D'Croz, K. Wiebe, B. L. Bodirsky, L. Lassaletta, … W. Willet (2018). Options for keeping the food system within environmental limits. *Nature* 562(7728), 519–525.

Steinfeld, H., P. Gerber, T. D. Wassenaar, V. Castel, M. Rosales, and C. de Haan (2006). *Livestock's long shadow: Environmental issues and options*. Rome: Food & Agriculture Organization of the United Nations.

Todisco, E. (2019). Arby's trolls vegans and Impossible Burger fans by making 'carrots' made entirely of meats. *People*. 26 June. https://bit.ly/3iUNtLf

Torres, B. (2007). *Making a killing: the political economy of animal rights*. Oakland, CA: AK Press.

Vatafuck (2012). Brazilian Prank: Sausages [video]. 28 November 2012. https://youtu.be/NG4WhppBNCM

Washington, H. and J. Cook (2011). *Climate Change Denial: Heads in the Sand*. New York: Earthscan.

Waxman, O. (2015). Arby's launches bacon hotline for 'tempted' vegetarians. *Time*. 7 July. https://time.com/3944920/arbys-vegetarian-support-hotline/

Wilson, L. (2014). Ag-gag laws: A shift in the wrong direction for animal welfare on farms. *Golden Gate University Law Review* 44(2014), 311.

1
Pink slime is good for you? The animal-industrial complex as neoliberal–neoconservative corporate ventriloquism

Norie Ross Singer

In the United States, much of the current discussion about the dire state of food and agriculture under the dominant industrial model is symptomatic of cultural anxiety about 'fake food'. Low-priced processed meat products (i.e. 'mystery meats') such as those found in the frozen food aisle, at fast food and buffet restaurants and in school lunch lines have long been a topic of concern. Media attention to what has been derogatorily described as the 'pink slime' product in some of the ground beef sold in the US has invigorated this discourse about mystery meat and shaken the beef industry to an extent seldom seen before.

When *ABC News* televised an investigative series on pink slime in 2012, critical media publicity that had been building since 2009 expanded into a full-blown national controversy. Borrowing from a US Department of Agriculture (USDA) scientist's email, the exposé used the expression pink slime to describe an inexpensive and low-grade, ground beef 'filler' that the industry calls 'lean finely textured beef' (LFTB).[1] Animal-industrial complex (AIC) public relations strategists had previously countered statements made by the *New York Times*, industrial food critic and television chef Jamie Oliver, and the acclaimed documentary *Food, Inc.*[2] However, it was the *ABC* series that

---

1 Greene 2012.
2 Greene 2012.

31

finally triggered a public relations crisis and had the most dramatic effect. Most impacted were LFTB processors, especially Beef Products Incorporated (BPI), the company on which the series focused.

BPI responded with one of the largest defamation suits in US history. BPI's lawsuit alleged that *ABC News*' use of the pink slime term hundreds of times as well as nearly two hundred false claims created three key misperceptions: LFTB is unsafe, is not nutritious and is hidden in ground beef.[3] In South Dakota, where BPI filed the lawsuit, unlawful food disparagement refers to knowingly disseminating:

> a false statement or implication that an agricultural food product is *not safe* for consumption by the public or that generally accepted agricultural and management practices make agricultural food products *unsafe* for consumption by the public.[4]

State-level food disparagement laws have long been criticised in the US as outcomes of the well-documented brute political lobbying influence of so-called Big Ag and Big Food.[5] Critics argue that 'food libel laws' as well as 'farm protection' or 'ag-gag laws' reflect corrupt corporate–state policymaking intended to stifle industry criticism.[6] Ag-gag laws make whistleblowing through undercover photography and video-recording of industrial animal agricultural production and processing facilities illegal.[7] Food libel laws have often been scrutinised for lowering barriers of entry for food and agricultural corporations to use frivolous lawsuits against critics. Such laws were widely publicised in 1996 when beef industry interest groups sued talk show celebrity Oprah Winfrey. The industry sued Winfrey due to an on-air segment about mad cow disease (bovine spongiform encephalopathy, or BSE) in which she exclaimed that she would no longer eat hamburger.

At minimum, the animal-industrial complex's brute legal and political economic power may intimidate citizens and journalists from

---

3   Beef Products Incorporated 2012.
4   United States District Court 2012, p. 10. Emphasis added.
5   Hooks 1990; Nestle 2002.
6   Broad 2016, p. 49.
7   Broad 2016.

practising free speech on food and agricultural issues directly affecting them. Pinpointing some of the exact effects of this dominance on public discourse can be challenging because their presence is marked by absence, or what is not said or made visible. At a very general level, it may be obvious that what scholars such as Annie Potts describe as contemporary meat culture propagates the same commercial ideology as the animal-industrial complex.[8] However, to the extent that representational practices that create and maintain this ideological linkage between the AIC and meat culture are acts of commodification, their less obvious function is to generate comfort by concealing oppression and exploitation. As Carol J. Adams notes, meat culture and the AIC typically erase any visible connection or symbolic reference to the animal from which meat and other animal-based products derive.[9]

As Adams also points out, occasionally exposed ruptures such as the 1986 discovery of mad cow disease in cattle in the United Kingdom (and later several nations including the US) are exceptions to this dominant representational pattern.[10] Rather than random or coincidental, these ruptures, too, are part of a longitudinal pattern. The 1996 identification of a human equivalent to mad cow disease (Creutzfeldt-Jakob disease) thought to be obtained by consuming beef contaminated with cattle's central nervous system tissue attests to this interconnectedness. The pink slime controversy is one of the more recent ruptures adding to this pattern.

One way of assessing the significance of such moments of rupture in the animal-industrial complex is through their tangible outcomes. As BPI's lawsuit against *ABC* approached five years of litigation, involved parties settled out of court to an undisclosed amount estimated at over $100 million, though much less than the $1.9 billion that BPI originally sought.[11] Despite this massive settlement, *ABC*'s steadfast unwillingness to rescind its reporting stands as a meaningful democratic act of journalistic resistance to agribusiness and food industry interest groups' coercive power. In a congressional report

---

8   Potts 2017.
9   Adams 2018.
10   Adams 2018.
11   Flynn 2017.

featuring a broad index of the pink slime debacle's effects on the US beef industry, Joel L. Greene writes that the 'controversy demonstrates that consumers' perceptions and understanding of modern food production can quickly affect markets and/or a company's business'.[12] Greene adds that media depiction of lean finely textured beef as pink slime 'raised the product's "yuck" factor and implied there were food safety issues with LFTB, mainly because ammonium gas is used as an antimicrobial intervention in the production of LFTB'.[13]

Consider the following gains that critical media publicity generated for animal-industrial complex reform. When citizens called for the USDA to eliminate lean finely textured beef from the school lunch program, the agency responded that it would change its policy to give schools the choice to purchase ground beef without the pink slime product in it.[14] By 2014, the USDA estimated that industry sales of LFTB to school lunch programs had declined by 94 per cent.[15] Also as a result of the controversy, major grocery chains announced they would stop selling ground beef with LFTB in it, while others such as Walmart followed the USDA, stating they would begin to give consumers the choice of buying pink-slime-free ground beef.[16] In the restaurant sector, fast food giant Wendy's ran a series of national newspaper ads clarifying that due to quality concerns, it had never used LFTB in its hamburgers. Wendy's followed other major chains, including McDonald's, Burger King and Taco Bell, which in 2011 responded to an initial wave of critical pink slime publicity by announcing they would no longer serve LFTB.[17] During this time, the price of LFTB sharply declined by 50 per cent as industry expectations for higher ground beef prices emerged. Within only a matter of weeks from the time the *ABC* series aired, AFA Foods, a LFTB producer annually selling nearly 500 million pounds of ground beef, filed for bankruptcy.[18] Other processors decided to begin to label ground beef

---

12 Greene 2012, p. 1.
13 Greene 2012, p. 1.
14 Greene 2012.
15 Bloomberg 2014.
16 Greene 2012; Walmart 2012.
17 Baertlein & Geller 2012; Andrews 2012.
18 Gleason & Berry 2012.

containing the product.[19] One of them, Cargill, announced that it would label all ground beef containing LFTB 'to enhance consumer awareness about ground beef products regarding how they are made and used'.[20] BPI suffered most, closing three of its four plants and laying off at least 650 employees.[21]

Even though there is no guarantee that some of these material effects of negative media publicity will be permanent, they are nonetheless striking. Although food defamation laws helped BPI reach a financially lucrative outcome, the opposition achieved meaningful gains outside the courtroom. The controversy vividly displays that a primary objective of institutions of industrial modernity such as the AIC is to manage perceptions of risk through means of social production such as public relations, marketing and lobbying.[22] Having co-produced a 'global risk society' characterised by new risks to human health and the environment, and constant development of new systems to manage them, such institutions are increasingly defending their claim to expertise to preserve public trust.[23] How the AIC has responded beyond the legal sphere, namely by using strategic discourse to defend and restore its image, is likely a major determinant of the nature of its post-crisis relationships with customers and other key audiences.

Despite the AIC's enormous influence, few studies have directly examined how the AIC uses careful rhetorical manoeuvring in ways that may shape to its advantage what counts as knowledge and ignorance about its animal-based products. Scholars Cathy B. Glenn, Ellen W. Gorsevski, and Garrett M. Broad stress the importance of further work on this discursive dimension of the AIC's power.[24] The critical reading of AIC 'meatsplaining' that I perform situates the animal-industrial complex's account of pink slime as a contextually adapted articulation of already-dominant ideological discourses and value frames. As Broad writes, close study of the AIC's narrative

---

19   Greene 2012.
20   Cargill 2013.
21   Andrews 2012.
22   Giddens 1990.
23   Beck 1999.
24   Glenn 2004; Gorsevski 2015; Broad 2016.

explanations of 'what industrial animal agriculture is, what it does, and what we should do about it' helps us carefully weigh the possible futures of food and the risks they present.[25] Following Broad, I take interest in how the AIC configures discourse and value systems, in this case to secure a particular understanding of LFTB. The AIC's defence of LFTB is reflective of what I contend is a troubling dependence upon what Jen Schneider, Steve Schwarze, Peter K. Bsumek, and Jennifer Peeples call rhetorical modes of corporate ventriloquism.[26] Before analysing the AIC's defence, I begin with a theoretical overview of their corporate ventriloquism model.

Corporate advocacy as ventriloquism

Corporate ventriloquism refers to a set of rhetorical modes that channel a corporate or industry voice through an agentic 'dummy/figure' (e.g. organisations, experts, ideologies) to generate public support or the appearance of it.[27] Ventriloquist modes generate an 'alternative ethos, voice, or identity' from which to speak that advances corporate interests.[28] The concept of corporate ventriloquism does not deny that corporations may also play the role of the dummy/figure, nor does it suggest that they are in complete control of their actions and destinies.

Francois Cooren writes that everyone acts as both ventriloquist and dummy/figure, though which one they perform depends on the moment of exchange. Dummies/figures, also called 'figures of authority', take various forms beyond the colloquial reference to a person of considerable power.[29] A law, a scientific study, a well-respected or otherwise power-holding organisation, citizen testimonies, or appeals to widely accepted values and beliefs are a few examples.

As I will demonstrate, the AIC's ventriloquising of figures of authority in its defence of LFTB activates three of the four corporate

---

25 Broad 2016, p. 46.
26 Schneider et al. 2016.
27 Cooren 2010, p. 90.
28 Schneider et al. 2016, p. 53.
29 Cooren 2012, p. 11.

ventriloquist modes that Jen Schneider et al. theorise: lateral appropriation, greenwashing and, to a lesser extent, astroturfing.[30] Lateral appropriation alludes to instances in which one group, who may be marginalised or dominant, uses means commonly associated with another similar or related group to further its own ends.[31] Powerful organisations such as corporations may use this strategy to adapt dominant ideological discourses to new circumstances. Rather than challenging or undermining the discourse that it appropriates (like greenwashing and astroturfing do), lateral appropriation extends this already-existing discourse into 'new discursive fields'.[32]

The animal-industrial complex's practice of lateral appropriation to address LFTB is an example of a powerful voice appropriating dominant ideological discourses of neoliberalism and neoconservativism. Neoliberal discourse emerged in the 1970s and 1980s through the installation of neoliberal/free market economic policies in various countries. Past scholarship theorises neoliberalism as a deeply consequential discursive formation of global political power taking various contextual forms.[33] Despite this variability, some conjoining features of neoliberalism make its fluid rhetorical repertoire identifiable.[34] Often using a realist or 'no-nonsense' rhetorical style, proponents of neoliberalism stress free trade, deregulated markets, faith in new technology, as well as privatisation of not only 'natural resources' but also social services and infrastructure. Neoliberal discourse also promises a near future of widened economic and cultural prosperity largely made possible by tax cuts for corporations and the wealthy.[35] Finally, neoliberalism redefines culture and citizenship as consumptive choice-making and meritocratic entrepreneurialism.[36]

Functioning as a political complement to neoliberalism, neoconservative discourse lends itself to stabilising the potential chaos of neoliberalism's ethic of individual freedoms and free market

---

30 Bsumek et al. 2014; Schneider et al. 2016.
31 Bsumek et al. 2014.
32 Bsumek et al. 2014, p. 25.
33 Chaput 2010; Couldry 2010; Singer 2010.
34 Aune 2001; Singer 2010; Singer 2017.
35 Aune 2001; Brown 2006; Harvey 2005.
36 Harvey 2005; Melamed 2006; Singer 2017.

accumulations of wide power disparities. According to Ann Norton and Wendy Brown, while not a unified or static discourse, neoconservatism is foremost committed to a strong state domestically and globally, in part through alliances of militarism, corporatism, anti-elitist (anti-decadence/anti-liberal latte) populism, theology and private virtue (e.g. traditional 'family values').[37] Brown suggests that although the two are in some ways at odds with each other (e.g. neoliberals envision borderless global commerce, neoconservatives want strong borders), neoliberal and neoconservative discourses unite in the form of a moral-market rationality.[38] The result, as Nick Couldry explains, is a potent rhetorical hybrid and a 'societal crisis of voice'.[39]

The lateral appropriation of ideological discourses such as those of neoconservativism and neoliberalism may be performed in tandem with other corporate ventriloquist modes, including astroturfing and greenwashing. Astroturfing entails creating the illusion of a largely spontaneous voice of grassroots citizen advocacy that, in reality, corporate or industry interests have rhetorically manufactured. In some instances, astroturfing appears in the temporary form of a public letter or other simulation of protest. In others, astroturfing may consist of a long-term project such as a front group or philanthropic organisation, which has been directly or indirectly funded or otherwise steered by industry.[40] Equally deceptive, the ventriloquist mode of greenwashing consists of what J. Robert Cox describes as 'the act of misleading consumers regarding the environmental practices of a company or the environmental benefits of a product or service'.[41] Greenwashing may also consist of disavowing or downplaying industrial environmental risks, threats and realised consequences.[42]

Despite the omnipresence of these corporate ventriloquist modes in everyday public discourse, the relatively little critical scholarship on the AIC's rhetorical practices tends to focus only on corporate

---

37 Brown 2006; Norton 2004.
38 Brown 2006.
39 Couldry 2010.
40 Bsumek et al. 2014, p. 26.
41 Cox 2010, p. 345.
42 Pezzullo 2003, p. 346.

advertising and branding, and without attention to multi-vocality.[43] Cathy B. Glenn argues that further inquiry on (animal) factory farm industry discourse will foster a better understanding of the relationship between this discourse and US audiences' perceptions.[44] Glenn adds that the effectiveness of pro-industry discursive strategies articulating a public 'image of a benevolently beneficial industry' may be a major contributor to society's historical failure to stop the industry's destructive practices.[45] Offering a similar rationale, Ellen W. Gorsevski lists several ethical and material violations for which the AIC is to blame as a rationale for studying 'meatwashing', or greenwashing of processes of meat production and consumption through expressions such as 'sustainable meat'.[46]

The animal-industrial complex's defence of pink slime: Voicing premium value

One of the AIC's foci in its LFTB discourse is to articulate a moral-market voice that reframes pink slime as a premium product at a low cost. The AIC suggests that LFTB is a great buy because of its exceptional leanness and nutritional content. This discourse is an outcome of the collective efforts of, among other agents, beef processors such as BPI and Cargill, non-profit industry trade associations such as the American Meat Institute (AMI; now the North American Meat Institute), and industry front groups such as the Center for Consumer Freedom (CCF). Ventriloquist modes organising this discourse include astroturfing and lateral appropriation.

Much of this discourse on LFTB as a premium value attempts to reduce the perceptual gap between high-quality and low-quality beef. In an online video released by AMI shortly after the *ABC* series aired, industry representative Janet M. Riley sits behind a counter with two

---

43   Adams, 2015; Buerkle 2009; Glenn 2004; Gorsevski 2015; Rogers 2008; Todd 2010.
44   Glenn 2004.
45   Glenn 2004, p. 64.
46   Gorsevski 2015, p. 203.

heaped plates of raw beef cuts, which look like lean steaks, sitting directly in front of her.[47] Riley insists that despite media sensationalism, 'Lean Finely Textured Beef isn't substandard beef, it's not scraps scooped from the floor. It's not so-called salvage meat.' Riley continues by reframing pink slime as nutritious and high-quality beef: 'Nutritionally it's equal to ground beef. It tastes like beef, and under a microscope it looks like other beef. The same two proteins are found in all beef', from steaks to LFTB. Here, consistent with the function of the corporate ventriloquist dummy/figure, the AMI appears to speak as an external (non-profit) voice of authority. In doing so, the industry trade association stages an alternative crisis management ethos for BPI and other corporate pink slime processors amidst a major public backlash.

This appeal to LFTB's high nutritional value also appears in Dr Russell Cross' online video remarks, posted by BeefFacts, a screen name concealing the video's sponsorship by the Cattlemen's Beef Board and National Cattlemen's Beef Association. Cross explains that in 1993 he approved LFTB for use in the beef industry, adding: 'those trimmings have pieces of lean [beef] and that lean [beef] is very high-quality protein'. Cross later adds that:

> The process of producing finely textured beef removes those lean pieces and concentrates them, if you will, into what could be a very red, 95% lean, very high percent protein … very high in heme iron, B vitamins.[48]

The mass media circulation of the testimonies of figures such as Cross and Riley equates to a staging of multiple corporate ventriloquist dummies. Through their shared persona of emotionally detached rational authority, these dummy/figures invite the perception of diverse and independent voices in agreement, beyond those directly involved in the dispute.

The uniformity across these voices in relation to LFTB processors such as BPI is noteworthy. Addressing the same topical themes of nutritional value and quality of meat as found in the

---

47 American Meat Institute 2012b.
48 Beef Products Incorporated 2013.

rhetoric of Riley and Cross, BPI directly addresses what it identifies as a misunderstanding:

> Our signature beef is lean finely textured beef. It is 100% beef and is key to making healthy ground beef. It is simply the lean beef trimmed from sirloins, ribeyes and other whole muscle cuts. No organs, tendons, bones or fillers are used.

BPI continues by speaking through statistics as figures of authority: 'When beef is divided into cuts, 53 per cent go to steaks and roasts and 47 per cent are cuts for ground beef known as beef trimmings.' The company explains that LFTB is a special form of beef trimming, however, because 'Once the fat is removed, this trimmed beef is 95 per cent lean.'[49]

The AMI's MeatSafety.org emphasises the same purity and leanness to clear up 'confusion':

> Recent media interest in lean finely textured beef (LFTB) has caused some confusion among consumers. LFTB is simply beef that has been separated from the fat in beef trimmings.[50]

This AIC discourse directly addresses specific charges that LFTB is low-grade filler and thus economic fraud. Appealing to ethical transparency, BPI asserts that LFTB is not a mysterious and dangerous concoction hidden in ground beef; it is pure and nutritious meat. BPI's promise is that it shares a belief in the virtue of the cost-benefit-savvy meat consumer and the industry's commitment to high quality at a low cost. In other words, BPI's implicit goal is to reassert its moral-market rationality.

Cargill has also stressed that LFTB is anything but a violation of moral-market rationality. Following the broader pattern in the AIC response, Cargill reminds consumers of its longstanding commitment to good consumer value as a basis for restoring public confidence: 'For more than two decades, Cargill has been safely removing this meat

---

49   Beef Products Incorporated 2016.
50   MeatSafety.org 2017.

from the fat to create ground beef at a much lower cost to consumers. This is Finely Textured Beef ... 100% pure beef.'[51] BPI co-founder and CEO Eldon Roth uses virtually the same rhetorical appeal to trustworthiness. Adding to this neoliberal appeal to consumer value and neoconservative appeal to safety, Roth integrates the neoconservative virtue of family:

> For more than 30 years, our family has built and operated companies that are committed to providing consumers with wholesome, safe and nutritious lean beef ... lean finely textured beef has made the leaner ground beef that consumers desire more affordable.[52]

Other animal-industrial-complex statements appeal to media sensationalism's threat to the industry's virtuous commitment to consumer value. The Center for Consumer Freedom's astroturfing response is one example:

> We predicted that the unscientific, hysterical calls to remove finely textured beef – tarred as 'pink slime' in the media – would result in higher hamburger prices ... The early results of the scare ... back us up.[53]

The CCF bemoans both the added cost of production and that cost-conscious consumers may get less nutritious meat as well:

> Without lean finely textured beef, or LFTB, the price of manually recovered lean beef trimmings [has] skyrocketed while the price of fatty trimmings (the raw ingredients for LFTB) [has] plummeted.[54]

51　Cargill 2013.
52　Pro Farmer Editors 2012.
53　Center for Consumer Freedom Team 2012b.
54　Center for Consumer Freedom Team 2012b.

Here, the CCF extends the noted rhetorical pattern of positioning the AIC as a virtuous provider of lean, nutritious meat at a low price.

In the discourse surveyed thus far, the AIC appeals to the threatened virtue of affordable consumer options for eating healthily and embodying personal responsibility. Consistent with what Julie Guthman and Melanie DuPuis conceptualise as popular neoliberal food discourse, this rhetoric hails a savvy consumer-citizen who is disciplined with their waistline and wallet but also deserves to indulge in high-quality, delicious food.[55] The rhetoric of fatness that both enables and haunts this disciplined/deserving neoliberal food trope is notable here because it unites neoliberalism with neoconservatism. This rhetoric circulates and is sustained within a dominant national discourse that has long mistakenly celebrated the consumption of *lean* animal-based protein as necessary for physical and mental fitness.[56] Neoliberal food culture takes this a step further by both retaining a focus on meat as strength and reducing sentient farmed animals to a select few numerical and/or nutritional values.[57] In the AIC's discourse at hand, protein takes centre stage as concerns about added hormones, steroids, antibiotics, beef's high saturated fat content and its elevation of risks such as that of chronic cardiovascular disease are sent backstage.[58] Given this neoliberal–neoconservative discourse, it follows that resistance to LFTB becomes an irrational violation of not only self-care, but also the collective virility of the body politic (i.e. families, economy, security, cultural traditions).

These complex ideological connections aside, the focus of AIC's rhetoric of premium value is straightforward. Although the AIC-preferred product name, lean finely textured beef, may not seem simple, its function is to simplify perceptions along the lines of moral-market common sense. While also appealing to gastronomic and nutritional value, the name strips away potential references to any possible unethical sources, processes or outcomes, and any

---

55 Guthman & DuPuis 2006.
56 Buerkle 2009; Shugart 2010.
57 Singer 2017.
58 Sweeney 2019.

connotation of strangeness, chemicalisation or mystery. As Luke Yoquinto states, however:

> 'lean, finely textured beef' sounds like the caviar of meat, and this product is among the lower quality types of beef sold for human consumption; pink slime is probably the less disingenuous term.[59]

From this viewpoint, the circulation of 'pink slime' as a counter-descriptor exposing a crude reality is consistent with Nick Couldry's recommendation that 'strategies [of neoliberal simplification] must be opposed, by name, in a reverse strategy of simplification'.[60] Below, I explicate a second corporate ventriloquist discourse.

Voicing corporate morality

The AIC's voicing of corporate morality consists of two appeals to a desire to 'do the right thing'. The first appeal greenwashes LFTB as an outcome of humane and sustainable meat production (i.e. animal and food conservation) made possible by private sector technological innovation and moral-market common sense. The rhetoric of cost-benefit rationality described above is in unison with this discourse. BPI's statement that 'More precise trimming means MORE beef from the same cattle and LESS fat' epitomises this rhetoric of rationality.[61] AMI's MeatSafety.org also speaks in this voice of moral-market greenwashing, claiming that previously 'trimmings were wasted … But 20 years ago, a new technology became available … today we can derive more beef from a beef animal with less waste.'[62] Elsewhere, the AMI makes a comparable appeal, stressing that LFTB production technology makes conservation possible: '[D]oing it by hand would be impossible. LFTB products prevent the waste of valuable, lean, nutritious, safe, beef.'[63] This rhetorical manoeuvring clearly exhibits that the AIC's

---

59   Yoquinto 2012.
60   Couldry 2010, p. 6.
61   Beef Products Incorporated 2017b.
62   Meat Safety 2017.

greenwashing ventriloquism is virtually inseparable from its lateral appropriation and voice of premium economic value explicated in the previous section. This institutional formation creates the false appearance that all relevant issues and interests and groups advocating for them enjoy equal voice. BPI and other LFTB processors are both the ventriloquist and the dummy. The discourse positions these companies as leading agents in the development and use of high technology, but also servants of virtue compelled by the best interests of animals, nature and consumers.

The animal-industrial complex's tendency in its LFTB greenwashing is to offer calm, collected and unemotional reassurance that all diverse voices have already been accommodated. Astroturfing organisation rhetoric is an exception. Given that Big Food and Ag front groups do not disclose that they are in fact creations of industry, this enables the use of ridicule in their greenwashing while assuming little risk to the industry. The Center for Consumer Freedom offers a vivid example of LFTB greenwashing characterised by defensive neoliberal ridicule:

> It shouldn't be wrong to use machines to remove more beef from a cow than people can do themselves, should it? Aren't we supposed to 'use every part of the animal' and reduce our environmental footprints? When did killing fewer cows to satisfy America's appetite for hamburgers become a bad thing?[64]

This excerpt exhibits a decidedly neoliberal view of conservation foregrounding consumer demand and market opportunity to co-opt and privatise environmentalism. David Helvarg notes that pro-AIC interest groups such as the National Cattlemen's Association and the American Farm Bureau Federation have long supported this 'wise use' free market rhetoric.[65]

CCF complements this neoliberal framing of LFTB as corporate morality by appropriating neoconservatism's anti-elitist populism:

---

63 American Meat Institute 2012a.
64 Center for Consumer Freedom Team 2012a.
65 Helvarg 2004.

> USDA reduces the school lunch program's annual cattle slaughter and environmental footprint by the equivalent of up to 12,000 animals by using 7 million pounds of boneless lean beef trimmings in hamburgers and ground beef. Despite this potential for savings, foodies demand it be banned (even, oddly, those who decry the numbers of animals raised for food).[66]

This moral dichotomisation of commonsense red meat populists and elitist foodies emerges as one industry proxy delegates its authority to another, and speaks through it like a ventriloquist. The problem is not the product. The CCF quips, 'So what is the problem? *Aesthetics* (snobbery might be a better word) seems to be the answer.'[67]

The neoconservative element of laterally appropriated moral-market appeals such as these in the AIC's greenwashing appears even more overtly as it articulates the second of its two corporate morality appeals. Here, the AIC frames LFTB's ammonia-based processing as consistent with nature's way and the normal chemical composition of many foods. BPI also stresses that ammonia processing is completely normal in relation to standard practices pioneered by LFTB processors. BPI claims that although using ammonia or 'any other substance sounds strange to the average person … it would be a mistake to stop using such an effective and proven safety measure.' The company is making two assertions. First, consistent with appeals noted in the AIC's rhetoric on premium value, BPI asserts its scientific ethos, invoking a 'trust us, we're experts' type of appeal that Sheldon Rampton and John C. Stauber find pervading corporate discourse about product-related risks.[68] Second, and more implicitly, BPI's warning that not using ammonia would be consequential affirms an 'it's too late to go back now; there are no alternatives' neoliberal–neoconservative message that has characterised pro-corporate, Western-led globalisation visions since the latter part of the 20th century. Rhetorically constituting a basis for LFTB's desirability, the AIC appeals

---

66 Center for Consumer Freedom Team 2012a.
67 Center for Consumer Freedom Team 2012a.
68 Rampton & Stauber 2001.

to its exclusive expertise regarding food risks that it and neoliberalism helped create or worsen.

It is through a two-step rhetorical manoeuvre that the case for the ammonia-based processing becomes a performance in greenwashing. The AIC first asserts technical expertise and then explains the mobilisation of that expertise in mass-scale beef production as motivated by a moral mandate to intervene in nature. Drawing upon the metaphor of sustainability-as-war, the animal-industrial complex rhetorically positions ammonia processing as natural and, more specifically, part of a larger battle between good nature (such as ammonia) and bad nature such as bacteria.[69] In other words, the beef industry keeps consumers safe and nature virtuous by protecting food from bad nature. The following statement from BPI illustrates the use of this dichotomous moral frame to defend LFTB:

> In our beef, the natural amount of pure ammonia, in the form of ammonium hydroxide, is increased by a minute amount because it is a powerful defense against potential germs. Although not required to make LFTB, we added this innovative step because it is important to us to provide the safest beef possible.

BPI elaborates by equating ammonia with the essence of life and its moral defence. The beef processor describes the use of ammonia in its mass production system as consistent with good nature's way – that is, as restoring beef's 'natural' composition:

> Ammonia is an essential component of all life. Simply put it is ... a key element in our entire ecosystem. So, it naturally occurs in all foods, in some cases at pretty high levels.[70]

Another set of statements in this greenwashing of ammonia processing addresses distortion in LFTB propaganda. Laterally appropriating neoconservative appeals, some of this discourse frames resistance to ammonia processing as a consequence of prioritising elitist (liberal

---

69   Larson 2011.
70   Beef Products Incorporated 2017a.

foodie) aesthetics over the wellbeing of consumers and industry employees and their families. An opinion-editorial column by Steve Dittmer, Executive Vice President of an astroturfing organisation, the Agribusiness Freedom Foundation, invokes the good nature–bad nature moral frame: 'The use of ammonium hydroxide gas to kill pathogens and provide an absolutely safe product left some viewers thinking liquid household ammonia was used.'[71] Unfortunately, 'fake news' and social media have maligned 'an industry sensitive to the need to eliminate *E. coli* and other harmful pathogens'.[72] Statements such as these laterally appropriate an expressed neoconservative populist disfavour for 'the vulgarity of mass culture'.[73]

The CCF, too, stresses the threat of petty aesthetics, but addresses its detriment to locally sourced beef – a more sustainable and 'American-made product'. CCF adds, 'US beef imports ... have skyrocketed' and the 'divine irony' is that the local food movement has helped to fuel fear. One major consequence of this is that '[n]ow, instead of consuming more meat from each US-raised animal, Americans will get more of their ground beef from the Southern Hemisphere'. [74]

The AMI likewise stresses the cruel irony of this disavowal of ammonia:

> If this beef is not used in fresh ground beef products, approximately 1.5 million additional head of cattle would need to be harvested annually to make up the difference, which is not a good use of natural resources, or modern technology, in a world where red meat consumption is rising.[75]

An AMI online video repeats this statement almost verbatim, while adding:

---

71   Dittmer 2017.
72   Dittmer 2017.
73   Norton 2004, p. 178.
74   Center for Consumer Freedom Team 2012b.
75   American Meat Institute 2012a.

lean finely textured beef is a sustainable product ... making sure that we harvest as much beef as possible from an animal ... is just the right thing to do ... And this helps keep beef ... affordable.[76]

In sum, animal-industrial-complex greenwashing recasts LFTB resistance as a threat to the virtues of nature, US workers and consumers, and modern science and technology. Below, I consider how this voicing of corporate morality fits within the broader rhetorical defence of pink slime in which the AIC engages, and summarise the insights emerging from the analysis that I have presented.

Lessons on the AIC's moral-market rhetoric of corporate expertise

This essay has constructed a critical reading of the US animal-industrial complex's public relations discourse within the controversy over LFTB, or what critics have called pink slime. Reading this discourse using Jen Schneider et al.'s corporate ventriloquism model, I show that the industry has relied heavily on three of the model's four rhetorical modes: lateral appropriation, greenwashing and astroturfing. The AIC's defence of pink slime enacts these modes in a way that foremost re-asserts beef processing corporations' expert authority and moral legitimacy. Lateral appropriation emerges in the examined discourse as the most prominent of these modes, and helps shape the discourse generated by the other two modes. The lateral appropriation of already-dominant neoliberal and neoconservative discourse proves central to the image that the AIC projects. This image positions pink slime processors, their proxies and their practices as simultaneously apolitical, rational and moral. More specifically, this image and the three ventriloquist modes illuminated articulate the counterargument that pink slime is actually a premium-value product in terms of cost, nutritional value and taste. This counterargument also states that this LFTB exemplifies a corporate moral commitment to 'do the right thing' in the areas of environmentalism, food conservation and food safety.

---

76   American Meat Institute 2012b.

One of the most recurring rhetorical features found across this AIC's response is a 'no nonsense', realist rhetorical style for which neoliberal discourse has long been known. According to James Arnt Aune, discourse crafted in the realist style derives much of its persuasive potency by dissociating the rhetor's self-proclaimed authority from emotion and politics. Furthermore, the realist rejects virtually all criticisms as rooted in these threats and in the faulty implementation of the normative vision set forth.[77] Even in its practice of greenwashing, little of the AIC's defence of pink slime features romantic imagery; instead, much of it uses carefully selected logical appeals. Most of the AIC's public relations greenwashing appeals studied here stress the scientific, mathematical and moral-market merit of defending 'good nature' with chemicals, sourcing beef domestically and conserving beef. This almost complete aversion from romance differs from what past studies such as those by Ellen W. Gorsevski and Anne Marie Todd have tended to find in corporate food industry greenwashing. Prior studies' focus on marketing and advertising may help explain this divergence.[78]

This consistent use of realist style in AIC public relations regarding LFTB is a cumulative accomplishment of multiple corporate ventriloquist figures/dummies. The enactment of multiple modes of corporate ventriloquism during the pink slime controversy generated the false appearance of a conversation characterised by openness, multi-vocality and the decentring of the voices of LFTB processors such as BPI and Cargill. This simulation portrays these corporations as taking an unemotional and apolitical stance, and as inviting seemingly external objective, rational and moral voices to weigh in on the merit of their practices. However, the multiple voices invited into the discussion prove to be dummies/figures of the meat industry's own making brought in to reclaim top-down 'expert' control over what counts as knowledge, ignorance and acceptable dissent.

As Jen Schneider et al. have already highlighted, corporate ventriloquism is perhaps foremost an art of this sort of anti-democratic muting and misdirection. As these scholars and the present study

---

77   Aune 2001.
78   Gorsevski 2015; Todd 2010.

animate, corporate ventriloquism may be especially handy when unsustainable and unjust industries are desperate to delay their own doom. In the pink slime controversy, animal-industrial complex public relations discourse functions to downplay, deflect, deny and dismiss raised concerns. The investigated discourse appeals to the AIC's self-created figures/dummies of authority, and they in turn offer half-truth counterarguments, shift the initial topics of discussion and/ or resort to cynicism and ridicule. The overall AIC message seems to be that there are no potential problems or legitimate questions regarding LFTB. The 'real' problem is that critics suffer from ignorance and/ or ideology and are missing the point. The animal-industrial complex suggests that beyond ignorance, an aesthetic (liberal foodie) ideological worldview is the only other possible explanation for finding LFTB unappealing or the case for it specious.

This conclusion regarding the AIC's defence of pink slime is consistent with a historical pattern when it comes to addressing criticism. The animal-industrial complex rarely publicly acknowledges that its own *systemic* practices, technologies, expertise and values are even a small part of the problem. More commonly, as exemplified during the mad cow disease crisis and the Oprah Winfrey trial, this institutional formation misdirects full blame toward libel and slander-induced public misunderstanding and hysteria. Wenonah Hauter observes that for decades the AIC has publicly denied its own failures while simultaneously advocating for quick 'technofixes' to manage the consequences of high-speed mass production. Though often making this case through government lobbying, the animal-industrial complex has also urged consumers to overcome a mere gut-level resistance to the use of chemicals and irradiation in meat production.[79]

Therefore, LFTB and the AIC's defence of it should not be read as extreme exceptions, but as reflective of extreme norms in a US food culture increasingly defined by conversations and practices organised by real food/fake food distinctions. Like so much of the food found on store shelves and in restaurants in the US, LFTB is part-real, part-fake. In a national food culture in which mysterious mass-produced food –

---

79   Hauter 2010, p. 287.

mysterious in terms of its production, processing, and effects – has been the norm for decades, outrage, crisis, and change do not typically arise from simply exposing food as fake. In the dispute over LFTB, critics decried it as not only fake but also grotesque, possibly dangerous and fraudulent. Among these charges, the *ABC News* series' attention to the question of fraudulence, or that LFTB is widely found in ground beef but not labelled, became a major focal point among alarmed viewers.

It may come as a surprise to many of these same viewers that such fraudulence is pervasive in the meat industry. Larry Olmsted writes that fraudulent food labelling and marketing is particularly heinous and widespread in the beef and seafood industries.[80] In Olmsted's investigation on beef industry fraud, it is telling that he focuses not on LFTB but on widely celebrated and seldom questioned beef products such as Kobe steak and gourmet Kobe burgers. To offer some background, Kobe beef is the world's most expensive and desired beef, and it is exclusively sourced from Japan. Due to mad cow disease concerns, Kobe beef was banned in the US for many years and is now only occasionally available at a select few restaurants in miniscule amounts. Yet, as Olmsted details, US beef has been fraudulently marketed as Kobe beef for decades.[81] Olmsted's troubling conclusion lends support to the claim that pink slime, fakeness and fraudulence are reflective of an extreme norm.

Given the norms I have identified, and my contention that the animal-industrial complex has staged ventriloquist dummies to offer testimony on its expertise and morality, the implications may seem grim. However, let us not forget that the controversy over pink slime has fostered considerable tangible gains for animal-industrial complex reform and has made an invaluable contribution toward the goal of critical food literacy in the United States. Given the well-supported scholarly conclusion that the cattle industry is by far more detrimental to human health and the planet than any other part of the animal agriculture system, widespread critical publicity regarding LFTB is especially important.[82] Critical scholarship must continue to identify and demonstrate how theoretical resources such as the corporate

---

80 Olmsted 2016.
81 Olmsted 2016.

ventriloquism model can aid such scrutiny toward the goal of permanently shuttering the animal-industrial complex. It is vital that we contribute to new ruptures and resist the vicious but fragile cycle of rhetorical self-legitimation that has long provided the AIC with cover for unsustainable and unjust practices. Instead of letting each other play the dummy, let us recognise, expose and get beyond the absurdity and desperation of the animal-industrial complex's voice of denial when it states, 'Trust us, pink slime is good for you!'[83]

References

Adams, C. J. (2018). *Burger*. New York: Bloomsbury Academic.

Adams, J. L. (2015). Family farms with happy cows: A narrative analysis of Horizon Organic dairy packaging labels. In S. Boerboom (Ed.), *The Political Language of Food* (pp. 183–200). Lanham: Lexington Books.

American Meat Institute (2012a). Questions and answers about lean finely textured beef. https://bit.ly/3aGGqTu

American Meat Institute (2012b). The facts about lean finely textured beef [video]. 16 March 2012. https://www.youtube.com/watch?v=GDiPjmsKeh8

Andrews, J. (2012). BPI, maker of 'pink slime', to close 3 of 4 plants. *Food Safety News*. 8 May. https://bit.ly/3gbEvr6

Aune, J. A. (2001). *Selling the Free Market: The Rhetoric of Economic Correctness*. New York: Guilford Press.

Baertlein, L. and M. Geller (2012). Wendy's jumps into pink slime public relations war. *Reuters*. 30 March. https://reut.rs/3hiuXMa

Beck, U. (1999). *World Risk Society*. Cambridge: Polity Press.

Beef Products Incorporated (2012). Beef Products Inc. sues ABC News [video]. 5 October 2012. https://www.youtube.com/watch?v=DxhmF-B8BbA

Beef Products Incorporated (2013). Dr Russell Cross talks about the safety of LFTB [video]. 24 September 2013. https://bit.ly/3aJKhPv

Beef Products Incorporated (2016). More lean from the same beef trim. https://www.beefproducts.com/ground-beef/

Beef Products Incorporated (2017a). Ammonium hydroxide. https://www.beefproducts.com/ammonium-hydroxide/

---

82 Gerber et al. 2013; Godfray et al. 2018; Imhoff 2010; Steinfeld et al. 2006; Sweeney 2019.

83 Quotation inspired by Stauber & Rampton 1995; Rampton & Stauber 2001.

Beef Products Incorporated (2017b). Simply beef: 100% beef, 95% lean. https://www.beefproducts.com/simply-beef/

Bloomberg Wire Services (2014). U.S. schools cut pink slime purchases by 94%, USDA says. *AgWeb*, 14 May. https://bit.ly/2QeHqoy

Broad, G. M. (2016). Animal production, ag-gag laws, and the social production of ignorance: Exploring the role of storytelling. *Environmental Communication* 10(1), 43–61. doi:10.1080/17524032.2014.968178

Brown, W. (2006). American nightmare: Neoliberalism, neoconservatism, and de-democratization. *Political Theory* 34(6): 690–714. doi:10.1177/0090591706290316

Bsumek, P. K., J. Schneider, S. Schwarze, and J. Peeples (2014). Corporate ventriloquism, corporate advocacy, the coal industry, and the appropriation of voice. In S. Depoe and J. Peeples (Eds.), *Voice and Environmental Communication* (pp. 21–43). New York: Palgrave Macmillan.

Buerkle, W. A. (2009). Metrosexuality can stuff it: Beef consumption as (heteromasculine) fortification. *Text and Performance Quarterly* 29(1): 77–93. doi:10.1080/10462930802514370

Cargill (2013). What is finely textured beef (FTB)? http://www.cargillgroundbeef.com/lean-textured.aspx

Center for Consumer Freedom Team (2012a). Foodie villain of the week. *Center for Consumer Freedom*. 15 March. https://bit.ly/2EnyOt3

Center for Consumer Freedom Team (2012b). The winners from the 'pink slime' scare are… Australian? *Center for Consumer Freedom*. 14 May. https://bit.ly/31gnR5B

Chaput, C. (2010). Rhetorical circulation in late capitalism: Neoliberalism and the overdetermination of affective energy. *Philosophy and Rhetoric* 43(1): 1–25. doi:10.5325/philrhet.43.1.0001

Cooren, F. (2010). *Action and Agency in Dialogue: Passion, Incarnation, and Ventriloquism*. Philadelphia: John Benjamins.

Cooren, F. (2012). Communication theory at the center: Ventriloquism and the communicative constitution of reality. *Journal of Communication* 62(1): 1–20. doi:10.1111/j.1460-2466.2011.01622.x

Couldry, N. (2010). *Why Voice Matters: Culture and Politics After Neoliberalism*. London: Sage.

Cox, R. J. (2010). *Environmental Communication and the Public Sphere* (2nd ed.). Thousand Oaks: Sage.

Dittmer, S. (2017). BPI near getting ABC & Avila in courtroom. *Oklahoma Farm Report*. 17 March. https://bit.ly/3aIOEKN

Flynn, D. (2017). Looks like BPI got ABC's insurance money plus $177 million. *Food Safety News*. 10 August. https://bit.ly/3aVv3Y5

Gerber, P. J., H. Steinfeld, B. Henderson, A. Mottet, C. Opio, J. Dijkman, ... G. Tempio (2013). *Tackling Climate Change Through Livestock: A Global Assessment of Emissions and Mitigation Opportunities.* Rome: Food and Agriculture Organization of the United Nations.

Giddens, A. (1990). *Consequences of Modernity.* Stanford: Stanford University Press.

Gleason, S. and I. Berry (2012). Beef processor falters amid 'slime'. *Wall Street Journal.* 4 April. https://on.wsj.com/3aIP5EV

Glenn, C. B. (2004). Constructing consumables and consent: A critical analysis of factory farm industry discourse. *Journal of Communication Inquiry* 28(1): 63–81. doi:10.1177/019685990325873

Godfray, H., J. Charles, P. Aveyard, T. Garnett, J. W. Hall, T. J. Key, ... S. A. Jebb (2018). Meat consumption, health, and the environment. *Science* 361(6399). doi:10.1126/science.aam5324

Gorsevski, E. W. (2015). Chipotle Mexican Grill's meatwashing propaganda: Corporate-speak hiding suffering of 'commodity' animals. In S. Boerboom (Ed.), *The Political Language of Food* (pp. 201–225). Lanham: Lexington Books.

Greene, J. L. (2012). *Lean Finely Textured Beef: The 'Pink Slime' Controversy.* Washington: Congressional Research Service.

Guthman, J., and M. DuPuis (2006). Embodying neoliberalism: Economy, culture, and the politics of fat. *Environment & Planning D: Society & Space* 24(3): 427–48. doi:10.1068/d3904

Harvey, D. (2005). *A Brief History of Neoliberalism.* New York: Oxford University Press.

Hauter, W. (2010). Nuclear meat: Using radiation and chemicals to make food safe. In D. Imhoff (Ed.), *The CAFO Reader: The Tragedy of Industrial Animal Factories* (pp. 287–294). Healdsburg: Watershed Media.

Helvarg, D. (2004). *The War Against the Greens: The 'Wise Use' Movement, the New Right, and the Browning of America* (revised ed.). San Francisco: Sierra Club Books.

Hooks, G. (1990). From an autonomous to a captured state agency: The decline of the New Deal in agriculture. *American Sociological Review* 55(1): 29–43.

Imhoff, D. (Ed.) (2010). *The CAFO Reader: The Tragedy of Industrial Animal Factories.* Healdsburg: Watershed Media.

Larson, B. (2011). *Metaphors for Environmental Sustainability: Redefining Our Relationship with Nature.* New Haven: Yale University Press.

Meat Safety (2017). Facts about lean finely textured beef. http://www.meatsafety.org/ht/d/sp/i/76540/pid/76540

Melamed, J. (2006). The spirit of neoliberalism: From racial liberalism to neoliberal multiculturalism. *Social Text* 24(4): 1–24. doi:10.1215/01642472-2006-009

Nestle, M. (2002). *Food Politics: How the Food Industry Influences Nutrition and Health*. Berkeley: University of California Press.

Norton, A. (2004). *Leo Strauss and the Politics of American Empire*. New Haven: Yale University Press.

Olmsted, L. (2016). *Real Food/Fake Food: Why You Don't Know What You're Eating and What You Can Do About It*. Chapel Hill: Algonquin Books of Chapel Hill.

Pezzullo, P. (2003). Resisting 'National Breast Cancer Awareness Month': The rhetoric of counterpublics and their cultural performances. *Quarterly Journal of Speech* 89(4): 345–65. doi:10.1080/0033563032000160981

Potts, A. (2017). What is meat culture? In A. Potts (Ed.), *Meat culture* (pp. 1–30). Leiden: Brill.

Pro Farmer Editors (2012). BPI files lawsuit against ABC. *AgWeb*. 13 September. http://www.agweb.com/mobile/article/bpi_files_lawsuit_against_abc_/

Rampton, S. and J. Stauber (2001). *Trust Us, We're Experts! How Industry Manipulates Science and Gambles with Your Future*. New York: Tarcher/Putnam.

Rogers, R. A. (2008). Beasts, burgers, and hummers: Meat and the crisis of masculinity in contemporary television advertisements. *Environmental Communication* 2(3): 281–301. doi:10.1080/17524030802390250

Schneider, J., S. Schwarze, P. K. Bsumek and J. Peeples (2016). *Under Pressure: Coal Industry Rhetoric and Neoliberalism*. New York: Palgrave MacMillan.

Shugart, H. A. (2010). Consuming citizen: Neoliberating the obese body. *Communication, Culture & Critique* 3(1): 105–26. doi:10.1111/j.1753.9137.2009.01060.x

Singer, R. (2017). Neoliberal backgrounding, the Meatless Monday campaign, and the rhetorical intersections of food, nature, and cultural identity. *Communication, Culture & Critique* 10(2): 344–64. doi:10.1111/cccr.12155

Singer, R. (2010). Neoliberal style, the American Re-Generation, and ecological jeremiad in Thomas Friedman's 'Code Green'. *Environmental Communication* 4(2): 135–51. doi:10.1080/17524031002775646

Stauber, J. C. and S. Rampton (1995). *Toxic Sludge is Good for You: Lies, Damn Lies, and the Public Relations Industry*. Monroe: Common Courage Press.

Steinfeld, H., P. Gerber, T. D. Wassenaar, V. Castel, M. Rosales, and C. de Haan (2006). *Livestock's long shadow: Environmental issues and options*. Rome: Food & Agriculture Organization of the United Nations.

Sweeney, C. (2019). Increasing red meat consumption linked with higher risk of premature death. *Harvard T.H. Chan School of Public Health.* 12 June. https://bit.ly/3hj6MNF

Todd, A. M. (2010). Happy cows and passionate beefscapes: Nature as landscape and lifestyle in food advertisements. In J. A. Sandlin and P. McLaren (Eds.), *Critical Pedagogies of Consumption: Living and Learning in the Shadow of Shopocalypse* (pp. 169–179). New York: Routledge.

United States District Court, District of South Dakota, Southern Division (2012). Memorandum in support of ABC defendants' motion to dismiss all claims of plaintiff Beef Products, Inc. 31 October. https://bit.ly/3aJL5nv

Walmart (2012). Walmart statement regarding lean finely textured beef. 21 March. https://bit.ly/3ghvgFN

Yoquinto, L. (2012). Is pink slime bad for your health? *Live Science.* 18 May. https://www.livescience.com/36367-pink-slime-bad-health-beef.htm

2

Grieg in the henhouse: 12 seconds at the contested intersections of human and nonhuman animal interests

Daniel Lees Fryer

> Opening shot: interior, henhouse, low light, hens, two rows of perches and nest boxes. Voiceover, subtitle: 'That's why we play music'. Close-up of human hand flicking switch and turning dial on old radio. Cue music: Edvard Grieg's 'Morning Mood'. Close-up of hens. Wider frame, man walks slowly between perches and nest boxes. Voiceover, subtitle: 'They become calm. They enjoy themselves'. Close-up of single hen shaking feathers. Low-angle shot, hens, man by open door, daylight. Man speaks, subtitle: 'Ba-pa-pa-pa!' Fade to black. Caption, white on black, top of frame: *'GOOD TASTE WITH A CLEAR CONSCIENCE.'* [Producer name], white on black, middle. Green logo, 'organic', lower right. Ends.

Introduction

Chances are you've seen and heard hundreds if not thousands of ads for animal-based products in your lifetime – ads for meat, dairy, eggs, clothing, cosmetics, medicine and entertainment.[1] If you spend any

---

1   A study published in the early 1990s (Kunkel & Gantz 1992) estimated that children in the United States were exposed to more than 40,000 television

time online, engaging in digital environments, you've probably seen many of those ads on social media, especially since the early 2000s.

Social media allow us, as users, to produce, distribute and respond to user-generated content, connecting people (and products) in potentially innovative ways. Whether it's sharing cat videos, sending personal messages or organising events, that connectivity can have transformative, liberating and emancipatory potential; it can also be controlled, manipulated and commodified in ways that can be difficult to fully appreciate.[2]

The ad described in the opening of this chapter is a short film I saw on social media in 2017. While seemingly unremarkable, the content, design, distribution and responses to the ad represent a microcosm of themes dealing with human–nonhuman animal relations. What I want to do in this paper is highlight and discuss some of those themes, identifying ways in which users position themselves in relation to the ad, in relation to each other and in relation to wider conversations about the use and abuse of nonhuman animals.

Communities of shared values

To do this, I draw on the work of Jay L. Lemke and others, and especially on Lemke's notions of 'stance' and 'heteroglossic relations'.[3] Stance, here, can be understood in three different, potentially

---

commercials per year. Around 70 per cent of those ads were for breakfast cereals, confectionery and fast food (Kunkel & Gantz 1992; Kunkel 2001; Wilcox et al. 2004). For more specific, qualitative studies on the advertising of animal-based products, see Delahoyde & Despenich 1994; Heinz & Lee 1998; Pendergrast & McGrath 2018, among others.

2 See, for example, van Dijck 2013; Allmer 2015; Pasquale 2018.

3 'Heteroglossia' is a term borrowed from Bakhtin 1981 [1935], which basically means different- or other-voiced. Bakhtin's heteroglossia is part of what has become more widely known as 'intertextuality' (see Kristeva 1984). Lemke's work (Lemke 1988, 1995, 1998) focuses on themes as diverse as homophobia, student–teacher relations and science discourse. While those themes do not extend to animal rights or human–nonhuman animal relations, I consider Lemke's work on stance and heteroglossic relations to be relevant and applicable to the themes and aims of this paper.

overlapping ways: how we position ourselves with regard to whatever it is we're talking about; how we position ourselves with regard to those we're talking to and their anticipated responses; and how we position ourselves with regard to the other people or texts we reference, respond to or invoke during those conversations.[4] The kinds of relations that are set up between different participants – speakers, listeners and any number of third parties – are ones of varying degrees of alliance or alignment and opposition or disalignment, around which groups or communities of shared values, feelings and interests can be co-constructed.[5] Those communities are 'imagined', not in the sense that they are not 'real' or don't matter, but in the sense that, while members may share similar interests, ideas, affinities and identities, they may not necessarily know each other or occupy the same physical or virtual spaces.[6] Membership of such groups or communities is not necessarily fixed or stable, and affiliation or identification with one group or community does not have to be mutually exclusive of another.

How exactly we construe and align ourselves with certain value positions depends on a variety of factors that include choices of expression (what we say, how we say it, what we could have said, what we don't say), the kinds of ideas and emotions we're trying to convey (what we're talking about, what feelings we express) and contextual variables such as the setting, the participants, and the roles and relations of those involved.[7] If we know something about some or all of those factors, we can make certain inferences about people's opinions and beliefs and the kinds of positions they might be willing or unwilling to take in relation to others.

---

4   See Lemke 1998, pp. 105–106; Baldry & Thibault 2006, pp. 89–90.

5   See Lemke 1988, 1995; Martin and White 2005. Note the considerable overlap here with related concepts such as communities of interest, communities of practice or discourse communities (e.g. Swales 1990; Lave & Wenger 1991).

6   Benedict Anderson uses the term 'imagined community' in reference to nationalism and national identity, but the concept can be usefully expanded to include other domains (Anderson 1991). Zappavigna (2012, 2014, 2018) uses the term 'ambient affiliation' to describe these relations in online exchanges.

7   See, for example, Halliday 2002, 2013; Lemke 1988; Martin & White 2005.

A microcosm of human–nonhuman animal relations

The film described above was posted on Facebook on 17 October 2017.[8] At the time of writing, the film had been viewed over 293,000 times, 'liked' 310 times and shared 16 times.[9] Thirty-eight comments had been added to the post by other Facebook users, including the publisher of the original post, a Norway-based food-and-drink producer and distributor.

The film is a 12-second-long advertisement for eggs, although its primary focus is on the producers of those eggs – the hens (as well as the farmer and the distributor) – rather than the products themselves. I first encountered the short film as part of Facebook's 'sponsored content', advertising material that appears alongside and in the same or similar style as other user-generated content. A longer version of the film (1 min 24 sec), from which this 12-second segment is excerpted and adapted, has been posted elsewhere online.[10]

A number of themes were identified in the film and in the comments sections. Those themes are discussed below and cover a range of issues that are likely to be familiar to those interested in or involved with animal rights and animal liberation. The themes – animal welfare, ethical consumerism, property relations, entertainment, vegaphobia and national identity – are not intended to be exhaustive. Nor is their ordering here a reflection of their perceived importance, although I have attempted to group them loosely together, since many of the themes are closely related.

---

8 The video can be viewed at https://bit.ly/3hj71s3 and https://bit.ly/3aQvkLF.
9 Facebook currently offers several single-click symbols that allow users to express a set of predefined responses or emotions: 'like' (a blue thumbs-up symbol), 'love' (a red heart-shaped symbol), 'haha' (a yellow laughing face), 'wow' (a yellow surprised face), 'sad' (a yellow frowning tearful face) and 'angry' (a yellow-red scowling face).
10 See URL https://vimeo.com/355950251.

Animal welfare and ethical consumerism: 'Good taste with a clear conscience'

As mentioned above, the film is not about eggs per se. There's only one egg in the 12-second film, in the opening shot, on the henhouse floor, in a scene dominated by the sight of 50 to 60 hens on perches. If you blink, you might miss it. Rather, the film is about the producers of those eggs and the kinds of conditions they live in. As the publisher of the original post writes: 'Nothing is better than eggs that come from happy hens. That's why we play classical music for them, and in return they give us delicious organic eggs.'[11] An additional comment reads: 'Classical music is just one of many measures our egg farmer has used to improve the comfort of the hens.' The post lists other measures such as being able to roam freely among fruit trees, access to water and showers, pebbles and sand-baths, and other 'installations that motivate increased activity and movement'. Some of these are shown in the longer version of the film.

The main theme, then, is animal welfare and, as the final caption in the film suggests, potential consumers can rest assured that if they buy and consume eggs from these hens, they're making the right ethical choice. The alternatives – presumably including large-scale farming and various battery-cage-like systems – are not made explicit in the film, but they are part of the backdrop for understanding why one might have a 'clear conscience' for buying eggs produced under these and not other conditions. Some users make this explicit in their comments on the video. For example, one writes

> [I] buy organic eggs because the hens seem to have a better life. Don't like hens in such large flocks. can't possibly be good. We humans don't like overcrowding either over time. there's too much stress for it to be natural. We like nature and need its fresh air and tranquillity. Same for the animals.

---

11 Unless stated otherwise, all user comments reproduced in this paper are translated from the original Norwegian. Wherever possible, I have tried to retain the original orthography. Translations are my own.

Without this backdrop – the overcrowding and stress – the (ethical) choice to buy organic, free-range eggs seems ambiguous. In response to a series of negative comments from other users (see sections below), the film producer replies: 'One can always ask questions about whether we should eat eggs, but if you want eggs we think this is the best way to do it.' Part of this response acknowledges a potentially different ethical choice, one that is not a choice between organic and non-organic and/ or between free-range and not free-range, but between eggs and not eggs. The film producer concedes the point, but the answers to questions about eating eggs are left to consumers to consider. Instead, the film producer argues that the choices it makes or offers are those ostensibly determined by the market and the individual consumer.[12]

From an animal rights perspective, animal welfare and ethical consumerism, while arguably more acceptable forms of exploitation, are still forms of exploitation. Animals exist for the purposes of human profit and consumption, and their lives are subordinate to those processes.[13] Playing classical music for hens sounds like a wonderful idea, but if the music is intended to calm their nerves, the implication is that those animals are in some way nervous or anxious and that, without the music, they would not be calm, or certainly less calm. Similarly, freedom to roam and access to water, pebbles and sand-baths are all intended to make the lives of hens better, but only insofar as they maintain the livelihoods and profits of humans. A better life would be one that was free from captivity and not contingent upon the amount or perceived quality of eggs a hen produces. That, however, is not a position that most egg farmers and distributors are likely to adopt.

The following sections take up various critical responses to the 'happy hens lay happy eggs' (or animal welfare as market branding) position advanced by the film.

---

12 This position is remarkably similar to the 'lesser evil' arguments often made by oil companies, arms manufacturers and political organisations in justifying some of the work they do and the kinds of choices they make or offer.

13 For a recent review and discussion of animal welfare and ethical consumerism, see Pendergrast & McGrath 2018. For discussion of some of the differences between animal welfare and animal rights, see Regan 1997.

Just doing their job: Animals as property, animals as (forced) labour

'If the hens are going to do their job, and lay good eggs, nice eggs, strong eggs, then they have to be happy.' The farmer's comment in the longer version of the film emphasises the importance not just of happy hens, but of happy workers. The hens work for the farmer, and in return for their labour and the products of their labour, they are given food and shelter.

The idea of animals as workers is discussed at length by Hribal, who argues that animals who perform and produce for human consumption should be considered part of the working class, part of the exploited and excluded in society.[14] Torres agrees to a certain extent, but also identifies aspects of animal slavery that go beyond the kind of 'wage slavery' typically associated with work.[15] Apart from food and shelter, animals receive no recompense for what they produce: their own bodies, their bodily secretions or the bodies of their offspring. Often held in captivity, and almost always 'on the job', these animals' lives are precarious and expendable, but, Torres argues, they are qualitatively different from those of human slaves and human wage labourers.[16]

The comment in the film may simply be a turn of phrase, of course. 'Doing one's job' could be equated more generally with a specific role, function or behaviour. It doesn't have to refer to contracted, uncontracted or forced labour. However, it serves as a reminder of how society values nonhuman animal lives and how those lives exist first and foremost to fulfil humans' perceived needs and desires. It also emphasises the role of animals as commodities, as property to be bought, sold or exchanged on the market. Egg-laying hens are not only producers; they are also products in the commodity chain of animal agriculture.

With regard to captivity, exploitation and violence, one user draws parallels between animal agriculture and Nazi concentration camps,

---

14 Hribal 2010.
15 Torres 2007.
16 Torres (2007, p. 39) argues that animals, unlike humans, are generally unable to 'resist, plan, revolt, and [...] struggle for their own freedom'. Hribal (2010) claims, on the contrary, that animals can and in fact do resist their incarceration and exploitation.

by posting an image of a group of prisoners alongside a comment that sardonically echoes that of the film: "'We play some music for them, so everything will be fine" <3'. The image depicts the cramped, overcrowded and intolerable living conditions of a concentration camp and the emaciated bodies of prisoners.[17] It highlights the plight of those prisoners, placed in captivity, forced into labour, abused and tortured, and awaiting possible execution. The post gets 20 'likes' and one 'haha'.

Comparison – the 'dreaded comparison' – with the plight of nonhuman animals is common, with well-known examples ranging from the relatively innocuous Chicken Run film to PETA's more provocative and divisive 'Holocaust on a Plate' or 'Captivity is Slavery' campaigns.[18] Such comparisons emphasise similarities between the horrifying abuses committed by humans against other humans and by humans against other animals. But these comparisons can be problematic. For example, they often fail to acknowledge or are less interested in highlighting the social, political, economic and historical reasons for such systematic oppression, persecution and slaughter and the qualitatively different conditions under which they occur. Moreover, as Aph and Syl Ko argue, '[n]ot only are these types of comparisons or connections absurd – even worse, these simplistic characterisations miss the ways in which these struggles and these wounded subjectivities relate to one another'.[19] A particularly relevant example here is provided by Nekeisha Alayna Alexis, who explores at length the parallels between the discourses around contemporary 'humane farming' and 19th-century 'slave romances', and their remarkably similar rationales or defences for distinct yet overlapping forms of violence and oppression.[20]

---

17 The specific photograph, taken in the Mauthausen-Gusen concentration camp complex, is a well-known image, taken in 1945 by Allied soldiers shortly after the camp was liberated.
18 See Spiegel 1988, as well as Molloy 2011, pp. 111–112, and Potts 2012, pp. 101–102.
19 Ko & Ko 2017.
20 Alexis 2018.

Entertainment: Why did the chicken cross the road?

'arf arf arf! tweet, tweet, tweet!' says one user in a GIF (graphics interchange format) image from the animated television show *Ed, Edd n Eddy* showing a character wearing shoes on its ears and flapping its arms like a bird. Another user writes 'Hens enjoying themselves' followed by a crying-laughing emoji, to which someone else replies 'Lol'. It's not difficult to understand who or what this laughter is aimed at, and it's clear from both versions of the film that, in addition to projecting a caring, ethical, welfarist position towards hens, the film is meant to entertain.[21]

The 'disnification' – or, in the above example, cartoon-networkification – of animals is part of a process of representation that trivialises and belittles their lives.[22] Animals, like other marginalised or oppressed groups, are often reduced to and portrayed as either 'dangerous threats to "civilized" society or as comic buffoons'.[23] Chickens are no exception: on the one hand, they carry the threat of avian flu and salmonella; on the other, they're the dim-witted butt of poultry-related jokes and derisions. This has not always been the case, however. Hens and cockerels have also been admired for 'their vigilance, courage and loyalty to family and flock'.[24] According to Potts, the relatively recent trivialisation of chickens and other animals is largely a result of the industrialisation of animal agriculture and the subsequent distancing or dissociation of humans from other animals.[25]

Nibert's point about the process of trivialisation applying to both human and nonhuman animals is an important one here.[26] In the film, the source of entertainment is not just the hens; it is also the farmer. It's the farmer who plays music for the hens, the farmer who talks to the hens, the farmer who paints landscapes and plays recorder, and the farmer who is, in the words of the film producer, 'unlike other egg

---

21   Among the 310 general 'likes' the film has received, 12 of these are laughing-face 'haha' symbols.
22   Baker 2001, p. 174.
23   Nibert 2002, p. 205.
24   Potts 2012, p. 98.
25   Potts 2012, p. 98.
26   Nibert 2002, p. 205.

farmers'. Farmers are often portrayed like this, as simple or eccentric folks, as country bumpkins whose lives, or livelihoods at least, are ridiculed and generally have low status. Although the example here is a relatively simple one, it demonstrates how the marginalisation and interests of different groups, across species, can overlap and intersect.

Vegaphobia: Veg*ns Gonna Hate

'They play music for hens = Vegans still rage', writes one user, who also includes a still image of a laughing Bryan Cranston from the television series *Breaking Bad*. Another user responds with 'TING GOES SKRRRAAA', based on a popular internet meme at the time featuring rap lyrics by comedian Michael Dapaah. (Each user gives the other a thumbs up.)[27] Both of these comments ridicule the idea that someone, in this case someone identifying as vegan, would find the video offensive and feel the need to express outrage.

This seems to be a relatively common sentiment regarding vegetarians and vegans, one that Cole and Morgan describe as a form of 'vegaphobia'.[28] In their study of British newspapers' representations of vegans and veganism, Cole and Morgan identify a series of derogatory discourses that include ridiculing veganism, as well as characterising veganism as asceticism, describing veganism as difficult or impossible to sustain, describing veganism as a fad, and characterising vegans as oversensitive and/or hostile. In a slightly longer comment by another user (see below), the criticism of veganism as a moralistic and elitist consumer practice is also raised, and the potential role of veganism in reducing hunger and pollution is dismissed in favour of 'local food movements' and self-sufficiency.

> Lots of vegans here. Had we lived in famine-inflicted regions
> … But [they] get exotic vegetables flown in and live 'morally/

---

27 Both posts are partly or fully written in English: 'Vegans still rage' and 'TING GOES SKRRRAAA'.
28 Cole & Morgan 2011.

vegan'.(?) [I] believe in local food and self-sufficiency in view of world hunger and global pollution <3.

So, do vegans rage, or are these comments directed more generally at some kind of vegan caricature? One of the longer negative responses to the film reads:

> Is there really anyone who falls for this? What kind of life do you think these hens have? Almost all male chicks are killed as soon as they hatch, only hens are allowed to live. It's good that [company name] is making more organic products available, but organic eggs are by no means 'good'.

The user also includes a hyperlink to a vegan-community website with the heading 'Why Don't Vegans Eat Eggs?' The post gets 47 'likes', two 'sad' faces and one 'love' heart, more than any other post in response to the film, and another user responds: 'Agree with you! Repulsive the whole thing!!' In a separate comment, one user writes, 'should I laugh or cry?? fucking hell', to which another responds, 'I'm doing both, bloody idiots the whole lot'. Among the primarily visual responses to the film are GIF images that include actor Ryan Reynolds facepalming, a participant on a US television talk show shouting the words LIE LIE LIE flashed in progressively larger typeface, and actor Ola Ray screaming in the music video for Michael Jackson's 'Thriller'. Still images include prisoners in a concentration camp (see above) and a dead, plucked, eviscerated chicken on a chopping board.

The above examples express a range of responses and emotions that include anger, disgust, disbelief and mockery. Some, like the first comment, try to present reasoned responses to the film; others, like the LIE LIE LIE GIF, offer snappier retorts; while examples like the concentration camp image are likely to be considered more confrontational. All of these comments are essentially responses to the filmmaker's overall claim that 'Nothing is better than eggs that come from happy hens'. The 'happy hens = happy eggs' logic is one that runs counter to animal rights discourses. Animal welfare, as discussed above, may be all well and good, but it ignores and potentially reinforces the acceptability of commodifying, confining and killing animals for human use – just so long as it's done humanely. While some of the above responses may seem inappropriate for this kind of forum and for this kind of film – after all, it's an ad for eggs, what would you expect? – the post is part of Facebook's 'sponsored content' and can potentially appear on anyone's feed, regardless of their interests (more on this below). If someone who identifies as vegan is presented with an ad for eggs, is it any wonder they respond? It may not be easy to engage critically in online forums that favour short-form responses and that are often portrayed as sites of incivility, 'flaming' or ' trolling', but ridiculing vegans or countering with appeals for sustainability seems to miss the point.[29] In the worst case, it can serve to marginalise veganism and obscure the exploitative and violent relations inherent in animal agriculture and the hidden or 'naturalised' ideology of consuming animal-based products that some users may be trying to highlight.[30]

National identity: Edvard Grieg's 'Morning Mood'

The production and consumption of animal-based products are sometimes associated with discourses of national identity. Stuart, for example, discusses how beef-eating became an important part of British culture in the 18th century, connected in part with the strength and virility of the nationalist personification of John Bull.[31] Similar narratives can be found around national dishes – most of which are animal-based – and meat, eggs and other animal-derived products are often emblazoned with flags, heraldry and other national symbols as part of marketing strategies to increase sales of domestically produced food and clothing.[32] With regard to the context of the short film discussed here, Norwegian state authorities generally pride themselves on the claim that Norwegian farms produce salmonella-free eggs and poultry, and that Norway is more

---

29 Papacharissi 2004; Anderson et al. 2014.
30 See Cole & Morgan 2011, p. 149; and discussions of 'carnism' in Joy 2010 and Francione 2012.
31 Stuart 2006.
32 See Molloy 2011, pp. 106–110.

or less self-sufficient with regard to egg production.[33] Organic eggs accounted for 3.5 per cent of total egg production and 5.3 per cent of all egg sales in Norway in 2012 (compared with 1.7 per cent for the sale of dairy, 2.2 per cent for vegetables, 0.9 per cent for grains and 0.3 per cent for meat), and food safety and animal welfare are central to the *Nyt Norge* (Enjoy Norway) campaign.[34]

In the comments section of the film, one user thanks producers and consumers for their commitment to animal welfare and takes the opportunity to criticise the treatment of animals in other parts of the world: 'Thanks to all of you who contributed to what's best for hens by buying eggs from free-range hens. Continue work by NOT buying fur clothing from China.' The common narrative of pitching one nation against another is upheld here through an animal welfare chauvinism that, like other forms of nationalism, tends to overlook or ignore historical and contemporary similarities and emphasise perceived differences.

A central motif in the film is the classical music of Edvard Grieg's 'Morning Mood'. The piece is from Grieg's incidental music for the Henrik Ibsen play *Peer Gynt* and is often associated with national romanticism and pastoral Norway.[35] The film's soundtrack is likely to be instantly recognisable to a broad Norwegian-speaking audience.

'Morning Mood' plays a crucial role in construing for the film a harmonious henhouse, helping to create an idyllic scene of hens in a peaceful, tranquil environment. 'All hens should have such a nice home <3', writes one user. 'Important to mix in a bit of jazz too', comments another. And in a spin on the national identity narrative set up by the use of Grieg's music, one user (also a hen-keeper) expresses a preference for Norwegian black metal band Dimmu Borgir and its recordings with the Norwegian Radio Orchestra, KORK: 'Well, I'm playing Dimmu Borgir with kork for them now, probably as close as I get to classical :)'

---

33 Norwegian Food Safety Authority 2018.
34 Bye & Løvberget 2013, p. 29; Matmerk 2018.
35 The pastoral tranquillity associated with 'Morning Mood' is contrasted with its use in a scene in *Peer Gynt* in which the protagonist, Peer, finds himself in a tree in north Africa, fighting off monkeys.

In the longer version of the film, first posted on 19 October 2017, the music played for hens is Mozart's 'Alla Turca' (often known as Turkish March) from Piano Sonata No. 11. Unlike the shorter version posted on Facebook, the longer film focuses as much on the unconventional farming techniques and lifestyle of the farmers as it does on the welfare of hens. The national and the pastoral are construed visually: a wide-angle shot of a fjord, hens wandering freely among fruit trees, a man painting a mountain scene, a ski hat bearing a Norwegian flag. Musically, Mozart's fast-paced rondo underscores the peculiarity or eccentricity of the farmers and the seemingly erratic head and body movements of the hens and cockerels (see section above on animals as entertainment).

It's not all about SoMe, or is it?

Social networking sites are commercial enterprises that profit from the commodification of social relations: the more a user engages in those spaces, the more data the platform can collect, and the more targeted subsequent advertising and promotion becomes. The kinds of 'sponsored content' promoted on those sites, however, can open up new (and possibly unintended) spaces for critical engagement. New texts and new situations can be created, and new alliances and oppositions can be formed. In the example discussed in this paper, users highlight and respond to a broad set of themes concerning human–nonhuman animal relations that critique and go beyond the issues of animal welfare and ethical consumerism presented in the promotional film itself. While all PR may be good PR, some of the 'talk around text' in this example may not be desirable or optimal for the content-promoter. The publisher of the original post is limited in how much it can manage or control the direction a particular discussion thread takes. Undesirable comments can be reported, deleted, ignored or otherwise contested, of course, but each of these options carries a certain risk, particularly if the content of the original post is intended to create goodwill. As an example of how discussions can unfold in new and potentially surprising ways, the film producer in this instance responds to user comments by choosing to acknowledge and concede the problems of egg consumption while also defending its position to supply perceived market needs.

Film plays an important role in portraying animals' lives, and in representing and reimagining the production and consumption of animal-based products. Social media provide us with platforms to share and respond to those audiovisual representations in potentially innovative ways. This paper has focused on one film, shared on one platform, as an instance of some of the contested intersections between human and nonhuman animal interests. The themes discussed herein, while not exhaustive, overlap and intersect in complex and interesting ways; for example, the nexus of animal welfare and national identity, and the trivialisation of different marginalised groups. The analyses and insights in this paper – although restricted to a single discussion – should be relevant and applicable to other texts and wider discourses concerning our relations with other animals. They may also serve as a useful point of reference for activists using social media and other online forums to advocate and campaign for the lives and interests of all animals.

Coda

In October 2017, I came across a short film on social media, nestled between posts from friends and family. As I scrolled past, the film began to roll. I paused, read the first line of subtitles ('That's why we play music') and clicked for sound (cue Grieg). I watched it three or maybe four times, showed it to my partner and saved it for later reference. Since then, I've watched the film many times and I've read and reread comments left by other users. The result of this is not just the paper before you, but a transformation of the kind of sponsored content that typically appears on my social media timeline or feed. Now, when I log on, I'm met with all kinds of chicken- and egg-related promotional material: tips on how to boil eggs, reasons why Norwegian hens and eggs are the best in the world, even a video of dancing broiler chickens. The reason I mention this is not simply to point out that Facebook's algorithms have detected I have an interest in chickens. Rather, or in addition, it is to ask what effect this might have on how and why users respond to this kind of content. When users encounter videos of dancing chickens or classical-music-listening hens, their responses to those videos may be cumulative responses to a series of similarly themed sponsored posts (as well as any number of offline encounters) they've recently experienced. Responding to a film that is ostensibly about playing music for hens may just be the tip of a much greater online and offline 'iceberg'. Moreover, as users respond to these and similar ads, regardless it seems of the sentiments expressed, the effect is likely to be amplified, generating more of the same ads and encouraging more of the same responses until such time as users ask the site to stop – assuming, that is, users know how to do that and it has the desired effect.

References

Alexis, N. A. (2018). There's something about the blood…: Tactics of evasion within narratives of violence. In L. Gruen and F. Probyn-Rapsey (Eds.), *Animaladies: Gender, Animals, and Madness*. New York: Bloomsbury.

Allmer, T. (2015). *Critical Theory and Social Media: Between Emancipation and Commodification*. Abingdon: Routledge.

Anderson, A. A., D. Brossard, D. A. Scheufele, M. A. Xenos and P. Ladwig (2014). The 'nasty effect': Online incivility and risk perceptions of emerging technologies. *Journal of Computer-Mediated Communication* 19(3), 373–387. doi:10.1111/jcc4.12009

Anderson, B. (1991). *Imagined Communities: Reflections on the Origin and Spread of Nationalism* (2nd ed.). London: Verso.

Baker, S. (2001). *Picturing the Beast: Animals, Identity, and Representation*. Champaign, IL: University of Illinois Press.

Bakhtin, M. M. (1981). *The Dialogic Imagination: Four Essays* (M. Holquist, Ed.). Austin, TX: University of Texas Press.

Baldry, A. and P. J. Thibault (2006). *Multimodal Transcription and Text Analysis*. London: Equinox.

Bye, A. S. and A. I. Løvberget (2013). Interessa for økologisk mat aukar [Interest in organic food is growing]. *Samfunnsspeilet* 2013(2), 28–33.

Cole, M. and K. Morgan (2011). Vegaphobia: Derogatory discourses of veganism and the reproduction of speciesism in UK national newspapers. *The British Journal of Sociology* 62(1), 134–153. doi:10.1111/j.1468-4446.2010.01348.x

Delahoyde, M. and S. C. Despenich (1994). Creating meat-eaters: The child as advertising target. *The Journal of Popular Culture* 28(1), 135–149. doi:10.1111/j.0022-3840.1994.2801_135.x

Francione, G. L. (2012). 'Carnism'? There is nothing 'invisible' about the ideology of animal exploitation. *Animal Rights: The Abolitionist Approach.* https://bit.ly/3hczTCm.

Halliday, M. A. K. (2002). Class in relation to the axes of chain and choice in language. In J. J. Webster (Ed.), *On Grammar. Volume 1 in the Collected Works of M. A. K. Halliday* (pp. 95–105). London: Continuum.

Halliday, M. A. K. (2013). Meaning as choice. In L. Fontaine, T. Bartlett and G. O'Grady (Eds.), *Systemic Functional Linguistics: Exploring Choice* (pp. 15–36). Cambridge: Cambridge University Press.

Heinz, B. and R. Lee (1998). Getting down to the meat: The symbolic construction of meat consumption. *Communication Studies* 49, 86–99. doi:10.1080/10510979809368520

Hribal, J. (2003). 'Animals are part of the working class': A challenge to labor history. *Labor History* 44(4), 435–53. doi:10.1080/0023656032000170069

Hribal, J. (2010). *Fear of the Animal Planet: The Hidden History of Animal Resistance.* Oakland: CounterPunch/AK Press.

Joy, M. (2010). *Why We Love Dogs, Eat Pigs, and Wear Cows: An Introduction to Carnism.* San Francisco: Conari Press.

Ko, A. and S. Ko (2017). *Aphro-Ism: Essays on Pop Culture, Feminism, and Black Veganism from Two Sisters* [e-book]. New York: Lantern Books.

Kristeva, J. (1984). *Desire in Language: A Semiotic Approach to Literature and Art.* London: Blackwell.

Kunkel, D. (2001). Children and television advertising. In D. G. Singer and J. L. Singer (Eds.), *Handbook of Children and the Media* (pp. 375–392). Thousand Oaks, CA: Sage.

Kunkel, D. and W. Gantz (1992). Children's television advertising in the multichannel environment. *Journal of Communication* 42(3), 134–152. doi:10.1111/j.1460.2466.1992.tb00803.x

Lave, J. and E. Wenger (1991). *Situated Learning: Legitimate Peripheral Participation.* Cambridge: Cambridge University Press.

Lemke, J. L. (1988). Discourses in conflict: Heteroglossia and text semantics. In J. Benson and W. Greaves (Eds.), *Systemic Functional Approaches To Discourse: Selected Papers From The 12th International Systemic Workshop* (pp. 29–50). Norwood, NJ: Ablex.

Lemke, J. L. (1995). Intertextuality and text semantics. In P. H. Fries and M. Gregory (Eds.), *Discourse in Society: Systemic Functional Perspectives.*

Meaning and Choice in Language: Studies for Michael Halliday (pp. 85–114). Norwood, NJ: Ablex.

Lemke, J. L. (1998). Multiplying meaning: Visual and verbal semiotics in scientific text. In J. R. Martin and R. Veel (Eds.), *Reading Science: Critical and Functional Perspectives on Discourses of Science* (pp. 87–113). London: Routledge.

Martin, J. R. and P. R. R. White (2005). *The Language of Evaluation: Appraisal in English*. Basingstoke: Palgrave Macmillan.

Matmerk (2018). Hva er Nyt Norge? [What is Enjoy Norway?]. https://www.matmerk.no/no/nytnorge/hva-er-nyt-norge.

Molloy, C. (2011). *Popular Media and Animals*. Basingstoke: Palgrave Macmillan.

Nibert, D. (2002). *Animal Rights/Human Rights: Entanglements of Oppression and Liberation*. Lanham, MD: Rowman and Littlefield.

Norwegian Food Safety Authority (2018). Egg og salmonella [Eggs and salmonella]. https://bit.ly/2EnzPBn

Papacharissi, Z. (2004). Democracy online: Civility, politeness, and the democratic potential of online political discussion groups. *New Media and Society* 6(2), 259–83. doi:10.1177/1461444804041444

Pasquale, F. (2018). Mettre fin au trafic des données personnelles [Stop the trafficking of personal data]. *Le Monde diplomatique*. May, pp. 16–17. https://www.monde-diplomatique.fr/2018/05/PASQUALE/58653.

Pendergrast, N. and S. McGrath (2018). The role of the ideology of animal welfare in the consumption and marketing of animal-origin products. In D. Bogueva, D. Marinova and T. Raphaely (Eds.), *Handbook of Research on Social Marketing and Its Influence on Animal Origin Food Product Consumption* (pp. 219–35). Hershey, PA: IGI Global.

Potts, A. (2012). *Chicken*. London: Reaktion Books.

Regan, T. (1997). The rights of humans and other animals. *Ethics & Behavior* 7(2), 103–11. doi:10.1207/s15327019eb0702_2

Spiegel, M. (1988). *The Dreaded Comparison: Human and Animal Slavery*. New York: Mirror Books.

Stuart, T. (2006). *The Bloodless Revolution: A Cultural History of Vegetarianism from 1600 to Modern Times*. London: W.W. Norton and Company.

Swales, J. M. (1990). *Genre Analysis: English in Academic and Research Settings*. Cambridge: Cambridge University Press.

Torres, B. (2007). *Making a Killing: The Political Economy of Animal Rights*. Oakland, CA: AK Press.

Van Dijck, J. (2013). *The Culture of Connectivity: A Critical History of Social Media*. Oxford: Oxford University Press.

Wilcox, B. L., D. Kunkel, J. Cantor, P. Dowrick, S. Linn and E. Palmer (2004). *Report of the APA Task Force on Advertising and Children*. Washington, DC: American Psychological Association.

Zappavigna, M. (2012). *Discourse of Twitter and Social Media: How We Use Language to Create Affiliation on the Web*. London: Bloomsbury.

Zappavigna, M. (2014). Enacting identity in microblogging through ambient affiliation. *Discourse & Communication* 8(2), 209–28. doi:10.1177/1750481313510816

Zappavigna, M. (2018). *Searchable Talk: Hashtags and Social Media Metadiscourse*. London: Bloomsbury.

3

Ethical meat from family farms? Transparency and proximity in a blog marketing campaign on broiler production

Saara Kupsala

Introduction: Transparency, animal visibility and meat marketing[1]

In Nordic countries, consumer connection to farming and the transparency of animal production have become increasingly important themes in meat and dairy marketing. Food companies have, for instance, organised open farm events, published online videos from farms and fostered interaction with animals on social

1   This research was conducted in a project 'Ambivalent images of animals: Finnish animal discussion in the 2010s', funded by the Finnish Cultural Foundation. I warmly thank the leader of the project, Elisa Aaltola, for guidance and valuable comments, and Birgitta Wahlberg for useful feedback. During the study, I was a visiting researcher in the Centre for Corporate Responsibility, Department of Marketing, Hanken School of Economics. I thank Martin Fougére and Nikodemus Solitander for organising my research visit, and colleagues in Hanken for discussions and feedback. I am grateful to Minna Kaljonen for valuable comments as a discussant of the manuscript in the working group 'Towards sustainable food system' in the 13th Nordic Environmental Social Science Conference (2017) and to Eija Vinnari as a discussant in the seminar 'Food, naturecultures and politics' (Tampere University, 2018). Additional thanks to Minna for useful advice in the early phase of the research. Thanks go also to the working group and seminar participants for helpful comments about the paper.

media.[2] This type of marketing is a part of the widening corporate responsibility (CR) communication of food companies as they seek to mitigate growing public criticism of industrial agriculture. In this chapter, based on a blog marketing campaign on broiler production in Finland, I analyse how the ideas of visibility and proximity of meat production are constructed in the marketing texts. In the marketing campaign, food and lifestyle bloggers visited a broiler farm and slaughterhouse and posted about their experiences on social media. Industrial poultry production and slaughtering are not typically depicted in advertising.[3] Consequently, this case study examines how the meat industry makes visible those production practices that are typically left hidden. The chapter also discusses how consumers negotiate the notions of proximity and visibility when engaging with marketing texts on social media.

In industrial agriculture, farmed animals and their killing are segregated in enclosed facilities, often justified on the grounds of disease prevention, but control of information also plays a role.[4] Visibility affects the protection of animals, hence the statutory rights of low-visibility animals, including farmed animals, tend to be weak.[5] Animal agriculture arguably benefits from the public's ignorance of modern farming practices, which is recurrently reinforced by advertisements where happy animals are depicted in pastoral landscapes.[6] The industry has also manifestly tightened its control of media access as farming has become increasingly industrialised.[7] In this situation, undercover investigations have become an important tool for activists to expose farming practices to the wider public. However, the industry has responded to the covert filming by prosecuting activists and demanding its criminalisation.[8] Regulatory transparency has also become a pertinent issue because industry standards have increasingly replaced legal standards for animal welfare. While governmental

---

2   Kaljonen & Lonkila 2013; Linné 2016; Linné & Pedersen 2016.
3   Borkfelt et al. 2015, p. 1067.
4   O'Sullivan 2011; Swabe 1999, pp. 137–141.
5   O'Sullivan 2011.
6   Borkfelt et al. 2015; Singer & Mason 2006, pp. 11–12.
7   Lappalainen 2012, pp. 14–19; Singer & Mason 2006, pp. 8–12.
8   Aaltola 2014, p. 29; Pachirat 2011, pp. 5–8.

legislation and control are open for public scrutiny, in industry's regulation of animal welfare, firms are not legally obligated to disclose the specific requirements of their standards nor farmers' compliance with them.[9]

Pictures of live animals rarely appear in meat marketing, particularly in chicken marketing where images of cooked chicken are common.[10] This reflects the tendency in the mainstream meat culture to dissociate meat from its animal origin. The invisibility of animals in meat marketing differs from dairy marketing where cows are highly visible because of cows' positive popular image and milk not being directly associated with slaughter.[11] In particular, consumers tend to have a negative perception of broiler welfare, which motivates advertisers to remove cues to live chickens.

Marketing, which promotes consumer connection with farming and the transparency of production, appears to conflict with this background where the industry has benefitted from consumer disconnection from production and has reinforced it actively by controlling the information flow and making animals invisible in marketing. However, the growing social criticism of industrial agriculture has forced animal industries to respond with new communications strategies,[12] which serves to highlight the reactive character of CR communications in managing crises that pose a threat to business.[13] In Finland, covert filming has been particularly damaging to the meat industry. Since 2007, undercover footage has been obtained from nearly two hundred farms and several slaughterhouses, published by the animal rights organisation Oikeutta Eläimille, and it has gained widespread exposure in the mainstream media.[14] The footage has contained graphic images, such as cruel treatment of animals in slaughterhouses. Furthermore, Finns' high level of meat consumption has been challenged also on environmental

---

9   Lundmark 2016, pp. 70–71.
10   Molloy 2011, pp. 110–111.
11   Molloy 2011, pp. 114–123.
12   Kaljonen & Lonkila 2013.
13   Fougère & Solitander 2009, p. 221.
14   Kaihovaara 2015; Vinnari & Laine 2017; Oikeutta Eläimille has published
      the footage on its website: https://www.elaintehtaat.fi/english.html.

and public health grounds, encouraging the public to participate in meat reduction campaigns.[15] The sales of vegan and vegetarian foods have increased considerably in recent years.[16] Moreover, growing international competition in the domestic markets has forced Finnish meat companies to renew their marketing strategies. To maintain their market position, they aim to distinguish domestic meat based on the ideas of responsibility and familiarity.[17]

Marketing campaigns on visibility and proximity seem to comprise a new strategy of persuasion that seeks to tackle growing public criticism and to protect the meat industry from further societal scrutiny. As an exemplar of the phenomenon of meatsplaining where various rhetorics of denial are employed by the meat industry to neutralise negative publicity,[18] notions of visibility and proximity are utilised to foster the idea of responsible production. In this marketing strategy, animal industries have opened the farm gates – virtually or physically – suggesting a possibility for consumers to witness for themselves the different aspects of the food chain. This type of marketing appropriates the popular theme of consumer alienation from food production for its own purposes, fostering intimacy between consumers and animals or consumers and farmers. Online stories, photos and videos of farmers enhance consumers' familiarity with them, providing industrial products with a story.[19] Furthermore, this type of marketing appropriates local food discourses where industrial farms are defined as local family farms and where consumers' contact with farming appears as a means to more ethical eating habits.[20]

In contemporary capitalism, consumers are distanced and ethically insulated from the conditions of production. Corporate transparency discourse suggests that it is possible for consumers to see more clearly different stages of commodity production, which typically have remained hidden. However, the notions of proximity and visibility

---

15 Mattila 2016.
16 Jallinoja, Vinnari & Niva 2018.
17 Kaljonen & Lonkila 2013; Kotilainen 2015.
18 See Hannan 2020 in this volume.
19 Kaljonen & Lonkila 2013; Kotilainen 2015.
20 Kotilainen 2015; Linné 2016, pp. 721–722.

constructed in the marketing of animal-based foods have become increasingly problematised in critical animal studies. In commercially scripted human–animal encounters, the visibility of animal production is carefully regulated, and animals can be distanced through various techniques, such as exoticisation and mechanistic portrayals, which serve to cement rather than disrupt the species gap.[21] The notion of transparency suggests direct perception and unlimited access to information, hence making companies' actions more visible to different stakeholders.[22] However, because firms control what information they provide, transparency communication is essentially 'staging' where selective disclosure of information has strategic importance for the firms.[23] Corporate transparency often suggests neutral viewing, yet it simultaneously manipulates perception, leaving some corporate actions opaque.[24] Ambiguity is inherent in the pursuit of transparency; while it makes some corporate actions visible, at the same time it creates new types of opacity.[25]

Aims and objectives

The review of the literature suggests that while marketing has traditionally promoted consumer–animal disconnection, its recent emphasis on animal visibility and proximity calls for critical unpacking of how these concepts are constructed in marketing. This study aims to contribute to the research on the meat industry's communicative strategies as it seeks to mitigate public criticism. Based on an analysis of the blog marketing campaign, and drawing on critical animal studies perspectives, the study brings additional insight into the scholarly analysis of meatsplaining by examining in detail how marketing constructs distance toward animals, despite its suggestions of closeness and visibility.

21　Linné & Pedersen 2016.
22　Christensen 2002; Torssonen 2019.
23　Christensen 2002, p. 162, pp. 166–167.
24　Christensen & Cheney 2015; Torssonen 2019.
25　Christensen & Cheney 2015; Pachirat 2011, pp. 253–255.

The chapter focuses on three research questions: First, how are visibility and proximity of broiler production constructed in the bloggers' textual and visual presentation of the tour? Second, by which processes are chickens and their killing distanced and concealed in the marketing texts? Third, how do consumers negotiate, reinforce and contest the notions of visibility and proximity constructed in the marketing texts?

I analyse the processes of constructing closeness to farming by making use of the literature on the commodification of intimacy in blog marketing. I also draw from theories of moral distancing and moral invisibility, particularly utilising the literature on the objectification, de-individualisation and fragmentation of animals and the theories of distancing killing in the slaughterhouses.

Theoretical starting points

Commodification of intimacy in blog marketing

There has been increasing research attention on the ways in which intimacy is harnessed for commercial purposes in blog marketing. Bloggers with a large following are described in the marketing industry as 'influencers' because their association with a brand or product is considered valuable advertising due to their cultural impact.[26] Promotions in blogs are highly personalised as the marketing message is woven into the narratives of bloggers' personal lives and their first-hand experiences and opinions of a product or a brand.[27] Bloggers' self-revelation regarding their private lives enhances the audience's sense of closeness with them.[28] The bloggers also appear relatable to their readers as ordinary people, enhanced by recurrent self-deprecation to minimise social distance from them.[29] Likewise, frequent responding to readers' comments online fosters the perceived

---

26 Berryman & Kavka 2017, p. 307.
27 Abidin & Gwynne 2017.
28 Abidin & Gwynne 2017; Berryman & Kavka 2017; Dejmanee 2016.
29 Abidin & Gwynne 2017; McQuarrie, Miller & Phillips 2013.

accessibility of the bloggers.[30] In this way, readers' closeness with bloggers is constructed in various ways in blog marketing, and this closeness is monetised by fostering readers' identification with commercial narratives.

Blog marketing is interactive marketing where the followers participate in the construction of the marketing message. Blogs provide a forum to promote positive recommendations in the digital media community where information is spread through social networks.[31] With their positive feedback, readers participate in reinforcing the marketing message, further enhanced by the bloggers' endorsements.[32] In this way, readers' engagement with marketing texts is monetised. However, readers can also challenge the marketing messages, producing counternarratives to the marketing campaign, which means firms must then employ various strategies to manage negative online discussions.[33]

Moral distance to animals

Zygmunt Bauman has examined 'morality silencing' mechanisms embedded in modern technocratic and bureaucratic societies that operate by replacing proximity with physical or mental distance.[34] Proximity breeds moral recognition and responsibility, while distance tends to erode them.[35] With increasing physical distance, moral attributes of the victim and the outcomes of action are rendered invisible.[36] In the absence of physical distance, mental distance can take place in the forms of objectification and de-individualisation of the victim, as well as clinical, technical jargon.[37] Ever longer and complex supply chains erode moral proximity in modern corporations. However, CR actions do not typically bridge the moral gaps inherent in this complexity, as moral issues are outsourced to

---

30 Abidin & Gwynne 2017; Berryman & Kavka 2017.
31 Liljander, Gummerus & Söderlund 2015.
32 Berryman & Kavka 2017.
33 Linné 2016, p. 727.
34 Bauman 1989, p. 174.
35 Bauman 1989, p. 184.
36 Bauman 1989, pp. 192–194.
37 Bauman 1989, pp. 25–27, pp. 196–198.

intermediaries, such as CR experts and rating agencies, which handle ethical issues as technical matters, erasing their moral substance.[38] While Bauman analysed 'morality-eroding mechanisms' in relation to humans,[39] his observations are applicable also in the nonhuman animal context.[40] As frequently pointed out in critical studies on animal industries, the slaughterhouse, industrial farm and animal laboratory are exemplary cases of sequestering violence toward animals via the processes of isolation, objectification and de-individualisation, hygiene practices and the compartmentalisation of labour to specialised tasks.[41]

Objectification generally refers to a process where inanimate features are attributed to living beings.[42] In objectification, the subjectivity of animals becomes invisible, and it is denied that they are agents with intentions and experiences. Objectification is facilitated by de-individualisation where animals become interchangeable units.[43] Furthermore, the slaughtering process removes the individuating characters of animals stage by stage.[44] Animals are further fragmented in the slaughter line where they become gradually de-animalised and transformed into food commodities.[45]

Hygiene practices and discourses of contamination are important techniques of moral demarcation.[46] Physical separation from animals is often encouraged for hygiene reasons.[47] Touch fosters regard and caring for animals,[48] while avoidance of physical contact and reduction of animals to mere objects of gaze enhance their remoteness.[49] Also in the slaughterhouse, hygiene practices are effective ways of concealing

---

38 Herlin & Solitander 2017.
39 Bauman 1989, p 199.
40 Hamilton & McCabe 2016; Pachirat 2011, p. 4.
41 Arluke 1988; Pachirat 2011; Vialles 1994.
42 Arluke 1988, p. 100.
43 Arluke 1988, p. 101; Wilkie 2010, p. 225.
44 Pachirat 2011, p. 40, p. 72.
45 Adams 1990, pp. 49–53; Hamilton & McCabe 2016; Pachirat 2011, pp. 20–84; Vialles 1994.
46 Douglas 2002.
47 Swabe 1999, pp. 137–141.
48 Haraway 2008, p. 36.
49 Berger 2009.

and neutralising large-scale killing.[50] Slaughtering becomes an issue of food safety and its technical and bureaucratic control rather than the mass destruction of sentient life.[51]

The case study: Bloggers visiting a broiler farm and slaughterhouse

In September 2016, Finnish meat company Atria Finland invited five lifestyle and food bloggers to visit its broiler slaughterhouse and contract chicken farm and paid them to post about their experiences on social media. Atria Finland is responsible for Atria Group's business activities in Finland, which forms the largest business area of the corporation. The blog marketing campaign was a part of the ongoing communication strategy of Atria Finland (henceforth Atria) to emphasise the transparency and responsibility of its production chains.[52] Atria is the largest meat company in Finland in terms of net sales, and its manufacturing share in poultry is 45 per cent.[53] In 2011, the company launched its Atria Family Farm brand (*Atria Perhetila*), which contains products traceable to specific farms, with the names of farmers appearing on the packaging.[54] Farmers are harnessed visibly to the marketing of the brand, featuring in advertisements and on social media.[55] The intention of the blog campaign was to strengthen consumer recognition of the brand.[56]

In the marketing event, the bloggers visited a broiler house that contained 30,000 chickens and a slaughterhouse where around 110,000 chickens were slaughtered daily. The bloggers interviewed the farmer and the company's managers and a veterinarian during the visit, took pictures and actively replied to readers' comments online. The

---

50 Pachirat 2011, pp. 206–207.
51 Pachirat 2011, p. 206.
52 Kaljonen & Lonkila 2013.
53 Atria 2017.
54 Atria 2018.
55 Ahlroth 2016.
56 Atria's communications and investor relations manager in the company's blog: https://bit.ly/2Qd0SBT.

campaign generated a lively discussion on social media, while also attracting attention in the mainstream media.[57] Criticism was particularly directed toward the campaign's inadequate marketing identifiers and misleading animal welfare claims. The Council of Ethics in Advertising issued a statement about one blog posting, proclaiming that the marketing identifier of the blog was not clear and understandable.[58] Because of the heated social media debate, the bloggers clarified the commercial content of their blogs in their replies to the readers.

All the bloggers were members of influencer marketing agencies with thousands of weekly readers, and two of them were award-winning bloggers. Reflecting the female dominance in food and lifestyle blogging,[59] the bloggers were women, and consequently, the marketing campaign targeted their predominantly female readership. Chicken is less masculinised than red meat.[60] In Finland, men on average eat considerably more red meat than women, but gender differences in poultry consumption are small.[61] Women also tend to express greater concern for farm animal welfare than men,[62] which may partly explain why the company targeted its marketing campaign at women. The cultural background of the bloggers varied, and they included, for instance, returning migrant backgrounds.

The data of the case study consists of the bloggers' blog postings (5), Facebook and Instagram postings (14), their responses to reader comments (184) and readers' comments to them (319). On the blog platforms, most comments were written by anonymous users or users with pseudonyms, while on Facebook and Instagram the participants were typically identifiable. Women or persons with female names or pseudonyms posted most of the comments. The visual analysis covered 58 pictures after duplicates between social media and blog postings were

---

57   Ahlroth 2016.
58   Council of Ethics in Advertising 2017.
59   Abidin & Gwynne 2017; Dejmanee 2016.
60   Cudworth 2011, p. 88.
61   Ovaskainen 2016, p. 42.
62   Kupsala, Vinnari, Jokinen & Räsänen 2015.

removed. The bloggers took most of the pictures, although three bloggers also used pictures taken by a photographer hired by the company.

I read the materials several times both online and as printouts. I transferred electronic printouts to the qualitative data analysis software program NVivo for thematic content analysis. Coding helped to identify important themes and supported the interpretative process. Different themes are illustrated with quotes from the data, translated from Finnish. The bloggers' postings and readers' comments are public, accessible to all those who have an internet connection, and therefore they can be used for research purposes like any other public material.[63] However, I refer to the bloggers with pseudonyms and I have anonymised all the users quoted in this article.

Constructing proximity and visibility in the blog marketing texts

'We saw every stage of the process with our own eyes.'[64]

Although the company did not brief the bloggers on what they should write in their blogs, the company framed their visitor experience in many ways. When the bloggers paid the visit, the chickens were three weeks old, half their eventual slaughter age. The farmer, the company's managers and the veterinarian appeared as authoritative sources of expert knowledge and they were the only source of information throughout the visit. Through reporting the interviews with them, the bloggers disseminated the marketing message of 'responsible domestic production'. For instance, Finnish production was distinguished from European production in terms of larger space allowance, minimal antibiotic use and the disallowance of beak trimming. The bloggers substantiated this company information with their own endorsements. For instance, they wrote how they became convinced about the responsibility of domestic production after seeing the whole chain. 'I'm convinced that Finnish meat is produced responsibly and cleanly' (Helena's blog, 17/9/2016). 'In future, I'll always choose domestic, quality meat, which is produced responsibly' (Anne's blog, 22/9/2016).

---

63   Hookway 2008.
64   Sonja's blog, 28 September 2016.

Although the readers' experience of broiler production was necessarily mediated by the bloggers' stories, the marketing texts constructed a sense of proximity to broiler production in various ways. The bloggers appeared to visit the facilities on behalf of their readers. 'Few have an opportunity to visit a farm and slaughterhouse, and my aim was to tell how things there are' (Sonja, blog comment, 28/9/2016). Following the style of intimate storytelling in the blogging genre,[65] the bloggers invite readers to identify with their experiences of broiler production by fostering a sense of closeness and relatability with them. In the first parts of the blog postings, they disclose their everyday food practices in a conversational tone. Three bloggers describe themselves as typical omnivores: Sonja is 'a gourmet', emphasising taste in her selection of food; Helena is 'a realistic mother', emphasising price, taste and domestic origin of food; and Anne regularly buys domestic broilers. In contrast, the two other bloggers position themselves as critical consumers. Heidi mentions that she has 'a very critical attitude' to broiler production, having avoided broiler meat for years, although still eating it occasionally. Nina had reduced her chicken consumption after reading a book about animal production. Interest in learning more about broiler production also motivated these critical consumers to participate.

The bloggers construct the idea of neutral viewing to broiler production by framing the visit as an educational event.[66] They write how consumers, including themselves, have become alienated from the origin of food. Consumers tend to hold many suppositions but have limited knowledge. The bloggers describe how their knowledge of broiler production increased considerably during the visit. 'After the farm visit, I know about broilers and their rearing much more than before' (Heidi's blog, 28/9/2016). The bloggers emphasise the importance of facts and information when forming opinions about food production. 'Based on facts (not only images) everyone can make their own conclusions and act accordingly' (Nina's blog, 23/9/2016).

The bloggers also seemed to provide an uncensored and realistic view of a normal weekday in broiler production. They appear as ordinary consumers who post their amateur, non-edited photos from

---

65   Abidin & Gwynne 2017; Berryman & Kavka 2017; Dejmanee 2016.
66   Linné & Pedersen 2016.

the visit. Photos that show thousands of chickens in a huge hall and red-coloured chicken wings on a conveyer belt seem to be far removed from the typical advertising images of happy meat. The bloggers also praise the company for its 'boldness', 'openness' and 'transparency' in showing them all the aspects of production. Sonja was even perplexed by the straightforwardness of the farmer when he described his morning routine of collecting dead chickens from the shed. The company appears to be ready to show even the darker aspects of production to the public as the bloggers report the mortality of chickens. Sonja writes on Instagram: '[T]his is truly transparent from Atria. We all were baffled by how honestly we were told about issues and that we could really go everywhere, including the slaughtering room' (comment, 14/9/2016).

Proximity to farming is fostered by the bloggers' emphasis on their personal experiences. Most bloggers mention having negative views about broiler production before the visit, but these 'prejudices' (Anne's blog) were not confirmed when they saw everything with their own eyes. Heidi writes in her Facebook posting: 'Before the visit, [it was] easier to be against factory farming and meat industry and view it super-critically. After the visit the feeling is a little bit different' (28/9/2016). The bloggers, for instance, write how the chickens appeared unstressed and calm. Chickens also had plenty of litter, which provided possibilities for scratching and bathing. This positive experience is confirmed with the bloggers' descriptions of eating chicken after the visit. For instance, Helena mentions eating chicken tortillas 'with good appetite', and Sonja orders broiler for lunch because the farm visit created such 'a good feeling'. In this way, promotions in the blogs are highly personalised, and they are based on the bloggers' direct experiences and eating habits. The bloggers are also frequently photographed during the visit, for instance, pictured gathering around the farmer and taking photos of the birds, further integrating the visit with the bloggers and their experiences.

Closeness with farming is also enhanced by the personalisation of the farmer, making industrial farming more relatable to the readers. As a part of the farmer-oriented marketing strategy of the Atria Family Farm brand, the bloggers describe their positive impressions of the farmer, characterising him as 'open', 'trustworthy' (Sonja's blog) and 'passionate' about his work (Heidi's blog). Additionally, bird welfare is a 'priority' for him (Helena's blog). Nearly one-third of the photos from the farm visit portray the farmer, for instance, talking to visitors and holding a chicken in his hands. The farmer's house and yard are also pictured.

Distancing and concealment of chickens and their killing

Even though the bloggers sought to convey a sense of proximity to broiler farming, the marketing texts distanced and concealed chickens and their killing in various ways. When reading the blog postings closely, one soon notes that chickens are remarkably absent in the written material. The bloggers describe mainly the conditions of the chickens as described by the farmer and the company representatives, and make only a few remarks about the actual chickens in the hall. None of them describes interacting with an individual chicken. In the written material, chickens appear as passive, displaying little subjective agency and versatility of living, effectively hindered by the monotonous living environment.

The chickens are also distanced through hygiene practices. The bloggers emphasise the stringent hygiene control, the tidiness of the farm and the cleanliness of the birds, conveying the message of 'clean' domestic meat. Before entering the broiler house, they dress in overalls and disinfect their boots and hands. Cross-contamination is prevented by maintaining physical distance from the chickens. Anne notes that some chickens try to sit in her lap, and she stands up to avoid touching them with bare skin, 'despite disinfection'. Touch fosters regard for animals and affectionate relations with them.[67] However, in this marketing event, the bloggers' experience of chickens was insulated, and the chickens were only looked at and photographed. The encounter is reminiscent of viewing animals in zoos; the human gaze governs the encounter where meaningful interaction between two agents is rendered marginal.[68]

Moreover, the chickens are distanced through de-individualisation. In the written material, no specific chicken stands out or is personalised, and chickens are talked of only in the plural. Because

---

67 Haraway 2008, p. 36; Kaarlenkaski 2014, p. 16.
68 Berger 2009, pp. 27–37.

of breeding and a batch-based production model, chickens appear markedly homogeneous.[69] They grow at a similar pace, and no differences in size or colour mark them out as individuals. A notable contradiction emerges in Helena's blog where she mentions her 'beloved pet chickens', each with its own name. In the visual material, the chickens are mostly portrayed in groups: as a whole flock (6), a smaller group of chickens (5) and the human visitors surrounded by the chickens (6). Only in five pictures (of 39 in all) from the farm does the photograph focus on an individual chicken.

Similarly, with regard to the visit to the slaughterhouse, hygiene practices were effective in distancing the killing of animals. The bloggers highlight the stringent hygiene measures and describe the slaughterhouse as a 'clean' place. They are dressed in white overalls, and every time they pass into a new area, they disinfect themselves. In compliance with hygiene rules, they tour the slaughterhouse 'from the cleanest area to the dirtiest' (Heidi's blog). The slaughterhouse is compartmentalised into a 'clean' side, where carcasses are being processed, and a 'dirty' side, where live animals are handled and killed and where excreta and litter form potential sources of pollution.[70]

The bloggers post photos only from the 'clean side', leaving out the photos of live chickens waiting for slaughter and the stunning, bleeding, de-feathering and evisceration of chickens. The photos portray a sterile image of the slaughterhouse; white walls, steel surfaces and machinery form a background to pictures where de-animalised chicken carcasses, without head, feathers, internal organs and feet, are gliding along on hooks. Cleanliness and white walls indicate professionalism, order and conformity to standards.[71] Although hygiene control is guided by practical motives to promote food safety, it works also on a metaphorical level, sanitising the violence of large-scale killing.[72] Live chickens and the materials that indicate their organic being become 'dirt' that can pollute the food their bodies

---

69   Arluke 1988, p. 101.
70   Hamilton & McCabe 2016, p. 339; Pachirat 2011, pp. 61–72; Vialles 1994, pp. 35–39.
71   Vialles 1994, 66.
72   Pachirat 2011; Vialles 1994, p. 66.

later become. Chickens in the 'dirty' side hold an indeterminate place between the categories of food and an animal,[73] hence appearing as 'matter out of place', which essentially characterises the concept of dirt.[74] Defining chickens as dirt functions also on the metaphorical level, denigrating them and hence legitimising their slaughter.

Moreover, focus on technology distances killing. The bloggers never use the word 'slaughterhouse'; instead, they use the terms 'factory', 'mill' and 'poultry line'. They are impressed by the quality-control measures and the efficiency of the machinery. 'As a group, we marvelled at the efficiency of the line and the engineering skill it represented' (Sonja's blog). In this way, the bloggers join 'the discourse of managerial success' where the celebration of the machinery obliterates the killing that takes place in the plant.[75]

Of course, the slaughterhouse tour was not devoid of emotions, and the bloggers describe their unease when encountering large numbers of chicken carcasses, since they indicated the sheer scale of the slaughter. The stunning and bleeding of chickens also generated anxiety. Anne writes in her blog: 'Those last moments stuck to my mind permanently. When watching the birds, I gulped, and the event brought tears to my eyes, after all.' However, the disquieting experiences did not lead to the moral questioning of large-scale killing. For instance, Helena and Heidi associate their anxiety with being 'alienated' from food production, and particularly Heidi downplays her emotional reaction as an urbanite's sense of shock. Sonja emphasises that meat-eaters must accept that animals die, despite feeling sympathy for them. By expressing their unease, the bloggers show they are not pitiless towards the animals. However, their way of negotiating their emotional reaction serves to normalise the mass killing of sentient life.[76]

---

73 Hamilton & McCabe 2016, p. 339.
74 Douglas 2002, p. 44.
75 Hamilton & McCabe 2016, p. 340.
76 Parry 2010.

Contested notions of proximity and visibility in the reader feedback

The bloggers' blog and social media postings received plenty of comments, and the readers actively debated the campaign on social media. Many readers wrote positive feedback to the bloggers, participating in strengthening the marketing message of the campaign. The readers thanked the bloggers for posting 'honest', 'objective', 'realistic' and 'impartial' texts about broiler production. 'Dispassionate' writing style was welcomed particularly because of the polemical nature of the topic. 'In my view this was a good text where you told dispassionately about the production conditions of poultry' (a comment on Sonja's blog, 30/9/2016). The readers also applauded the bloggers and the company for their openness and transparency. 'Interesting and important. High five to Atria and the family farm for transparency' (a comment on Helena's blog, 18/9/2016).

Some readers strengthened the bloggers' positive visitor experience by bringing up their own positive experiences at Finnish farms. 'I study agricultural sciences at the university, and there I realised how well things are in Finland! … I did my internship on a big … beef farm, and it really did leave a good feeling' (a comment on Heidi's blog, 28/9/2016). The readers were glad that the bloggers saw food production in practice, instead of seeing a mere 'rose-tinted slideshow' of it (a comment on Sonja's blog, 28/9/2016). They applauded the bloggers for giving a realistic portrayal of Finnish production to consumers.

The readers also participated in reinforcing the marketing message concerning the purchasing of Finnish meat. They emphasised how important it is to buy domestic meat and demand it also in restaurants. 'Things are done so damn well in our country. In the future, I will watch more carefully that the broiler I eat is definitely domestic' (a comment on Nina's blog, 24/9/2016). In their replies, the bloggers emphasised how they value domestic meat much more after the visit.

However, there was an overflow of critical feedback where the readers contested the notions of visibility and proximity. Negative feedback was directed particularly at two of the bloggers as both had shown a critical attitude in their blogging and hence their readers were disappointed that they participated in 'meat lobbying'. For instance, one of the bloggers had covered feminist issues, and therefore her participation in the campaign was considered contradictory to a feminist stance against oppression.[77] Many readers suggested that the blog campaign was just about greenwashing where broiler production was painted as ethical despite its various problems. 'Readers are disappointed because the bloggers have participated in this Atria family farm / neighbour's chicken greenwashing ... The bloggers are lobbying [on behalf of an] ecologically and ethically questionable business, for money' (a comment on Heidi's blog, 30/9/2016).

The readers contested the suggestions of openness and neutrality put forward in the campaign. For them, the postings were evidently one-sided; only the farmer's and the company's perspectives were brought up in the blogs, while all other perspectives were left out. The readers noted that the bloggers had come to a conclusion about the 'ethicality' of broiler production based on a single visit, arranged and scripted by the company, and made few comparisons between different production systems.

The readers also contested the value of the bloggers' personal experience in terms of verifying animal welfare on Finnish farms. For them, personal testimonials had little value if the bloggers' understanding of chickens' needs was limited. The readers also pointed out that the bloggers did not witness all the phases of production (such as transport) and that probably sick birds were removed before the visit. It was noted that the bloggers omitted key welfare issues from their postings, such as leg disorders and heart-related illnesses related to fast growth.

The bloggers responded to the critical comments in varying ways. Some bloggers left many of the critical comments without a response. When they did respond, the bloggers defended their postings, for instance by emphasising their own subjective experience and that they had tried to report honestly what they saw and learned during the visit. '[I] feel at ease in passing on what I saw in the farm and in the factory because, based on my experience, Finnish broiler farming is not that horrible as it has been suggested. It's my opinion' (Helena, blog comment, 29/9/2016).

---

77 In fact, a year later Heidi wrote that she would no longer join a commercial co-operative venture with a meat company because her thoughts had changed (Facebook posting, 8 November 2017).

Conclusion: Transparency as concealment

In the blog marketing campaign analysed in this chapter, the Finnish meat company Atria appeared to be open to consumers by inviting popular bloggers to visit its slaughterhouse and contract broiler farm. The campaign seemed to counteract the invisibility of intensively farmed animals and their slaughtering. The meat industry, which has been criticised for disseminating only fairy-tale images of happy meat, no longer shies away from showing thousands of animals in a production hall and hundreds of carcasses in the slaughter line, as the marketing case study evinced. The marketing campaign suggested that the meat company had shown different stages of meat production to consumers via the bloggers, who were external to the industry and told their readers about what they saw and posted their own pictures about the visit, instead of the company's polished PR material. The consumers were reassured about the responsibility of Finnish production practices by the bloggers' positive endorsements and willingness to eat domestic meat after having witnessed the process.

The images presented in the marketing campaign appeared to counteract activists' undercover images. In the marketing images, the industrial facilities for animal production were shown, but all cues to evident suffering (such as chickens with severe leg disorders) were removed. While the campaign suggested full visibility, it was not acknowledged that some phases of production, such as the stunning and bleeding of chickens, were not pictured. By producing a sanitised image of broiler rearing and slaughtering, and emphasising the cleanliness of production, the campaign sought to purify the ethical image of the industry.

The bloggers constructed their authority to speak about the industry through personally visiting the broiler farm and slaughterhouse. First-hand testimonials gave them a position to explain production conditions to wider audiences and to discredit those industry critics who lack personal experience of industrial meat production. After all, as the campaign suggested, videos circulating on social media can create misconceptions about the industry and they do not equate to direct exposure. In the campaign, the company strived for high credibility regarding its claims on responsible Finnish meat production by recruiting female bloggers with varied cultural backgrounds – some even describing critical attitudes towards the industry before the visit – to engage in meatsplaining and to endorse domestic meat.

While the campaign appeared to bring chickens and their production closer to consumers, this proximity was created from the anthropocentric perspective where consumers were invited to find out how animals end up on their plates. The chickens that had become visible were already objectified as food in waiting, while they remained unseen as morally valuable beings. In this marketing campaign, empathy for animals was dampened through the objectification and de-individualisation of chickens as well as through hygiene practices. As is well established in the literature on the photographic representation of suffering, visibility as such does not ensure moral recognition and action.[78] Comprehending suffering requires both factual knowledge and moral reflection.[79] If pictures of suffering are not anchored to moral frameworks, they can foster detachment rather than caring.[80]

The contentious character of social responsibility marketing became evident as the readers discussed the campaign on social media. Some readers reinforced the constructed visibility of broiler production by praising the bloggers for writing about the visit realistically. However, there was an overflow of negative feedback where readers contested the notions of visibility and proximity. Indeed, the abundance of negative feedback indicates vulnerabilities in the meat industry's communications around responsibility as social media marketing provides a platform to produce counternarratives on animal visibility.

As the meat industry is increasingly eager to show its own 'truth' of production, there is a need to critically unpack the visibility constructed by the industry. In the societal discussion, the transparency measures of the animal foods industries are often applauded without acknowledging the political nature of constructed visibility. In the commercially scripted human–animal encounter, 'visibility also functions as concealment', sequestering violence toward

---

78 Aaltola 2014.
79 Aaltola 2014, p. 27.
80 Aaltola 2014.

animals.[81] Marketing on visibility and proximity comprises a rhetorical strategy of meatsplaining where ideas of 'transparency' and 'openness' are used to deny severe violence against animals and hence to cancel out public criticism of the meat industry. It can be expected that the meat industry will employ increasingly sophisticated marketing tactics to suggest transparency of production in order to mitigate future risks posed by undercover investigations and other negative publicity.[82] Hence, activists are well advised to deconstruct the visibility put forward in the marketing texts and to demonstrate how the devices for enhancing transparency serve to conceal, rather than illuminate, key moral issues in meat production.

References

Aaltola, E. (2014). Animal suffering: Representations and the act of looking. *Anthrozoös* 27(1), 19–31.

Adams, C. J. (1990). *The Sexual Politics of Meat: A Feminist-Vegetarian Critical Theory*. New York: Continuum.

Ahlroth, J. (2016). Ruokabloggarit kävivät broileritilalla ja pitivät näkemästään – lihayhtiö maksoi bloggareille, yleisöltä sataa kritiikkiä. *Helsingin Sanomat, Nyt-liite*. 30 September. https://www.hs.fi/nyt/art-2000002923406.html

Arluke, A. (1988). Sacrificial symbolism in animal experimentation: Object or pet? *Anthrozoös* 2(2), 98–117.

Atria (2017). Annual report 2016. https://bit.ly/31h3hSl

Atria (2018). The first 114 years of Atria. https://bit.ly/3aGWpB0

Bauman, Z. (1989). *Modernity and the Holocaust*. Cambridge: Polity Press.

Berger, J. (2009). *Why Look at Animals?* London: Penguin Books.

Berryman, R. and M. Kavka (2017). 'I guess a lot of people see me as a big sister or a friend': The role of intimacy in the celebrification of beauty vloggers. *Journal of Gender Studies* 26(3), 307–320.

Borkfelt, S., S. Kondrup, H. Röcklinsberg, K. Bjørkdahl and M. Gjerris (2015). Closer to nature? A critical discussion of the marketing of 'ethical' animal products. *Journal of Agricultural and Environmental Ethics* 28(6), 1053–1073.

---

81 Linné & Pedersen 2016, p. 117.
82 Comp. Fougère & Solitander 2009.

Christensen, L.T. (2002). Corporate communication: The challenge of transparency. *Corporate Communications: An International Journal* 7(3), 162–168.

Christensen, L.T. and G. Cheney (2015). Peering into transparency: Challenging ideals, proxies, and organizational practices. *Communication Theory* 25(1): 70–90.

Council of Ethics in Advertising (2017). *MEN 1/2017: Markkinoinnin tunnistettavuus, blogi*. https://bit.ly/2FKy4Ph

Cudworth, E. (2011). *Social Lives with Other Animals: Tales of Sex, Death and Love*. Basingstoke: Palgrave Macmillan.

Dejmanee, T. (2016). 'Food porn' as postfeminist play. *Television & New Media* 17(5), 429–448.

Douglas, M. (2002). *Purity and Danger: An Analysis of the Concepts of Pollution and Taboo*. Oxon: Routledge.

Fougère, M. and N. Solitander (2009). Against corporate responsibility: Critical reflections on thinking, practice, content and consequences. *Corporate Social Responsibility and Environmental Management* 16(4), 217–227.

Hamilton, L. and D. McCabe (2016). 'It's just a job': Understanding emotion work, de-animalization and the compartmentalization of organized animal slaughter. *Organization* 23(3), 330–350.

Hannan, J. (2020). Introduction: The meat industry explains things to us. In J. Hannan, *Meatsplaining: The Animal Agriculture Industry and the Rhetoric of Denial*. Sydney: Sydney University Press.

Haraway, D. (2008). *When Species Meet*. Minneapolis: University of Minnesota Press.

Herlin, H. and N. Solitander (2017). Corporate social responsibility as relief from responsibility: NPO legitimizations for corporate partnerships in contested terrains. *Critical Perspectives on International Business* 13(1), 2–22.

Hookway, N. (2008). 'Entering the blogosphere': Some strategies for using blogs in social research. *Qualitative Research* 8(1), 91–113.

Jallinoja, P., M. Vinnari and M. Niva (2018). Veganism and plant-based eating: Analysis of interplay between discursive strategies and lifestyle political consumerism. In M. Boström, M. Micheletti and P. Oosterveer (Eds.), *Oxford Handbook of Political Consumerism*. Oxford: Oxford University Press.

Kaarlenkaski, T. (2014). Of cows and women: Gendered human–animal relationships in Finnish agriculture. *Relations: Beyond Anthropocentrism* 2(2), 9–26.

Kaihovaara, R. (2015). MOT:n haltuunsa saama videomateriaali paljastaa vakavia epäkohtia suomalaisissa teurastamoissa. *Yle*. 22 October. https://bit.ly/3lclloX.

Kaljonen, M. and A. Lonkila (2013). Tuttu ja turvallinen kotimainen – huomioita lihatalojen vastuullisuusviestinnästä. *Maaseudun uusi aika* 21(2–3), 91–98.

Kotilainen, N. (2015). Puhdasta, suomalaista, nationalistista lihaa. In E. Aaltola and S. Keto (Eds.), *Eläimet yhteiskunnassa* (pp. 37–56). Helsinki: Into Kustannus.

Kupsala, S., M. Vinnari, P. Jokinen and P. Räsänen (2015). Citizen attitudes to farm animals in Finland: A population-based study. *Journal of Agricultural and Environmental Ethics* 28(4), 601–620.

Lappalainen, E. (2012). *Syötäväksi kasvatetut: miten ruokasi eli elämänsä*. Jyväskylä: Atena.

Liljander, V., J. Gummerus and M. Söderlund (2015). Young consumers' responses to suspected covert and overt blog marketing. *Internet Research* 25(4), 610–632.

Linné, T. (2016). Cows on Facebook and Instagram: Interspecies intimacy in the social media spaces of the Swedish dairy industry. *Television & New Media* 17(8), 719–733.

Linné, T. and H. Pedersen (2016). With care for cows and a love for milk: affect and performance in Swedish dairy industry marketing strategies. In A. Potts, *Meat Culture* (pp. 111–128). Leiden: Brill.

Lundmark, F. (2016). Mind the gaps! From intentions to practice in animal welfare legislation and private standards [Doctoral thesis]. Skara: Swedish University of Agricultural Sciences.

Mattila, H. (Ed.) (2016). *Vähemmän lihaa: kohti kestävää ruokakulttuuria*. Helsinki: Gaudeamus.

McQuarrie, E. F., J. Miller and B. J. Phillips (2013). The megaphone effect: Taste and audience in fashion blogging. *Journal of Consumer Research* 40(1), 136–158.

Molloy, C. (2011). *Popular Media and Animals*. Basingstoke: Palgrave Macmillan.

O'Sullivan, S. (2011). *Animals, Equality and Democracy*. Basingstoke: Palgrave Macmillan.

Ovaskainen, M. L. (2016). Lihankulutus numeroina. In H. Mattila, *Vähemmän lihaa: kohti kestävää ruokakulttuuria* (pp. 36–49). Helsinki: Gaudeamus.

Pachirat, T. (2011). *Every Twelve Seconds: Industrialized Slaughter and the Politics of Sight*. New Haven: Yale University Press.

Parry, J. (2010). Gender and slaughter in popular gastronomy. *Feminism & Psychology* 20(3): 381–396.

Singer, P. and J. Mason (2006). *The Ethics of What We Eat: Why Our Food Choices Matter*. New York: Rodale.

Swabe, J. (1999). *Animals, Disease and Human Society: Human–Animal Relations and the Rise of Veterinary Medicine*. London: Routledge.

Torssonen, S. (2019). A history of ideological transparency. *Rethinking Marxism* 31 (4), 472–492.

Vialles, N. (1994). *Animal to Edible* (J. A. Underwood, Trans.). Cambridge: Cambridge University Press.

Vinnari, E. and M. Laine (2017). The moral mechanism of counter accounts: The case of industrial animal production. *Accounting, Organizations and Society* 57(1), 1–17.

Wilkie, R. (2010). *Livestock/Deadstock: Working with Farm Animals from Birth to Slaughter.* Philadelphia: Temple University Press.

4

Whose land? Whose beef? Marketing beef in Canada

Kelsey Speakman

'Canadian beef is not simply a premium food ... it is an embodiment of what it is to be Canadian.'[1]

Birthday beaver

While doing rounds on a spring day in Saskatchewan, rancher Adrienne Ivey was surprised to find a beaver positioned at the front of a herd of heifers. Ivey described the scene as the 'most Canadian moment of all moments',[2] since the Canadian-raised cattle were being herded by an animal that is a national symbol for Canada.[3] Moreover, the herd included 150 heifers – a noteworthy number, considering the encounter took place in 2017 when Canada was celebrating the 150th anniversary of its confederation. Along with a video posted to Twitter, Ivey included the hashtag for the trade organisation Canada Beef (#CDNbeef).[4] Indeed, Canada Beef could not have asked for a

---

1   Canada Beef 2016f, p. 11.
2   Coorsh 2017.
3   Berland 2015.
4   Adrienneivey 2017.

more fitting promotion, given that the meeting of Canada and beef represents the core of the brand.

Canada Beef was formed in 2011 when the Canadian beef industry consolidated research and marketing bodies into a single organisation with a 'mission' to: 'Strategically position the "Canadian Beef Advantage" to stimulate and sustain our premium global Canadian beef brand'.[5] Reasoning that consumer loyalty to Canadian beef would result in economic growth, the industry highlighted the product's origins as its key selling feature. Mobilising images of frontier landscapes and testimonials from ranching families, the 'Canadian Beef Advantage' positions Canada itself as the source of Canadian beef's high quality.

What national narratives does Canada Beef reproduce in selling Canada as an integral component of the country's beef industry? The chapter addresses this question by bringing together a political economic overview[6] of the current landscape of the Canadian beef industry with a critical discourse[7] and visual analysis[8] of Canada Beef's promotional materials. I situate Canada Beef within the 'animal-industrial complex'[9] – a partially concealed web of actors and relationships that normalise humans' use of other animals[10] for food, entertainment, science and profit. Following from Twine's methodological recommendation that critical animal researchers employ case studies of specific companies to illuminate the inner workings of the broader complex,[11] I focus on Canada Beef's nationalistic rhetoric in the service of revealing the mechanisms by which 'meatsplaining' operates in this particular context. Building on

---

5   Canada Beef 2016e.

6   Sayer 2001.

7   Willig 2013.

8   Rose 2001.

9   Noske 1989; Twine 2012.

10   Scholars and activists have indicated that the use of the term 'animal' to distinguish between humans and all other animals is a practice that maintains human exceptionalism. At the same time, alternative terms such as 'nonhuman' and 'more than human' continue to centre the human in the comparison (Fudge 2002; Nibert 2002). While recognising the term's limitations, I consciously use 'animal' to capture the contradictions and complex cultural meanings that are embedded in this constructed category.

11   Twine 2012.

the concept of 'mansplaining',[12] meatsplaining suggests that the patriarchal structures that empower men as experts also support the contemporary meat industry's position as a food authority. Drawing on feminist insights, I recognise that the human domination of animals reinforces and is reinforced by other relationships of power.[13] I foreground Belcourt's assertion that the power dynamics of settler colonialism are inextricably tied to the anthropocentric (human-centred) logics of capitalism in Canada, in that the colonial regulation of Indigenous bodies and lands has enabled the spatial and ideological expansion of animal agriculture as a profitable enterprise.[14]

To begin, I outline the political economic challenges that the Canadian beef industry is facing in terms of production barriers and declining consumption. Coupled with the increasing consolidation of industry and government, these conditions have necessitated the maintenance of positive connections between beef and Canada. Next, I identify three main themes about Canada's landscape, people and culture that emerged in my analysis of Canada Beef's marketing. These themes also function as components of metanarratives about Canada's national identity, which position Canada as a moral liberal democracy that industrious settlers built from an untamed wilderness. As consumers have turned to industry actors to provide guidance about food choices,[15] the narratives that are embedded in branding discourses are increasingly influential. I argue that the Canadian Beef Advantage perpetuates colonial perspectives on food and animals in Canada by tying the value of beef to a homogenous vision of Canadian national identity.

---

12 The term 'mansplaining' has caught on in the past decade to name the practice of 'explain[ing] something to someone, typically a man to a woman, in a manner regarded as condescending or patronising' (Steinmetz 2014).
13 Donovan & Adams 2007.
14 Belcourt 2015.
15 Dixon 2003; Dixon 2007.

The political economy of beef in Canada: Challenges and responses

As a commodity, beef is shaped by the landscape of international trade. Evidenced by the world food crisis of 2007/2008, which saw severe food price spikes that led to civil unrest,[16] the food industry has been subject to the trend towards financialisation that has characterised the global economy since the 1980s.[17] Relocating the source of profit from the accumulation of material resources to the exchange of financial instruments, financialisation intensifies the capitalist abstraction of plants, animals and ecological systems into units of value.[18] Corn has become increasingly valuable as a commodity for speculation, for example, as the agrofuel industry has developed. With resources and investments diverted to ethanol production and the future agrofuel market, feed has become less available and more expensive for livestock.[19]

Even though beef is abstracted in the marketplace, it comes from live animals who are subject to organic limitations. Dry conditions in the Canadian Prairies depressed cattle herd numbers in the mid-2010s. These conditions compounded the pattern of low herd numbers that had been in place since cases of bovine spongiform encephalopathy (BSE) in 2003 led to 'one of the largest liquidation phases in [the industry's] history',[20] as countries closed their borders to Canadian beef and potentially infected cattle were exterminated. The recent climatic blow to the already diminished herds translated into record high beef prices.[21]

Challenging weather patterns are exacerbated by the intensive practices of the industry. In addition to being a top consumer of land and water resources, the livestock industry is a major contributor to soil erosion, deforestation, water pollution and greenhouse gas emissions.[22] The beef industry accounts for the largest proportion of these emissions

---

16 Bello & Baviera 2010.
17 Clapp & Isakson 2018; Harvey 2005.
18 Sanbonmatsu 2011.
19 Bello & Baviera 2010; National Beef Strategic Planning Group 2015.
20 National Beef Strategic Planning Group 2015, p. 4.
21 Canadian Press 2015a.
22 Steinfeld et al. 2006.

in Canada and worldwide.[23] Responding to these issues, the multi-stakeholder organisation Canadian Roundtable for Sustainable Beef (CRSB) launched a framework for certified sustainable beef in 2017.[24]

Beyond environmental worries, consumer perceptions about the health of beef have taken a hit. In 2015, the World Health Organization classified processed meat as 'carcinogenic to humans' and red meat as 'probably carcinogenic to humans'.[25] In response, industry defended the healthy components of red meat like iron and protein, and encouraged consumers to weigh these benefits against perceived risks.[26]

The treatment of animals in beef production has also come under scrutiny, with consumers becoming more invested in animal welfare improvements.[27] In April of 2016, Canadian restaurant chain Earls announced that it would begin sourcing beef from a US supplier with a Certified Humane designation in the absence of comprehensive national animal welfare certifications in Canada. Facing backlash from the Canadian beef industry, Alberta government and patriotic consumers,[28] Earls characterised the move as a 'mistake',[29] and the company recommitted to Canadian sourcing.

In this climate of increased public concern and record high prices, per capita beef consumption is falling in Canada.[30] Although cattle numbers and consumer demand are both down domestically, global demand for beef is projected to increase.[31] While scholars have questioned the inevitability of this prediction,[32] populations have historically consumed more animal products as their countries have industrialised.[33]

The Canadian beef industry views this development as an opportunity to diversify its global portfolio and has formulated

---

23 Gerber et al. 2013, p. 23; Vergé, Dyer, Desjardins & Worth 2008, p. 132.
24 Canadian Roundtable for Sustainable Beef 2017.
25 Bouvard et al. 2015, p. 1600.
26 Canadian Press 2015c.
27 Canadian Centre for Food Integrity 2016.
28 Canadian Press 2016a.
29 Canadian Press 2016b.
30 Agriculture and Agri-Food Canada 2019a.
31 Alexandratos & Bruinsma 2012.
32 Boscardin 2017; Twine 2010.
33 Popkin 2003.

a National Beef Strategy to take advantage of this growth. The aggressive pursuit of trade agreements like the Canada–Korea Free Trade Agreement (CKFTA) and the Comprehensive Economic and Trade Agreement (CETA) is a key part of this plan.[34] The opening of international markets has become even more significant as the Canadian beef industry's relationship with its biggest trading partner – the United States – has become more contentious. As Canada became a net importer of beef in relation to the United States in 2012 and 2013,[35] the beef industry is eager to retain the positive trade balance that has since been restored. Given the increasing economic tensions between the United States and its other trading partners in Asia and Europe, opportunities are opening up for Canada to take advantage of these international markets[36] while maintaining a beneficial trade relationship with the United States.[37] Even as tariffs are being eliminated, non-tariff trade barriers are being erected.[38] For example, the Country of Origin Labeling (COOL) law that was in place in the United States required that meat be labelled with the country in which it was produced. Declared by the World Trade Organization as a violation of trade obligations, COOL placed Canadian meat at a disadvantage in the US market before its appeal.[39]

Canada Beef's operations are funded by import levies and a 'National Check-off' that collects $1 per head from the sale of cattle.[40] Considering this financial partnership, Canada Beef benefits from presenting both beef and Canada in a favourable light. Blue advises that such marketing efforts 'warrant critical attention because they signal a

---

34 National Beef Strategic Planning Group 2015.
35 Agriculture and Agri-Food Canada 2019b.
36 Charlebois et al. 2019.
37 Of significance for many economic sectors including the beef industry, Canada, Mexico and the United States are in the process of replacing the North American Free Trade Agreement (NAFTA), which has been in force since 1994, with the Canada–United States–Mexico Agreement (CUSMA) (Haywood-Farmer 2018).
38 National Beef Strategic Planning Group 2015.
39 Canadian Press 2015b; Jalonick 2015.
40 Canada Beef 2016a, p. 21.

deepening convergence between industry and government promotion of agricultural commodities'.[41]

Beyond funding, this convergence is part of a broader shift in policymaking towards 'governance arrangements beyond the state',[42] as a diversity of actors from civil society organisations to industry have participated in decision making and regulatory processes traditionally associated with the government.[43] With the erosion of state-funded food programs,[44] for example, consumers have turned to corporate actors for food advice.[45] As consumers are distanced from the sources of globally produced food, brands increasingly fill the responsibility of mediating between producers and consumers. Although branding does not control consumer behaviour, it does draw on existing cultural beliefs and systems of meaning with the goal of shaping consumer experience. As such, Moor characterises 'branding as a form of *governance*' that uses design as a 'managerial technique' to advance the interests of corporate and state actors.[46]

While globalisation and free markets may seem to signal the end of the nation state's relevance, 'nation branding'[47] reinvents national culture as a form of added economic value. Nation-branding strategies rely on the 'country of origin effect', which associates particular products and services with 'stereotypes, metaphors, and structuring fictions'[48] of a nation. Elliott and McCready observe that food that has strong associations to its 'place of origin' is coded as 'good'[49] and is positioned in contrast to the negative connotations of globally processed food. Constructed by the dairy lobby as an essential part of Swedish national identity,[50] for example, the dairy industry occupies a position of trust in the Swedish public imagination and functions

---

41 Blue 2009, p. 231.
42 Bancerz 2016, p. 132.
43 Andrée, Clark, Levkoe & Lowitt 2019; Mendes 2017.
44 Koç, MacRae, Desjardins & Roberts 2008.
45 Dixon 2003; Dixon 2007.
46 Moor 2007, p. 38, 88.
47 Aronczyk 2013, p. 160.
48 Aronczyk 2013, p. 165.
49 Elliott & McCready 2016, p. 23.
50 Canavan 2017.

'rather like a semi-authority'.[51] This trust becomes essential for the industry during trying economic times, as Swedish origins become 'added value'[52] for milk.

Nation branding was an important part of seeing the Canadian beef industry through its biggest crisis – the BSE outbreak of the early 2000s. Public support was partly garnered through leveraging already existing feelings of provincial and national pride in beef. Earlier tourist marketing campaigns by Alberta Beef Producers had popularised the concept of 'Alberta Beef' through the use of cowboy imagery that associated contemporary cattle farming with the appeal of small-scale, pre-industrial methods.[53] In the face of BSE, a wave of 'mad cow nationalism'[54] swept the nation. Beyond a show of support for the industry, eating beef became a patriotic act.[55] Restaurants highlighted local beef dishes; businesses raised money for beef producers;[56] and government officials publicly chowed down on steaks and burgers.[57]

Industry commentators suggest that the beef sector has emerged out of the other side of the BSE crisis.[58] At the same time, the Canadian beef industry is at a turning point, facing increased public scrutiny alongside expanding global markets. Addressing the twin goals of protecting the domestic market from US imports and growing the export market, Canada's National Beef Strategy aims to situate

---

51   Linné & Pedersen 2017, p. 114.

52   Canavan 2017, p. 35.

53   Blue 2007.

54   Plantinga 2003.

55   The collectiveness of 'mad cow nationalism' could not exist without its flipside, 'mad cow xenophobia' (Plantinga 2003). While Plantinga uses this terminology as a metaphor to refer to 'the distrust of beef from elsewhere', the weight of the comparison deserves further elaboration. Scholars have examined the ways in which pride in national food can be accompanied by fears of food from elsewhere, converging with negative attitudes towards non-local people (Dalziell & Wadiwel 2017; Stănescu 2011).

56   Blue 2007.

57   Adams 2003; Kaufman 2003.

58   Canadian Agri-Food Policy Institute 2012; National Beef Strategic Planning Group 2015.

Canadian beef in a 'differentiated brand position'[59] by emphasising the unique features of Canada through the Canadian Beef Advantage.

The brand: 'Canada + Beef'[60]

Canada Beef is not responsible for raising, processing or selling cattle. The way that the organisation 'adds tangible value to Canadian beef'[61] is by telling an 'amazing story'.[62] In the remainder of the chapter, I share a critical discourse and visual analysis of this story, examining the ways in which it constructs Canada as a source of added value for the brand.

Discourse analysis considers the ways in which language and communication shape and perpetuate shared understandings of the world. Not confined to linguistic representations, discourse analysis can be conducted on 'texts' in a broader sense, including images.[63] Critical discourse analysis and critical visual analysis bring a focus on power to this exploration, analysing how certain ways of knowing perpetuate social inequalities.[64]

In critical research, an awareness of the researcher's position within these power structures should also be foregrounded, as the researcher does not exist outside of the world they are studying.[65] While I question the narratives about Canada that the Canadian Beef Advantage presents, I have also benefitted from these constructions of the nation, as a white settler and lifelong Canadian citizen. Moreover, as an eater who lives primarily in an urban environment, I remain grateful to the people who work to provide food, often facing great economic strain and personal hardship.[66]

Drawing on Twine's endorsement of corporate websites as a source of 'important data'[67] about the animal-industrial complex, I ground

---

59   National Beef Strategic Planning Group 2015, p. 8.
60   Canada Beef 2016d, p. 3.
61   Canada Beef 2016d, p. 6.
62   Canada Beef 2016f, p. 8.
63   Willig 2013, p. 343.
64   Rose 2001.
65   Madison 2005; Rose 2001.
66   Qualman 2011.

my analysis of the Canadian Beef Advantage in empirical details I obtained from Canada Beef's website. I gathered screenshots of images and text that were publicly available on the website between the summer of 2016 and spring of 2017. Paying special attention to representations of the Canadian Beef Advantage, I categorised screenshots according to repeated patterns that emerged. Next, I grouped these textual and visual repetitions under broad thematic categories. In this chapter, I present the themes that deal with constructions of Canada. Applying a theoretical framework to the empirical findings, I explore connections between these dominant themes and existing metanarratives about Canada.

Asking 'What's so great about Canadian beef?', Canada Beef answers: 'It is Canada'.[68] Beyond technical components that appeal to industry actors, Canada Beef aims to make the Canadian Beef Advantage 'an emotional differentiator'[69] that appeals to consumers. This affective addition was the goal of the brand's recent refresh, which features the tagline: 'We put the best of Canada into our beef'.[70]

What does Canada Beef consider to be 'the best of Canada'? Initially framed as a 'Checklist for Canada's Beef Advantage',[71] Canada Beef reformulated a list of bullet points to make up the 'criteria for the perfect place for raising beef'. Canada Beef recommends that readers 'consider these criteria against the landscape, people and culture of Canada, and [they] will understand why [the organisation] believe[s] Canada is truly the world's perfect place for raising beef'.[72] In analysing the attributes of the Canadian landscape, people and culture that Canada Beef uses to constitute the Canadian Beef Advantage, I determined three main characterisations: bountiful landscapes, pioneering people and a tolerant culture. Relying on intertwined metanarratives about Canada's national identity, the themes constitute

---

67   Twine 2012, p. 27.
68   Canada Beef 2016b, pp. 2–3.
69   Harris 2016.
70   Canada Beef 2016h.
71   Canada Beef 2015b.
72   Canada Beef 2016b, p. 5.

a positive characterisation of Canada that Canada Beef can use to add value to products.

The landscape: 'Our Land. Our Beef.'[73]

Claiming that Canada's 'climate and environment' are 'perfectly suited for grazing cattle',[74] Canada Beef presents the Canadian landscape as both abundant and vast. This depiction resonates with founding myths that underpinned European colonial expansion into the 'New World'. Imagined as a 'sort of spare continent, to use for parts',[75] Canada provided raw materials for European commodities, which bolstered the spread of colonial empires.[76]

In the context of Canada, settler colonialism is a significant form that colonisation takes. Settler colonialism is distinct 'in that settlers come with the intention of making a new home on the land, a homemaking that insists on settler sovereignty over all things in their new domain'.[77] Settler colonialism is an ongoing structure rather than an isolated historical event,[78] and contemporary reconstructions of these founding narratives continue to justify the occupation.

Abundant

According to the 'perfect place' criteria, Canada's environment contains: 'An abundance of fresh air, clean water, and fertile soil'.[79] These descriptions of Canada's 'rich ... natural resources'[80] are repeated throughout Canada Beef's materials, highlighting in particular the cleanliness of the Canadian environment.[81] In addition, Canada is

---

73   Canada Beef 2015d.
74   Canada Beef 2016b, p. 3.
75   Klein 2016.
76   Innis 1967.
77   Tuck & Yang 2012, p. 5.
78   Wolfe 2006, p. 388.
79   Canada Beef 2016b, p. 5.
80   Canada Beef 2015b.
81   Canada Beef 2016b, p. 8, 15; Canada Beef 2015d.

described as an ecological niche that provides the precise climatic ingredients for raising cattle:

> Canadian beef is the 'True North.' This northern attribute identifies a competitive advantage in terms of climate and genetics that goes to the quality of the product. It is because of where Canada is geographically that we are able to raise great quality beef.[82]

Described in a promotional video as 'nature's cattle ranch',[83] the Canadian environment seems to be primed and waiting for ranching.

The 'True North' – or 'The Great White North', as it is also known – is 'an enduring Canadian myth'[84] that functions as a critical component of colonial founding narratives. On one hand, Canada Beef's reference to 'our True North'[85] invokes an apolitical commons. At the same time, it reveals an ownership orientation towards the land that privileges colonial thinking. Baldwin, Cameron and Kobayashi argue that the persistence of white settler normativity in Canada depends on universalised constructions of nature as an untouched domain, and as the backdrop for quintessential Canadian wilderness experiences.[86]

Despite the recent challenges with herd sizes, 'our True North' is described as 'that place where herds grow and thrive'.[87] Like Canada's natural elements, cattle are positioned as property. Referencing the practice of branding cattle with irons 'to show ownership', Canada Beef differentiates between 'a branded cow [which] may be the property of Canada Beef's stakeholders' and 'our true Canadian beef brand … [which] is not something we can own'.[88] When cattle are not displayed as a distant herd,[89] closer shots reveal numbered ear tags – another method of cattle identification.[90]

---

82   Canada Beef 2015b.
83   Love Canadian Beef 2016.
84   Baldwin, Cameron & Kobayashi 2011, 1.
85   Canada Beef 2015d.
86   Baldwin, Cameron & Kobayashi 2011.
87   Canada Beef 2015d.
88   Canada Beef 2015b.
89   Canada Beef 2016b, p. 2, 4, 18; Canada Beef 2016d, p. 11, 14, 17.
90   Canada Beef 2016f, p. 5, 7, 11; Canada Beef 2016d p. 12, 24.

Despite the implicit violence of these identification practices, people are also shown displaying care towards cattle – feeding and/or petting them.[91] The concept of stewardship is used to characterise these relationships: 'There are beef farmers and ranchers in every province in Canada … working to be good stewards of the land and animals in their care.'[92] Stewardship connects an attitude towards cattle to a broader responsibility for the environment, and serves as a guarantee of sustainability. Elaborating on 'sustainability' as a 'brand pillar', Canada Beef promises: 'We take on the responsibility for the resources in our care. Stewardship is the mindset, sustainability is the practice.'[93]

Canada Beef positions ranching as a natural component of the Canadian ecosystem. This attitude exemplifies 'a narrative of balance and co-constitution' that Ellis calls 'the symbiotic ideology'.[94] Ellis argues that the concepts of stewardship and husbandry work to conceal the relationships of domination that are at play in animal agriculture. Instead, animal agriculture is presented as a 'pact', in Canada Beef's words, between 'Mother Nature … ourselves as humans and the animals we look after'.[95] With an emphasis on reciprocity, stewardship and husbandry situate the environment and animals in relation to humans. This anthropocentric perspective suggests that problems with animal agriculture can be solved through improved management, and 'leave[s] no room for questioning the system itself'.[96]

Vast

The colonial worldview of 'our True North' is repeated in the tagline: 'Our Land. Our Beef.'[97] 'Our Beef' implies human ownership of animals,[98] while 'Our Land' has associations with the concept of private property. These perspectives have been instrumental in the colonial

---

91   Canada Beef 2016d, p. 5, 11.
92   Canada Beef 2016b, p. 11.
93   Canada Beef 2016h.
94   Ellis 2013, p. 429.
95   Canada Beef 2016b, p. 26.
96   Ellis 2013, p. 444.
97   Canada Beef 2015d.

project of displacing Indigenous peoples from land. In order to justify the exploitation of Canada's 'abundant resources',[99] land has to be constructed as empty of beings who could be negatively affected, and as outside of time or ecological limits. Transposing European property laws onto the 'New World', colonists ascribed to a belief that investing in land through agriculture gave them rights over the 'empty' landscape,[100] which was not being 'productively' managed by Indigenous peoples.[101]

Even with industrial developments since this period, the image of Canada as empty of inhabitants perseveres. In describing Canada, Canada Beef proclaims:

> It is a land that stretches across seven and a half time zones, touches three seas and embraces 2.5 million lakes and rivers. It is a place as lofty as the Rocky Mountains, as vast and fertile as the Prairies and as ancient and enduring as the Canadian Shield.[102]

Accompanying such descriptions are panoramic images of landscapes. To introduce provincial beef producer organisations, for instance, the Canada Beef website displays panoramas from each province, from the forests of British Columbia to the shores of the Maritimes.[103]

Much like the natural elements, this vast landscape is conceptualised as if it was made for cattle. The 'perfect place' criteria also include: 'Wide open spaces for cattle to graze: an environment that's been conducive to grazing herds since time began.'[104] While Indigenous peoples do trace relationships with 'grazing herds' back to creation,[105] these herds were made up of bison rather than cattle. Canada Beef situates cattle as if they were the natural descendants

---

98 As a kind of euphemism for 'cow flesh', the term 'beef' adds a further layer of ownership, as it defines animals as food for humans (Adams 1990).
99 Beef Cattle Research Council 2016, p. 3.
100 Anderson 2004, p. 79.
101 Kepkiewicz 2015, p. 189.
102 Canada Beef 2016b, p. 3.
103 Canada Beef 2015d.
104 Canada Beef 2016b, p. 5.
105 Zontek 2007, p. 3.

of bison. In reality, cattle ranching was integral to the project of clearing the plains of bison and Indigenous peoples, so that the environment more closely resembled the empty landscape of the colonial imagination.[106]

Introducing diseases and providing competition for forage, cattle replaced bison on the plains during the late 19th century.[107] Since Indigenous peoples have crucial spiritual relationships with bison as a food source, the elimination of bison from the landscape amounted to an attack on Indigenous peoples' cultures and survival.[108] Legitimising human dominance over domesticated animals, anthropocentrism is a key mechanism of settler colonialism because it allows for 'the insertion of animals into ... vacated spaces',[109] which facilitates the initial and continued occupation of land.

The people: 'Our Heritage, Our Future'[110]

According to Canada Beef: 'Canadian farmers and ranchers produce Canadian beef with integrity, and personify the brand.'[111] Given that the brand represents 'the best of Canada', a personification of the brand symbolises the epitome of Canadian identity. Canada Beef depicts producers as hardworking cowboys and as family farmers. These representations situate Canada Beef's marketing materials as a retelling of one of the 'master narratives of Canadian nationalism', which Furniss labels the 'frontier myth'.[112] This narrative positions white European settlers as the original inhabitants of Canada,[113] and is maintained through widespread reverence for early pioneer life.[114]

---

106 Daschuk 2013.
107 Anderson 2004; Daschuk 2013.
108 Daschuk 2013; Zontek 2007.
109 Belcourt 2015, p. 3.
110 Canada Beef 2016f, p. 2.
111 Canada Beef 2016b, p. 11.
112 Furniss 1999, p. 53.
113 O'Connell 2010.
114 Furniss 1999.

Hardworking cowboys

Introducing the 'producer' as a second 'brand pillar', Canada Beef characterises Canadian beef producers as 'active, hardworking, dedicated, honest, careful, kind, friendly and diligent'.[115] Among these many adjectives, 'hardworking' is frequently repeated.[116] A close-up image of cupped, earth-covered hands,[117] for example, connects this notion of effort to the patience that is required to 'hand craft' beef 'from start to finish'.[118] The emphasis on beef as an 'artisanal product' that develops in line with 'seasonal changes'[119] resonates with depictions of early settlers as persistent, patient people who worked the land without the help of modern technologies.

The most iconic protagonist of the frontier narrative is the cowboy. Cowboy imagery is ubiquitous in Canada Beef's promotional materials, even though cowboys were only active during a brief period of open ranching from the 1860s to 1880s.[120] Rounding up cattle on horseback[121] and surveying the landscape,[122] Canada Beef producers regularly appear in cowboy attire. The central video of the brand's 2016 refresh features Canadian country music star Paul Brandt as the spokesperson, sporting a cowboy hat and gesturing to the landscape of open fields behind him.[123]

This iconography appeals to a particular kind of Canadian rurality, which celebrates the homogeneity of the rural space as a bastion for the enduring ideals of pioneer life.[124] Framed as representative of 'traditional Canadian values'[125], the frontier narrative naturalises white settlement while obscuring the colonial and racial tensions that have been part of Canada's history.[126] By representing farmers as white

---

115 Canada Beef 2016b, p. 11.
116 Canada Beef 2016b, p. 5; Canada Beef 2016d, p. 14; Canada Beef 2016f, p. 5.
117 Canada Beef 2015c.
118 Canada Beef 2016b, p. 17, 11.
119 Canada Beef 2015b.
120 Blue 2007.
121 Canada Beef 2016f, p. 4.
122 Canada Beef 2016b, p. 10.
123 Canada Beef 2016h; Love Canadian Beef 2016.
124 O'Connell 2010.
125 Canada Beef 2016f, p. 2.

cowboys,[127] Canada Beef participates in the 'white farm imaginary'[128] that heroicises white farm owners while ignoring the efforts of racialised, precarious farm workers.

A significant proportion of farm labour is performed by participants in Canada's Seasonal Agricultural Workers Program (CSAWP). This program brings individuals from international countries for eight months of the year to work in Canadian agriculture.[129] While the program is framed as necessary for industry,[130] it is based on inequitable hierarchies between Canadian citizens and migrant workers. As contracts are tied to individual employers, migrant farm workers have limited mobility rights, and while they pay into federal Employment Insurance, they are unable to access these benefits.[131] Perry characterises the CSAWP as a 'relic of Canada's racist and colonial past'[132] that has persisted even as Canada has enacted anti-racist immigration policies. Racialised workers are responsible for feeding 'the Canadian "host" population'[133] by performing tasks in which 'many Canadians are simply not interested'.[134]

In addition to on-farm labour, the meat industry is highly dependent on temporary foreign workers to perform slaughtering and butchering activities in the processing sector.[135] While ranching work is highlighted and chefs are shown[136] preparing eye-catching dishes,[137] the middle portion of the production process remains unpublicised in

---

126 O'Connell 2010.
127 My analysis understands race as a social and political construct, rather than as a biological occurrence (Omi & Winant 1986; Yudell 2014). Recognising that racial identifications are not readily legible in photographs, my visual analysis is based on the cultural codings of the photographs, rather than on the experiences of the individuals pictured.
128 Alkon & McCullen 2011, p. 938.
129 Lenard & Staehle 2012.
130 Cotter 2014; Laws 2013.
131 Perry 2012; Preibisch & Grez 2010.
132 Perry 2012, p. 189.
133 Perry 2012, p. 197.
134 Laws 2013, p. 5.
135 Cotter 2014.
136 Canada Beef 2016d, pp. 22–23.
137 Canada Beef 2016d, p. 11, 25.

Canada Beef's marketing. This absence is part of a long tradition of concealing from public view the messiness of animal death as well as the people who perform this work.[138]

Family farmers

Even as many workers in the value chain remain obscured, Canada Beef purports to reveal 'the people behind the Canadian beef story'[139] in their public materials. Behind this caption, two smiling families are pictured, posing in front of a pasture. Homogenous in style and in subject, similar family portraits are peppered throughout Canada Beef's materials.[140] Highlighting that '98% of Canadian farms are family-owned', Canada Beef maintains: 'Agriculture is not just a business, but a way of life for many Canadian families.'[141]

More than the production of meat, Ellis proposes that ranching produces a particular version of the self.[142] Here again, the concept of stewardship is essential to this process, as it situates the self in relation to a shared history and an imagined future. In this way, stewardship and sustainability include the goal of maintaining the ranching way of life in addition to ensuring the stability of the environment.

As well as the frontier life invoked through cowboy imagery, Canada Beef makes frequent reference to the past in the form of family 'heritage' and 'legacy'.[143] In addition to depictions of young people performing ranching tasks that will equip them to be future beef producers,[144] Canada Beef points to the future consumers of Canadian beef. In the 'Recipes' portion of the website, Canada Beef recommends that parents 'Put Beef on the menu!' Typifying the consolidation of food system governance, the page offers beef-related nutritional information based on Health Canada guidelines alongside the assurance: 'If you're a new parent, you've come to the right place!'[145]

---

138 Fitzgerald 2010; Pachirat 2011; Vialles 1994.
139 Canada Beef 2016b, p. 11.
140 Canada Beef 2015b; Canada Beef 2016d, p. 6; Canada Beef 2016f, p. 4.
141 Canada Beef 2016f, p. 11.
142 Ellis 2013.
143 Canada Beef 2016b, p. 5, 11.
144 Canada Beef 2016d; Canada Beef 2016b, p. 31.

Canada Beef frames the brand as representative of 'Our Heritage, Our Future'.[146] Though claimed as a shared history, the frontier myth foregrounds the experiences of settlers while glossing over the colonial implications of this heritage. Land is conceived of as a responsibility that has been rightfully passed down to the current generation of farmers, rather than as a sacred gift that was stolen from Indigenous peoples.[147] Canada Beef affirms: 'Canadian beef is raised with great pride and tradition. The greatness of Canadian beef has been built up by generations of ranchers and farmers.'[148]

In addition to valorising the frontier past, Canada Beef's emphasis on the 'intergenerational continuity'[149] of the family farm is implicated in the project of white settler futurity. More than presenting farmers as relatable members of the community, Cairns et al. argue that images of heteronormative families serve as assurances that future farmland will continue to be held by the descendants of settlers.[150] Encapsulated in the image of a child reaching up to hold the pinky finger of an adult as they walk together beside a barn,[151] Canada Beef promises to maintain this legacy.

The culture: 'Our country, our nation and our people'[152]

Representing more than a product for Canada Beef, Canadian beef 'is at the heart of the Canadian way of life and a way of living'.[153] While the 'way of living' is embodied by Canada's beef producers, the 'Canadian way of life' extends to Canadian beef consumers. Canada Beef characterises the broader Canadian culture as being made up of a responsible government and multicultural citizens.

---

145 Canada Beef 2016g.
146 Canada Beef 2016f, p. 2.
147 Morrison 2011; Rotz 2017.
148 Canada Beef 2015e.
149 Cairns, McPhail, Chevrier & Bucklaschuk 2015, p. 1186.
150 Cairns et al. 2015.
151 Canada Beef 2016f, p. 9.
152 Canada Beef 2016b, p. 30.
153 Canada Beef 2016, p. 26.

The presentation of Canada as a diverse and tolerant society is necessary for upholding the integrity of Canada's founding narratives. While the frontier myth conjures up depictions of early settlers, contemporary Canadians are conceptualised using:

> a master narrative of the nation, which takes as its point of departure the essentially law-abiding character of its enterprising nationals, who are presented (for the most part) as responsible citizens, compassionate, caring, and committed to the values of diversity and multiculturalism.[154]

These subjects participate in the construction of Canada as a liberal democracy that operates according to the beliefs and interests of its citizens.

Responsible government

Canada Beef portrays Canada as 'a nation that has become an example to the world for understanding the role of humans and animals in nature, and working at home and abroad for peace, order, and doing what's right'.[155] Operating according to the same logic that has protected the Canadian beef industry during times of crisis, the morality of Canada serves as a guarantee of the trustworthiness of Canada Beef. The 'Canadian Beef Promise' repeats a variation on the moral idiom in its last line: 'We will do what is right.'[156]

This attitude extends the concept of stewardship to the relationship between the Canadian government and Canadian citizens. According to this reasoning, Canada remains at peace because the government takes care of its citizens. Framing the economic system as an integrated component of the natural environment, the 'perfect place' criteria identify: 'A caring and effective government capable of ensuring the highest standards of quality and safety, and with sophisticated and enlightened trade policies.'[157]

---

154 Thobani 2007, p. 4.
155 Canada Beef 2016b, p. 3.
156 Canada Beef 2016f, p. 1.
157 Canada Beef 2016b, p. 5.

Beyond Canada Beef's conceptualisations of Canadian citizens in its marketing materials, it also directly harnesses the voices of Canadian citizens through social media interactions. In honour of the 150th anniversary of Canada's confederation, for example, Canada Beef held a social media contest that asked participants to respond to the prompt: 'What Canadian Beef dish would you bring to a Canada 150 celebration this summer?'[158] Perusing some of the organisation's 'favourite entries'[159] offers a perspective on the particular version of Canadian identity that Canada Beef encourages beef consumers to celebrate. One featured user suggests they would bring Canada Beef's 'lazy cheeseburger sliders' to a Canada 150 celebration 'because [the sliders] encapsulate the Canadian spirit: easy going, hardy, and puts a smile on everyone's face!'[160] Canada Beef uses these imagined qualities of Canadian citizenship along with the words, images and labour[161] of Canadian media users as a reflection of the brand. Taking on the stereotype of the polite Canadian, Canada Beef quips that it is 'not proclaiming that Canadian beef is the best in the world' as 'it wouldn't be Canadian to make such a claim against another country's product'.[162]

Multicultural citizens

Canada Beef names the project of linking producers and consumers as a major role of the brand:

> Through the deeply satisfying experience of Canadian beef, tens of thousands of farmers and ranchers and millions of consumers connect with one another and with the spirit of our country, our nation and our people.[163]

---

158 Canada Beef 2017a.
159 Canada Beef 2017c.
160 Canada Beef 2017c.
161 As companies surveil the activities of digital media users who also provide content for digital platforms, scholars have theorised digital media use as a form of labour (Andrejevic 2009; Cohen 2013).
162 Canada Beef 2015b.
163 Canada Beef 2016b, p. 30.

Unlike the homogeneous images of Canada Beef producers, consumers are portrayed as diverse. Accompanying a description of the long-term goals of the brand, a group of intergenerational, multiethnic friends are pictured enjoying a picnic.[164] These diverse diners are the consumers referenced in the 'perfect place' criteria: 'A globally savvy, multicultural people who understand the different roles and meaning of beef in different cultures and nationalities.'[165]

The Canadian government established policies on multiculturalism in the 1980s with the inclusion of multiculturalism in the *Canadian Charter of Rights and Freedoms* and the passing of the *Multiculturalism Act*. While Canada Beef presents a celebratory view of this diversity, scholars have argued that official multiculturalism also works to maintain white dominance by allowing for difference without dismantling structures of oppression.[166]

Like Canada Beef's other appeals to unity, 'our country, our nation and our people'[167] suggests that all people in Canada exist on an equal playing field, and yet the rhetoric of multiculturalism positions whiteness as the norm against which 'other' Canadians are measured. In the featured Canada 150 contest posts, participants describe white-coded Euro-American foods like steak and roast beef with gravy as 'traditional' and 'classically Canadian', while foods such as Thai lettuce cups and curry represent multiculturalism.[168] Even as Canada Beef declares that all of the recipes in their online collection are 'perfectly Canadian',[169] filtering the recipes by the category 'comfort foods' leads to predominantly white-coded Euro-American recipes, while filtering by 'exotic' results in recipes from racialised cultural traditions.[170] A particularly stark contrast situates the 'Oriental Beef Bottom Sirloin Tri-Tip' recipe from the 'exotic' category opposite the

---

164 Canada Beef 2015a.
165 Canada Beef 2016b, p. 5.
166 Baldwin, Cameron & Kobayashi 2011; O'Connell 2010; Thobani 2007.
167 Canada Beef 2016b, p. 30.
168 Canada Beef 2017c.
169 Canada Beef 2016c.
170 Canada Beef 2017b.

'Cowboy Ground Beef and Bean Casserole' from the 'comfort foods' section.[171]

This comparison recalls 'Orientalist'[172] discourses that positioned colonisers as stronger than people in colonised countries because of their diets of beef versus rice or corn.[173] Even though both Canada Beef recipes contain beef, the 'Oriental' dish is exoticised as 'other', while the 'cowboy' dish reflects the nostalgia of childhood foods. Beyond beef, the common ingredient in all of these dishes is expressed in Adams' description of the 'main ingredient' in a hamburger: 'colonialism'.[174]

B(earth)day bison

While Adrienne Ivey was admiring the Canadian herd in Saskatchewan, another marvel was taking place during that same April in Alberta – the first bison calf in 140 years was born in Banff National Park.[175] The birth took place two months after Parks Canada had translocated 16 bison from Elk Island National Park.[176] Born on Earth Day, the calf symbolised the initial success of the wild bison restoration program, which Parks Canada characterised as 'a momentous way to celebrate the 150th anniversary of Canada's Confederation'.[177]

Zontek identifies a pattern of settlers taking credit for bison restoration based on 'their efforts to establish parks and refuges for the buffalo'[178] while ignoring ongoing endeavours of Indigenous peoples. Although Parks Canada acknowledges the 'great spiritual meaning'[179] that buffalo have for Indigenous communities, this significance is overshadowed by the celebration of Canada's colonial founding and ecological programs. Moreover, the conservationist mentality is

---

171 Canada Beef 2017b.
172 Said 1978.
173 Adams 2018; Stănescu 2017.
174 Adams 2018, p. 31.
175 CBC News 2017.
176 Parks Canada 2017.
177 Boushy 2017.
178 Zontek 2007, p. 147.
179 Boushy 2017.

contrary to the Indigenous vision of a 'widespread bison landscape'.[180] A 'bison landscape' reimagines the concept of stewardship at the heart of the Canada Beef brand story, as it redistributes care, agency and responsibility throughout a network of human and nonhuman actors. In contrast to the human management of colonial cattle ranching, the 'bison landscape' is sustained through collaborative experiences between humans, bison and the land.[181]

As part of the animal-industrial complex, Canada Beef is firmly tied to the imperatives of the capitalist economy. As such, a necessary function of the brand is to maintain the economic position of the Canadian beef industry in the face of decreased domestic demand and increased public critique. In this context, 'the best of Canada' adds more value to the brand than the country's colonial injustices. At the same time, as brands reach into the realm of governance, branding narratives become increasingly entrenched in public discourse. Canada Beef's presentation of Canada as a spacious and tolerant frontier nation reinforces harmful colonial narratives that continue to structure attitudes and policies towards Indigenous peoples, migrant farm workers, agricultural animals and the environment.

While this chapter has troubled the colonial discourses that are central to Canada Beef's brand message, Tuck and Yang emphasise that critical perspectives on colonial structures are not the same as approaches to decolonisation. Decolonising the ranching landscape would 'involve the repatriation of land simultaneous to the recognition of how land and relations to land have always already been differently understood and enacted'.[182] As land ownership is at the core of ranching lifestyle, this process would create a fundamental shift not only in agricultural practice, but 'in the central being of everyone and everything involved',[183] including Canada Beef, Canadian beef and Canada itself.

---

180 Zontek 2007, p. 147.
181 Zontek 2007.
182 Tuck and Yang 2012, p. 7.
183 Ellis 2013, pp. 445–446.

References

Adams, C. J. (1990). *The Sexual Politics of Meat: A Feminist-Vegetarian Critical Theory*. New York: Continuum.

Adams, C. J. (2018). *Burger*. New York: Bloomsbury Academic.

Adams, J. (2003). Barbecue heats up as premiers show their mussels. *Globe and Mail*. 31 July. https://tgam.ca/3l6EY1h

Adrienneivey (2017, 15 April). How do we move 150 heifers in Canada? Just need a better trained beaver [Twitter post]. http://tiny.cc/twitter-adrienneivey.

Agriculture and Agri-Food Canada (2019a). Protein disappearance and demand by species. http://tiny.cc/aafc-proteindisappearance

Agriculture and Agri-Food Canada (2019b). Red meat trade balance reports. http://tiny.cc/aafc-redmeat-tradebalance

Alexandratos, N., and J. Bruinsma (2012). *World Agriculture Towards 2030/2050: The 2012 Revision*. ESA Working paper No. 12–03. Rome: Food and Agriculture Organization of the United Nations.

Alkon, A. H. and C. G. McCullen (2011). Whiteness and farmers markets: Performances, perpetuations... contestations? *Antipode* 43(2), 937–59. doi:10.1111/j.1467-8330.2010.00818.x

Anderson, V. D. (2004). *Creatures of Empire: How Domestic Animals Transformed Early America*. New York: Oxford University Press.

Andrée, P., J. K. Clark, C. Z. Levkoe and K. Lowitt (2019). Traversing theory and practice: Social movement engagement in food systems governance for sustainability, justice, and democracy. In P. Andrée, J. K. Clark, C. Z. Levkoe and K. Lowitt (Eds.), *Civil Society and Social Movements in Food System Governance* (pp. 1–18). Abingdon: Routledge.

Andrejevic, M. (2009). The work of being watched: Interactive media and the exploitation of self-disclosure. In J. Turow and M. P. McAllister (Eds.), *The Advertising and Consumer Culture Reader* (pp. 385–401). New York: Routledge.

Aronczyk, M. (2013). The transnational promotional class and the circulation of value(s). In M. P. McAllister and E. West (Eds.), *The Routledge Companion to Advertising and Promotional Culture* (pp. 159–173). New York: Routledge.

Baldwin, A., L. Cameron and A. Kobayashi (2011). Where is the great white north? Spatializing history, historicizing whiteness. In A. Baldwin, L. Cameron and A. Kobayashi (Eds.), *Rethinking the Great White North: Race Nature, and the Historical Geographies of Whiteness in Canada* (pp. 1–15). Vancouver: University of British Columbia Press.

Bancerz, M. (2016). New CSR in the food system: Industry and non-traditional corporate food interests. *Canadian Food Studies* 3(2), 127–44. doi:10.15353/cfs-rcea.v3i2.171

Beef Cattle Research Council (2016). *2016/17 Business Plan: Submitted to Canadian Beef Cattle Research, Market Development and Promotion Agency.* Calgary: Canadian Cattlemen's Association. https://bit.ly/3l6BJqI

Bello, W. and M. Baviera (2010). Capitalist agriculture, the food price crisis and peasant resistance. In H. Wittman, A. A. Desmarais and N. Wiebe (Eds.), *Food Sovereignty: Reconnecting Food, Nature and Community* (pp. 62–75). Winnipeg: Fernwood Publishing.

Belcourt, B. (2015). Animal bodies, colonial subjects: (Re)locating animality in decolonial thought. *Societies* 5(1), 1–11. doi:10.3390/soc5010001

Berland, J. (2015). The work of the beaver. In J. Blair (Ed.), *Material Cultures in Canada*. Jennifer Blair (pp. 25–49). Waterloo: Wilfrid Laurier University Press.

Blue, G. (2007). If it ain't Alberta, it ain't beef: Local food, regional identity, (inter)national politics. *Food, Culture & Society* 11(1): 69–85. doi:10.2752/155280107X23

Blue, G. (2009). Branding beef: Marketing, food safety, and the governance of risk. *Canadian Journal of Communication* 34(2), 229–44. doi:10.22230/cjc.2009v34n2a2057

Boscardin, L. (2017). Capitalizing on nature, naturalizing capitalism: An analysis of the 'livestock revolution,' planetary boundaries, and green tendencies in the animal-industrial complex. In D. Nibert (Ed.), *Animal Oppression and Capitalism, Volume 1: The Oppression of Nonhuman Animals as Sources of Food (pp. 259–276)*. Santa Barbara: Praeger.

Boushy, D. (2017). Wild bison back in Banff National Park. *Global News*. 6 February. https://bit.ly/3lclysf

Bouvard, V., D. Loomis, K. Z. Guyton, Y. Grosse, F. E. Ghissassi, L. Benbrahim-Tallaa, N. Guha, H. Mattock, K. Straif (2015). Carcinogenicity of consumption of red and processed meat. *Lancet Oncology* 16, 1599–1600. doi:10.1016/S1470-2045(15)00444-1

Cairns, K., D. McPhail, C. Chevrier and J. Bucklaschuk (2015). The family behind the farm: Race and the affective geographies of Manitoba pork production. *Antipode* 47(5), 1184–1202. doi:10.1111/anti.12147

Canada Beef (2015a). 30,000 ft view. http://www.ourlandourbeef.ca/30000-ft-view/

Canada Beef (2015b). *Canada: The World's Perfect Place for Raising Beef – Canada Beef Strategic Storyline*. Calgary: Canada Beef. https://bit.ly/34kdzmT

Canada Beef (2015c). How it works. http://www.ourlandourbeef.ca/how-it-works/

Canada Beef (2015d). Our land. Our beef. https://bit.ly/31e41b2

Canada Beef (2015e). Transitional branding. https://bit.ly/31hyuoo

Canada Beef (2016a). *Canada Beef Business Plan 2016/17*. Calgary: Canada Beef. https://bit.ly/3l7OYay

Canada Beef (2016b). *Brand Story*. Calgary: Canada Beef. https://bit.ly/2EjfqgG

Canada Beef (2016c). Make it beef. https://canadabeef.ca/make-it-beef/

Canada Beef (2016d). *Media Kit*. Calgary: Canada Beef. https://bit.ly/31eFUsz

Canada Beef (2016e). Our history. https://canadabeef.ca/our-history/

Canada Beef (2016f). *Producer Kit*. Calgary: Canada Beef. https://bit.ly/31fyxB8

Canada Beef (2016g). Starting solids? https://canadabeef.ca/starting-solids/

Canada Beef (2016h). Why Canadian beef? https://bit.ly/3hmlGTu

Canada Beef (2017a). Canadian beef at my table Canada 150 contest ends March 30th. https://canadabeef.ca/makeitbeef/canadian-beef-at-my-table-canada-150-contest-ends-march-30th/

Canada Beef (2017b). Recipes. https://canadabeef.ca/recipes/

Canada Beef (2017c). Some of our favourite entries, thank you to all who entered our contest. https://canadabeef.ca/canada150/

Canadian Agri-Food Policy Institute (2012). *Canada's Beef Food System: A Roadmap for Dialogue on Strategy*. Ottawa: Canadian Agri-Food Policy Institute.

Canadian Centre for Food Integrity (2016). *2016 Canadian Public Trust Research: With Insights from Moms, Millennials and Foodies*. Guelph: CCFI. https://bit.ly/3hhamrD

Canadian Press (2015a). Beef prices reach new high as dry conditions persist in the Prairies. *Canadian Grocer*. 6 July. https://bit.ly/3hto0YI.

Canadian Press (2015b). Canada won't back down on meat labelling rules. *Canadian Grocer*. 22 May. https://bit.ly/31gU3pq

Canadian Press (2015c). Cattlemen's group says no reason to stop eating meat in moderation. *Canadian Grocer*. 27 October. https://bit.ly/2EkO1uM

Canadian Press (2016a). Restaurant faces backlash after dropping Alberta beef for U.S. cattle. *Canadian Grocer*. 28 April. https://bit.ly/2QePjKG

Canadian Press (2016b). Where's the beef? Earls restaurants says it's back in Canada after 'mistake'. *Canadian Grocer*. 4 May. https://bit.ly/2QeV1fk

Canadian Roundtable for Sustainable Beef (2017). CRSB launches Certified Sustainable Beef framework. *Canadian Roundtable for Sustainable Beef*. 7 December. https://bit.ly/2CPBlM8

Canavan, J. (2017). 'Happy cow' welfarist ideology and the Swedish crisis: A crisis of romanticized oppression. In D. Nibert (Ed.), *Animal Oppression and Capitalism, Volume 1: The Oppression of Nonhuman Animals as Sources of Food* (pp. 34–55). Santa Barbara: Praeger.

CBC News (2017). Wild bison calves born in Banff National Park 'a huge step' to reintroduction. *CBC*. 25 April. https://bit.ly/2Q9Ly9j

Charlebois, S., E. McGuinty, V. Keselj, C. Mah, A. Giusto, J. Music, … J. Son (2019). *Canada's Food Price Report*. Halifax, Canada: Dalhousie University.

Clapp, J. and S. R. Isakson (2018). *Speculative Harvests: Financialization, Food, and Agriculture*. Black Point: Fernwood Publishing.

Coorsh, K. (2017). Herding cattle in Saskatchewan? Leave it to beaver. *CTV News*. 18 April. https://bit.ly/2Qc0gfN

Cohen, N. S. (2013). Commodifying free labor online: Social media, audiences, and advertising. In M. P. McAllister and E. West (Eds.), *The Routledge Companion to Advertising and Promotional Culture* (pp. 177–191). New York: Routledge.

Cotter, J. (2014). Canada's meat industry says it needs temporary foreign workers to fill jobs. *Globe and Mail*. 10 June. https://tgam.ca/3hhaJ5v

Dalziell, J. and D. J. Wadiwel (2017). Live export, animal advocacy, race and 'animal nationalism'. In A. Potts (Ed.), *Meat Culture* (pp. 73–89). Leiden: Brill.

Daschuk, J. (2013). *Clearing the Plains: Disease, Politics of Starvation, and the Loss of Aboriginal Life*. Regina: University of Regina Press.

Dixon, J. (2003). Authority, power and value in contemporary industrial food systems. *International Journal of Sociology of Agriculture and Food* 11(1): 31–40. https://www.ijsaf.org/index.php/ijsaf

Dixon, J. (2007). Supermarkets as new food authorities. In D. Burch and G. Lawrence (Eds.), *Supermarkets and Agri-Food Supply Chains: Transformations in the Production and Consumption of Food* (pp. 29–50). Cheltenham: Edward Elgar.

Donovan, J. and C. J. Adams (2007). Introduction. In J. Donovan and C. J. Adams (Eds.), *The Feminist Care Tradition in Animal Ethics* (pp. 1–20). New York: Columbia University Press.

Elliott, C. and W. McCready (2016). Communication food quality: Food, packaging, and place. In C. Elliott (Ed.), *How Canadians Communicate VI: Food Promotion, Consumption, and Controversy* (pp. 21–34). Edmonton: Athabasca University Press.

Ellis, C. (2013). The symbiotic ideology: Stewardship, husbandry, and dominion in beef production. *Rural Sociology* 78(4), 429–49. doi:10.1111/ruso.12031

Fitzgerald, A. J. (2010). A social history of the slaughterhouse: From inception to contemporary implications. *Human Ecology Review* 17(1), 58–69. http://w.humanecologyreview.org/pastissues/her171/Fitzgerald.pdf

Fudge, E. (2002). *Animal*. London: Reaktion Books.

Furniss, E. (1999). *The Burden of History: Colonialism and the Frontier Myth in a Rural Canadian Community*. Vancouver: University of British Columbia Press.

Gerber, P. J., H. Steinfeld, B. Henderson, A. Mottet, C. Opio, J. Dijkman, … G. Tempio (2013). *Tackling Climate Change Through Livestock: A Global Assessment of Emissions and Mitigation Opportunities*. Rome: Food and Agriculture Organization of the United Nations.

Harris, R. (2016). Canada Beef links cattle farmers and food with brand refresh. *Canadian Grocer*. 26 April. https://bit.ly/3hkC5Yz

Harvey, D. (2005). *A Brief History of Neoliberalism*. Oxford: Oxford University Press.

Haywood-Farmer, D. (2018). CCA Report: USMCA is good news. *Canadian Cattlemen*. 22 Oct. https://bit.ly/3hikOPO

Innis, H. (1967). *The Fur Trade in Canada: An Introduction to Canadian Economic History* (S. D. Clark and W. T. Easterbrook, Eds.). Toronto: University of Toronto Press.

Jalonick, M. C. (2015). U.S. votes to scrap meat labelling law. *Canadian Grocer*. 12 June. https://bit.ly/3aGOOSY

Kaufman, M. (2003). Canada moves to contain mad cow disease. *Washington Post*. 22 May. http://tiny.cc/washingtonpost-can-madcow

Kepkiewicz, L. (2015). Pedagogy lost? Possibilities for adult learning and solidarity in food activism. *Studies in the Education of Adults* 47(2), 185–198. doi:10.1080/02660830.2015.11661684

Klein, N. (2016). Canada's founding myths hold us back from addressing climate change. *Globe and Mail*. 23 September. http://tiny.cc/canada-foundingmyths

Koç, M., R. MacRae, E. Desjardins and W. Roberts (2008). Getting civil about food: The interaction between civil society and the state to advance sustainable food systems in Canada. *Journal of Hunger and Environmental Nutrition* 3(2–3), 122–44. doi:10.1080/19320240802243175

Laws, J. (2013). Canada's meat industry needs foreign workers. *Canadian Meat Business: The Beef, Pork & Poultry Magazine* 12(5), 5. https://bit.ly/2Es6a9V

Lenard, P. T. and C. Staehle (2012). Introduction. In P. T. Lenard and C. Staehle (Eds.), *Legislated Inequality: Temporary Labour Migration in Canada* (pp. 3–25). Montreal: McGill-Queen's University Press.

Linné, T. and H. Pedersen (2017). With care for cows and a love for milk: Affect and performance in Swedish dairy industry marketing strategies. In A. Potts (Ed.), *Meat Culture* (pp. 109–128). Leiden: Brill.

Love Canadian Beef (2016). We put the best of Canada into our beef [video]. 7 April 2016. https://www.youtube.com/watch?v=v_IH4egPtDk

Madison, D. S. (2005). *Critical Ethnography: Method, Ethics, and Performance.* Thousand Oaks: SAGE Publications.

Mendes, W. (2017). Municipal governance and urban food systems. In M. Koç, J. Sumner and A. Winson (Eds.), *Critical perspectives in food studies* (2nd ed.) (pp. 286–304). Don Mills: Oxford University Press.

Moor, L. (2007). *The Rise of Brands.* Oxford: Berg.

Morrison, D. (2011). Indigenous food sovereignty: A model for social learning. In A. A. Desmarais, N. Wiebe and H. Wittman (Eds.), *Food Sovereignty in Canada: Creating Just and Sustainable Food Systems* (pp. 97–113). Halifax: Fernwood Publishing.

Noske, B. (1989). *Human and Other Animals: Beyond the Boundaries of Anthropology.* London: Pluto Press.

National Beef Strategic Planning Group (2015). *Canada's National Beef Strategy.* 5 January. https://bit.ly/3ghDoWP

Nibert, D. (2002). *Animal Rights/Human Rights: Entanglements of Oppression and Liberation.* Lanham: Rowman & Littlefield.

O'Connell, A. (2010). An exploration of redneck whiteness in multicultural Canada. *Social Politics: International Studies in Gender, State and Society* 17(4), 536–63. doi:10.1093/sp/jxq019

Omi, M. and H. Winant (1986). *Racial Formation in the United States: From the 1960s to the 1980s.* New York: Routledge & Kegan Paul.

Pachirat, T. (2011). *Every Twelve Seconds: Industrialized Slaughter and the Politics of Sight.* New Haven: Yale University Press.

Parks Canada. (2017). Plains bison have officially returned to Banff National Park. *Banff National Park.* 6 February. https://bit.ly/3hjftaL.

Perry, J. A. (2012). Barely legal: Racism and migrant farm labour in the context of Canadian multiculturalism. *Citizenship Studies* 16(2), 189–201. doi:10.1080/13621025.2012.667611

Plantinga, T. (2003). Mad cow nationalism. *Myodicy.* 20 December. http://www.plantinga.ca/m/MCO.HTM

Popkin, B. (2003). The nutrition transition in the developing world. *Development Policy Review* 21(5–6), 581–97. doi:10.1111/j.1467-8659.2003.00225.x

Preibisch, K. L. and E. E. Grez (2010). The other side of el Otro Lado: Mexican migrant women and labor flexibility in Canadian agriculture. *Signs: Journal of Women in Culture and Society* 35(2), 289–316. doi:10.1086/605483

Qualman, D. (2011). Advancing agriculture by destroying farms? The state of agriculture in Canada. In A. A. Desmarais, N. Wiebe and H. Wittman (Eds.), *Food Sovereignty in Canada: Creating Just and Sustainable Food Systems* (pp. 20–42). Halifax: Fernwood Publishing.

Rose, G. (2001). *Visual Methodologies: An Introduction to the Interpretation of Visual Materials*. London: SAGE Publications.

Rotz, S. (2017). 'They took our beads, it was a fair trade, get over it': Settler colonial logics, racial hierarchies and material dominance in Canadian agriculture. *Geoforum* 82, 158–169. doi:10.1016/j.geoforum.2017.04.010

Said, E. (1978). *Orientalism*. New York: Pantheon.

Sanbonmatsu, J. (2011). Introduction. In J. Sanbonmatsu (Ed.), *Critical Theory and Animal Liberation* (pp. 1–32). Lanham: Rowman & Littlefield.

Sayer, A. (2001). For a critical cultural political economy. *Antipode* 33(4), 687–708. doi:10.1111/1467-8330.00206

Stănescu, V. (2011). Green eggs and ham? The myth of sustainable meat and the danger of the local. In J. Sanbonmatsu (Ed.), *Critical Theory and Animal Liberation* (pp. 239–55). Lanham: Rowman & Littlefield.

Stănescu, V. (2017). The whopper virgins: Hamburgers, gender, and xenophobia in Burger King's hamburger advertising. In A. Potts (Ed.), *Meat Culture* (pp. 90–108). Leiden: Brill.

Steinfeld, H., P. Gerber, T. D. Wassenaar, V. Castel, M. Rosales, and C. de Haan (2006). *Livestock's long shadow: Environmental issues and options*. Rome: Food & Agriculture Organization of the United Nations.

Steinmetz, K. (2014). Clickbait, normcore, mansplain: Runners-up for Oxford's word of the year. *Time*. 18 November. https://bit.ly/2QgbqA4

Thobani, S. (2007). *Exalted Subjects: Studies in the Making of Race and Nation*. Toronto: University of Toronto Press.

Tuck, E. and K. W. Yang (2012). Decolonization is not a metaphor. *Decolonization: Indigeneity, Education & Society* 1(1), 1–40. https://bit.ly/2CMfuVT

Twine, R. (2010). *Animals as Biotechnology: Ethics, Sustainability and Critical Animal Studies*. London: Routledge

Twine, R. (2012). Revealing the 'animal-industrial complex' – A concept & method for critical animal studies? *Journal for Critical Animal Studies* 10(1), 12–39. http://www.criticalanimalstudies.org/volume-10-issue-1-2012/

Vergé, X. P. C., J. A. Dyer, R. L. Desjardins and D. E. Worth (2008). Greenhouse gas emissions from the Canadian beef industry. *Agricultural Systems* 98(2), 126–34. doi:10.1016/j.agsy.2008.05.003

Vialles, N. (1994). *Animal to Edible* (J. A. Underwood, Trans.). Cambridge: Cambridge University Press.

Willig, C. (2013). Discourses and discourse analysis. In U. Flick (Ed.), *The SAGE Handbook of Qualitative Data Analysis* (pp. 341–53). London: SAGE Publications.

Wolfe, P. (2006). Settler colonialism and the elimination of the native. *Journal of Genocide Research* 8(4), 387–409. doi:10.1080/14623520601056240

Yudell, M. (2014). *Race Unmasked: Biology and Race in the Twentieth Century.* New York: Columbia University Press.

Zontek, K. (2007). *Buffalo Nation: American Indian Efforts to Restore the Bison.* Lincoln: University of Nebraska.

5

Colouring outside the lines: Symbolic legitimacy and the Dietary Guidelines for Americans

Barbara Willard

Eating animals and their by-products is one of the most devastating practices humans engage in for a host of reasons. One of the main ones is the impact it has on our environment. The Western diet, heavily reliant on meat and animal products, is not a sustainable diet and poses significant negative impacts to the environment.[1] Because the production of this diet contributes about 24 per cent of anthropogenic GHG emissions (greenhouse gas) to the atmosphere, it is a major driver of climate change.[2] [3] Worldwide meat consumption has tripled over the last four decades[4] and demand for animal products for human consumption continues to increase, placing further stress on our planet.[5] Of most concern to the human population, these environmental impacts pose significant threats to the health, food and

---

1 Foley et al. 2011; Poore & Nemecek 2018; Rojas-Downing, Nejadhashemi, Harrigan and Woznicki 2017; Edenhofer et al. 2014.
2 Intergovernmental Panel on Climate Change 2014.
3 The 24 per cent figure includes agriculture, forestry and other land use and is primarily from deforestation and agricultural emissions due to the raising of livestock. Therefore, diets high in meat and other animal products, requiring lots of range land and clearing of forest land, are a significant source of GHG emissions.
4 Stoll-Kleemann & O'Riordan 2015.
5 Rojas-Downing, Nejadhashemi, Harrigan and Woznicki 2017.

nutrition security of millions of vulnerable populations around the world, specifically women and children.[6] Given the impact that the American diet has on our environment, a primary challenge faced by the US in its 21st-century food policy is how it will address food security and sustainability. A main way to mitigate the potentially disastrous effects of this diet is to transition towards sustainable farming and develop national nutrition guidelines based on a sustainable diet.

With this in mind, the USDA Dietary Guidelines Advisory Committee (DGAC) released their report on recommendations for the 2015 Dietary Guidelines for Americans (DGAs) in February 2015. This august body of 15 scientists, including physicians and nutrition experts from elite university programs such as the Harvard and Yale School of Public Health, drew upon overwhelming scientific evidence to advocate for the inclusion of sustainability in the revised guidelines. Including this new category would suggest a significant reduction in meat and animal products to create a more sustainable food supply for future generations. In response, the North American Meat Institute and the National Cattlemen's Beef Association, among other meat industry trade associations, began a rhetorical meatsplaining offensive against the report and its findings to keep sustainability out of the new guidelines. They deployed an extensive rhetoric of denial against any negative meat-consumption messages contained in the proposed DGAs that could threaten their monopoly over the agricultural-industrial complex. The very concept of sustainability, as it relates to health and the environment, calls into question the legitimacy of the central place that meat holds in the US diet. As a reply to the increasing controversy surrounding sustainability and meat consumption, then US Secretary of Agriculture Tom Vilsack stated: 'The final 2015 Guidelines are still being drafted, but because this is a matter of scope, we do not believe that the DGAs [Dietary Guidelines for Americans] are the appropriate vehicle for this important policy conversation about sustainability.'[7]

The DGAs have historically been a site of rhetorical struggle; as a result, the final products 'are political compromises between what

---

6   Intergovernmental Panel on Climate Change 2014.
7   Vilsack & Burwell 2015.

science tells us about nutrition and health and what is good for the food industry'.[8] This chapter examines the discursive intervention, the meatsplaining, of the meat lobby and the political compromises that resulted when drafting the 2015 Dietary Guidelines. I argue that their erection of symbolic boundaries around what counts as *sound science* served to create doubt and illegitimacy around the scientific consensus that links meat production and consumption to increased GHG production, thus hastening warming and overall climate change. Much like climate deniers have challenged the science of climate scientists, the meat industry has done the same to discredit the symbolic legitimacy of nutrition and medical scientists regarding dietary discourse throughout history. Their discursive efforts, primarily through lobbying and advertising, have consistently influenced US dietary guidelines since their inception in 1980. While it might appear that these guidelines don't have much impact on US citizens' day-to-day diet, there are billions of dollars at stake in what these guidelines include. Several government programs are legally bound to follow them, including the Women, Infants, and Children Program serving approximately 8.5 million, the National School Lunch Program serving about 30 million and rations for American Military personnel.[9] The population of these institutions alone serves to create an enduring message about what constitutes a healthy diet. As nutritionist Marion Nestle explains:

> Dietary recommendations can be exploited to sell food products, but they also can turn the public away from entire categories of food. The danger of such a catastrophe is sufficient to explain the ferocity of food-industry arguments over the most minute, subtle and seemingly inconsequential aspects of dietary advice.[10]

Consequently, the meat industry has consistently had a significant role in influencing the amount of meat consumed and the messages our public institutions convey about meat consumption.

---

8   Nestle 2013, p. 30.
9   McCarthy 2016.
10   Nestle 2013, p. 29.

The meat industry has gained control of the discourse about what constitutes a healthy diet and, therefore, has influenced the upkeep and maintenance of one of the most destructive environmental practices of our time, the production and consumption of the Western American diet. By examining the strategies they have used to exert their rhetorical power, we can understand how institutions are able to delegitimise and gain the upper ground in environmental battles that favour the economy rather than the health of the planet and its inhabitants. We can also comprehend the rhetorical method that has not only placed the health of humans in jeopardy, but perhaps of more concern, has allowed the continuous abuse, torture and suffering of innocent animals that are subject to the practices of factory farms. By uncovering these strategies, we can subvert them by shining a light on the real motive behind their efforts: profit above all – human health, nonhuman animal health and environmental health.

Before exploring the controversy over the 2015 Dietary Guidelines, I will provide a theoretical perspective from which to analyse the rhetorical struggle. I then offer a brief history of the US dietary guidelines and the various revisions, and the subsequent battles over those revisions that have occurred over the years. I detail how those changes were influenced at various stages by the meat and dairy industries. I then describe the 2015 Dietary Guidelines suggested by the advisory board along with the meat and dairy industries responses to explain how they functioned to delegitimise the advisory board's recommendation through interrogation of their rightful role in constructing the dietary guidelines.

Crafting symbolic legitimacy

Robert Cox defines symbolic legitimacy as 'the perceived authority of a policy, source of knowledge, or an approach to a problem'.[11] It is a particularly significant concept for any scientist whose research serves to regulate industry such as environment, health and nutrition scientists. Because this legitimacy is *perceived*, it is rhetorically constructed and

---

11   Cox 2010, p. 301.

therefore is open to contestation, deliberation and transformation. Cox describes a time in the early 20th century when Americans put their faith in scientific discourse and trusted the expertise of those who had specialised knowledge and would inform the public about the best course of action on technical matters and help shape public policy. However, in the 1960s and 1970s when health and environmental regulation became more prevalent, the legitimacy of scientists was challenged by industry and politicians, their expertise was questioned and the boundaries of their symbolic legitimacy were narrowed. Policies, sources of knowledge or approaches to problems that exist within the legitimate symbolic boundary are perceived as 'reasonable, appropriate, or acceptable'.[12] The converse is true for policies, sources of knowledge or approaches to problems that are outside those boundaries. When industry and/or politicians engage in rhetorical battles over scientific findings, they often do so because the research could result in policy or regulation that harms profits to their business or, by extension, their campaign funds. Consequently, it is in the best interest of the industry to challenge the boundaries of what constitutes symbolic legitimacy.

Symbolic legitimacy and the erection of boundaries around that legitimacy is a highly relevant concept with regards to nutrition science and policy in the United States. As stated earlier, the science that informs public policy and nutrition guidelines for US citizens has significant economic consequences. The DGAs are the foundation of federal nutrition and policy programs, are used by health professionals and policy makers to create dietary plans for a host of private and public institutions and influence local, state and national health-promotion initiatives. Additionally, the publication and promotion of the guidelines send a clear message to ordinary Americans about what they should be eating for optimal health. All of this translates into dollars spent on certain foods, those foods that are targeted by the DGAs as health promoting. The health–food connection has been a primary factor in the construction of symbolic legitimacy boundaries for some time now, ever since the development of the nutrition paradigm of 'negative nutrition'.[13] This is the nutritional perspective that some foods

---

12 Cox 2010, p. 65.
13 Belasco 1989, p. 175.

contribute to chronic diseases such as cardiovascular disease and type 2 diabetes and should therefore be limited or even eliminated from one's diet. When certain foods are singled out because of their negative nutritional consequences, such as meat and animal products, there is a potential threat to the overall profit for producers of that food. Prior to the 2015 DGAs, the threat to corporate profits only came from the symbolic legitimacy boundaries of nutrition science; however, with the potential addition of sustainability added to the guidelines, environmental science became another factor that had to be policed to contain threats to the meat and dairy industries.

History of dietary guidelines and meatsplaining interventions

The USDA has been publishing nutrition and dietary guides of several types since 1894 when chemist Wilbur Atwater, the USDA's first director of research, wrote in the *Farmers' Bulletin* of 'the importance of variety, proportionality, and moderation in healthful eating'.[14] He warned of the 'evils of overeating', which could eventually result in negative health consequences. It is important to note that food guides that followed Atwater's for the next several decades did not recommend reducing food intake but rather, the emphasis was on consuming enough food so that one was assured of adequate nutrient intake. The nutrition guidelines disseminated by the USDA in 1917 recommended food groups according to their nutritional components. For the remainder of the early part of the 20th century, the main dietary advice was to 'eat more' as nutritionists focused on helping the poor obtain adequate nutrients and helping citizens avoid communicable diseases by building a strong immune system.[15] This was important for all agricultural products because the food guides acted as an official form of nutritional endorsement; there never was any threat to the agricultural industry. In 1958, the longest standing food guide was released with the goal of helping Americans select the most nutritious food in a straightforward manner. The Basic Four (food groups) guide

---

14   Davis & Saltos 1999.
15   Nestle 2013.

recommended minimum levels of daily servings in four categories: milk, meat, vegetable/fruit and bread/cereal. Because the guide recommended only minimum daily servings and no maximum, the 'eat more' mantra was still a clear message in the USDA nutrition guides and all were satisfied. Anyone growing up between 1958 and 1980 would remember the enthusiastic endorsement of these four food groups and their visual graphics that graced the walls of elementary schools throughout the country.

But in the 1960s and 1970s, trouble was brewing in nutrition circles. Research was consistently finding the connection between high rates of consumption of red meat and animal products and chronic disease such as cardiovascular disease and type 2 diabetes.[16] The 'diseases of affluence' pointed to a diet rich in saturated fats and cholesterol, which came from foods of animal origin, especially red meat. The evidence was mounting, and nutritionists were starting to speak out about this dietary connection, urging the American public to 'eat less' of these foods. It was only a matter of time before the 'eat less' dictum found its way into the USDA dietary guidelines. The first suggestion to eat less of certain foods by the US government came out in January 1977 when the *Dietary Goals for the United States* was produced by a Senate Select Subcommittee, led by Senator George McGovern. These guidelines recommended dietary changes including reducing intake of saturated fat (to 10 per cent of diet) and cholesterol (to 300 milligrams daily). This would require limiting the consumption of meat, eggs and whole milk products. McGovern's committee was very clear in their guidance: 'decrease consumption of meat' and other products high in saturated fat. To say 'decrease' or 'eat less' or 'limit' was an affront to the meat, dairy and egg industries, which responded in full force. This was the first major effort to develop meatsplaining rhetoric that can be found in direct connection to the dietary guidelines. They organised to stop these guidelines gaining approval and dissemination, demanding special hearings on the report before the select committee to discuss the language used and recommendations set forth. One moment in the hearings was particularly revealing when Wray Finney, then president of the National Cattlemen's Beef Association, stated that

---

16   Oppenheimer & Benrubi 2014.

'decrease is a bad word' in response to the recommendation that Americans 'decrease consumption of meat'.[17] With this statement the censorship of US dietary guidelines began.

This first attempt by the meat industry to challenge the symbolic legitimacy of the US government and its scientists to create nutrition guidelines for Americans revealed one primary strategy: question the consensus around the science. The *Dietary Goals for the United States* was the first set of comprehensive guidelines to establish dietary restrictions based on ample scientific research on risk factors associated with chronic disease.[18] Knowing that their product was a major risk factor, the meat industry had to develop a strategy to dismantle the legitimacy of these guidelines and their capacity to threaten their market position and, consequently, financial wellbeing. Without going into too much detail here, meat industry lobbyists were most successful at arguing there was a lack of scientific consensus around medical evidence that found the causality between high intake of saturated fats and coronary heart disease. They based their arguments on interpretation of data and scientific validity in the research.[19] Because all science has some degree of uncertainty and is constantly being tested and updated, it is easy for sceptics or deniers to exploit this characteristic and find the weak link in a policy based on scientific evidence, the unsettled science. There will always be those who argue over interpretation of data and the validity of findings, but there is also the need to establish the degree to which consensus exists around findings. For example, the regular reports of the Intergovernmental Panel on Climate Change (IPCC) use 'confidence terminology' to indicate the degree of confidence in findings being correct based on consensus around interpretation of data and validity, among other factors. When they report that a finding has 'very high confidence', this translates into a 90–100 per cent chance of it being correct. A 'high confidence' translates into an 80–100 per cent chance of being correct and so on. However, the possibility always exists that there is room for

---

17 Nestle 2013, p. 41.
18 McGovern 1977.
19 Oppenheimer & Benrubi 2014.

error. Those who seek to benefit from exploiting this room for error will capitalise on the uncertainty of scientific findings.

Robert Cox calls this 'trope of uncertainty' a way to challenge the symbolic legitimacy of environmental science by suggesting there is not enough evidence to call for action or a certain policy.[20] The trope of uncertainty is often a stall tactic or a way of delaying policy measures so that interested parties, often industry, can come up with a new strategy to halt proposed policy or regulation. In the case of the Dietary Goals for the United States, the meat industry was successful in using the trope of uncertainty to question a call to reduce meat intake based on unsettled science around the link between saturated fat and coronary heart disease. They drew upon witnesses that included nutrition experts and medical doctors to testify at the Senate hearings to challenge the well-documented scientific consensus.[21]

Ultimately, the recommendations were dismissed by the Senate, primarily due to their economic implications for the food industry. Many attribute this dismissal to the lobbying efforts of the National Cattlemen's Beef Association and the National Dairy Council. However, the Senate claimed they abandoned the guidelines because they were too stringent and that there was a lack of scientific consensus around the connection between red meat and other animal products and coronary heart disease.[22]

Despite the challenge to their symbolic legitimacy from the meat and dairy industries, the US government did not abandon the idea of formalising nutrition guidelines and in 1978 the Department of Health and Human Services and the United States Department of Agriculture formed a joint committee made up of scientists from both units to craft a set of nutrition guidelines. These two units came together for several reasons, but one was due to the complaints that the USDA had a conflict of interest in developing dietary guidelines because of its role as both primary producer of nutrition education information and promoter of food products, including those of the meat, egg and dairy industries. Nutrition educators expressed concern that the USDA was

---

20   Cox 2010, p. 309.
21   Mayer & Dwyer 1978.
22   Oppenheimer & Benrubi 2014.

susceptible to food-industry lobbying. With this joint effort of the two federal departments, the Dietary Guidelines for Americans (DGAs) was first released in 1980 and has been released every five years since that time. The purpose of the DGAs is 'to make recommendations about the components of a healthy and nutritionally adequate diet to help promote health and prevent chronic disease for current and future generations'.[23] These guidelines have changed over the years based on changes in nutrition science, but one thing remains consistent: none of the DGAs has ever suggested Americans *eat less* meat of any kind. However, there was one USDA guideline that drew the largest controversy to date over its visual depiction of the protein food group.

This heated debate concerning nutrition education and policy occurred at the beginning of the 1990s over the release of the food pyramid. Encouraged by findings of a federal advisory committee and what former Secretary of Health and Human Services Louis W. Sullivan declared was a 'strong public demand for more understandable nutritional guidance', the USDA released the Food Guide Pyramid in 1991.[24] This pyramid had been the subject of dispute among health-care professionals, environmentalists and animal rights activists on one side, and the beef and dairy industries on the other. The primary problem was that the pyramid gave a visual suggestion, although not a verbal one, that Americans reduce their meat, dairy and animal-fat consumption in order to decrease saturated fat and cholesterol. At the same time, the pyramid suggested that Americans should increase their consumption of grains, fruits and vegetables. The food industry saw this as an indication that the USDA was beginning to group foods into *good* foods and *bad* foods, and animal products did not fare well in this categorisation.

The guide was presented in the form of a pyramid with grains forming the base of the pyramid, and the foundation of the diet, the vegetable and fruit groups forming the next layer, dairy and meat products on the next level, and the fats group forming the apex of the triangle. The pyramid was somewhat similar to the older Basic Four food groups, but the graphic gave pictorial emphasis to those foods that should be consumed more than others, stressing the consumption

---

23 United States Department of Agriculture 2015, 'Introduction'.
24 A pyramid topples, 1991.

of grains, fruits and vegetables. Further, the pyramid added another food group by breaking up the vegetables and fruit group into two separate categories. Serving suggestions for each group were as follows: 6–11 servings of grains, 3–5 servings of vegetables, 2–4 servings of fruit, 2–3 servings of milk, 2–3 servings of meat and other protein sources (including beans, peas, nuts and seeds) and minimal use of fats, oils and sweets. The pyramid visually suggested that the foods forming the foundation of a well-balanced diet should be grains, fruits and vegetables, a radical departure from previous food guides. While the Basic Four food guide offered serving suggestions, all minimum servings, its graphic did not set dietary priorities or serving limits. This was not the case with the pyramid, which gave more graphic space to grains, fruits and vegetables.

When it was announced that the Food Guide Pyramid, designed to provide up-to-date nutritional information, was to replace the Basic Four, the response from the lobbyists of the National Cattlemen's Beef Association, the North American Meat Institute and the National Milk Producers Federation was immediate. They met with then Secretary of Agriculture Edward Madigan to protest the graphic that gave visual preference to grains, vegetables and fruits while undermining the primary role that meat and dairy played in the American diet. The groups complained that the pyramid was misleading and might encourage individuals to reduce their daily meat and dairy intake, which was, of course, the intended effect.

The Basic Four, which had been represented by a pie chart consisting of four equivalent pieces representing each food group, suggested that no one food was better than any other. Government and media, relying on campaign and advertising funds from the food industry, benefitted from the use of the Basic Four because it supported the notion of a 'balanced diet' and allowed them to avoid playing food favourites, thus avoiding any potential political problems.[25] The pyramid graphic redefining sound nutrition was highly objectionable to the meat, dairy and egg industries because it no longer allowed for equality among all foods. They felt that their products would be viewed as *bad* when compared with the *good* grains, vegetables and fruits which enjoyed

---

25   Levenstein 1993, p. 206.

a more privileged position at the base of the pyramid. Gary Wilson, director of research and food policy for the National Cattlemen's Beef Association at the time, stated that his association 'wanted to be sure that consumers did not misinterpret the pyramid to be a ranking of food ... We wanted to avoid a good-food, bad-food ranking and the de-emphasis of meat.'[26] Jeannie Kenney, then a lobbyist for the National Milk Producers Federation, expressed dismay that the pyramid 'stigmatizes dairy products because they are next to fats and oils ... it emphasises the foods on the bottom more than those on the top and it encourages people to consider some food groups better than others.'[27]

The nutritional guidance offered by the Food Guide Pyramid reflected a trend in rhetorical redefinition that had been growing over the years: the villainisation of dietary fats. By extension, or guilt by association, this also produced a villainisation of the previous dietary hero, animal protein.[28] Over the second half of the 20th century, saturated fat had increasingly been accused of contributing to obesity, coronary heart disease, strokes and a variety of cancers.[29] However, even in 1991 it was still not the policy of the USDA to link particular foods to saturated fat, thereby framing those foods as unhealthy. They responded to criticisms of the pyramid by stating that 'it was intended only to reflect the relative daily recommended consumption of each of the four groups.'[30]

After 12 days of lobbying against the Food Guide Pyramid that 'demonized' the products of the meat and dairy industries, Madigan held a press conference to announce that he would be halting the distribution of the new Food Guide Pyramid. He stated that the guide needed further study to determine if it would mislead children and even some adults due to its 'complex' visual presentation. Nutrition and consumer groups denounced this decision because research for the pyramid had already been taking place for three years at the cost of $100,000. In order to avoid a 'conflict of interest' between the USDA

---

26   Burros 1991, p. 9.
27   Burros 1991, p. 9.
28   Stacey 1994, p. 157.
29   O'Neill 1996.
30   Burros 1991, p. 9.

and the meat industry, the testing was supervised and partially funded by the Department of Health and Human Services. The final decision about the dietary guidelines graphic was made by Secretary Madigan with the help of Secretary Sullivan. One anonymous HHS employee said that their involvement in the selection of the graphic was motivated by an effort to 'keep USDA honest'.[31] Secretary Madigan and representatives of the meat and dairy industries had preferred a bowl pictorial that did not appear to rank the food groups, but the research supporting the superiority of the pyramid as an educational tool was overwhelming.[32] In 1992, one year and almost a million dollars later, the pyramid was re-released in its original form after extensive research testing alternative graphics on over 3,000 people. The USDA assured the meat and dairy industries that consumers would not see food as *good* or *bad*. Meanwhile, these food industries had time to react to the pyramid's unveiling by starting rigorous ad campaigns of their own convincing the public that despite what the pyramid had to say, 'Beef. It's what's for dinner.'[33]

Interrogating the boundaries of legitimacy: Moving towards the 2015 DGAs

The meat and dairy industries lost their battle with the pyramid and for the first time, the USDA suggested limiting the intake of its products without actually saying the forbidden words to *limit* or *eat less*. The pyramid's graphic spoke for itself. However, the boundaries around the legitimacy of the nutrition guidelines remained in force. The DGAs still did not state that foods were *good* or *bad*, nor that one should eat

---

31 Burros 1992.
32 Burros 1992.
33 "Beef. It's what's for dinner" was an advertising slogan developed by the beef industry and used for decades in the United States to promote meat consumption. The dairy industry developed a similarly successful ad campaign, "Got Milk?" that also ran for decades, finally being replaced by another in 2014. These slogans are widely recognized among English-speaking North Americans and the ad campaigns were considered highly successful in promoting the products.

less of a certain food. The guidelines would only state that Americans should eat less of specific nutrients, such as fats, but foods linked to these fats were never mentioned. It was the job of the consumer to find this out. In this sense, the meat and dairy industries were highly successful at policing the symbolic boundaries, making sure that the USDA and HHS did not speak out of turn. No controversies arose over the ensuing years and the symbolic legitimacy of the Dietary Guidelines Advisory Committee remained intact, so long as they remained within their proper purview of recommending nutrition guidelines.

However, a new threat was on the horizon for the meat and dairy industries that had little to do with nutrition and had a much larger impact on the world stage: the environmental impacts of eating a meat- and dairy-heavy diet due to their production intensity. The United Nations' Food and Agriculture Organization (FAO) had been calling for a reduction in consumption of meat and dairy products due to its function as a significant driver of negative environmental changes. Their 2006 report, Livestock's Long Shadow, gave damning evidence that linked 18 per cent of all greenhouse gas emissions to the livestock industrial sector (9 per cent total anthropogenic CO_2, 37 per cent methane and 65 per cent nitrous oxide).[34] It described the link between the production of meat and animal products and their contribution to global warming, water pollution, habitat destruction and loss of biodiversity. Warning that meat production was predicted to grow worldwide by 2050, they made major policy suggestions regarding how to decrease consumption as well as mitigate the problems of intensive animal production practices. This report made headline news worldwide and was expectedly met with harsh criticism from the meat and dairy industries who questioned the veracity of the scientific methodology. However, the main criticism was based on a publication by an agronomy professor at the University of California, Davis, whose research was funded in part by the livestock industry.[35] Perhaps what was most significant about this report was that it recommended dietary policy intervention as a way to mitigate the environmental harms detailed by the report. If eating substantial amounts of meat and other

---

34 Steinfield 2006.
35 Hickman 2010.

animal products threatened the environmental stability of a country, then by extension it could threaten the food security of a country's population and should be factored into dietary recommendations. So, countries started to take notice.

While public health and nutrition experts had never considered food security as a primary issue before, the environmental challenges of the 21st century made it a central concern for nutrition policy in countries worldwide. The question lingered: How would a country create a food supply for a growing population, under inadequate environmental conditions, that provided the necessary nutritional requirements for human health? Influenced by this question, a theme developed in food policy discourse, 'Eco-Nutrition or Environmental Nutrition, which conceives … nutritional dependency on biophysical factors such as soil, biodiversity, water and climate'.[36] If intensive animal production for meat and dairy food sources threatened the food supply due to its environmental impact, there should be a suitable policy response among nutrition experts.

The World Health Organization (WHO) and the FAO had been suggesting global dietary recommendations for decades but more recently have made specific statements regarding nutrition and environmental stability. In 2010, the FAO published Sustainable Diets and Biodiversity: *Directions and Solutions for Policy, Research and Action* to encourage countries to develop nutrition policy that included sustainable diets. They defined sustainable diets as follows:

> Sustainable diets are those diets with low environmental impacts which contribute to food and nutrition security and to healthy life for present and future generations. Sustainable diets are respectful of biodiversity and ecosystems, culturally acceptable, accessible, economically fair and affordable; nutritionally adequate, safe and healthy; while optimizing natural and human resources.[37]

In 2014, the WHO released the Rome Declaration on Nutrition that included the following statements addressing the challenges

---

36   Lang & Barling 2013, p. 2.
37   Burlingame 2012, p. 7.

obstructing the right of all people to have access to 'safe, sufficient and nutritious food':

> the impacts of climate change and other environmental factors on food security and nutrition, in particular on the quantity, quality and diversity of food produced, taking appropriate action to tackle negative effects.[38]

and:

> [C]urrent food systems are being increasingly challenged to provide adequate, safe, diversified and nutrient rich food for all that contribute to healthy diets due to, *inter alia*, constraints posed by resource scarcity and environmental degradation, as well as by unsustainable production and consumption patterns, food losses and waste, and unbalanced distribution.[39]

The document was endorsed by 170 participating countries and the WHO went on to make a set of policy recommendations that included developing sustainable food systems that ensured adequate nutrition. Without mentioning a reduction in meat and animal products, most recommendations for a sustainable diet maintain that a reduction in saturated fat is a necessity, which translates into a reduction in consumption of animal fat. With the publication of these two documents, the message was sent on a global scale that environmental sustainability was a legitimate factor to consider when developing national nutrition policy.

Given the charge from these international organisations, countries began to follow suit and develop nutrition guidelines that included sustainability. To date, the Nordic countries, The Netherlands, Germany, and Brazil have developed dietary guidelines with a sustainability component. Sweden considered the environmental impact of specific food groups when creating their guidelines in 2015. Along with other factors, such as nutrition and accessibility, the

---

38 World Health Organization 2014.
39 World Health Organization 2014.

Swedish Food Agency (SFA) developed a brochure with the tagline 'Eat greener, not too much and be active'. Included in this new diet philosophy is the advice to 'eat less red and processed meat [including] beef, pork, lamb, reindeer and game'. While the guidelines mention the health reason for reducing intake of these meats, they also state the environmental reasons for cutting back:

> Of all foods, meat has the greatest impact on our climate and environment. This is why it's important for us to cut back on meat and be careful about what meat we do choose to eat.[40]

It should be noted that Sweden tried to implement sustainability into their guidelines as early as 2009 but was blocked by objections from the European Union who protested the recommendation of consuming locally produced foods. Doing so would privilege Swedish food products over other EU goods and would therefore disobey EU regulations, undermining free trade. However, after years of negotiations, the SFA came out with their nutrition guidelines including environmental impacts, but not mentioning eating locally produced foods.

2015 DGAs

With the international precedent established to include sustainability in nutrition guidelines, the DGAC had legitimate grounds on which to consider inclusion for the DGAs. Sustainability had been recognised as a topic of relevance in the 2010 DGAs but did not appear in that DGAC report and never was included as a nutritional recommendation. However, the 2015 DGAC felt that it was necessary to incorporate sustainability in the guidelines because of the relationship between long-term food sustainability and, thus, nutrition and health. Simply put, you can't have a healthy population without food security and sustainability; therefore, any committee charged with developing nutrition guidelines should consider sustainability. The DGAC felt it was

---

40   Livsmedelsverket 2015.

time to expand the boundaries of their symbolic legitimacy and bring sustainability into their sphere of expertise and authoritative voice.

In their report to the USDA and HHS, the DGAC defined sustainable diets as 'a pattern of eating that promotes health and wellbeing and provides food security for the present population while sustaining human and natural resources for future generations'.[41] The report states that being able to stabilise the food supply and create food security will require two primary actions: changing individual dietary patterns and changing agricultural production practices. Because of the committee's charge and their members' expertise, they focus on the former to remain within their authoritative sphere. The primary way in which they recommend dietary patterns change is to shift to a diet higher in plant-based foods:

> [A] diet higher in plant-based foods, such as vegetables, fruits, whole grains, legumes, nuts, and seeds, and lower in calories and animal based foods is more health promoting and is associated with less environmental impact than is the current U.S. diet. This pattern of eating can be achieved through a variety of dietary patterns, including the Healthy U.S.-style Pattern, the Healthy Mediterranean-style Pattern, and the Healthy Vegetarian Pattern. All of these dietary patterns are aligned with lower environmental impacts and provide options that can be adopted by the U.S. population.[42]

The membership of the DGAC consisting of reputable scientists, physicians and nutritionists from the US, along with reliance on high-impact, science-based evidence, laid the foundation for their symbolic legitimacy. The recommendations were based on 'the systematic review and analysis of the evidence published since the last DGAC deliberations'.[43] For nutrition content, much of the science-based evidence is drawn from the USDA's Nutrition Evidence Library[44] and is readily available to the public. For the sustainability

---

41   Dietary Guidelines Advisory Committee 2015, p. 375.
42   Dietary Guidelines Advisory Committee 2015, p. 19.
43   Dietary Guidelines Advisory Committee 2015, p. 51.
44   See www.nel.gov

chapter, they also relied on 15 global studies published between 2003 and 2014 focusing on 'dietary pattern modeling' along with agricultural production and its environmental impacts. All studies were published in prominent peer-reviewed scientific journals or by reports from intergovernmental organisations such as the United Nations Environmental Program (UNEP) or FAO. The report contains a section on their methodology to further substantiate the manner in which they came to their conclusions, providing full transparency in their process.

Despite these efforts, the meat and dairy industries responded in full force in an attempt to delegitimise the DGAC's authority and their report through interrogation of their rightful role in allowing sustainability to be part of the dietary guidelines. They secured the borders of the DGAC's legitimacy, drawing a firm line around their right to recommend policy in the 'Life Sciences Nutrition', the dominant understanding of nutrition based on the biochemical understanding of nutrients and their impact on the human body.[45] However, their expansion into the territory of Environmental Nutrition was characterised as a breach of their symbolic legitimacy. The meat and dairy industries policed the symbolic boundaries of the DGAs with an assiduous effort to censor the 2015 DGAC report and expel the sustainability recommendations and their suggestion to *eat less* meat from its contents.

The rhetorical battle came on several fronts. First was 'The Hearing to Review the Development of the Dietary Guidelines for Americans' with Secretary of Agriculture Tom Vilsack and Secretary of Health and Human Services Sylvia Burwell in a hearing before the Committee on Agriculture. The main arguments against the DGAC report focused on Chapter 5: Food Sustainability and Safety, which recommended the reduction of animal-based products. Prior to the hearing, an unprecedented 29,000 public comments were submitted to the USDA and HHS weighing in on the report. Many of these comments, 19,000, were about the sustainability recommendations, with 97 per cent supportive of including them in the guidelines.[46] Despite this public support, Secretary Vilsack, Secretary Burwell and several congressional

---

45 Lang & Barling 2013.
46 US Government Publishing Office 2015.

representatives felt otherwise. One representative was quite forthcoming about his reasons for objections. US House of Representative Tim Walz (DFL – MN) stated:

> [I]n full disclosure, I have the ninth largest agricultural district in America. We produce lots of pork, lots of milk, lots of turkeys, and all those things. When we make those decisions [about lean meat in the DGAs] they have an economic impact.[47]

The financial interests at stake when including sustainability were significant and the hearings, public comments and statements from elected and appointed officials reflected this. In some cases, those who objected were forthright, as with Walz, but in most cases, the objections came in the form of attacks against moving beyond perceived symbolic legitimacy boundaries. Several congressional representatives at the hearings summarised their constituencies' concerns that the DGAC was going outside the scope of their mandate by making recommendations regarding sustainability. However, some pointed out that the DGAs had started including Physical Fitness recommendations in 2010 and therefore had already begun recognising a need to broaden the scope of their authority. Challenging the scientific legitimacy of the DGAC's findings regarding red meat consumption, 30 US Senators sent a letter to Secretaries Vilsack and Burwell strongly urging that they exclude the recommendation to decrease consumption of red and processed meat on the grounds that it 'ignores peer-reviewed and published scientific evidence that shows the role of red meats as part of a healthy diet'.[48] The letter also chastised the DGAC for 'going beyond its purview of nutrition and health research' by including sustainability, asserting that they should remain 'within their statutory authority'.[49] The DGAC report explained the precedent for including sustainability in national dietary guidelines by referencing the UN and FAO reports along with the nutrition guidelines of Germany, Brazil and Nordic countries. They also justified why they were expanding their

---

47 US Government Publishing Office 2015.
48 Thune et al. 2015.
49 Thune et al. 2015.

boundaries of authority, showing the link between nutrition and food security. Nevertheless, this justification was ignored in the objections.

Secretary Vilsack heard the call to keep DGAC within its symbolic borders and at the March 2015 Pork Industry forum he stated that they needed to colour 'within the lines'. He explained:

> My three-year-old granddaughter has the privilege of coloring outside the lines. My grandson, who is in preschool, is learning a little bit about coloring inside the lines. I think that's a significant difference. I think the advisory group has the freedom of coloring outside the lines … our job is to color inside the lines. We don't necessarily have the freedom to color outside the lines.[50]

This was a clear indication of how Vilsack viewed the legitimacy of DGAC to enter into the science of sustainable diets; he likened them to three-year-olds exploring new ground. His job, as influenced by significant pressure from lobbyists and elected officials, was to rein in any exploratory deviance and remain within the scope of standard Life Sciences Nutrition.

Outside of the hearings and public comments, the meat industry was busy making their own public comments to the press and to Congress. The North American Meat Institute (NAMI) President said of the DGAC report upon its release that the members had entered 'into the murky waters of sustainability [which] is well beyond its scope and expertise. It's akin to having a dermatologist provide recommendations about cardiac care.'[51] Carpenter also criticised the scientific advice as 'contradictory' and 'nonsensical', all typical strategies at delegitimising symbolic authority. In hearings before Congress, NAMI Vice-President of Scientific Affairs Betsy Booren argued that more than 70 per cent of DGAC's 2015 recommendations were not based on the USDA's nutrition library (NEL) and complained about the lack of expertise on sustainability, stating, '[i]t is not appropriate for the person designing a better light bulb to be telling Americans how to make

---

50   Tosh Farms 2015.
51   Shanker 2015.

a better sandwich.'[52] Once again, an industry association spoke out about the boundaries of legitimacy being transgressed. Booren and Vice-President of NAMI Foundation Susan Backus also submitted a letter to the congressional subcommittee on the DGAC 2015 report. In it they used the uncertainty trope to question the science around sustainability and diets. They argued:

> Sustainability is a complex issue that is being addressed by various experts in a number of other forums. Until those expert panels have drawn more concrete conclusions it would be premature for the Committee to incorporate such considerations into its dietary guidance recommendations. To do so runs the risk the Committee will act on incomplete data.[53]

Framing the science of a particular body of research, like sustainability or climate change, as 'unsettled' or incomplete and ongoing often shuts down debate or conversation about what should be done in light of current research findings. It is an effective meatsplaining strategy because it appears to be rational; policy should not be based on unsettled or uncertain science. However, science is always unsettled and ever evolving, so it is a deceptively rational statement to say no action should be taken based on this premise. Action and policy are always based on unsettled and evolving science. However, when there are special interests at stake, this uncertainty trope proves to be very successful at stifling action. This is the case with sustainability and nutrition policy. The meat and dairy industries are stakeholders that stand to lose a great deal, so the uncertainty trope is a convenient rhetorical strategy on which to rely.

Overall, despite public support for the inclusion of sustainability in the 2015 DGAs, Vilsack and Burwell reported in their blog post of 6 October 2015 that the sustainability recommendations would not be included. The meat industry won a 'round in war over federal nutrition advice' to reduce red meat for sustainability reasons, or any reason at all for that matter.[54] Their carefully choreographed efforts at meatsplaining

---

52 North American Meat Institute 2015.
53 Booren & Backus 2014.
54 Bottemiller Evich 2016.

had prevailed, this time around. However, the debate over sustainability and nutrition guidelines was placed in the public spotlight. The conversation had begun.

Conclusion

This chapter illustrates how the Dietary Guidelines for Americans are hardly neutral sources of nutritional and sustainable eating practices. They are highly influential and contested discourses where those who support and benefit from the practice of eating animal flesh and other animal by-products gain entrance into the minds of the public through federal policy, directly influencing their eating habits.

Given the severity of our current environmental problems, especially in regard to climate change, and the relationship that dietary patterns have to contributing to these problems, there must be a concerted effort on the part of all countries to educate their citizens about how diet plays a role not only in creating health for humans but health for the planet. The United States, as one of the largest consumers of meat per capita in the world, has an ethical obligation to adopt sustainability guidelines in its federal nutrition recommendations as other countries have done. Given the history of interrogation and dismantling of symbolic legitimacy of the Dietary Guidelines for Americans, it is perhaps time to take away the task from the USDA, which has a conflict of interest in its charge, and hand over the creation of dietary guidelines to the office of Health and Human Services. As journalist and food activist Michael Pollan describes:

> The Department of Agriculture ... has a conflict of interest at the heart of its mission. Its mission is to promote sales of US agricultural products, sell more food, while the dietary guidelines are about helping us curb our appetite for certain foods. The idea that the Department of Agriculture has anything to do with advising Americans on nutrition is absurd.[55]

---

55 Belluz 2016.

Moreover, because food security is going to become an increasingly significant aspect of nutrition policy, perhaps it is time to have the Environmental Protection Agency provide input to the DGAs given its charge of protecting human health and the environment. Although, given the way in which the EPA has been compromised under leadership in the Trump Administration, it appears this agency is also open to corruption and susceptible to corporate influence.

In their comprehensive study of approximately 38,000 farms around the world producing 40 agricultural goods to examine foods' impacts on the environment, Joseph Poore and Thomas Nemecek concluded that the biggest change that needs to be made to avoid environmental calamity is to convince people to change their diet and significantly reduce their consumption of meat and dairy products. They maintain that accomplishing this dietary change will be a mammoth undertaking and require major communication efforts by several countries. They state:

> Communicating average product impacts to consumers enables dietary change and should be pursued. Though dietary change is realistic for any individual, widespread behavioral change will be hard to achieve in the narrow timeframe remaining to limit global warming and prevent further, irreversible biodiversity loss. Communicating producer impacts allows access to the second scenario, which multiplies the effects of smaller consumer changes.[56]

In an effort to make the world population aware of what is at stake when consuming a diet rich in meat and dairy, Poore and Nemecek contend that there will need to be broad education on the true cost of these food products. As the evidence pointing to the unsustainability of meat- and dairy-heavy diets mounts, the interrogation of the symbolic legitimacy of those scientists, nutritionists and environmentalists that build this case will be an inevitable outcome. We can only hope, for the sake of the planet, our health and most importantly the animals that suffer due to

---

56   Poore & Nemecek 2018, p. 991.

our unsustainable dietary patterns that we will uphold that legitimacy, listen to the science and change our diets for the good of all.

References

A pyramid topples at the USDA. (1991). *Consumer Reports* 56(10), 663–666.

Belasco, W. (1989). *Appetite for Change*. New York: Pantheon.

Belluz, J. (2016). Michael Pollan on how America got so screwed up about food. *Vox*. 7 January. https://bit.ly/2QccDbN

Booren, B. L. and S. L. Backus (2014). RE: Subcommittee request for public comments [Letter to Dr. Olson and Dietary Guidelines Advisory Committee]. 3 March. https://bit.ly/3hcKddA

Bottemiller Evich, H. (2016). Meat industry wins round in war over federal nutrition advice. *Politico*. 7 January. https://politi.co/3hkDCOj

Burlingame, B. (2012). Preface. In B. Burlingame and S. Dernini (Eds.), *Sustainable Diets and Biodiversity: Directions and Solutions for Policy, Research and Action* (pp. 7–8). Rome: Food and Agriculture Organization.

Burros, M. (1992). Eating well: Testing of the food pyramid comes full circle. *New York Times*. 25 March. https://nyti.ms/3aIOm6E

Burros, M. (1991). U.S. delays issuing nutrition chart. *New York Times*. 27 April. https://nyti.ms/2Ek2ffA

Cox, R. (2010). *Environmental Communication and the Public Sphere* (2nd ed.). Los Angeles: Sage Publications, Inc.

Davis, C. and E. Saltos (1999). Dietary recommendations and how they have changed over time. In E. Frazao (Ed.), *America's Eating Habits: Changes and Consequences* (pp. 33– 50). United States Department of Agriculture, Economic Research Service, Food and Rural Economics Division.

Dietary Guidelines Advisory Committee (2015). *Scientific report of the 2015 Dietary Guidelines Advisory Committee*. Agricultural Research Service. https://health.gov/dietaryguidelines/2015-scientific-report/

Edenhofer, O., R. Pichs-Madruga, Y. Sokona, E. Farahani, S. Kadner, K. Seyboth, ... J. C. Minx (Eds.) (2014). *Climate Change 2014: Mitigation of Climate Change: Contribution of Working Group III to the Fifth Assessment Report of the Intergovernmental Panel on Climate Change*. Cambridge: Cambridge University Press.

Foley, J. A., N. Ramankutty, K. A. Brauman, E. S. Cassidy, J. S. Gerber, M. Johnson, ... D. P. M. Zaks (2011). Solutions for a cultivated planet. *Nature* 478(7369), 337–342. doi:10.1038/nature10452

US Government Publishing Office (2015). Hearing to review the development of the Dietary Guidelines for Americans. 7 October. https://bit.ly/2QbVUp3

Hickman, L. (2010). Do critics of UN meat report have a beef with transparency? *The Guardian*. 24 March. https://bit.ly/3aIh1IU

Lang, T. and D. Barling (2013). Nutrition and sustainability: An emerging food policy discourse. *Proceedings of the Nutrition Society* 72(1), 1–12. doi:10.1017/S002966511200290X

Tosh Farms (2015). Lawmakers to Vilsack: Keep meat on dinner plates. *Tosh Farms*. 17 March. https://bit.ly/3hh8sYj

Thune, J., S. Daines, D. Fischer, J. Ernst, J. M. Inhofe, M. B. Ezi, ... J. Moran (2015). Dear Secretaries Burwell and Vilsack [Letter from the U.S. Senate]. 12 March. https://bit.ly/2EkQzJm

Levenstein, H. (1993). *The Paradox of Plenty*. New York: Oxford University Press.

Livsmedelsverket (2015). *Find Your Way to Eat Greener, Not Too Much and Be Active. Livemedelsverket Swedish Food Agency*. https://bit.ly/3aLePR4

Mayer, J. and J. Dwyer (1978). Experts polled on diet, heart disease. *Los Angeles Times*. 10 August.

McCarthy, D. E. (2016). Incorporating sustainability into America's Dietary Guidelines. *Yale Environment Review*. 11 April. https://bit.ly/3hnNO8Y

McGovern, G. (1977). Statement of Senator George McGovern on the publication of Dietary Goals for the United States. In Senate Select Committee on Nutrition and Human Needs, *Dietary Goals for the United States* (pp. xiii-xiv). Washington, DC: US Government Printing Office. https://bit.ly/3geOAn1

Nestle, M. (2013). *Food Politics: How the Food Industry Influences Nutrition and Health* (10th ed.). Berkeley, CA: University of CA Press.

North American Meat Institute (2015). North American Meat Institute argues for scientific evidence as foundation of nutrition policy. *North American Meat Institute*. 24 March. https://bit.ly/2EmLws0

Oppenheimer, G. M. and I. D. Benrubi (2014). McGovern's Senate Select Committee on Nutrition and Human Needs versus the meat industry on the diet-heart question (1976–1977). *American Journal of Public Health* 104(1), 59–69. doi:10.2105/AJPH.2013.301464.

O'Neill, M. (1996). The Morality of Fat. *New York Times Magazine*. 10 March. https://www.nytimes.com/1996/03/10/magazine/the-morality-of-fat.html

Poore, J. and T. Nemecek (2018). Reducing food's environmental impacts through producers and consumers. *Science* 360(6392), 987–992. doi:10.1126/science.aaq0216

Rojas-Downing, M., A. P. Nejadhashemi, T. Harrigan, and S. A. Woznicki (2017). Climate change and livestock: impacts, adaptations, and mitigation. *Climate Risk Management* 16(1),145–16. doi:10.1016/j.crm.2017.02.001

Shanker, D. (2015). Meat wins: Sustainability won't factor into the U.S. Government's new dietary guidelines. *Quartz*. 6 October. https://bit.ly/2Ek3ooW

Stacey, M. (1994). *Consumed: Why Americans Love, Hate, and Fear Food*. New York: Simon & Schuster.

Steinfeld, H., P. Gerber, T. D. Wassenaar, V. Castel, M. Rosales, and C. de Haan (2006). *Livestock's long shadow: Environmental issues and options*. Rome: Food & Agriculture Organization of the United Nations.

Stoll-Kleemann, S. and T. O'Riordan (2015). The sustainability challenges of our meat and dairy diets. *Environment: Science and Policy for Sustainable Development* 57(3), 34–48. doi:10.1080/00139157.2015.1025644

Vilsack, T. and S. Burwell (2015). 2015 dietary guidelines: Giving you the tools you need to make healthy choices. *United States Department of Agriculture*. 6 October. https://bit.ly/2CPRIZ8

Welsh, S. O., C. Davies and A. Shaw (1993). *USDA's Food Guide: Background and development*. United States Department of Agriculture, Miscellaneous Publication Number 1514.

United States Department of Agriculture (2015). *Dietary Guidelines for Americans 2015–2020* (8th ed.). United States Department of Agriculture. https://health.gov/dietaryguidelines/2015/guidelines/

World Health Organization (2014). Conference outcome document: Rome declaration on nutrition. *Food and Agriculture Organization of the United Nations*. October. http://www.fao.org/3/a-ml542e.pdf

6

Meat taboo: Climate change and the EU meat lobby[1]

Núria Almiron

In the year 2006, and despite timid and delayed media coverage,[2] the publication of the Food and Agricultural Organization of the United Nations (FAO) report Livestock's Long Shadow[3] produced a worldwide commotion. For the first time, a governmental organisation confirmed what an increasing number of independent experts had been reporting:[4] that the animal agriculture industrial complex[5] is one of the major causes of human-induced global greenhouse gas emissions. From that date onwards, the role of animal agriculture in climate change became a hot topic of research and investigators plunged into it in relevant numbers. Today there is already a substantial amount

1   This research was funded by the Spanish State Research Agency (Agencia Estatal de Investigación, AEI) and the European Regional Development Fund (ERDF) under grant CSO2016-78421-R (THINKClima project). The author is also grateful for the assistance provided in the data collection by Fortunat Miarintsoa Andrianimanana, THINKClima's research assistant and PhD student in the Department of Communication at the Universitat Pompeu Fabra.
2   Almiron & Zoppeddu 2014.
3   Steinfeld 2006.
4   For example, see Eshel & Martin 2006; World Watch Institute 2004.
5   By 'animal agriculture industrial complex', I refer here to all the industries directly involved in the exploitation of nonhuman animals to produce food commodities for humans. This includes extensive and intensive farming.

of literature supporting this negative impact, including more governmental reports, nongovernmental green organisations' accounts, scientific papers, books, think-tank research and even political party output[6] as well as a countless number of media reports and research.

With very few exceptions, the majority of this research has been mostly oriented to climate change mitigation or adaption – including assessing the real impact of animal agriculture and devising ways of reducing this impact before or after it occurs (for instance, manipulating diets to reduce nonhuman animals' emissions or manipulating the nonhuman animals' bodies or their waste to reduce the impact of emissions). Human health has also been considered in these researches, yet the violence and suffering perpetrated on nonhuman animals in agriculture – that is, the confinement, exploitation and murder of trillions of beings (if we include fishing) – is only mentioned in climate change reports produced by animal defence organisations or animal advocates.[7] Overall, however, all of these efforts agree on the fact that the animal-industrial complex has a very important role in global greenhouse gas emissions and therefore must be addressed by any strategy that is serious about fighting climate change.

Different research projects provide different figures for the impact of animal exploitation on global warming, from the 10–12 per cent of direct global greenhouse gas (GHG) emissions as assessed by the IPCC[8] to the 51 per cent of GHG worldwide emissions estimated by Goodland

---

6   For example see Gerber et al. 2013; Intergovernmental Panel on Climate Change 2019; Leip et al. 2010; Schwarzer 2012 for governmental reports; Bellarby, Foereid, Hastings & Smith 2008; Greenpeace International 2018; Hamerschlag 2011; Thomas 2010 for NGOs reports; Aleksandrowicz et al. 2016; Carlsson-Kanyama & Gonzalez 2009; Eshel, Shepon, Makov & Milob 2014; McMichael, Powles, Butler & Uauy 2007; Poore & Nemecek 2018; Rosi et al. 2017; Scarborough et al. 2014; Springmann, Godfray, Rayner & Scarborough 2016; Westhoek et al. 2014 for scientific papers; Kemmerer 2014; Hedges 2016; Lymbery 2017; Lymbery & Oakeshott 2014 for books; Bailey, Froggatt & Wellesley 2014; Goodland & Anhang 2009; Pew Environment Group 2011; Ranganathan et al. 2016; Renner 2014 for think-tanks research; Holm & Jokkala 2007; Soeters & Zwanikken 2007 for political parties output.

7   For example, see Freeman 2010; Humane Society International 2008.

8   Intergovernmental Panel on Climate Change 2014.

and Anhang,[9] including what these authors define as 'uncounted, overlooked and misallocated' animal agriculture-related GHG emissions. Of the 23 per cent of total anthropogenic greenhouse gas emissions derived from agriculture, forestry and other land use as estimated by the IPCC by 2019, the major portion of it related to the exploitation of other animals.[10] The largest sources of CO_2 from animal agriculture come not from the animals themselves (through respiration and waste), but from the inputs and land-use changes necessary to maintain and feed them, including: burning fossil fuels to produce fertilisers used in feed production; maintaining intensive animal production facilities; growing the associated animal feed; transporting the animal feed; and processing and transporting the animal products. Furthermore, clearing land to graze *livestock*[11] and grow feed is the largest single cause of deforestation and among the major causes of land degradation and desertification.

However, despite such a significant scientific consensus on the contribution of the animal-industrial complex in global warming, the Intergovernmental Panel on Climate Change (IPCC), the major authority on the issue, systematically neglected stressing plant-based diets in its suggested pack of solutions until 2019.[12] Until that date, and bizarrely, IPCC reports had routinely highlighted that among the main drivers of increases in global warming emissions are lifestyle choices and, notably, diet choices (alongside economic and human population growth). However, when it came to solutions, the IPCC reports did not explicitly recommend a shift to a plant-based diet. Rather, all scenarios for climate change adaptation and mitigation heavily relied on technology – with a strong emphasis on technological solutions that involve a large number of adverse side effects and uncertainties (such as carbon dioxide capture and storage, nuclear power or geoengineering)

---

9   Goodland & Anhang 2009.
10   Intergovernmental Panel on Climate Change 2019.
11   Words like *livestock*, *meat* and *dairy*, usually employed to refer to the nonhuman animals exploited in agriculture or the products obtained from them, are used only in this paper in italics in an effort to reject language that devalues nonhuman animals by objectifying them (*livestock*, for instance, literally means *stock*, i.e. merchandise, which is *alive*).
12   Intergovernmental Panel on Climate Change 2019.

– and on cultural patterns that despite being important have a lesser impact on the environment than population, the economy and, most of all, diet. Due to the fact that the IPCC serves as the main reference for mainstream and popular science literature on climate change, this failure to recommend solutions that fully match the problem is widespread and consistently endorsed by celebrities and the political class. Hence, major bestsellers such as Naomi Klein's *This Changes Everything*[13] and the main policies deployed by governments to fight climate change simply reproduce this failure. Similarly, the United Nations Framework Convention on Climate Change (UNFCCC), the most important intergovernmental arena for the discussion of anthropogenic global warming, has time and again resisted even discussing the topic and it was not until the Paris Climate Conference (COP21) in 2015 that animal agriculture was for the first time specifically addressed, although informally (outside the official political talks) and without concrete results.

In this respect, it is worth noting that, outside the scientific sphere, advocates for animal rights and animal liberation have been the most active in stressing the links between global warming and the animal agriculture industry, in an attempt to get a reduction of consumption of animal products by taking advantage of the widespread concern for the environment. Besides the reports published by animal rights organisations[14] and the word spread through their websites (see, for instance, PETA.org or AnimalEquality.net), other advocacy activities have included documentaries like the well-known *Cowspiracy*[15] and above-mentioned books. All of them gather and disseminate scientific evidence using plain language and, although it is not clear that the aggregation of global warming arguments to the ethical claim made by animal advocates has any relevant impact on the consumption of animal products, they certainly have helped to visualise and erode the animal agriculture taboo.

---

13 Klein 2015.
14 For instance, see CIWF 2008; CIWF 2015; Humane Society International 2008.
15 Andersen & Kuhn 2014.

This taboo, as scholars have pointed out,[16] is a cultural taboo but also, and probably firstly, an economic taboo, which promotes and nourishes the ideological denial that prevents most humans from accepting that the consumption of animal product is not a matter of personal choice but a social justice issue in capitalist societies.[17] The economic basis of the taboo is so powerful that it has even prevented green NGOs from including animal agriculture in their campaigns until very recently, and even then, still very timidly. These NGOs – for example, Greenpeace, Sierra Club or the World Wildlife Fund – have not provided any explicit justification of their reluctance to address what probably is the most relevant source of GHG, but Al Gore, aligned with these NGOs' objectives, has actually done so. In an interview about the launching of his documentary *An Inconvenient Sequel: Truth to Power*,[18] Gore was asked why he did not put more emphasis on eating habits and on the consumption of animal products. Gore, who according to himself has been vegan since 2012, provided two reasons for this: first, personal habits are very difficult to change and, second, any emphasis on animal products could be seen as an attack on the animal agriculture and food industry. That is, he recognised that he did not emphasise *meat*-eating so as to not bother big business and citizens. We can infer from this that green NGOs and advocates are strongly reluctant to send messages that may expose the contradictions of society probably out of fear of losing support, which could severely damage their finances. Thus, their denial is also essentially economically oriented.

However, of course, where economic interests are much more influential is in the arena of politics and the media. In these contexts, vested interests have been the major barrier in the fight against climate change from the very beginning. The 'denial machine' organised by the US right-wing countermovement to mostly protect the interests of the fossil fuel industry[19] is the best example of how corporate interests,

---

16 Joy 2011.
17 Almiron 2020; Nibert 2017a; Nibert 2017b.
18 Gore 2017.
19 For instance, see Boykoff 2016; Dunlap & McCright 2015; McCright & Dunlap 2010.

through interest groups and public relations (PR),[20] can prevent action from even occurring. However, how the biggest taboo of all has been perpetuated by the animal agriculture lobby is still to be fully uncovered. This chapter unveils one of the mechanisms that works in its favour: the strategy and rhetoric deployed in the EU by the *meat* lobby to safeguard its environmentally unsustainable business while avoiding the ethical implications of it for both the animals exploited and for the planet.

In particular, this text analyses the extent to which the EU *meat* lobby's strategy regarding the ecological footprint of *meat* aligns with the strategy deployed by the tobacco and climate change denial countermovements, the latter working within the logic of the *merchants of doubt*,[21] which was also identified in the vivisection industrial complex.[22] That is, the logic of the dissemination of information devoted to maintaining controversy and keeping the debate alive on the basis of claims that are contrary to most scientific evidence and ethics. In this respect, the communication strategy of the two main lobbyists of the EU *meat* industry – UECBV (European Livestock and Meat Trades Union) and CLITRAVI (Liaison Centre for the Meat Processing Industry in the European Union) – has been analysed to expose the *meat* industry's counternarrative on the ecological impact of *meat*.

Data for this chapter was gathered during 2018 and 2019, but the analysis covers the period starting with publication of the FAO Livestock's Long Shadow report in 2006. The approach taken by the author is a critical animal studies perspective – aimed at introducing a critical animal standpoint in the phenomenon of *meat*splaining, in this case to unveil how EU corporate lobbying justifies and normalises human violence against other animals by means of a rhetoric of denial.

---

20   Almiron & Xifra 2020.
21   Oreskes & Conway 2010.
22   Almiron & Khazaal 2016.

The European *meat* lobbies

The lobbies registered in the EU Transparency Register[23] that are interested in agricultural issues number in the hundreds. Agriculture, through the Common Agricultural Policy (CAP), receives 40 per cent of the total EU budget every year (in the mid-1980s the figure was over 70 per cent)[24] and represents a huge industry whose size translates into major political influence. Animal agriculture is the biggest sector within the industry, including both the *meat* and *dairy* sectors, with the former being the larger.[25] Among all the trade associations, two umbrella organisations represent the interests of the main *meat* industries in the EU: the UECBV and the CLITRAVI.

The UECBV is the lobby group of the *livestock* and *meat* industry, including the animal protein trade and market, slaughterhouses, cutting and preparation plants, the wholesale *meat* trade and international *meat* traders. It represents more than 50 national federations from 24 EU member states as well as certain EFTA (European Free Trade Association) countries and EU candidate countries (Turkey) – that is, around 20,000 firms of medium and small sizes according to their own description. The UECBV was created in

---

23 The Transparency Register is a voluntary lobbyist register operated jointly by the European Parliament and the EU Commission since June 2011. Its coverage extends beyond lobbyists to law firms, NGOs and think-tanks, and it includes information on staff numbers, the legislative proposals they have attempted to influence and the amount of EU funding they have received. However, the transparency gained by this register is seen as minor, since entries are voluntary and have been withdrawn arbitrarily by lobbyists in the past and incorrect information (which the co-signed code of conduct does not officially allow) is not sanctioned in practice. In fact, the UECBV was included in the 2015 list of five complaints in which ALTER-EU (the Alliance for Lobbying Transparency and Ethics Regulation) revealed reporting of incorrect information by the lobbyists. In particular, the UECBV was accused of reporting less than €9999 in annual lobby expenditure, despite declaring a staff of eight full-time lobbyists, an office in Brussels, extensive interests in influencing the decision making of the European institutions, publication of several position papers and far higher declared lobby expenditures in the previous year (ALTER-EU 2015).
24 Agriculture and Rural Development of the European Commission 2017.
25 Fooddrink Europe 2017.

Switzerland in 1952 and opened an office in Brussels in 1980 to be close to four of the European institutions, as explained by its website. CLITRAVI was established in 1958 and is the lobby group representing the interests of the European *meat* processing industry. According to its website, CLITRAVI represents about 15,000 companies through 26 federations which together manufacture around 13.5 million tons of *meat* products and account for an annual turnover of more than 75 billion euros in the EU. Both lobby groups have joined efforts to address climate change issues in the last decade to compensate for the increasing popularisation of their negative impact on the environment.

Since their main goal is to influence policy making at the EU level to protect their interests, both trade organisations are pure lobbyists. Aligned with a typical lobbying mantra, they claim to aim to legitimately 'achieve an optimum business climate' and to engage 'in a constant dialogue' with EU institutions to have their voice democratically heard. However, this euphemistic language masks a permanent and very well-funded campaign to prevent changes at the regulatory level that may put their business at risk while simultaneously encouraging others that may increase the consumption of *meat* products and therefore their profits. As is usual with lobbying activities, transparency is low, much lower in the EU than in the US, and the full account of their lobbying activities is unknown.

However, the Transparency Register provides us with a list of the main interests lobbied by UECBV and CLITRAVI in the EU, which in 2018 included: food information regulation, TTIP (Transatlantic Trade and Investment Partnership) negotiations, animal welfare policies, additives and enzymes, trade and international market access, sustainability, environment and climate change, food information to consumers, public health, the food chain and the image of *meat*.

Animal agriculture lobbying includes the usual portfolio of lobbying strategies. First, lobbies make financial contributions to political campaigns to cultivate good relationships with the political parties in office. This is done differently from country to country because of varying regulations across the EU.

Second, and obviously, lobbies conduct pure direct lobbying following established patterns. One consists of building and maintaining a network of contacts. The lobbies nurture traditional links with political elites, visit the offices of new politicians and invite old and new contacts to discuss soft issues. When a specific legislative opportunity or threat arises, lobbyists use their established networks to push their agenda. As stated by the UECBV and CLITRAVI themselves, their main targets are the European institutions (including the European Commission, the European Parliament, the Council of the European Union, the European and Economic Social Committee and the European Food Safety Authority) and international organisations (such as the Food and Agriculture Organization or the World Health Organization). In 2016, for instance, in the Transparency Register, the UECBV declared it had held up to 32 meetings with members of the European Commission alone. The UECB also often works in sections and committees in which decision makers are regularly invited. EU policy makers thus participate in their working groups and section meetings, allowing participants to have direct contact with them.

Third, these lobbies try to capture as many seats as possible in the forums created by EU authorities to gather opinions regarding specific topics and foster discussions that assist them in policy development. Actually, lobbies are usually disproportionately influential in these official forums. These social, professional and expert groups are devised as discussion platforms where nongovernmental organisations, including non-profit ones, have the opportunity to help prepare legislation or policy definitions in a transparent model very much open to public scrutiny. Yet, although they are open to all organised stakeholders in society, these forums end up being largely dominated by industry. In 2018, the UECBV and CLITRAVI reported in the Transparency Register that they were members of at least five such platforms created by the European Commission alone.[26]

Lobbies also try to become primary advisors of public officers, the media and public opinion by means of their own dissemination of apparently scientific, objective knowledge. This is carried out by

---

26 The Civil Dialogue Group on food supply chain, animal and plant health; the EU Animal Welfare Platform; the Expert group on the exchange of information on Best Available Techniques related to industrial emissions; the Expert group on *Meat* Market Observatory; and the High Level Forum for a better functioning food supply chain.

means of the creation of taskforces, research groups, observatories or even full institutes or think-tanks that often are funded and supported by European institutions. These platforms also are able to send spokespersons to represent their interest in multiple events. The UECBV, for instance, regularly sends members to participate in conferences, seminars, press debriefings and lectures with key EU officials and other stakeholders in Brussels and across the EU.[27]

Finally, lobbies also work in coalition among themselves and co-operate in networks in order to combine their efforts and increase their influence and capacity for disseminating their discourses. In 2018, besides CLITRAVI, the UECBV also reported working in alliance with a number of other key trade organisations from the *meat* industry, including: COCERAL,[28] Codex Alimentarius,[29] COPA-COGECA,[30] EuroCommerce,[31] EuropaBio,[32] CEJA,[33] CELCAA,[34] FVE[35] and FEFAC.[36]

In the EU, as in the US, the agriculture lobby – and particularly the animal agriculture business within it – is the largest single lobbying

27 UECBV nd.
28 COCERAL is the European association representing the trade in cereals, rice, feedstuffs, oilseeds, olive oil, oils and fats and agrosupply.
29 Codex Alimentarius is a collection of internationally recognised standards, codes of practice, guidelines and other recommendations relating to foods, food production and food safety maintained by the FAO and the WHO under a commission that is recognised by the World Trade Organization as an international reference point for the resolution of disputes concerning food safety and consumer protection.
30 COPA-COGECA are two trade organisations representing the European agri-cooperatives and European farmers.
31 EuroCommerce is the trade association representing over six million retail, wholesale and other trading companies.
32 EuropaBio is the European Association for Bioindustries, the lobby group of the biotechnology industry, whose members include Solvay S.A., Monsanto, Bayer and other biotechnology companies.
33 CEJA, the European Council of Young Farmers, is the lobby group for young farmers in Europe.
34 CELCAA is the European Liaison Committee for Agriculture and Agri-Food Trade.
35 FVE is the Federation of Veterinarians of Europe.
36 FEFAC is the European Feed Manufacturers' Federation.

force (Corporate Europe, for instance, reported its comparative lobbying weight for the TTIP negotiations, with agriculture having a higher lobbying effort than the telecommunications, automobile or finance industries[37]).

Meat lobbying and climate change: Kidnapping the discussion in the guise of science

Although the FAO's 2006 Livestock's Long Shadow report went apparently rather unnoticed by the press, alarms rang within the industry. Shortly after its publication, the *meat* industries in the EU and the US started to launch major lobbying efforts to address their negative environmental image. What follows is the timeline of the reaction publicly available for UECBV and CLITRAVI, gathered from a number of news reports on the two lobbies and from documents authored by them and accessible online.[38]

In 2009, three years after the issuing of the FAO's report, the UECBV and CLITRAVI gathered to fight back and launched a taskforce on climate change with the aim of becoming a privileged discussion partner for the European Commission on issues regarding climate change policy that could impact the agriculture business. This taskforce has issued several memorandums that will be discussed in the next section.

In 2012, both lobbies became leading stakeholders in the public–private partnership co-ordinated by the FAO animal production and health division launched to assess the best way to estimate the environmental performance of EU *livestock*. This was a great success of the *meat* lobbies, who have been claiming from 2006 that FAO estimations were wrong for the EU and a new method of calculation was needed.

In 2014, the EU Commission (DG Environment) launched a call for volunteers to suggest Product Environment Footprint Category

---

37 Corporate Europe Observatory 2014.
38 Only a small number of lobbyists' documents are open to the public; the ones used for this paper include: CLITRAVI-UECBV 2010, CLITRAVI-UECBV 2012, UECBV nd, UECBV 2012, UECBV 2016.

Rules,[39] dedicated to food, feed, drinks, packaging for foods, fertilisers, catering services and drink products. Eleven projects were selected and funded, including one for *meat* prepared by a consortium led by the UECBV that was developed to, among other things, prevent third parties from settling the basis for assessment of the sustainability of *livestock–meat* production and consumption. The funded project (called Product Environmental Footprint or PEF) was aimed at the 'development of a harmonised methodology for the calculation of the environmental footprint' of *meat* products.[40]

At the end of 2019 no scientific output had emerged from any of the previous partnerships beyond press releases and memorandums of positions. In short, the strategy followed seems to merely replicate a common pattern: make great efforts to become a privileged partner in discussions on what has to be changed in order to prevent such change as much as possible by forcing in one's narrative and interests. In this sense, the animal agriculture strategy parallels the tobacco and oil lobby strategy in the mid and late 20th century, in their efforts to delay what can clearly no longer be delayed. As shown in the next section, the discursive tools used were the same – sowing the seeds of doubt and constructing a counternarrative[41] – but also parallel that of the vivisection lobbies' narratives at the beginning of the 21st century.[42]

A counternarrative of denial

The first and main element of the EU *meat* lobby strategy regarding climate change is a complete replication of the tobacco and climate change lobbying strategies: scientific denial. From 2006, the UECBV and CLITRAVI, and the whole industry they represent, have denied that the FAO's estimation has any validity, arguing that the method used for calculating animal agriculture's GHG emissions was not valid for

---

39   The Environmental Footprint Pilots by the European Commission: http://ec.europa.eu/environment/eussd/smgp/ef_pilots.htm.

40   UECBV 2016.

41   Oreskes & Conway 2010.

42   Almiron & Khazaal 2016.

the EU and that a new assessment method had to be developed. As we have seen, their efforts in this direction have been very successful, as the EU institutions and FAO itself are currently supporting platforms to develop news methods of assessment and all of these platforms have already been captured by the industry through the acquisition of leading positions in them.

The *meat* lobbies also cast doubt on the role of the *meat* industry in global warming by introducing the idea, so successful in the case of climate change denial in general, of a lack of consensus. In this case, what is presented as a controversial issue: what a 'sustainable food system' actually is. The *meat* industry suggests that the right definition is one that takes into consideration a list of issues that, not surprisingly, have little to do with the environment and much to do with the industry's fears and needs. In order to produce a definition of sustainability in the case of food, the lobbies request policy makers to consider the role of *meat* in human health, the role of *livestock* in the environment, the alleged efforts already made by the industry in sustainability and the need to reinforce the role of red *meat* in a sustainable and resource-efficient food system. This is not the place to discuss the veracity of these remarks, but this list does show the multidimensional denial it implies. Besides not recognising the real extent of the impact of the industry on the environment, they recognise neither its negative impact on human health nor the economic inefficiency of the industry (which is highly subsidised). However, the real agenda behind this green rhetoric is made apparent when the lobbyists directly appeal to policy makers. Even if this is done in a memorandum referring to climate change, the lobbyists forget about the environment when making their claims for CAP (Common Agricultural Policy) reform. According to this, a CAP reform shouldn't put the *meat* business at risk, should 'stop losing animal production' in the EU and should always listen to the *meat* industry when conducting discussions for reform.[43]

In general, the contradictions in the discourse are many. For instance, in one memorandum the *meat* lobbies recognise that the populations of Western countries tend to exceed *meat* intake

---

43   CLITRAVI-UECBV 2010.

recommendations (mostly men); however, they also produce an unsupported alarming argument to neutralise this: the alleged fact that 'sub-clinical micronutrient deficiencies are increasingly prevalent' in Western societies (and thus reducing *meat* intake can worsen this alleged deficiency).[44] Their arguments for the contributions of animal agriculture to the environment and the efforts by the industry for improvement are examples of simple discursive distractions.

Beyond the issue of climate change, the industry also casts doubt on other issues that harm its image. For instance, after the 2014 WHO report on carcinogenicity associated with the consumption of red and processed *meat*, CLITRAVI criticised the scientific quality of the WHO report and insisted on the number of experts recommending a varied diet; here the old mantra of 'moderation is what counts' is used again. As revealed by Nestle,[45] the food industry has been steadily conforming to three principles of advice that lobbying has successfully embedded into public policy: promoting balance, variety and moderation in the diet. These three principles are the result of strong ideological battles against any attempt to recommend that people eat less food or classify certain foods as being good or bad. The resulting interpretation is that any food that supplies calories or nutrients should be recognised as useful in a nutritious diet. This is a broad enough framework to accommodate all industrial interests, notably the sectors directly involved in nonhuman animal exploitation. This mantra is widely found in their climate change counternarrative as well: overconsumption is the problem and a balanced, varied diet is what is needed.[46]

Two other main issues are found in the *meat* lobby's counternarrative, both of which have already been identified in the vivisection lobby. The first has been abundantly used by the *meat* industry to mask the cruelty of their business and includes the adoption of a welfare-friendly rhetoric to claim that they do care for the animals they exploit. In the case of climate change, the rhetoric is similar, though the claim here is that they do care for the environment and that, actually, the environment needs their business since exploiting

---

44 CLITRAVI-UECBV 2012.
45 Nestle 2007.
46 EURO Meat News 2017; CLITRAVI-UECBV 2012.

nonhuman animals, they argue, contributes to the agronomy, food security, the maintenance of soils, and the economic and social vitality of rural areas.

The second parallel with the vivisection lobby's discourse refers to the claim that the industry is under attack by the media, which allegedly misinforms the public and policy makers. Thus, a major portion of the problem, according to the *meat* lobby's narrative, is that they receive negative coverage by the media and a lack of reporting on the many positive things one of the most polluting industries in the world insists it does regarding climate change. The global reduction in *meat* consumption is explained by a *meat* lobbyist as being the result of such a campaign against the *meat* industry (particularly after the WHO's report on the links between carcinogenicity and red and processed *meat*).[47] In one of the references to such a 'misleading communication' we also find the single mention of ethical issues regarding animal cruelty in all the climate change memorandums analysed. The mention is used, however, to diminish the moral claim by mixing the moral concern of society with the alleged manipulation of the media.[48]

Also worth mentioning is the deterrent character of the *meat* lobby's arguments regarding plant-based diets. Vegans and vegetarians are mentioned as belonging to subgroups at risk of micronutrient and B_{12} deficiencies when the lobbies argue for the need for eating red *meat*.[49] Furthermore, the *meat* lobby resorts to moral pluralism in defining veganism simply as a personal choice. This is evident, for instance, in an interview with a top CLITRAVI executive[50] that refers to 'democracy on the table' and implicitly labels vegans as radicals that do not respect *meat*-eaters. In this way, it is not that the industry only takes a defensive stance, it also goes on the offensive. The attack strategy of the *meat* industry towards veganism and vegetarianism can also be clearly seen in the *meat* lobby's campaign to ban plant-based products from using *meat* terms on packaging and advertising.[51] The reason

---

47 Euro Meat News 2017.
48 CLITRAVI-UECBV 2010.
49 CLITRAVI-UECBV 2012.
50 Euro Meat News 2017.
51 Brehaut 2017; Michail 2017; Plant Based News 2017.

given for such a campaign is that using *meat* terminology deceives consumers. A top CLITRAVI executive even stated that veganism is having a market impact because they confound the consumers with *meaty* names and health claims.[52]

In spite of the propaganda aims of the *meat* lobby discourse, language carefully stresses commitment to science by acknowledging the whole industry's heavy reliance on scientific research behind the formulation of much public policy and media discourse.[53] Yet, in spite of this language, what they call *science* is tantamount to lobbying. For instance, in a memorandum the joint CLITRAVI- UECBV climate change taskforce states that their aim is 'tracing and discriminating scientific facts from non-reliable figures' while at the same time acknowledging that 'a core part of this group's activity is the promotion of consistent messaging on environmental issues concerning the livestock-meat chain'. In short, the allegedly scientific platform created by the *meat* lobbies admits that it mainly seeks to improve the image of the *meat* industry and prevent climate change policies from harming business.[54] It seems as if the apparent contradiction of their rhetoric is irrelevant to them. The scientific and green rhetoric is also much in contradiction with the threats issued by the industry at some points, like the warning sent by one of the partners of the UECBV in 2015 before the European Parliament voted on national caps on emissions of key pollutants. Before the vote, COPA-COGECA lobbied MEPs hard and were accused by the European Environmental Bureau of blackmail because of a warning that if emissions caps were too restrictive, the demand (for *meat* and *dairy* products) in Europe would be satisfied by moving the production to countries with less stringent environmental laws.[55]

---

52   Euro Meat News 2017.
53   Almiron 2016.
54   CLITRAVI-UECB 2010.
55   Animal Equality 2015; Ryan 2015.

A two-pronged strategy devoid of ethics

For years, other animals' exploitation for food has been climate action's greatest taboo. Eating *meat* on a daily basis across social classes is a recent phenomenon in Europe, which has flourished only since the end of the Second World War and introduction of the Common Agricultural Policy (CAP). Through the CAP, the EU has massively subsidised the wrong sort of food: not only extremely cruel, but also intolerably polluting, import dependent and export harming for developing countries. However, as a journalist covering the Bonn climate summit put it, 'there is very little appetite' in the EU to encourage people to eat less *meat*, the same little appetite that the climate change summits have shown so far.[56] As the author of this chapter could also confirm first-hand in 2019, the UN climate change conferences are not committed to a real diet change in their own facilities.[57]

This lack of enthusiasm for promoting a much less polluting and less violent diet is to a large degree not the result of scientific and political discussions but of very powerful interest groups shaping policy making, the media and public opinion. This inaction shows the power of lobbying, not of science, which in the EU case mostly follows a two-pronged strategy that nearly replicates the strategies used by the tobacco, oil and vivisection industries.

This dual strategy pursues, on the one hand, stepping up lobbying efforts to protect corporate interests by blocking real climate change action. This is done by means of casting doubt on the actual greenhouse gases emitted, very much in the same way as the *meat* industry is acting in the US,[58] and by capturing as much attention and initiative of public officers as possible to delay real change and to prevent other stakeholders (such as green or animal advocates) from being influential. On the other hand, and in contrast, the *meat* lobbies adopt a pro-scientific, greenwashing narrative to suggest that the industry cares for the environment and is already investing in its improvement.

---

56   Teffer 2017.
57   Almiron 2019.
58   Duhaime-Ross 2016; Shanker 2015; Sharma 2016.

The latter is partially true. The problem is that these improvements are so far very speculative and they do not address the unethical root of the business, the exploitation of other animals, but rather exacerbate it (including increased genetic manipulation of animals' bodies and feed in the form of *technological* solutions).

Sadly, the industry has convinced policy makers to focus on *technological* solutions to reduce emissions while increasing their business. Governments are rapidly embracing the key notion behind the *meat* lobby's rhetoric: that of continuing the current economic model of production while producing fewer emissions. In this case, this means exacting even more *meat* from animals than we currently do, following the assumption that the more efficiently an animal turns feed into muscle, the less intensely it emits greenhouse gases. Thus, animal bodies, feed and waste instantiate the largest part of the so-called *innovation* in the field.

This view of course reinforces the notion of human supremacy and is instrumental in building a narrative which is mere propaganda, a facade that allows business to continue as usual. Thus, it is easy to see that the big taboo is not actually animal exploitation in itself, but the widespread social addiction to *meat* and the manufactured consent to avoid talking about what is really at stake here, the immorality of the habit of eating other animals' bodies.

References

Aleksandrowicz, L., R. Green, E. J. M. Joy, P. Smith and A. Haines (2016). The impacts of dietary change on greenhouse gas emissions, land use, water use, and health: A systematic review. *PLOS ONE* 11(11), e0165797. doi:10.1371/journal.pone.0165797

Almiron, N. (2020). Rethinking the ethical challenge in climate change lobbying: A discussion of ideological denial. In N. Almiron and J. Xifra (Eds.), *Climate Change Denial and Public Relations: Strategic Communication and Interest Groups in Climate Inaction* (pp. 9–25). London: Routledge

Almiron, N. (2019). The UNFCCC and the animal agriculture entanglement. *The IECA Blogs*. 7 July. https://theieca.org/blog/3515

Almiron, N. (2016). The political economy behind the oppression of other animals: Interest and influence. In N. Almiron, M. Cole and C. P. Freeman

(Eds.), *Critical Animal and Media Studies: Communication for Nonhuman Animal Advocacy* (pp. 26–41). New York: Routledge.

Almiron, N. and M. Zoppeddu (2014). Eating meat and climate change: The media blind spot – a study of Spanish and Italian press coverage. *Environmental Communication* 9(3), 307–325. doi:10.1080/17524032.2014.953968

Almiron, N. and N. Khazaal (2016). Lobbying against compassion: Speciesist discourse in the vivisection industrial complex. *American Behavioral Scientist* 60(3), 256–275. doi:10.1177/0002764215613402

Almiron, N. and J. Xifra (Eds.) (2020). *Climate Change Denial and Public Relations. Strategic Communication and Interest Groups in Climate Inaction.* London: Routledge.

ALTER-EU (2015). ALTER-EU complaints to the EU transparency register regarding misleading entries. *ALTER-EU.* 27 July. https://bit.ly/3hh9ofh

Andersen, K. and K. Kuhn (Directors) (2014). *Cowspiracy. The Sustainability Secret* [film]. Los Angeles: A.U.M. Films.

Animal Equality (2015). *Factory Farming and Blackmail in the European Union.* Los Angeles, CA: Animal Equality.

Bailey, R., A. Froggatt and L. Wellesley (2014). *Livestock – Climate Change's Forgotten Sector Global Public Opinion on Meat and Dairy Consumption.* London: The Royal Institute of International Affairs Chatham House.

Bellarby, J., B. Foereid, A. Hastings and P. Smith (2008). *Cool Farming: Climate Impacts of Agriculture and Mitigation Potential.* Amsterdam: Greenpeace.

Boykoff, M. T. (2016). Consensus and contrarianism on climate change. How the USA case informs dynamics elsewhere. *Mètode Science Studies Journal* 6, 89–95. doi:10.7203/metode.85.4182

Brehaut, L. (2017). Is that vegan 'bacon' or the real, porky product? EU meat industry says mock meat is deceiving consumers. *National Post.* 12 June. https://bit.ly/3hjhuDR.

Carlsson-Kanyama, A. and A. D. González (2009). Potential contributions of food consumption patterns to climate change. *Epidemiology* 20(6), s238. doi:10.1097/01.ede.0000362799.46174.56

Corporate Europe Observatory (2014). Who lobbies most on TTIP? *Corporate Europe Observatory.* 8 July. https://bit.ly/31ivPLw

Compassion in World Farming (2008). *Global Warning: Climate Change and Farm Animal Welfare. Summary Report.* Godalming, Surrey: Compassion in World Farming. https://bit.ly/3hgFnw5

Compassion in World Farming (2015). In defence of factory farming: How a ruinous system is kept afloat. *Compassion in World Farming.* https://bit.ly/3aLnO4L

CLITRAVI-UECBV (2012). *CLITRAVI-UECBV Joint Meat Sector Taskforce on Climate Change Issues: The Role of Meat as a Component of a Sustainable Food System*. Brussels: CLITRAVI-UECBV.

CLITRAVI-UECBV (2010). *Climate Change Taskforce position vis-à-vis the environmental challenges*. Brussels: CLITRAVI & UECBV.

Duhaime-Ross, A. (2016). New US food guidelines show the power of lobbying, not science. *The Verge*. 7 January. https://bit.ly/2EkRRnG

Dunlap, R. E. and A. M. McCright (2015). Challenging climate change: The denial countermovement. In R. E. Dunlap and R. Brulle (Eds.), *Climate Change and Society: Sociological Perspectives*. New York: Oxford University Press.

Eshel, G., and P. A. Martin (2006). Diet, energy, and global warming. *Earth Interactions* 10(9), 1–17. doi:10.1175/EI167.1

Eshel, G., A. Shepon, T. Makovc, and R. Milob (2014). Land, irrigation water, greenhouse gas, and reactive nitrogen burdens of meat, eggs, and dairy production in the United States. *PNAS* 111(33), 11996–12001. doi:10.1073/pnas.1402183111

Agriculture and Rural Development of the European Commission (2017). *CAP Explained. Direct Payments for Farmers 2015–2020*. Brussels: European Commission.

Euro Meat News (2017). Exclusive interview with Paolo Patruno, CLITRAVI. *Euro Meat News*. 15 November. https://bit.ly/2Qay7Wn

FoodDrink Europe (2017). *Economic Bulletin Q4 2017*. Brussels: FoodDrink Europe.

Freeman, C. P. (2010). Meat's place on the campaign menu: How U.S. environmental discourse negotiates vegetarianism. *Environmental Communication: A Journal of Nature and Culture* 4(3), 255–276. doi:10.1080/17524032.2010.501998

Gerber, P. J., H. Steinfeld, B. Henderson, A. Mottet, C. Opio, J. Dijkman, … G. Tempio (2013). *Tackling Climate Change Through Livestock: A Global Assessment of Emissions and Mitigation Opportunities*. Rome: Food and Agriculture Organization of the United Nations.

Goodland, R. and J. Anhang (2009). Livestock and climate change. What if the key actors in climate change are… cows, pigs, and chickens? *World Watch Magazine* 22(6), 10–19.

Gore, A. in Paramount Pictures UK (2017). An inconvenient sequel: Truth to power | Live in conversation with Al Gore [video]. 13 August 2017. https://www.youtube.com/watch?v=o0Bgikppynw

Greenpeace International (2018). *Less Is More. Scientific Background for the Greenpeace Vision of the Meat and Dairy System Towards 2050*. Amsterdam: Greenpeace. https://bit.ly/3hg1xyw

Hamerschlag, K. (2011). Meat eater's guide to climate change + health. https://www.ewg.org/meateatersguide/

Hedges, C. (2016). *The Sustainability Secret. The Cowspiracy Companion*. San Rafael, CA: Earth Aware.

Holm, J. and T. Jokkala (2007). *The Livestock Industry and Climate – EU Makes Bad Worse*. Brussels: Delegation of the Swedish Left Party in GUE/NGL.

Humane Society International (2008). An HSI Report: The impact of animal agriculture on global warming and climate change. *HIS Reports: Farm Animal Protection* 2, 1–27. https://animalstudiesrepository.org/hsi_reps_fap/2/

Intergovernmental Panel on Climate Change (2014). *Climate Change 2014: Mitigation of Climate Change. Contribution of Working Group III to the Fifth Assessment Report of the Intergovernmental Panel on Climate Change*. Cambridge: Cambridge University Press, Cambridge. https://bit.ly/2CRm3Xi

Intergovernmental Panel on Climate Change (2019). Summary for Policy Makers. In IPCC, *Climate Change and Land: An IPCC Special Report on Climate Change, Desertification, Land Degradation, Sustainable Land Management, Food Security, and Greenhouse Gas Fluxes in Terrestrial Ecosystems*. Geneva: IPCC. https://www.ipcc.ch/srccl/chapter/summary-for-policymakers/

Joy, M. (2011). *Why We Love Dogs, Eat Pigs, and Wear Cows: An Introduction to Carnism*. San Francisco: Conari Press.

Kemmerer, L. (2014). *Eating Earth: Environmental Ethics and Dietary Choice*. New York: Oxford University Press.

Klein, N. (2015). *This Changes Everything. Capitalism Vs the Climate*. New York: Simon & Schuster.

Leip, A., F. Weiss, T. Wassenaar, I. Perez, T. Fellmann, P. Loudjani, … K. Biala (2010). *Evaluation of the Livestock Sector's Contribution to the EU Greenhouse Gas Emissions (GGELS) – Final Report*. Brussels: European Commission, Joint Research Centre.

Lymbery, P. (2017). *Dead Zone: Where the Wild Things Were*. London: Bloomsbury Publishing.

Lymbery, P. and I. Oakeshott (2014). *Farmageddon: The True Cost of Cheap Meat*. London: Bloomsbury Publishing.

McCright, A. M. and R. E. Dunlap (2010). Anti-reflexivity: The American conservative movement's success in undermining climate science and policy. *Theory, Culture and Society* 26, 100–133. doi:10.1177/0263276409356001

McMichael, A. J., J. W. Powles, C. D. Butler and R. Uauy (2007). Food, livestock production, energy, climate change, and health. *The Lancet* 370, 1253–1263. doi:10.1016/S0140-6736(07)61256-2

Michail, N. (2017). Clash of the Seitans: Lobbies locked in plant-based stalemate but near EU definition of vegetarian. *FoodNavigator*. 23 May. https://bit.ly/3ghMfIj

Nestle, M. (2007). *Food politics: How the food industry influences nutrition and health*. Los Angeles: University of California Press.

Nibert, D. A. (Ed.) (2017a). *Animal Oppression and Capitalism. Volume One: The Oppression of Nonhuman Animals as Sources of Food*. Santa Barbara: Praeger Press.

Nibert, D. A. (Ed.) (2017b). *Animal Oppression and Capitalism. Volume Two: The Oppressive and Destructive Role of Capitalism*. Santa Barbara: Praeger Press.

Oreskes, N. and E. M. Conway (2010). *Merchants of Doubt*. London: Bloomsbury Publishing.

Pew Environment Group (2011). *Big Chicken. Pollution and Industrial Poultry Production in America*. Washington: The Pew Charitable Trust. https://bit.ly/31eqrsA

Plant Based News (2017). Now animal ag lobby says vegan plant meat 'can't be called meat'. *Plant Based News*. 6 June. https://bit.ly/3hiQC70

Politico (2016). How to fix European farming. *Politico*. 13 June. https://politi.co/3aLgu9g

Poore, J. and Nemecek, T. (2018). Reducing food's environmental impacts through producers and consumers. *Science* 360(6392), 987–992. doi:10.1126/science.aaq0216

Ranganathan, J., D. Vennard, R. Waite, P. Dumas, B. Lipinski and T. Searchinger (2016). *Working Paper: Shifting Diets for a Sustainable Food Future*. Washington: World Resources Institute.

Renner, M. (2014). *Peak Meat Production Strains Land and Water Resources*. Washington: World Watch Institute.

Rosi, A., P. Mena, N. Pellegrini, S. Turroni, E. Neviani, I. Ferrocino … F. Scazzina (2017). Environmental impact of omnivorous, ovo-lacto-vegetarian, and vegan diet. *Scientific Reports* 7(6105). doi:10.1038/s41598-017-06466-8.

Ryan, C. (2015). Air quality review warning for European farmers. *Global Meat News*. 2 November. https://bit.ly/3hgG4Wd.

Scarborough, P., P. N. Appleby, A. Mizdrak, A. D. M. Briggs, R. C. Travis, K. E. Bradbury and T. J. Key (2014). Dietary greenhouse gas emissions of meat-eaters, fish-eaters, vegetarians and vegans in the UK. *Climatic Change* 125, 179–192. doi:10.1007/s10584-014-1169-1

Schwarzer, S. (2012). *Growing Greenhouse Gas Emissions Due to Meat Production*. Nairobi: UNEP Global Environmental Alert Service (GEAS). https://na.unep.net/geas/archive/pdfs/GEAS_Oct2012_meatproduction.pdf

Shanker, D. (2015). How meat producers have influenced nutrition guidelines for decades. *Atlantic*. 24 October. https://bit.ly/2CJYFL4

Sharma, S. (2016). *Climate, Livestock, Carbon and the Lobby*. Minneapolis: Institute for Agriculture, Trade and Policy. https://bit.ly/2EkSoWI

Soeters, K. and G. Zwanikken (Directors) (2007). *Meat the Truth* [film]. The Netherlands: Alalena, Nicolaas G. Pierson Foundation.

Springmann, M., H. C. J. Godfray, M. Rayner and P. Scarborough (2016). Analysis and valuation of the health and climate change cobenefits of dietary change. *PNAS* 113(15), 4146-4151. doi:10.1073/pnas.1523119113

Steinfeld, H., P. Gerber, T. D. Wassenaar, V. Castel, M. Rosales, and C. de Haan (2006). *Livestock's long shadow: Environmental issues and options*. Rome: Food & Agriculture Organization of the United Nations.

Teffer, P. (2017). Meat 'taboo' debated at Bonn climate summit. *EuObserver*. 14 November. https://euobserver.com/environment/139869

Thomas, P. (2010). *Healthy Planet Eating. How Lower Meat Diets Can Save Lives and the Planet*. London: Friends of the Earth.

UECBV (2012). *Meat is a major player in resource efficiency EU's 2020 strategy to reach a sustainable food system* [press release]. Brussels: UECBV. http://www.uecbv.eu/.

UECBV (2016). *UECBV Factsheets – Info. Red Meat PEF – Trends towards a greener future*. Brussels: UECBV. https://bit.ly/2Q9WdRl

UECBV (n.d.). *The European Livestock and Meats Trade Union*. Brussels: UECBV. http://www.uecbv.eu/UECBV/documents/UECBVBrochureEN7027.pdf

Westhoek, H., J.P. Lesschen, T. Rood, S. Wagner, A. De Marco, D. Murphy-Bokern … O. Oenema (2014). Food choices, health and environment: Effects of cutting Europe's meat and dairy intake. *Global Environmental Change* 26, 196–205. doi:10.1016/j.gloenvcha.2014.02.004

World Health Organization (2014). *Q&A on the Carcinogenicity of the Consumption of Red Meat and Processed Meat*. Lyon: International Agency for Research on Cancer. http://www.who.int/features/qa/cancer-red-meat/en/

World Watch Institute (2004). Is meat sustainable? *World Watch Magazine* 17(4), 12–20.

7

Exporting meat, exporting progress? The Australian meat export industry and discourses of development and modernisation

Eliza Waters and Gonzalo Villanueva[1]

We are currently living in an era that is increasingly referred to as the Anthropocene, a human-dominated, geological epoch. Human population has contributed to the emergence of the Anthropocene and to many ecological problems. Today, there are 7.3 billion people on the planet and that number is due to climb to 9.7 billion by 2050. Affluent societies rear and slaughter billions of animals each year for their flesh and products, and they consume it at abundant, unsustainable levels: in recent years, the average per capita rate of meat consumption in developed countries was 76.2 kg, compared to 33.5 kg in developing countries. However, in Australia, the average person eats about 111 kg of meat each year.[2] Meanwhile, meat consumption in nations like India and China, with their large and growing populations, is on the rise.

---

1 Eliza Waters would like to acknowledge Dr Daniel McCarthy, University of Melbourne, for supervision of her Honours thesis, which formed the basis for this chapter.
2 Food and Agriculture Organization 2014; Wong, Selvanathan & Selvanathan 2013, p. 11.

The fate of the world's farmed animals, particularly those reared in industrial settings, is one of the most significant ethical issues in the era of the Anthropocene. According to historian Yuval Noah Harari, nonhuman animals 'are the main victims of history, and the treatment of domesticated animals in industrial farms is perhaps the worst crime in history'.[3] There are more domesticated animals than humans living today. Animal agriculture, argues Harari, is responsible for more pain and suffering than all the wars and conflicts throughout human history put together. Unfortunately, the number of animals suffering in farms across the world is growing, not declining. Nations like Australia play a significant role in stimulating and promoting the use and consumption of animals.

Alongside India and Brazil, Australia is one of the largest 'red meat' exporters in the world. In 2017, Australia shipped 10.3 million tonnes of chilled and frozen meat – beef, veal, mutton, lamb, goat and pork – to all corners of the globe. Exports to Asia and the Middle East currently make up 70 per cent of this industry, which makes them major, lucrative markets.[4] Meat exports is a $12.3 billion a year industry and it is likely to continue growing. It is expected that rising incomes in Asia and the Middle East will create economic opportunities and booming demand for Australian meat products.[5] Policy makers have consistently sought to pursue Asian markets for agricultural exports, including meat and livestock.

In addition to the 'carcass-only' trade, Australia is also involved in live animal exports. In 2017, Australia exported around 2.6 million live animals – cattle, sheep and buffalo. These animals were transported via ship, and most of them were sent to the Middle East and South-East Asia, where they underwent ritual slaughter.[6] Live animal exports is a highly contentious issue. The controversial industry is routinely discussed on television shows like *60 Minutes*, which have broadcast exposés showing undercover footage of sheep suffering and dying from heat stress onboard a livestock carrier during the long three-week sea

---

3   Harari 2015, p. 1.
4   Department of Agriculture and Water Resources 2018a.
5   Johnson 2017, pp. 3–4.
6   Department of Agriculture and Water Resources, 2018b.

voyages.[7] This has often sparked public outrage, protest, government inquiries and renewed calls for the trade to be abolished.

This chapter explores the phenomenon of meatsplaining in the Australian meat industry and how narratives of modernisation and development are entangled with assumptions around meat consumption. It critically analyses discourses of development, progress and modernisation. Developing nations are rapidly increasing their consumption and importation of meat, and Australia seeks to capitalise on this increased demand. While this global trend has been extensively documented, few scholars have examined or problematised how rising meat consumption may be constructed within a wider project of modernity and development. This chapter starts with a broad exposition of critical meat studies. The discussion then shifts to considering the concept of modernisation and development. The final section presents the results of critical discourse analysis of Australian meat industry institutions. Although considered a marker of 'progress', rising meat consumption, modernisation and development constitute powerful discourses in meatsplaining, which are implicated in the production and reproduction of unequal power relations, hierarchies and animal exploitation.

What is meat?

Meat is pervasive in our global society and its analysis has been central to human-animal studies and critical animal studies. Nick Fiddes refers to meat as a 'natural symbol' because it is a central organising idea. Above its nutritional value, one of the most important features of meat, argues Fiddes, is that it represents human domination and control of the natural world. 'Consuming the muscle flesh of other highly evolved animals,' claims Fiddes, 'is a potent statement of our supreme power.'[8] The marketing of meat, according to Fiddes, becomes essentially similar to other commodities, although there are implicit values that emphasise power and control.[9] Furthermore, meat-eating is often more

---

7   Bartlett 2018.
8   Fiddes 1991, p. 2.
9   Fiddes 1991, pp. 84–86.

than the simple act of sustenance, of putting food in one's mouth; it is symbolically linked to patriarchy, masculinity and virility.[10]

Australia's meat and livestock industry, its exporting institutions and the discourses they deploy are part of a wider animal-industrial complex. This complex is defined by Richard Twine as 'a partly opaque and multiple set of networks and relationships between the corporate (agricultural) sector, governments, and public and private science'.[11] It is a diverse network made up of different stakeholders, with economic, social and cultural dimensions, which includes a range of practices, technologies and markets. Similarly, Erika Calvo refers to this kind of human supremacy as 'anthroparchy', a term that denotes human domination over the nonhuman world through social organisation that privileges humans. For Calvo, production relations, domestication, political institutions, systemic violence and cultures of exclusive humanism combine to form anthroparchy.

Following Twine and Calvo, sociologists have argued that meat is a form of cultural hegemony, which makes the consumption of animal flesh a perceived necessity.[12] In a study that is similar to this chapter, sociologists Amy J. Fitzgerald and Nik Taylor analysed meat exporter websites and advertisements in cooking magazines and discovered that animals are absent, manipulated or used to maintain cultural hegemony.[13] Similarly, Annie Potts refers to this social phenomenon as a 'meat culture', which encompasses practicalities, discourses, behaviours, tastes and shared beliefs about meat.[14] Like any culture, meat culture varies across different times, places, regions and populations. Contemporary meat culture is different to its historical antecedents, although some continuations may remain. For example, Australia's colonial past was built on a large sheep economy, a trend which remains important, although not as central, to the modern-day agriculture sector. Ultimately, meat culture, argues Potts, is widespread and ingrained.[15]

---

10   Adams 2010.
11   Twine 2012, p. 23.
12   Fitzgerald & Taylor 2014, p. 166.
13   Fitzgerald & Taylor 2014.
14   Potts 2016, p. 20.
15   Potts 2016, p. 20.

Underpinning Australia's meat culture, as sociologist Adrian Franklin's survey of consumers observed, is the idea that it is acceptable to eat meat so long as animals are reared and killed 'humanely'.[16]

Humane slaughter presumes that animals are of less moral value and that, therefore, it is justifiable to kill them, so long as it is done so without inflicting unnecessary pain and suffering. Drawing on Foucault's ideas of disciplinary power, Matthew Cole has examined the discursive shift of farmed animals, from 'animal machines' to 'happy meat'. Intensive farms act as sites of biopower where 'docile' animal bodies are produced, through spatial distribution, surveillance and control. Animal welfare institutions, or what Cole terms 'pastoral power', attempt to mobilise knowledge of animal bodies in order to claim that farmed animals enjoy good welfare and have good lives. Happy meat discourse, a type of greenwashing, involves the use of 'animal welfare' to further pastoral power. It 'reassures consumers that they *know* the needs and desires of "farmed animals", and that those needs and desires are fulfilled precisely *because* they eat the flesh of those animals'.[17] Ultimately, humane slaughter is not only ethically flawed[18] but also impossible in modern industrial slaughterhouses, where animal suffering is not only routine but hidden from public sight.[19]

It is important to emphasise that the production and consumption of animals and meat, particularly in Australia, has unfolded, and continues to unfold, in the context of settler-colonialism. Both settler-colonialism and white supremacy are mechanisms that work because they are intricately connected to the exploitation of animal and Indigenous bodies.[20] Colonial animalities, argues Billy-Ray Belcourt, are 'inseparable from the colonized spaces in which they are subjected and labored'.[21] Contemporary animal historians are increasingly showing the complex and specific entanglements between animals and empire, and how they were vital

---

16   Franklin 2007, p. 22.
17   Cole 2011, pp. 95–96.
18   Singer 1975; Singer 1979.
19   Pachirat 2011.
20   Belcourt 2015, p. 3.
21   Belcourt 2015, p. 4.

actors to the imperial state and capitalism.[22] As Jonathan Saha argues, the British Empire ruled over nonhuman animals as well as humans, and through complex hierarchies and processes, certain species and peoples 'become subjugated, marginalised, disempowered, and endangered'.[23] In recent times, Australia has been at the forefront of land clearing and deforestation, most of which is transformed into pastoral land for animal grazing.[24] Land clearing by settler-colonialists furthers Indigenous dispossession and harms animals. One recent study estimated that 'land clearing in Queensland and New South Wales combined kills more than 50 million birds, mammals and reptiles each year'.[25]

Development and modernisation

The hegemonic meat culture that has arisen in settler-colonial nations like Australia has led some theorists to observe that this is a common trajectory of modernity, which other developing nations will inevitably emulate. Development theories that emerged in the mid-20th century often presented narratives of economic and political progress, which placed the Western model as the summit for all other nations to reach.[26] Notably, the American economist Walt Rostow contended that there were five stages of economic growth, entailing gradual progression from a traditional society with limited production to a period of 'high mass consumption' featuring a proliferation of consumer goods.[27] Another key proponent of modernisation theory, Daniel Lerner, posited that American economic, political and social models should be emulated by Middle Eastern countries in order to achieve development. Lerner also emphasised the crucial role of mass media in the modernisation

---

22   DeJohn Anderson 2004; Roy 2015, pp. 66–75; Skabelund 2011; Woods 2015, pp. 117–36; Saha 2017, pp. 1–27.
23   Saha 2017, p. 20.
24   Preece & van Oosterzee 2017.
25   Finn 2017.
26   Bhambra 2007, p. 141.
27   Rostow 1959, pp. 4–12.

process.[28] These broader theories of modernisation are echoed by the assumption that modernising societies will adopt the Western diet, which is high in saturated fat (especially from animal products), sugar, refined foods and meat and dairy, and low in fibre.[29] Nutritional scientist Barry M. Popkin theorised that these 'nutrition transitions' are universal, occurring in conjunction with economic, social, demographic and health developments.[30]

The modernisation paradigm has been heavily criticised. Such narratives, argues geographer Tony Weis, have a naturalising and legitimising effect – they suggest that different countries are at certain stages of development working towards the same destination.[31] Weis refers to the assumption that there *will* be more meat consumed and food production *must* double, which is frequently peddled by powerful stakeholders, as the 'meatification' of diets.[32] Weis' challenge to the idea of 'meatification' as an inevitable phase of development parallels the broader critiques of theorists such as Arturo Escobar, Gilbert Rist and Wolfgang Sachs. These theorists argue that modernisation discourses entrench hierarchies, by further embedding Western economic, political and social hegemony. Escobar argues that these discourses are produced and reproduced 'under conditions of unequal power'.[33] It is through the obfuscation of the 'culturally and historically specific' origins of the idea that societal advancement takes particular forms that this idea gains its traction.[34] Because accounts of modernisation and development are presented as universal, akin to the maturation of natural organisms,[35] they serve to uphold certain socio-economic processes as natural and necessary.[36] Those processes which are situated as the core constituents of modernisation and development – such as the accumulation of material goods, indefinite economic growth and

---

28 Lerner 1958.
29 Popkin 1993, pp. 138–157.
30 Popkin 1993.
31 Weis 2013, p. 3.
32 Weis 2013, p. 4.
33 Escobar 2012, p. 9.
34 Escobar 2012, p. 13.
35 Rist 2014, p. 27.
36 Rist 2014, p. 43.

the use of more efficient technologies – are also depicted as universally essential.[37] Although modernisation theory has lost its scholarly currency, Wolfgang Knöbl suggests that it still stubbornly persists as a group of assumptions about the development trajectories of states.[38] This chapter argues that these enduring assumptions are reflected in discourses around Australian meat and animal exports.

Meatsplaining in the Australian meat industry

The following section discusses the results of a critical discourse analysis of 75 Australian industry and government texts, where discursive constructions of modernisation, development and meat were examined.[39] As the remainder of this chapter will show, ideas around modernisation and development are entangled with meat consumption in complex ways.

The Australian meat industry positions development in Asian and Middle Eastern countries as important to the successful export of Australian meat products. The notion that certain countries are 'less developed', 'developing', 'emerging' and 'currently industrialising'[40] explicitly draws on assumptions of modernisation theory, that nations will unlock a series of achievements already reached by advanced capitalist societies. The mantra of growth and emergence dominates the concept of development, and central to this is the idea that increased meat consumption is linked to economic development. Notably, the Australia in the Asian Century government White Paper – a document published by the Labor government in 2012 during a period of increased attention to Australia's economic place in the Asia-Pacific region – states that:

> With rising incomes in Asian economies, there will be structural change in global consumption to higher value food products and

---

37 Rist 2014, p. 270.
38 Knolb 2003, p. 105.
39 This analysis followed the approach developed by Fairclough 2013.
40 Barnard 2014, pp. 6–7.

services. Strong demand is expected to continue for the foreseeable future, especially for higher quality produce and protein-rich foods such as meat and dairy products.[41]

The White Paper suggests a causal relationship between rising incomes in Asia and changes in food consumption patterns, including strengthening demand for meat. Similar predictions have been made by the meat industry, with the former Managing Director of Meat & Livestock Australia (MLA) asserting that: 'the growth of the middle and upper classes in emerging economies means ... more available income to be spent on food', a positive indicator 'for future demand for red meat'.[42] Causality between other specific kinds of economic, social and cultural change associated with development and increased consumption of Australian meat products is widely suggested in industry literature, with growing middle classes, urbanisation, growth in 'modern retail', the proliferation of luxury hotels and restaurants and Western influences each being identified as drivers of demand.[43] Naturalistic metaphors buttress Australia's role and suggest that rising demand for meat is unstoppable: 'Australia's beef export industry is riding the "tidal wave" that has been called the "developing Asia" era'.[44] It is noteworthy that in many instances these processes are not attributed to any social actors or agents. For example, an article in the MLA magazine about the Middle East/North Africa region describes the 'burgeoning modernisation and sophistication borne of the region's rich fossil fuel reserves'.[45] The 'burgeoning modernisation' is attributed to natural resources, but the complex processes behind this – the roles of government, transnational corporations, workers, technology and other institutions – are absent. Rising meat consumption across the Middle East and Asia is constructed as inevitable and natural, and the role of the Australian meat industry is to capitalise on it.

---

41 Australian Government 2012.
42 Hansen 2012, p. 1.
43 AusTrade 2015; Department of Agriculture 2014; Edmonds 2014; Thomas 2015; AusTrade 2014; Meat and Livestock Institute 2012c, p. 34; AusTrade 2007.
44 The Beef Export Evolution 2015, p. 6.
45 MENA's Melting Pot Brews Opportunity 2012, pp. 34–35.

Australian meat industry literature implies that ideas around development and modernisation can be harnessed to promote the consumption of Australian meat in target markets. A presentation – titled 'Red Obesssion' – which was delivered to an industry audience by Michael Edmonds, former General Manager for Global Marketing at MLA – associates the consumption of Australian meat in Asia with concepts of luxury, consumption and progress. As Edmonds explains how MLA will realise 'value for Australian red meat in Asia', he draws attention to aspects of economic and social change in China, referring to China's 'growing middle classes', increasing household incomes and growing 'luxury good consumption'. Here, Australian red meat is depicted as a luxury good and is compared to fine French wine and high-end German cars. The presentation conveys to its industry audience that 'Brand Australia' can harness Chinese consumers' demand for luxury products and those consumers' conceptions of meat so as to successfully market Australian red meat.[46] Similar ideas are found elsewhere. Meat-marketing initiatives are often described as having taken place in spaces evocative of wealth and modernisation – major financial centres, supermarket chains, five-star hotels etc.[47] Other Western icons of conspicuous consumption are also mobilised, such as the popular television show *MasterChef* and magazines like *Martha Stewart Living* and *Elle à Table*. In this way, meat is constructed as a desirable consumer good.[48]

In the meat industry literature, Australian identity is a key concept that is mobilised. Australian culture and ways of life are sometimes represented as part of the 'story' which must be told to market Australian red meat products.[49] Indeed, in a 'market insight' piece concerning the Middle East and North Africa Region, it is stated that 'another vehicle used by MLA to drive sheepmeat consumption and loyalty to Australian product is the "Live the Good Life" barbecue. Held as close as possible to Australia Day … '.[50] The Australian way of life

---

46 Edmonds 2014.
47 Meat and Livestock Australia 2012a, pp. 32–33; Meat and Livestock Australia 2013, pp. 34–35; Meat and Livestock Australia 2014a, pp. 34–35.
48 AusTrade 2013; Meat and Livestock Australia 2012d, pp. 32–33.
49 The Premium Sales Pitch 2014, pp. 6–7.
50 Meat and Livestock Australia 2012b, pp. 34–35.

is represented as constituting 'the Good Life', with the consumption of red meat being positioned as emblematic of this high standard of living. Australia's 'aspirational way of life' is emphatically used to market meat products.[51] In this way, Australian lifestyles and meat-eating are constructed as interlinked aspirations for consumers in Middle Eastern societies undergoing modernisation.

Greenwashing is also evident in the way the Australian meat industry portrays itself. The Australian environment is sometimes represented as a selling point, with references being made to the 'clean and green' nature of the landscape and the production process.[52] In an industry article, MLA Regional Manager for Korea Michael Finucan explains that the terms 'clean and green' were developed to communicate that Australian agriculture is unaffected by bovine diseases which have blighted other meat-exporting countries.[53] However, as the terms are ill-defined, they can be imbued with virtually any meaning, thus functioning as empty signifiers. Thus, in a global context of concern regarding climatic change, the phrase 'clean and green' may connote credentials of sustainable development or ecological modernisation. For example, in the 'Red Obsession' presentation, the heading 'desire for clean and green' is set against a picture of a traffic jam surrounded by thick smog, along with the text: 'Industrial pollution and food safety issues are sending affluent consumers to imported products'.[54] In this case, the presenter contrasts environmental problems associated with industrialisation in developing Asian countries with the supposedly 'clean and green' landscape of Australia. Through comparisons to the environmental challenges faced by industrialising countries, the ostensibly sustainable nature of Australian production becomes another aspirational aspect of Australian identity, which is harnessed to promote the consumption of Australian meat products. At the same time, the depiction of Australia as a 'clean and green' haven ignores Australia's extremely high

---

51   Meat and Livestock Australia 2014b, pp. 7–9.
52   AusTrade 2015; Joyce 2015; Meat and Livestock Australia 2014b, pp. 7–9.
53   Meat and Livestock Australia 2012e, p. 34.
54   Edmonds 2014.

per-capita greenhouse gas emissions, not to mention the environmental impact of Australian red meat production.

The production processes behind Australian meat are also represented in language connotative of modernisation and industrialisation, with emphasis being placed on efficiency, traceability and hygiene. In the video 'Asian chefs tour Australia', the narrator describes 24 chefs from China being brought to Australia as part of an MLA 'Red Majesty Chef program', 'designed to educate these masters of Chinese cuisine on the benefits and uses of our prime Australian red meat'. The chefs are taken on tours of farms and are shown being 'educated' about the qualities of red meat. In addition, footage of the chefs changing into white biohazard suits and walking past skinned carcasses suspended among clean, stainless steel fixtures is shown as the narrator states that 'the chefs are impressed by the efficiency and sanitation of the plant'. Then the video cuts to footage of a MLA Red Majesty Chef who exclaims that 'Everything is so clean, perfectly run, and … look at the set-up here, it's like being [in] a hospital.'[55] He also extols the virtues of the land, water and climate, which produces 'great' Australian red meat. As this is one of few texts in which the process of slaughtering animals in Australia is momentarily represented in relation to the export of Australian beef to Asian consumers, the highly sanitised depiction of the process is significant, as it adds legitimacy and confidence. The animals in the video are only ever seen in the background: roaming pastureland, or being disembodied after a slaughter the viewer never sees. Meat production is represented as a high-quality, clean, modernised, efficient process.

Similar associations are constructed on the MLA True Aussie Beef and Lamb website, which promotes Australian red meat to Asian consumers: 'Australian producers are at the forefront of technological advancements in livestock genetics and reproduction efficiencies', with the online format of the text reinforcing associations with advanced technology.[56] Australia is often referred to as a world leader and Australian livestock and products are situated as the 'best' of their kind.[57]

---

55   MLA Feedback TV 2011.
56   MLA 2015.
57   Burke 2009; Joyce 2015.

These superlative assertions imply comparisons to meat products from other nations; however some of the industry literature explicitly compares Australian products to those from rival suppliers. Notably, food marketing professor David Hughes is quoted as warning that Australian suppliers must differentiate their products otherwise 'you'll be down the bottom of the commodity market, arm wrestling with buffalo meat from India'.[58] This implies a hierarchy of meat products with buffalo meat positioned as emblematic of an inferior product on the basis of its provenance and species-origin. Thus, Australian livestock animals are represented as superior, positioning the species as living technologies. Australia often comes to stand for an exemplar of modernisation, and its meat products as consumable symbols of this modernised society.

Although links between meat, modernisation and development emphasise connections to economic growth and progress conceived in terms of increased wealth and luxury spending, there are some industry and government texts which feature language connotative of other ideas around development, such as poverty alleviation, food security and sustainable development. Indeed, the title of the Red Meat Advisory Council Strategic Plan 2010–2015 was 'Meat Industry Strategic Plan 2010–2015: guaranteeing vital food for the nation and the world', which stresses that the Australian meat industry has an essential role in meeting the food requirements of the world's population.[59] Other articles draw on discourses associated with development organisations involved in the provision of food aid to the 'developing' world, along with the following call to action: 'Sustainably feeding nine billion people will require action at the global, national, regional and local levels.' This sets out a problem but then paves the way for a solution, a structure reminiscent of development agency appeals for support. This resemblance to development agency appeals is heightened by the accompanying photo of a row of outstretched hands, symbolising desperation for food.[60] The National Farmers' Federation, a representative organisation for the agricultural sector, has similar claims about poverty alleviation.[61] In these

---

58 The Premium Sales Pitch 2014, pp. 6–7.
59 Red Meat Advisory Council 2009.
60 Barnard 2014, pp. 6–7.
61 National Farmers' Federation 2015.

cases, Australia's neighbouring Asian countries, who 'do not have the resources or geography to efficiently produce livestock to feed their people',[62] are depicted as passive and dependent recipients of Australian assistance. In this example, the Australian industry draws on patronising, paternalistic and racist rhetoric, which is akin to a civilising mission.

Australia's red meat industry positions itself as part of the solution to feeding a growing world population. The idea that certain countries are better suited to food production is first introduced in general terms: 'It makes economic and environmental sense to focus production in the most suitable areas.'[63] Once the reasoning of 'comparative advantage' has been laid out, the statement that this is 'why Australia produces surplus beef and lamb and exports it to the world' appears to follow on logically, as does the conclusion that 'freeing up trade' is necessary for a sustainable global food supply. Furthermore, Indonesia's own policy of beef self-sufficiency is suggested as a misguided approach to supplying food to populations.[64] However, given that this protectionist policy has resulted in reduced demand for Australian live exported cattle, the emphasis on a free market approach seems consistent with the Australian meat industry's position as an exporter. These arguments are tied to neoliberal economic discourse; that is, to assumptions about an 'increased role for markets, an enhanced role for the private sector and voluntary regulation'.[65]

Finally, in the context of live animal exports, certain Australian institutions claim that Australian presence in Asian and Middle Eastern markets contributes to improved standards of slaughter. The Australian Live Exporters' Council frames the Australian live export industry as having a holistic positive impact, which extends to both technical and moral advancement:

Increasingly our efforts to help improve animal welfare is recognised as contributing to wider social and ethical change,

---

62   National Farmers' Federation 2015.
63   Barnard 2014, pp. 6–7.
64   Barnard 2014, pp. 6–7.
65   Humphreys 2009, p. 319.

better treatment of local livestock, improved worker safety and better meat quality.[66]

This claim positions Australia's animal welfare standards as aspirational, despite the extreme animal suffering which has been documented on the very ships which transport Australian animals to overseas markets. As Jacqueline Dalziell and Dinesh Wadiwel argue, this sentiment of modernising welfare standards is shaped by epistemologies based on civilised/uncivilised actors, where the alleviation of cruelty is a 'redemptive act by those same civilised actors'. Here, Australians know how to kill 'our' animals in a civilised, humane way, while non-white others do not. The live exports issue therefore emerges from and is challenged through the 'geopolitics of animal slaughter and racialized subjectivities'.[67]

Discussion and conclusion

Discourses of development, progress and modernisation within the Australian meat industry literature are mobilised in diverse ways. The most pervasive linkages between meat and modernisation relate to the emulation of Western capitalism. As these interlinkages depend on the universalisation of certain Eurocentric conceptions of progress, they depend upon the production and reproduction of assumptions about hegemonic meat culture, which are shaped both by the particular context and by actors' positions within the social structure. The observations in this chapter are consistent with representations of modernisation as the global replication of Western trajectories of development and the widespread adoption of practices which first emerged in industrialised Western countries, especially those associated with 'capitalist modernity'.[68] Despite ostensible shifts in development theory, it remains underpinned by ethnocentric assumptions that progress equates to Westernisation, including the

---

66   Australian Livestock Exporters' Council 2018.
67   Dalziell & Wadiwel 2016, pp. 81–82.
68   Escobar 2012, p. xxxii.

adoption of meat culture, and remains tied to dominant neoliberal economic ideas.[69]

The Australian meat industry literature reveals that representations of rising meat consumption in Asian and Middle Eastern nations are reminiscent of 'nutrition transition' accounts. Higher meat diets in these regions are often depicted as a correlate of other forms of social transition, such as urbanisation and the emergence of a richer middle class, thus situating increased meat consumption within a broader process of modernisation. Just as the observed discourses linking meat and modernisation are underpinned by assumptions about the nature of societal progress, they also depend on assumptions about meat itself. Similar to Fiddes' account,[70] meat is transformed from a protein source, consumed in larger and larger quantities, to a symbol for progress. Therefore, this universalisation of the desire to eat more meat masks its culturally and socially contingent nature, just as it obscures the specific historical origins of narratives of modernisation. However, the persistence of dramatic inequalities in the consumption of meat between different countries and social classes suggest that such ostensible benefits of development are far from universal.[71]

Far from being a natural process, 'meatification' flows from the exercise of capital within a hierarchical global order. Jeremy Rifkin argues that meat industries' trade practices play a crucial role in creating the conditions for rising global meat consumption, a perspective which stands in contrast to representations of rising meat consumption as an inevitable component of development.[72] The discursive framing deployed by the Australian meat industry, as this chapter reveals, reinforces the notion that rising meat consumption is entangled with economic and social growth, which in turn reifies the association between meat and modernity. Australian meat institutions are also implicated in the legitimation of certain social relations, especially class stratification. In the literature examined, the potential

---

69 Kothari & Minogue 2002; Sidaway 2007, pp. 345–361; Simon & Närman 2014.
70 Fiddes 1991.
71 McMichael & Butler 2010, p. 204.
72 Rifkin 1992.

to consume meat differentiated certain classes and state populations from others. For example, Australia was constructed as a modernised state with enviable lifestyles of high meat consumption. However, this representation also requires a problematic binary opposition: that other nations with lower consumption patterns are not modern and civilised. Consequently, the Australian meat industry positions itself as a saviour to those less-modern countries. When tied to Australian identity, meat is transformed as an aspirational symbol, implying that emulating Western diets elevates class and national status. However, as other scholars argue, such discourses contribute to the construction of hierarchies between 'developed' and 'developing' states, and entrench power differences.[73]

The Australian meat industry literature upholds a number of assumptions and in doing so ignores some vital factors. It maintains the speciesist assumption that humans are entitled to dominate, exploit and commodify animals. Furthermore, it entrenches the role of industrial animal agriculture in the narrative of 'development' and 'growth' and legitimises the 'naturalness' of consuming meat. Whether it is meat-exporting institutions or cooking magazines, various actors in the animal-industrial complex work 'skilfully to normalise and rationalise' the exploitation and violence inflicted upon domesticated animals in order to make them 'consumable'.[74] Sentient animal bodies are transformed both physically and conceptually into tradable consumer goods. Moreover, the Australian meat industry either greenwashes or ignores the environmental costs of more people consuming a high-meat diet. As Susan Baker asserts, the Western model of development 'is blind to the fact that it is not possible to achieve a global replication of the resource-intensive, affluent lifestyle of the high consumption economies of the North'.[75] The notion promoted by the Australian meat industry that its meat is 'clean and green' ignores the deforestation, pollution, carbon emissions, loss of biodiversity and other environmental harms associated with animal agriculture. Instead, the meat industry co-opts and diminishes the language of sustainability.

---

73   Dirlik 2009, pp. 119–135; Escobar 2012; Sachs 2010.
74   Fitzgerald & Taylor 2014, pp. 179–180.
75   Baker 2016, p. 4.

Ultimately, the entanglement of modernisation and meat is implicated in the production and reproduction of hierarchies between states, social groups and the dichotomy between human and nonhuman animals.

References

Adams, C. J. (2010). *The Sexual Politics of Meat: A Feminist-Vegetarian Critical Theory*. New York: Continuum.

AusTrade (2007). Meat and meat products overview. *Australian Trade Commission*. 12 July. https://bit.ly/2QwVwBT.

AusTrade (2013). India ready to put Australian meat on the menu. *Australian Trade Commission*. https://bit.ly/34tdgWY

AusTrade (2014). Agribusiness to Indonesia: Trends and opportunities. *Australian Trade Commission*. https://bit.ly/3l9LZyt

AusTrade (2015). Meat and meat products to the Philippines. *Australian Trade Commission*. https://bit.ly/3l9MwjX

Australian Government (2012). *Australia in the Asian Century: White paper*. Canberra: Australia in the Asian Century Implementation Task Force. https://bit.ly/2FLZZhD

Australian Livestock Exporters' Council (n.d.). Live Trade FAQS. *Australian Livestock Exporter's Council*. https://bit.ly/2YssfMG

Baker, S. (2016). *Sustainable Development*. Abingdon: Routledge.

Barnard, P. (2014). How to feed 9 billion people. *Feedback: MLA Magazine* December 2014, 6–7.

Bartlett, L. (2018). Why the live export industry must change. *Nine Now: 60 Minutes*. 8 April. https://bit.ly/2YoYI6I

Belcourt, B. (2015). Animal bodies, colonial subjects: (Re)locating animality in decolonial thought. *Societies* 5(1), 1–11. doi:10.3390/soc5010001

Bhambra, G. (2007). *Rethinking Modernity: Postcolonisation and the Sociological Imagination*. Basingstoke: Palgrave Macmillan.

Burke, T. (2009). Australia's Role in Feeding the World: a Focus on World Food Day [media release]. *Department of Agriculture Fisheries and Forestry*. October. https://bit.ly/2YvmJct.

Calvo, E. (2008). 'Most farmers prefer blondes': The dynamics of anthroparchy in animals' becoming meat. *Journal for Critical Animal Studies* 7(1), 32–45.

Cole, M. (2011). From 'Animal Machines' to 'Happy Meat'? Foucault's ideas of disciplinary and pastoral power applied to 'animal-centred' welfare discourse. *Animals* 1, 83–101.

Dalziell, J. and D. J. Wadiwel (2016). Live exports, animal advocacy, race and 'Animal Nationalism.' In A. Potts (Ed.), *Meat Culture* (pp. 73–89). Leiden: Brill.

DeJohn Anderson, V. (2004). *Creatures of Empire: How Domestic Animals Transformed Early America*. Oxford: Oxford University Press.

Department of Agriculture (2014). 'Clean and Green': The key to future export markets for Australian meat [media release]. http://www.agriculture.gov.au/abares/media-releases/2014/clean-and-green.

Department of Agriculture and Water Resources (2018a). Red Meat Export Statistics 2018. https://bit.ly/2EklpSL.

Department of Agriculture and Water Resources (2018b). Reports to Parliament. https://bit.ly/3huQrG4.

Dirlik, A. (2009). Spectres of the third world: Global modernity and the end of the three worlds. In M. T. Berger (Ed.), *After the Third World?* (pp. 119–135). Abingdon, Oxon: Routledge.

Edmonds, M. (2014). Red obsession: Realising value for Australian red meat in Asia [conference presentation]. *Department of Agriculture ABARES*. http://www.daff.gov.au/abares/outlook-2014/Documents/presentation-slides/michael-edmonds-presentation.pdf.

Escobar, A. (2012). *The Making and Unmaking of the Third World*. Princeton: Princeton University Press.

Fairclough, N. (2013). *Critical Discourse Analysis: The Critical Study of Language*. Hoboken: Taylor and Francis.

Fiddes, N. (1991). *Meat: A Natural Symbol*. London: Routledge.

Finn, H. (2017). Land clearing isn't just about trees – It's an animal welfare issue too. *The Conversation*. 5 July. https://bit.ly/2FVd3S4

Fitzgerald, A. J. and N. Taylor (2014). The cultural hegemony of meat and the animal industrial complex. In N. Taylor and R. Twine (Eds.), *The Rise of Critical Animal Studies* (pp. 165–182). Abingdon, Oxon: Routledge.

Food and Agriculture Organization (2014). Meat Consumption. http://www.fao.org/ag/againfo/themes/en/meat/background.html.

Franklin, A. (2007). Human–nonhuman animal relationships in Australia: An overview of results from the first national survey and follow-up case studies 2000–2004. *Society and Animals* 15(1), 7–27.

Hansen, S. A. (2012). Note from the MD. *Feedback: MLA Magazine* April 2012, 1. https://bit.ly/31shlc5

Harari, Y. N. (2015). Introduction. In P. Singer (Ed.), *Animal Liberation*. London: Vintage Publishing.

Humphreys, D. (2009). Discourse as ideology: Neoliberalism and the limits of international forest policy. *Forest Policy and Economics* 11, 319–325.

Johnson, S. (2017). *Meat Processing in Australia* (IBIS World Industry Report). www.ibisworld.com.au

Joyce, B. (2015). Beef Australia 2015: Celebrating an iconic Australian industry [media release]. *Minister for Agriculture.* http://www.agricultureminister.gov.au/pages/media-releases/beef-oz-2015.aspx.

Knöbl, W. (2003). Theories that won't pass away: The never-ending story of modernisation theory. In G. Delanty and E. F. Isin (Eds.), *Handbook of Historical Sociology* (pp. 96–107). London: Sage Publications.

Kothari, U. and M. Minogue (Eds.) (2002). *Development Theory and Practice: Critical Perspectives.* Basingstoke: Palgrave Macmillan.

Lerner, D. (1958). *The Passing of Traditional Society: Modernising Middle East.* New York: Free Press of Glencoe.

McMichael, A. J. and A. J. Butler (2010). Environmentally sustainable and equitable meat consumption in a climate change world. In J. D'Silva and J. Webster (Eds.), *The Meat Crisis: Developing More Sustainable Production and Consumption* (pp. 204–21). Abingdon: Earthscan.

Meat and Livestock Australia (2012a). Around the globe. *Feedback: MLA Magazine* March 2012, 32–33. https://bit.ly/3j9rvUN

Meat and Livestock Australia (2012b). MENA's Melting Pot Brews Opportunity. *Feedback: MLA Magazine* March 2012, 34–35.

Meat and Livestock Australia (2012c). On the Ground: Philippines. *Feedback: MLA Magazine* June 2012, 34. https://bit.ly/32yxrAf

Meat and Livestock Australia (2012d). Around the globe. *Feedback: MLA Magazine* August 2012, 32–33. https://bit.ly/32lTvOa

Meat and Livestock Australia (2012e). On the Ground: Korea. *Feedback: MLA Magazine* August 2012, 34. https://bit.ly/32lTvOa

Meat and Livestock Australia (2013). Around the globe. *Feedback: MLA Magazine* April 2013, 34–35. https://bit.ly/3j8KRtk

Meat and Livestock Australia (2014a). Around the globe. *Feedback: MLA Magazine* November/December 2014, 34–35. https://bit.ly/32efXZC

Meat and Livestock Australia (2014b) Aussie, Aussie, Aussie; Beef, Lamb, Goat! *Feedback: MLA Magazine* June 2014, 7–9. https://bit.ly/3lc2A4G

Meat and Livestock Australia (2014c). The Premium Sales Pitch. *Feedback: MLA Magazine* June 2014, 6–7. https://bit.ly/3lc2A4G

Meat and Livestock Australia (2015) The Beef Export Evolution. *Feedback: MLA Magazine* May/June 2015, 6. https://bit.ly/2FHJxPt

MLA (2015). Product Information. *Love Australian Beef and Lamb.* 13 August 2015. https://bit.ly/32egnza

MLA Feedback TV (2011). Asian Chefs Tour Australia (Episode 13) [video]. 28 February 2011. https://youtu.be/bKe6uHKWbJk

National Farmers' Federation (2015). Support Live Exports. http://www.nff.org.au/supportliveexports.html.

Pachirat, T. (2011). *Every Twelve Seconds: Industrialized Slaughter and the Politics of Sight*. New Haven: Yale University Press.

Popkin, B. M. (1993). Nutritional patterns and transitions. *Population and Development Review* 19(1), 138–157.

Potts, A. (2016). What is meat culture? In A. Potts (Ed.), *Meat Culture* (pp. 1–30). Leiden: Brill.

Preece, N. D. and P. van Oosterzee (2017). Australia is a global top-ten deforester – and Queensland is leading the way. *The Conversation*. 17 November. https://bit.ly/3j5rQI4

Red Meat Advisory Council (2009). Meat industry strategic plan 2010–2015: Guaranteeing vital food for the nation and the world. 20 August. https://bit.ly/32egquQ

Rifkin, J. (1992). *Beyond beef: The rise and fall of cattle culture*. New York: Plume.

Rist, G. (2014). *The History of Development from Western Origins to Global Faith* (4th ed.). London: Zed Books.

Rostow, W. W. (1959). The stages of economic growth. *The Economic History Review* 12(1), 1–16.

Roy, R. D. (2015). Nonhuman empires. *Comparative Studies of South Asia, Africa and the Middle East* 31(1), 66–75.

Sachs, W. (2010). *The Development Dictionary: A Guide to Knowledge as Power*. London: Zed Books.

Saha, J. (2017). Colonizing elephants: Animal agency, Undead capital and imperial science in British Burma. *British Society for the History of Science*, 1–27.

Sidaway, J. D. (2007). Spaces of postdevelopment. *Progress in Human Geography* 31(3), 345–361.

Simon, D., and A. Närman (Eds.) (2014). *Development as Theory and Practice*. London: Routledge.

Singer, P. (1975). *Animal Liberation: A New Ethics for Our Treatment of Animals*. New York: Random House, Inc.

Singer, P. (1979). *Practical Ethics*. Cambridge: Cambridge University Press.

Skabelund, A. (2011). *Empire of Dogs: Canines, Japan, and the Making of the Modern Imperial World*. Ithaca: Cornell University Press.

Thomas, B. (2015). Australian Cattle Industry Projections 2015. *Meat & Livestock Australia*. 4 August. http://www.mla.com.au/Prices-and-markets/Trends-and-analysis/Beef/Forecasts/MLA-Australian-cattle-industry-projections-2015

Twine, R. (2012). Revealing the 'Animal-Industrial Complex' – A concept & method for critical animal studies? *Journal for Critical Animal Studies* 10(1), 12–39.

Weis, T. (2013). *The Ecological Hoofprint: The Global Burden of Industrial Livestock.* London: Zed Books.

Wong, L., E. A. Selvanathan and S. Selvanathan (2013). Changing pattern of meat consumption in Australia. *Australian Conference of Economists.* Perth: Murdoch University.

Woods, R. J. H. (2015). Building an empire of sheep in New Zealand, ca. 1800–1900. *Comparative Studies of South Asia, Africa and the Middle East* 35(1), 117–36.

8

'Stewed in mighty symbolism of wealth, power and masculinity': The legitimation of 'meat'-eating through anti-vegan rhetoric in mainstream US news

Lisa Barca

Veganism is an ethical position and way of living that renounces exploitation of and cruelty towards nonhuman animals for food or any other purpose.[1] As such, it poses a challenge to speciesism, the pervasive cultural belief system that views nonhuman animals as less morally important than humans and sees their value as lying in their potential to serve human interests. At its core, veganism is about compassion for nonhuman beings, grounded in the recognition that, like humans, other animals prefer to stay alive, have autonomy, engage in chosen social relationships and avoid suffering. Just about anyone who has lived with animal companions such as dogs or cats can recognise these qualities in them; vegans extend this acknowledgement to equally sentient and sensitive nonhuman animals used for food. Because nonhuman animal agriculture causes well-documented harms, and mainstream health organisations such as the Academy of Nutrition and Dietetics have recently deemed vegan diets healthful for all life stages,[2] vegans' efforts to bring reasoned examination of current animal-consuming practices into public discourse seem appropriate and necessary.

---

1   For a full, foundational definition, see Vegan Society n.d.
2   Melina, Craig & Levin 2016.

As veganism becomes more culturally visible, mainstream media, the mass-communicative arm of corporate power and the capitalism-friendly state apparatuses supporting it, sporadically invoke veganism in ways that reinforce speciesist ideology and reposition meat-eating as normative. This essay analyses a selection of articles mentioning veganism as a central theme, signalled by its presence in headlines, in major US newspapers from October 2017 to March 2018.

The term 'vegan' was most often used in news texts as a descriptor of food, in which case it was generally accompanied by positive evaluation.[3] When used as a descriptor for people, however (the focus of this essay), 'vegan' most often signalled negative evaluation.[4] This points towards the double-edged nature of the recent mainstreaming of dietary veganism: on the one hand, the growing availability of vegan food provides people with necessary alternatives to 'meat'-based diets; yet this culinary development has not ushered in accurate or sympathetic representation of the views, motivations or experiences of ethical vegans. This can be explained at least partly by capitalist media's embeddedness with nonhuman animal-products industries – for instance, through reliance on advertising revenues – and the media's general reflection of dominant cultural values.[5] Vegan philosophy, which takes a position about the moral worth of other animals and is thus more than a diet, arguably poses a deeper challenge to carnivory than does the presence or praise of plant-based food. Likely for this

---

3   This is consistent with results from Cole & Morgan 2011.

4   The most notable exception was Severson 2017. While largely focused on food and personal health, it also references struggles for racial justice and contains two mentions of 'animal welfare' as a motive for veganism. Severson is a white journalist visible in LGBT advocacy, and, while apparently not vegan (her publications contain many nonhuman-animal-food-based recipes), is apparently supportive of some social-justice aspects of veganism. This provides an anecdotal indication that connecting veganism with justice for marginalised human groups may currently be a more media-friendly topic (so long as capitalist sources of oppression or the corrupt practices of animal agriculture are not seriously critiqued) than discussion of veganism's grounding in nonhuman animal rights.

5   On the pro-establishment orientation of corporate media, see Chomsky 2002; McChesney 2015. On capitalist values and speciesism in media, see Almiron, Cole & Freeman 2016; Nibert 2013; Sorenson 2016.

reason, when vegans are discussed in news, the ethical content of veganism is routinely deflected by a focus on food as a matter of personal consumer 'choice', thereby evading the need to justify exploitative practices.

There are two main reasons why it is important to examine the media's representations of veganism. One is the impact media have in shaping public opinion; although people do not passively receive and automatically agree with media narratives, elite publications like the *New York Times* and other high-circulation newspapers, through their authoritative and pervasive presence, play a role in setting boundaries for public discourse and legitimating certain ideological viewpoints while excluding others. The other compelling reason to look at veganism in media is the frightening magnitude of humans' oppression of other animals and the consequent urgency of a cultural shift towards veganism. David Nibert has eloquently summarised the violence of the current human–nonhuman relationship as follows:

> Countless other animals are hunted and killed, trapped, subjected to laboratory experimentation, or exploited for human entertainment. The oppression of other animals for food is unquestionably the deadliest practice; globally, more than 65 billion land-based beings are killed to be consumed as food every year, while the water-based other animals killed for food number in the hundreds of millions. The physical and emotional suffering from such horrific treatment experienced by each individual being, multiplied by the billions of individual animals who undergo it, results in a degree of severe distress and pain – every second – that defies comprehension.[6]

When the media stigmatise vegans, the small minority of citizens committed to resisting these atrocities, they do more than fuel petty cultural quarrels: they make themselves complicit in the continuance of systematised violence by using their rhetorical power to discredit and impede the work of advocating for nonhuman animals as a matter of justice. When, added to the violence perpetrated against these beings,

---

6   Nibert 2017, p. xi.

we take into account animal agriculture's massive role in contributing to impending environmental catastrophe,[7] the need to scrutinise the rhetoric of influential commentators who malign and misrepresent veganism becomes undeniable.

Throughout this essay, rather than referring to animals other than humans simply as 'animals', I generally employ the terms 'other animals' and 'nonhuman animals', which, although still imperfect insofar as they position humanness as the norm from which other animals deviate, encourage attention to the fact that humans are also animals by avoiding the 'human vs. animal' rhetorical and ontological divide that has played a role in fostering the distorted thinking that undergirds humans' catastrophic treatment of other animals. I use scare quotes around terms that commodify other animals, such as 'meat', 'beef', 'dairy' and 'poultry'; this serves to mark out and critique oppressive language that normalises systematised violence.[8] When objectifying terms appear in quoted material, I generally follow them with [*sic*] to problematise their use. These linguistic choices are part of a critical animal studies (CAS) perspective, which does not pretend 'objectivity' about the plight of nonhuman animals and other matters of injustice, giving voice instead to an explicitly vegan commitment to liberating all sentient beings from systems of oppression.

Literature review

Previous analyses of speciesism in news media have made crucial contributions to understanding this widespread and deeply harmful phenomenon. Matthew Cole and Karen Morgan (2011) examined discourses of veganism in UK national newspapers in 2007, summarising their findings as follows: 'Newspapers tend to discredit veganism through ridicule, or as being difficult or impossible to maintain in practice. Vegans are variously stereotyped as ascetics, faddists, sentimentalists, or in some cases, hostile extremists.' They

---

7   See Poore & Nemecek 2018; Glaser, Romaniello & Moskowitz 2015;
      Hyner 2015; Goodland & Anhang 2009; Steinfeld 2006.
8   See Nibert 2017, p. xviii.

interpret derogatory discourses of veganism as 'evidence of the cultural reproduction of speciesism, through which veganism is dissociated from its connection with debates concerning nonhuman animals' rights or liberation'.[9] This is consistent with my findings here, with the exception that US newspapers in 2017–2018 revealed more characterisations of vegans as 'preachy' or 'proselytizing' compared to Cole and Morgan's investigation of UK newspapers in 2007. (This is perhaps attributable to the rapid growth of veganism in the intervening years, with the result that the dominant culture and the journalists working within it may more recently have come to see vegans as a countercultural force effectively disrupting the normalcy of 'meat'-eating, rather than as mere quirky and easily dismissible outsiders. More research would be needed to substantiate such a hypothesis, however.)

Carrie P. Freeman's (2009/2016) seminal study of how nonhuman animals exploited for food were represented in US national print and broadcast news from 2000 to 2003 found a predominance of 'anthropocentric news frames' that marginalise animal rights as a topic of public debate.[10] Freeman calls for the press to adhere to its social responsibility to represent the perspectives of all groups affected by the issues on which it reports; this mandates including the perspectives of nonhuman animals in news stories on agricultural practices in which they are exploited.[11] While Freeman's study looks at news stories on agriculture rather than primarily on veganism, her findings and assertions are relevant here, since she found that the press, with few exceptions, 'disregards animal sentience and creates imbalanced coverage' that favours 'advocates for the status quo'.[12] This correlates with Cole and Morgan's (2011) findings on the reinforcement of speciesism in news stories on veganism, and with my own findings.

In her analysis of journalistic discourse on nonhuman animals exploited for food, Karen Davis (2018) found, with few exceptions, a disturbing 'moral disengagement' on the part of journalists. The news

---

9   Cole & Morgan 2011, p. 134.
10   Freeman 2009, p. 169.
11   Freeman 2009, p.169.
12   Freeman 2009, p. 180.

articles she examined reinforce the 'meat'-eating status quo while superficially purporting to attend to the interests of nonhuman animals.[13] Her investigation suggests that 'journalists do not always feel obligated to adhere to standards of precise language where farmed animals are concerned'. Congruent with Freeman's (2009/2016) findings, Davis discovered that anthropocentric concerns, such as financial loss or gain, predominated in stories on farmed animal exploitation and suffering.[14] Perhaps most relevant for the current essay's discussion, Davis identified a pattern of 'dominance through mentioning', a process by which 'disturbing truths and iconoclastic viewpoints are "mentioned" so that the opinion makers cannot be accused of omitting them'; these truths are then satirised, diluted or dismissed.[15] This is in line with a central feature of *meatsplaining*: a rhetoric of denial (as the title of the present volume indicates) wherein the realities of human violence, nonhuman suffering, harms to health and environmental devastation wrought by animal agriculture are occasionally evoked only to be summarily overridden by less pressing concerns, such as 'convenience' or the trivial desire to taste the flesh of nonhuman beings.

Text selection

In compiling relevant texts for this analysis, I searched for the terms 'vegan', 'vegans' and 'veganism' in the online editions of the *New York Times, Wall Street Journal, Washington Post, New York Daily News, New York Post, LA Times* and *USA Today*. The date range of the search was 1 October 2017 to 31 March 2018. These papers were selected for their high circulation and their public image as credible, professional and mainstream US news sources. Of 34 total articles examined, three were selected as representative for analysis. They were selected because they discussed vegans as individuals or veganism as a practice, rather than simply referring to vegan food (food reviews were omitted from

---

13   Davis 2018, p. 73.
14   Davis 2018, p. 75.
15   Davis 2018, p. 88.

analysis). They were also chosen because they were long and detailed enough to provide rich opportunities for analysis.

In these articles, anti-vegan rhetoric constructs itself through multiple levels of denial: of the meaning of veganism as not just a diet but an ethical position rejecting use of nonhuman animals, of these animals' subjectivities and sufferings, and of the harms to the environment and human health caused by meat production and consumption. Two of the articles are editorial in nature and penned by authors with popular-cultural visibility beyond newspaper journalism. The third is a sensationalised story covered across international media concerning a small, nonviolent, animal rights protest at a 'locavore' restaurant in Toronto, Canada. All three are representative of rhetoric that maligns vegans who go beyond quietly enjoying plant-based food (an apparently acceptable topic for capitalist media these days) to posing difficult questions about the speciesism that allows most people to keep consuming other animals despite the culinary alternatives largely acknowledged to be satisfactory by this same media. These articles show a pattern of framing their subject matter from a non-vegan perspective and referencing, in passing, the harms caused by eating other animals and then dismissing these as less significant than people's desire to eat 'meat'. They bury superficial references to the harms (apparently so well known these days as to require lip service) within a discourse that is most conspicuously anti-vegan.

'Good vegan, bad vegan' and the double-speak of denial

The first article I will look at, which bears the polarising headline 'Good vegan, bad vegan', is by Jane Brody, popular food author and *New York Times* health columnist since 1976. Brody begins by trying to establish herself as reasonable and credible, but she does this through a series of argumentative moves that, once examined, may have the opposite effect. The first of these rhetorical sleights-of-hand occurs in the opening sentence: 'I have no argument with people who adopt a vegetarian or vegan diet for health, religious, environmental or ethical reasons.'[16] The

---

16   Brody 2017.

sole function of this generic, apparently mollifying remark is to set the stage for discrediting people in this group who speak about their reasons for adopting such a diet: 'But I object vehemently to proselytizers who distort science or the support for dietary advice offered to the more than 90 per cent of us who choose to consume animal foods, including poultry and red meat [*sic*], in reasonable amounts.'[17] This employs the *argumentum ad populum* fallacy, which holds that a proposition must be true simply because many people believe it. If '90 per cent of us' (a vegan reader is positioned as not one of 'us') receive medical advice that supports continued consumption of 'poultry and red meat' (in 'reasonable amounts', whatever that might mean to different individuals), then that advice must be sound and 'we' must be justified in continuing these practices.

Concerning the hackneyed characterisation of vegans who educate others as 'proselytizers', it should be noted that it is rare to see this term assigned to advocates of other social justice movements.[18] It is drawn from a lexicon of evangelical religion, to which veganism – an ethical position based not upon faith in an unseen deity or transcendent reality but on demonstrable facts concerning nonhuman-animal oppression and its effects on the physical world – bears no plausible resemblance. The vegan-proselytiser cliché facilitates, and contains as its unmentioned foundational assumption, the framing of 'meat'-eating as a 'personal choice' rather than a behaviour with profound political and ethical ramifications. Elaborating on why she 'object[s] vehemently' to these kinds of vegans, Brody proclaims:

> Such [proselytizing] is the case with a recently released Netflix documentary called 'What the Health' that several well-meaning, health-conscious young friends have urged me to watch. And I did try, until I became so infuriated by misstatements – like eating an egg a day is as bad as smoking five cigarettes, or that a daily

---

17 Brody 2017.
18 On the tendency to claim that vegans are 'preachy', and the rarity of this accusation being made of others working for justice, see Grillo 2016, p. 148; Joy 2014, p. 82, 86.

serving of processed meat raises the risk of diabetes 51 percent – that I had to quit for the sake of *my* health.[19]

In precipitously refuting data presented in the film, Brody substitutes personal indignation for medical credentials. According to her biography on the *New York Times* website, her only scientific training is a BSc degree in biochemistry earned in 1962 from the New York State College of Agriculture at Cornell, followed by a master's in science writing in 1963.[20] (Brody's agriculture-school degree and her support of GMO food[21] indicate her sympathies with big food/agricultural industries.) Despite lacking medical training, Brody positions herself as qualified to discredit *What the Health*'s presentation of recent findings by medical doctors published in peer-reviewed journals.[22]

Most importantly, had Brody continued watching the documentary, she would have seen that it is about more than individual health. The filmmakers take viewers to marginalised communities near chicken-slaughtering operations in North Carolina, interviewing the predominantly African American citizens of these communities about the emotional, economic, environmental and health hardships they endure living near these polluting, fetid sites of industrialised violence. *What the Health* also exposes the escalation of public health-care costs related to preventable diseases exacerbated by other-animal consumption. The most relevant topic of the film, and the one most likely to be lost on corporate media commentators like Brody, is its exposé of the corrupt and profitable collusions between government and the pharmaceutical, food and medical industries to aggressively

---

19 Brody 2017.
20 See New York Times n.d.
21 In 1971, the school at Cornell became the New York State College of Agriculture and Life Sciences; when Brody attended, agriculture was the only discipline included in the college's name; see Cornell College of Agriculture and Life Sciences, n.d. In addition to her agriculture degree, an editorial Brody wrote for the *Times* supporting GMO food indicates her alliance with food industry interests (Brody 2015).
22 What the Health n.d. My goal is not to debate health-based arguments, but rather to point out the rash denial underpinning Brody's rhetoric.

promote a diet they know to be harmful, disregarding the public good in the name of private profit for a few.

Breaking away fleetingly from her focus on personal health and consumer choice, Brody makes shaky appeals that discount the validity of veganism's rationales while pretending to acknowledge them:

> Please understand: I do not endorse inhumane treatment of farm animals [*sic*] or wanton pollution of the environment with animal wastes and misused antibiotics and pesticides. Agricultural research has long shown better ways to assure the nation of an adequate food supply if only regulators would force commercial operations to adopt them.[23]

If one were to rephrase the first sentence above in the affirmative – I endorse inhumane treatment of farm animals and wanton pollution of the environment with animal wastes and misused antibiotics and pesticides – we see that the original sentence ('I do not endorse ...') is an empty statement. An unsuspecting reader might even process this as a meaningful concession to a counterargument. Rejecting an ethical position that can only be characterised as monstrous or absurd does not boost a writer's credibility, no matter how magnanimous it is dressed up to seem. What this sentence really communicates, correctly, is that these atrocities are occurring without abatement across the global animal-industrial complex, but veiling the admission in a hollow counterview circumvents any need to discuss this seriously. The second sentence above vaguely references 'agricultural research' without mentioning particular studies or which investigating entities carried them out (has this research been carried out by the 'meat' industry, for instance?). There is vague allusion to 'better ways to assure the nation of an adequate food supply' but no mention of a shift towards dietary veganism, arguably the best way to achieve this in that it would free up the nearly 50 per cent of land in the contiguous US devoted to animal agriculture,[24] allowing room and resources to grow plant-foods

---

23 Brody 2017.
24 See Glaser, Romaniello & Moskowitz 2015; Nickerson, Ebel, Borchers & Carriazo 2011.

for the human population rather than for nonhuman animals exploited in agriculture. Blame for 'inhumane treatment' is placed on 'regulators' and 'commercial operations', ambiguously pitted against each other when, given the well-documented history of government complicity with animal industries, both are part-and-parcel of the animal-industrial complex.[25]

After her attempts at conciliation ('I do not endorse inhumane treatment of farm animals', etc.), Brody continues:

> Nor do I endorse careless adoption of vegetarian or vegan diets for their name's sake … A vegan diet laden with refined grains like white rice and bread; juices and sweetened drinks; cookies, chips and crackers; and dairy-free ice cream is hardly a healthful way to eat.[26]

Why anyone would change their diet just for the privilege of adopting an identity label frequently denigrated in mainstream culture, including by articles such as Brody's, is a question the reader is left to ponder. In short, this is a strawman argument, or argumentation against a position that one's opponent/s (in Brody's case, 'proselytizing' vegans) do not actually hold. What is more, if Brody had watched *What the Health* in its entirety before reviewing it (recall her admission of not having done so cited above), she would have seen that the diet she impugns is not the one promoted in the film, which advises a whole-foods, plant-based diet, making this another strawman argument.

Another aspect of this and other news articles (see the discussion of Marta Zaraska's opinion piece in the next section, for instance) that may contribute to misrepresenting veganism is the persistent conflation of 'vegetarian' and 'vegan', referenced as merged or interchangeable categories. While veganism eschews all use of other animals, vegetarianism (at least in the way the term is generally used today) allows for consumption of 'dairy' and chickens' eggs, the products of violent and exploitative industries that require the reproductive enslavement of mother cows and hens, harsh confinement of hens and the

---

25 On government–industry collusion and the animal-industrial complex, see Sorenson 2016, pp. 11–14; Nibert 2011, pp. 197–209; Noske 1997.

26 Brody 2017.

amputation of their sensitive beaks, repeated sexual violation, forced impregnation and attaching of painful milking machines to cows' udders, the traumatic abduction of their young, the slaughter of every cow and hen used for 'milk' and 'eggs', the prompt killing of male offspring, who are of no use to the industries, and other abuses of nonhuman beings. While many vegans were vegetarian first and the categories are thus interrelated, routinely fusing them without explanation may enable continued public misunderstanding of veganism's ethical (i.e. its only relevant defining) content.

A final example of anti-vegan/vegetarian rhetoric in Brody's article follows, somewhat surprisingly, upon her citing of studies showing the coronary benefits of plant-based diets. Brody reports that

> you don't have to become a strict vegetarian to protect your heart. Simply reducing your dependence on animal foods, and especially avoiding those high in fat, is helpful. In fact, 'a diet that emphasized both healthy plant and healthy animal foods' was associated with a coronary risk only slightly higher than a diet based almost entirely on healthy plant foods, the researchers found.[27]

As Cole and Morgan (2011) noted in evaluating anti-vegan rhetoric in UK newspapers, Brody's article recurrently invokes a non-vegan *you*,[28] grounding the discourse in an assumption that the reader is not vegan and inviting audiences to identify with that non-vegan position rather than the unflattering 'vegan' identities fabricated. Also present here and consistent with Cole and Morgan's observations is the characterisation of veganism/vegetarianism as 'strict' or requiring asceticism when in fact vegans enjoy an abundant array of delicious foods.[29] Despite these veganism-unfriendly locutions, Brody's own statements above indicate that eliminating 'animal foods' from one's diet is the most healthful course: an omnivorous diet 'was associated with a coronary risk *only slightly higher* than a diet based almost entirely on healthy plant foods', meaning that the plant diet posed

27 Brody 2017.
28 Cole & Morgan 2011, p. 142.
29 Cole & Morgan 2011, pp. 142–143.

the least risk. Brody's closing argument delivers a media-friendly 'reducetarian' message that leaves veganism unmentioned and deems vegetarianism unnecessary.

In considering the broader question of the *rhetoric of denial* that this volume on meatsplaining poses, it is instructive to contemplate how a news text that is ultimately unable to deny the benefits of dietary veganism nonetheless makes anti-vegan rhetoric its most emphatic feature, overshadowing its veiled admissions of the preferability of plant diets. Given this predominance of anti-vegan rhetoric, it would appear that the 'bad vegan' of the article's headline is not the fictitious figure who adopts veganism for its 'name' and eats little other than cookies and chips, but rather the 'proselytizer' assailed in the opening paragraph, who talks about topics such as violence against nonhuman animals, animal agriculture's calamitous ecological impacts, and the diet of addiction and disease relentlessly and profitably promoted by the animal-industrial complex.

'Skip the veganism lecture': Meatsplaining to vegans

The rhetorical strategies leveraged in Brody's article – condemning vegans' 'proselytizing', slipping admissions of veganism's merits into anti-vegan rhetoric, diminishing the importance of nonhuman suffering, privileging personal choice over ethical considerations and framing discourse from a non-vegan perspective – also appear in a *New York Daily News* opinion piece headlined 'Skip the veganism lecture today'. Presumably addressed to vegans (who else would give a 'veganism lecture'?), this piece offers a laundry list of justifications for eating other animals and reasons why vegans should keep their views to themselves. This initially may seem odd given that the writer, Marta Zaraska, is author of the 2016 book *Meathooked: The history and science of our 2.5-million-year obsession with meat*, ostensibly a critique of carnivory. But Zaraska's book and her TED Talk based on it, while pointing out problems with 'meat'-eating, are at their core more supportive of the inevitability of 'our' addiction to and 'obsession with meat' than of truly tackling these in fact surmountable issues.[30] Consistently with this, Zaraska's *New York Daily News* opinion piece begins:

> 'No citizen of the U.S. shall refrain from turkey on Thanksgiving Day'. When founding father Alexander Hamilton made that remark, he was thinking not of vegetarians but of meat as a symbol of prosperity. Still, today, to ardent vegetarians – some of whom may be poised to proselytize – we could issue a similar call: 'No citizen of the U.S. shall coerce others to refrain from turkey on Thanksgiving Day'.[31]

In delivering a lecture on the importance of not lecturing, these commands to 'ardent vegetarians' (the switch from 'vegan' in the headline to 'vegetarian' in the first sentences is perhaps due to the sensationalised attraction of media that visibly, e.g. in a headline, uses

---

30 In her book's introduction, Zaraska miscategorises herself as vegetarian: 'I'm one of those sloppy vegetarians. First of all, I eat fish. I do it mostly because I'm lazy … Sometimes when no one is looking—and this is really difficult to admit—I nibble on a slice of sausage or a piece of bacon' (Zaraska 2016, p. 5). The book contains many descriptions of the deliciousness and irresistibility of 'meat' and dwells with little critique on people's purported reasons for eating it. Zaraska begins her 2017 TED Talk by asking how many audience members are vegetarian or vegan. Quite a few raise their hands. She then asks of those self-identified vegans/ vegetarians, 'how many of you have eaten meat in the last twenty-four hours?' When no one raises their hand, she says, 'that's surprising! Because surveys tend to show something else. One such survey done in the United States has found that 60 per cent of vegetarians and vegans have actually eaten meat within the last twenty-four hours. And a similar thing has been found in Canada. We know that in the United Kingdom almost 40 per cent of vegetarians say whenever they get drunk, they do eat meat' (Zaraska 2017b, 15:28). The evidence in the room belied Zaraska's evidence from the 'surveys', occasioning an instance of the 'denial-despite-contrary-evidence' trope noted throughout the analysis in this essay. Zaraska's rhetoric is of the kind used by meat-industry interests and other anti-vegan commenters to promulgate the idea that vegans are hypocritical and that the flesh of nonhuman animals is irresistible, giving the public two deceptive excuses for other-animal consumption.

31 Zaraska 2017a.

the term 'vegan', especially negatively) contain a few logical fallacies. One is an appeal to tradition, which assumes that old ways of thinking were sound when they actually could have been flawed and that past justifications for a practice are valid now, when relevant circumstances may have changed. Both of these are applicable to a practice like killing tens of millions of sentient avian individuals in order to celebrate a holiday when there is nothing about a bird corpse per se that is pertinent to the celebration. And while killing turkeys has always been a violent and unnecessary act, the mechanised mass brutality and ecological damage wrought by contemporary nonhuman animal agriculture are harms particular to our own rather than Hamilton's time. Zaraska also makes an appeal to authority – another logical fallacy – with the Hamilton quote, assuming that one should automatically accept the legitimacy of an idea because a well-known person, in this case a patriarchal 'founding father', articulated it. Whether or not Hamilton was 'thinking of vegetarians' is irrelevant to what we might find it important to do today. The characterisation of 'vegetarians' as 'ardent' (interpretable in this context as rigid and zealous; they are later called 'hardened'[32]) and the anticipation that they will 'proselytize' recall Brody's deployment of these themes.

The claim that Hamilton was 'thinking' (how would one know what he was thinking?) of 'meat as a symbol of prosperity' seems to offer this as a sound justification for consuming it without examining the tenuous grounds for this; that is, that harming other animals is acceptable as long as one imagines that it confers culturally desirable qualities upon the consumer. The notion that vegans/vegetarians have the power to 'coerce others to refrain from [sic] turkey' is equally problematic: a turkey is coerced into having a human worker ejaculate him (if male); coerced into having a human artificially inseminate her and take her eggs and young away (if female); mutilated and coerced into living in crowded, fetid, disease-filled conditions with no fresh air or sunlight; coerced onto crowded, stress-inducing trucks to the slaughterhouse; coerced into metal shackles while her or his throat is coercively slit. But talking about the ethics of eating these turkeys' flesh

---

32 Zaraska 2017a.

is hard to characterise as 'coercion' according to any workable definition of that term.[33]

Like Brody, Zaraska tucks admissions of the harms caused by 'meat'-eating into her overall anti-vegan rhetoric:

> Yes, it's true that many studies have linked meat-eating to cancer, heart disease, diabetes. It is also true that those 50 million turkeys that get slaughtered each year for Thanksgiving have likely suffered before their deaths – packed in three square feet of space per bird, their bodies so overgrown they could barely walk.[34]

That turkeys have 'likely' suffered (is there a possibility they have *not* suffered through being 'packed in three square feet of space per bird, their bodies so overgrown they could barely walk', in addition to the myriad other horrors they endure?) and that eating their tormented bodies harms human health and the environment seem to pale in comparison to the rationalisations that family members may have for eating turkeys' flesh. These justifications include the notion that '[m]eat is a food like no other. Since 2.5 million years ago, when our ancestors started eating it, it's been stewed in mighty symbolism: of wealth, power and masculinity'.[35] In other words, we should not mention the harmfulness of these unnecessary practices because people entertain notions of being affluent and manly while eating a relatively cheaply available bird who had no chance of escaping her or his fate to end up on the plate. The pun '*stewed* in mighty symbolism' makes light of a dire topic and does not compensate for these arguments' feebleness. And insofar as the historical associations between the control of domesticated animals and the patriarchal power of their owners are truthful (there are indeed links between the historical advent of nonhuman-animal 'herding' and the development of patriarchal, militaristic societies), this should reinforce the case for *discontinuing* these practices, since the domination-based worldview underpinning

---

33 See Grillo 2016, p. 149 on the idea of vegans 'forcing' their views.
34 Zaraska 2017a.
35 Zaraska 2017a.

these historical turns has led humanity into the precarious and self-destructive condition in which it finds itself in today.[36]

Whether the holiday dinner table is an apt setting for vegan advocacy is a worthwhile discussion for vegans to have, and many of us have, on at least some occasions, chosen to either quietly tolerate or altogether skip gatherings where nonhuman animals' flesh is consumed so as to avoid conflicts, awkwardness or distress. But that is not the kind of discussion this article engages in; rather, it is framed so as to rationalise the unchallenged continuance of a tradition that should be critically examined, while ordering vegans into unconditional silence.

The article skirts the boundaries of Anglocentric bigotry in its appeals to the Americanness of eating turkeys' flesh: 'Meat is a powerful pillar of national cultural identity. For a Zambian, mopane caterpillars are [a] vital piece of being Zambian, and so is a Thanksgiving turkey for an American.' Apparently attempting to support this pseudo-anthropological analogy, Zaraska continues:

> When sociologist Melanie Wallendorf and anthropologist Eric Arnould conducted extensive research on Thanksgiving, they discovered that this particular holiday is all about togetherness, continuity and simplicity ... What's more, Thanksgiving is also about simplicity. No wonder then that suggestions of swapping stuffed turkey for a Gardein Savory Stuffed Turk'y or Field Roast Celebration Roast are, in general, not met with enthusiasm. Such foods are anything but simple.[37]

That an anthropologist and a sociologist must be cited to arrive at the truism that Thanksgiving is 'all about togetherness, continuity and simplicity' is curious, since such an analysis can be retrieved from a Hallmark card. Even odder is the assertion that vegan alternatives to turkeys' flesh are 'anything but simple'. That handling a slippery,

---

36 On the links between animal domestication (or *domesecration*, as Nibert aptly terms it) and the development of hierarchical and warlike patriarchal societies, as well as the domination of female human and nonhuman animals, see Nibert 2013, pp. 9–42; Tuttle 2016, pp. 17–24, 109–134.

37 Zaraska 2017a.

heavy and decomposing bird cadaver that may harbour food-borne pathogens, taking the entrails out of her or his defeated body, 'stuffing' that body with separately prepared viands, getting that body into and out of the oven with the right timing, etc. is infinitely simpler than preparing a vegan dish is a claim too far-fetched to take seriously.

The article ends by recommending moral inconsistency, especially when dining on holidays:

> By all means, it would be best if we, in the West, cut down considerably on our meat consumption – for the sake of our health and the health of our planet. But that doesn't mean we all have to feel guilty about each and every bite of animal muscle, or about maintaining a powerful connection to certain kinds of meat on certain days, like Thanksgiving … If you are considering going vegetarian, my humble advice is this: Give yourself a 'get-out-of-jail' card for Thanksgiving, allowing yourself a bite of that turkey.[38]

This inclusion of yet another admission of 'meat' consumption's harmfulness (couched in a hollow 'reduction' message) illustrates the pattern of denial-despite-presented-evidence-to-the-contrary in much of the anti-vegan rhetoric looked at in this essay. Also congruent with a pattern noted earlier is the invocation of a 'meat'-eating 'you' in 'If *you* are considering going vegetarian'. From a headline that seemed to address vegans (albeit sanctimoniously), the article has devolved into addressing a reader who is not even vegetarian. The moral inconsistency the article enjoins readers to cultivate seems to spill over into its own rhetorical inconsistency.

Vegans vs. chef-hunter: Spectacle to re-establish the supremacy of 'meat'

A major source of denial of harm to other animals and legitimation of speciesist violence comes from locavore and other 'sustainable' and

---

38   Zaraska 2017a.

'humane' nonhuman animal exploitation trends. Vasile Stănescu (2010), after documenting the unsustainability of these trends and their promoters' hostility towards veganism, concludes that 'many of the proponents of the locavore movement seek to re-inscribe the very speciesism it first seems to draw into question'.[39] Stănescu acknowledges that his focus on locavorism and 'humane' farming may seem misplaced because of the tiny fraction of other animals exploited in these contexts compared to the global industrial system. He then clarifies, however, that his 'worry, in part, is that by drawing an increasing focus to these statistically wholly unrepresentative examples of the theoretical "ideal" farm serves to hide from the average consumer the reality of the life of nonhuman animals and our species' relation to them'.[40] Locavorism and other 'humane' imaginings serve as marketing gimmicks that falsely assuage the consciences of people concerned about the violence done to nonhumans. The animals exploited in these local or do-it-yourself operations are generally subjected to the same mutilations, separations of families, painful slaughter at a fraction of their natural lifespan and other injustices visited upon their cousins in standard industrial agriculture.[41]

I present this as background for examining an article in the *Washington Post* that was representative of a burst of coverage across the media about a small, nonviolent, animal rights protest at a 'locavore' restaurant in Toronto. Like the articles analysed previously, it frames discourse from a non-vegan perspective and contains denials and distortions that reposition 'meat'-eating as normative.

The article's headline, 'The vegans came to protest his restaurant. So this chef carved a deer leg in the window', sensationalistically appeals to a non-vegan public by summoning 'the vegans' as cultural others. The phrase '*this* chef', suggesting proximity or familiarity, positions audiences to identify with him, as does placing reference to his retaliation in a rhetorical emphasis position, at the end of the headline. The article begins:

---

39 Stănescu 2010, p. 27.
40 Stănescu 2010, p. 27.
41 See Bohanec 2013.

The vegans planned their protest for the middle of the restaurant's busy dinnertime shift. The group of animal rights activists were incensed that Antler Kitchen & Bar, a locavore restaurant in Toronto that says it highlights regional ingredients, served foie gras and farmed meat 'meant to run in the wild'.[42]

Depicting activists as 'incensed' utilises the stereotype of vegans as angry, a characterisation often used to discredit proponents of social justice movements. This is a mistaking of object for subject in the reference to 'farmed meat "meant to run in the wild"', since 'meat' is incapable of running (and less obviously, 'meat' is not 'farmed', a process imposed on beings, including the deer served at the restaurant, while living).[43] Reducing nonhuman individuals to 'meat' even while alive is a kind of speciesist metonym (a metonym occurring when part of an entity or process stands in for the whole; in this case, the end product 'meat' stands in for the whole animal's lifetime of experiences).[44] The journalist's presentation of the phrase, with only 'meant to run in the wild' in quotes and not 'meat', suggests that this illogical wording is a product of the journalist's rather than the activists' rhetoric. That foie gras requires torturous force-feeding of birds is not mentioned; later the article notes that 'the restaurant served foie gras, the dish made from the liver of fattened ducks or geese that has long drawn complaints', using the euphemism 'fattened' and calling objections to this reprehensible practice 'complaints', which portrays ethical responsiveness as something closer to personal grievance.

After setting up this scenario of unsympathetically portrayed vegans protesting at a restaurant labelled 'locavore' (an attribute likely to resonate positively with many members of the public, especially in comparison to the descriptor 'vegan'), the article continues:

---

42   Rosenberg 2018.
43   On mistaking of the object 'meat' for a sentient subject, see Cole 2016, pp. 109–110, 112–113.
44   On the use of similar speciesist metonyms in animal agriculture trade publications, see Stibbe 2001, pp. 154–155.

Then came the counterprotest. Michael Hunter, a chef and co-owner of the restaurant, appeared in its window with a raw deer leg and a sharp knife, when he began to carve up the meat in full view of the protesters, some of whom later said they were disturbed for days, according to news reports. 'I figured, I'll show them,' Hunter told the Globe and Mail. 'I'm going to have my own protest.'[45]

Framing the exhibition of a dominant cultural identity – that of 'meat'-eater – as a 'protest' entails abandoning a politicised definition of *protest* as a challenge to dominant ideologies and practices. It implies that butchering and eating other-animal bodies is radical or countercultural, when in fact nothing could be more conformist. The mention of the actual protesters being 'disturbed for days' (contradicted elsewhere by protester Marni Ugar[46]) encourages a schadenfreude delight at their humiliation and alleged traumatisation. The article makes clear later that Hunter is 'an avid hunter', a masculinised identity which cements his association with locavore (and in the minds of some, 'ethical') 'meat'-eating.

The protesters' viewpoints were poorly represented here and in other mainstream US news sources,[47] but a search through 'independent' media[48] uncovered an in-depth interview with two of the protesters on *Unilad*, a UK-based 'news and opinion' website. Although

---

45   Rosenberg 2018.
46   Marsh (2018) reported for *The Guardian*: 'Marni Ugar, the activist who planned the original protest, insists the whole incident has been sensationalised by media that saw outraged vegans as irresistible fodder for news. Ugar says she and her fellow activists were not as appalled as a number of local headlines made them out to be. 'Everyone thinks the vegans were freaking out. We weren't,' she says. 'I go to vigils at slaughterhouses,' Ugar says. 'I've seen so much worse. Chickens and cows en route to slaughter, missing limbs, alive. The deer, at least, was no longer suffering' (Marsh 2018).
47   Texts examined included the *Washington Post* article under discussion and similar pieces in the *New York Post* (Seidel 2018) and *The Daily Meal* (Rock 2018).
48   I place 'independent' in quotes because virtually all media outlets, including those outside the mainstream press, have advertising revenue from and promotional tie-ins with corporate sponsors. See for example the subsequent note concerning *Unilad*'s recent partnership with McDonald's.

its glib headline, 'Restaurant owner tucks into steak in front of vegan protesters', marks an inauspicious start, *Unilad*'s article generously quoted organiser Marni Ugar, who reflected:

> I chose Antler because their patrons feel good about eating ethical meat. I believe there's no such thing; for that one animal, no matter what kind of animal and how they were raised, that's their life and they don't want to die. We're being attacked for protesting a small business who has a couple of vegan options however, if they were serving dogs and cats with vegan options, there would be an outcry of support. When Michael came to the window carving into the leg of a deer, he looked like a crazed man unravelling in front of us, taunting a group who were there because they care about animal welfare.[49]

Ugar's explanation of her rationale, her calling attention to the contradictions inherent in many Westerners' idealisation of dogs and cats and discounting of the interests of equally sensitive animals exploited for food, and her disquieting description of the chef/hunter as he unfurled his aggression upon the 'meat' at least open the way for audiences to ponder veganism's challenge to speciesism rather than dismissing the incident as a sensationalistic conflict. *Unilad* also quoted Len Goldberg, identified as an activist videographer for the protest:

> It's enough the poor deer had her life taken and had her family destroyed. That was an individual, she may have had a family, she may have had children, she may have had a partner. She had her herd, her friends, her personality, her desires, her feelings, her wants, her fears, her loves, her character, her heart, her soul.

---

49 Tailor 2018. Despite this rare inclusion of pro-animal-rights perspectives when reporting on the Antler protest, *Unilad* should not be mistaken for a pro-vegan platform. A more recent article is essentially an advertisement for McDonald's products targeted at World Cup 2018 enthusiasts; it explicitly discloses a financial partnership between the website and the fast food juggernaut: 'In further celebration of the World Cup, McDonald's has also partnered up with UNILAD to create the ultimate tray so you can watch the footie with your mates in style' (Murry 2018).

It's enough all of that was taken from her, but now we have her body being defiled and degraded to taunt people who ... simply advocated for her kind. We chose that particular location to do our vegan outreach because that restaurant goes beyond the profound problem of serving the bodies of murdered animals, to actually celebrating the murder of animals.[50]

By using the personal pronouns *her* and *she* for the deer (rather than the impersonal 'it' conventionally used for nonhuman animals in mainstream discourses); attributing to her emotions, relationships and a soul; and pointing out the hypocrisy of the restaurant's 'humane' posturing, Goldberg presents an anti-speciesist perspective rarely seen in mainstream media.

Instead of including such views, mainstream US news engaged in mudslinging and shallow conflict frames, helping to instigate an anti-vegan backlash in response to the Antler protest story. For instance, the *Washington Post* article discussed earlier included a link to the protesters' Facebook event page, reporting that the page 'has since been inundated with comments, many harshly critical of their cause',[51] and also featured a punchline ending about the restaurant's increased popularity following the incident, including a screenshot of a Twitter post by US comedian Patton Oswalt: 'Next time I'm in Toronto I'm dining at Antler.'[52] These rhetorical choices invite news audiences to harass 'the vegans' and to feel reaffirmed in eating 'meat', since a minor celebrity tells them it is acceptable and even (in Oswalt's likely estimation of his own wittiness at least) clever to brag about doing so.

The most sensationalistic image of this story, which helped impel its widespread media coverage, is Hunter's public hacking of a dead deer's leg as a form of supposed psychological warfare against vegans. One might interpret his displaced violence against 'meat' as a visible proxy for violence against living animals. Carol Adams' concept of the *absent referent* (the absence of the identity and life story of the

---

50   Tailor 2018.
51   Rosenberg 2018.
52   Rosenberg 2018.

nonhuman animal killed for 'meat') sheds light on the politics of visibility this entails. In a 2013 interview, Adams argued:

> The locavore movement and other friendly slaughter assertions are not making the entirety of the (dead) animal visible. The animal's history is what is not available, it is not available to us to know exactly how she lived her life, nor how she experienced her death. What we have is the pretence and premise that sufficient information is available for us to conclude that eating her dead body is okay.[53]

Adams' analysis exposes the ruse of visibility leveraged to quell discussion about violence and exploitation. Slashing the deer's leg in a storefront window can be seen as flaunting 'ethical' slaughter's most powerful public-relations tool; that is, its claim to make the process transparent. However, as Adams notes, what is absolutely not visible is the animal's life and subjectivity, erased through her reduction to 'meat' and, in the case of Hunter's display and the media's reporting, a mere 'leg'.

Also discernible here is the intersection of culturally conditioned codes of masculinity with the positioning of meat-eating as normative. Speaking about the visibility of other animals killed in locavorism and hunting, Adams finds that 'the performative value of killing is working to communicate not just something about humans against domesticated animals, but about gender ... The need to make "the kill" present ... is a hypermasculine reinscription of the sexual politics of meat.'[54] Hunter's exhibition of his dominion over the deer's fragmented body in order to antagonise vegans is a fitting instance of this gendered reinscription of carnivory's supremacy. Although not actually killing the deer in that moment, his public butchering is readable as a re-presentation of the killing that happened offstage (he is an 'avid hunter' after all); either way, the deer's life and subjectivity are rendered irrelevant. This absence of nonhuman animals' identities and subjectivity is an overriding feature of anti-vegan discourse's maintenance of speciesist ideology.

---

53 Adams 2013, p. 120.
54 Adams 2013, p. 121.

Conclusion

Through a rhetoric that deflects the ethical dimensions of veganism in favour of a concept of nonhuman animal-product consumption as a matter of personal choice, mainstream news stories about vegans legitimise 'meat'-eating while denying or minimising the harms inflicted on nonhuman animals. They implicitly and explicitly portray vegans as cultural others, creating an identification between non-vegan journalists and readers by focusing on vegans' supposed personal characteristics rather than substantially citing the ethical views of vegans themselves. This has the effect of reaffirming the speciesist ideologies central to current capitalist power structures, of which the mass media are an integral part.

Given the embeddedness of dominant media with these ideologies, it may be unrealistic to expect improved coverage of veganism, at least until public opinion turns more pervasively against the exploitation of other animals and many vegans themselves occupy positions as prominent journalists. In the meantime, it is worth outlining a preliminary, albeit incomplete, list of recommendations based on the foregoing analysis. To improve representations of veganism, journalists might:

- Clearly define veganism as an ethical philosophy based on nonviolence rather than merely a diet or personal-health issue.
- Include in-depth commentary from ethical vegans, including noted experts where appropriate.
- Consider whether clichés characterising vegans as 'proselytizing', 'incensed', irrational or unhealthy are truthful, and whether they are at least balanced with portrayals of the diverse and positive behaviours and traits seen among vegans.
- Take more seriously the perspectives of nonhuman animals by personalising them and giving weight to their suffering whenever possible, rather than dismissing their moral importance in a discussion centred on human interests.
- Acknowledge that individuals' food decisions have tremendous impacts on human and nonhuman beings other than the consumer, thus avoiding the inaccurate framing of food as purely a matter of personal choice.

- Take vegan readers into account by acknowledging their perspectives, explicitly or tacitly, rather than assuming news audiences are entirely non-vegan.

For an extensive resource on covering issues related to nonhuman animals and their advocates, journalists can consult www.animalsandmedia.org, authored by Debra Merskin and Carrie P. Freeman (n.d.), which contains a host of insightful recommendations, including style guidelines.

As veganism grows and the public becomes increasingly disillusioned with the inherent cruelties of animal agriculture, these changes are likely to become evident, however gradually. Until then, educating media consumers to be more aware of the speciesist bias in media texts is a step in the right direction.

References

Adams, C. (2013). Interview by Lindgren Johnson and Susan Thomas. *Journal of Critical Animal Studies* 11(1), 108–132.

Almiron, N., M. Cole and C. P. Freeman (Eds.) (2016). *Critical Animal and Media Studies*. New York: Routledge.

Bohanec, H. (2013). *The Ultimate Betrayal: Is There Happy Meat?* Bloomington, IN: iUniverse.

Brody, J. (2015). Fear, not facts, support GMO-free food. *New York Times*. 8 June. https://nyti.ms/32h5QDr

Brody, J. (2017). Good vegan, bad vegan. *New York Times*. 2 October. https://www.nytimes.com/2017/10/02/well/eat/good-vegan-bad-vegan.html

Chomsky, N. (2002). *Manufacturing Consent*. New York: Pantheon Books.

Cole, M. (2016). Getting 'green' beef: Anti-vegan rhetoric and the legitimizing of eco-friendly oppression. In N. Almiron, M. Cole and C. P. Freeman (Eds.), *Critical animal and media studies* (pp. 107–123). New York: Routledge.

Cole, M. and K. Morgan (2011). Vegaphobia: Derogatory discourses of veganism and the reproduction of speciesism in UK national newspapers. *British Journal of Sociology* 62(1), 134–153.

Cornell College of Agriculture and Life Sciences (n.d.). A Brief History of CALS. https://cals.cornell.edu/about/history

Davis, K. (2018). The disengagement of journalistic discourse about nonhuman animals: An analysis. In A. Matsuoka and J. Sorenson (Eds.), *Critical Animal*

Studies: Toward Trans-Species Social Justice (pp. 73–93). London: Rowman & Littlefield.

Freeman, C. P. (2009). This little piggy went to press: The American news media's construction of animals in agriculture. In N. Almiron, M. Cole and C. P. Freeman (Eds.), *Critical Animal and Media Studies* (pp. 169–184). New York: Routledge.

Glaser, C., C. Romaniello, and K. Moskowitz (2015). Costs and consequences: The real price of livestock grazing on America's public lands. *Center for Biological Diversity*. https://bit.ly/3aP2r2B

Goodland, R. and J. Anhang (2009). Livestock and climate change. World Watch Institute. *World Watch Magazine* 22(6).

Grillo, R. (2016). *Farm to Fable: The Fictions of Our Animal Consuming Culture.* Danvers: Vegan Publishers.

Hyner, C. (2015). A leading cause of everything: One industry that is destroying our planet and our ability to thrive on it. *Harvard Environmental Law Review Syndicate*. 26 October.

Joy, M. (2014). Carnism: why eating animals is a social justice issue. In W. Tuttle (Ed.), *Circles of Compassion*. Davners: Vegan Publishers.

Marsh, C. (2018). Chef who butchered a deer leg in front of vegan protesters: 'we won't change'. *The Guardian*. 12 April. https://bit.ly/3aPXCG8

McChesney, R. (2015). *Rich Media, Poor Democracy*. New York: The New Press.

Melina, V., W. Craig and S. Levin (2016). Position of the academy of nutrition and dietetics: Vegetarian diets. *Journal of the Academy of Nutrition and Dietetics* 116(12), 1970–1980.

Merskin, D. and C. P. Freeman (n.d.). Animals and media: A style guide for giving voice to the voiceless. *Animals and Media*. http://www.animalsandmedia.org/main/

Murry, E. (2018). McDonald's launch 15 piece shareboxes of chicken selects and cheese bites. *Unilad*. 8 June. https://bit.ly/2Eu68yq

New York Times (n.d.) Jane E. Brody. https://www.nytimes.com/by/jane-e-brody

Nibert, D. (2011). Origins and consequences of the animal industrial complex. In S. Best, R. Kahn, A. J. Nocella II and P. McLaren (Eds.), *The Global Industrial Complex* (pp. 197–209). Lanham: Lexington Books.

Nibert, D. (2013). *Animal Oppression and Human Violence*. New York: Columbia University Press.

Nibert, D. (2017). Introduction. In D. Nibert (Ed.), *Animal Oppression and Capitalism* (pp. xi–xxv). Santa Barbara: Prager.

Nickerson, C., R. Ebel, A. Borchers, and F. Carriazo (2011). Major uses of land in the United States, 2007. *United States Department of Agriculture: Economic Research Service* 89, June. https://bit.ly/2Qk4G4q

Noske, B. (1997). *Beyond Boundaries: Humans and Animals*. Montreal: Black Rose Books.

Poore, J. and T. Nemecek (2018). Reducing food's environmental impacts through producers and consumers. *Science* 360, 987–992.

Rock, T. (2018). Toronto chef carves dead deer in front of animal rights protesters. *The Daily Meal*. 28 March. https://bit.ly/3gwkFap

Rosenberg, E. (2018). The vegans came to protest his restaurant. So this chef carved a deer leg in the window. *Washington Post*. 28 March. https://wapo.st/3aQ8xQ9

Seidel, J. (2018). This chef was ruthless in trying to shut up his vegan protesters. *New York Post*. 3 April. https://bit.ly/3hpTQ8O

Severson, K. (2017). Black vegans step out, for their health and other causes. *New York Times*. 28 November. https://www.nytimes.com/2017/11/28/dining/black-vegan-cooking.html

Sorenson, J. (2016). *Constructing Ecoterrorism: Capitalism, Speciesism and Animal Rights*. Black Point, Nova Scotia: Fernwood Books.

Stănescu, V. (2010). 'Green' eggs and ham? The myth of sustainable meat and the danger of the local. *Journal for Critical Animal Studies* 58(1/2), 8–32.

Steinfeld, H., P. Gerber, T. D. Wassenaar, V. Castel, M. Rosales, and C. de Haan (2006). *Livestock's long shadow: Environmental issues and options*. Rome: Food & Agriculture Organization of the United Nations.

Stibbe, A. (2001). Language, power, and the social construction of animals. *Society & Animals* 9(2), 145–161.

Tailor, N. (2018). Restaurant owner tucks into steak in front of vegan protesters. *Unilad*. 27 March. https://bit.ly/2YqMFFS

Tuttle, W. (2016). *The World Peace Diet*. New York: Lantern Books.

Vegan Society (n.d.). Definition of veganism. https://www.vegansociety.com/go-vegan/definition-veganism

What the Health (n.d.) Sources and statistics. http://www.whatthehealthfilm.com/facts/

Zaraska, M. (2016). *Meathooked*. New York: Basic Books.

Zaraska, M. (2017a). Skip the veganism lecture today. *New York Daily News*. 23 November. https://bit.ly/2EbBfze

Zaraska, M. (2017b). Why is mankind obsessed with meat? [video]. 6 September 2017. https://www.youtube.com/watch?v=3craFw_NcP0

9
Veganism and Mi'kmaq legends

Margaret Robinson

This article proposes a postcolonial eco-feminist reading of Mi'kmaq legends as the basis for a vegan diet rooted in Indigenous culture. I refer primarily to veganism throughout this work because unlike vegetarianism, it is not only a diet but a lifestyle that, for ethical reasons, eschews the use of animal products. Constructing an Aboriginal veganism faces two significant barriers – the first being the association of veganism with whiteness.

In a joke at the beginning of his documentary, *Redskins, Tricksters and Puppy Stew*, Ojibwa playwright Drew Hayden Taylor asks, 'What do you call a Native vegetarian?' His answer: 'A very bad hunter.'[1] The implication is that for an Aboriginal person, choosing a non-meat diet is a kind of failure. In *Stuff White People Like*, satirical author Christian Lander portrays veganism as a tactic for maintaining white supremacy. He writes: 'As with many white-people activities, being vegan/ vegetarian enables them to feel as though they are helping the environment and it gives them a sweet way to feel superior to others.'[2] Ecologist Robert Hunter depicts vegans as 'Eco-Jesuits' and 'veggie fundamentalists' who 'force Natives to do things the white man's way.'[3]

---

1   Taylor 2000b. See also Taylor 200a.
2   Lander 2008, p. 38.
3   Hunter 1999, pp. 100–113.

By projecting white imperialism onto vegans, Hunter enables white omnivores, such as himself, to bond with Aboriginal people over meat-eating. When veganism is constructed as white, Aboriginal people who eschew the use of animal products are depicted as sacrificing our cultural authenticity. This presents a challenge for those of us who view our veganism as ethically, spiritually and culturally compatible with our indigeneity.

A second barrier to Aboriginal veganism is the portrayal of veganism as a product of class privilege. Opponents claim that a vegan diet is an indulgence since the poor (among whom Aboriginal people are disproportionately represented) must eat whatever is available and cannot afford to be so picky. This argument assumes that highly processed specialty products make up the bulk of a vegan diet. Such an argument also overlooks the economic and environmental cost of meat, and assumes that the subsidised meat and dairy industries in North America are representative of the world.

My proposal is not that we replace a vibrant traditional food culture with one associated with privileged white culture. The eating habits of the majority of the Mi'kmaq have already been colonised, and are further complicated by poverty. As a participant in Bonita Lawrence's study of mixed-blood urban Native identity explained, 'people have been habituated to think that poverty is Native – and so your macaroni soup and your poor diet is Native.'[4] Lack of access to nutrient-rich foods is a problem Aboriginal people have in common with other racialised and economically oppressed groups. Konju Briggs Jr. argues, 'In the US, poor communities of colour are often bereft of access to fresh healthy foods, and disproportionately find themselves afflicted with the diseases of Western diets and lifestyles'. He identifies this as a tactic of class warfare, aimed at 'keeping the most chronically impoverished from being able to be healthy, long-lived and highly functioning, and from excelling as human beings'.[5] Several researchers have noted that the reserve system has begotten a diet high in sugar and carbohydrates and low in protein and fibre.[6] As a result, Mi'kmaq

---

4   Lawrence 2004, p. 235.
5   Briggs 2010, p. 28.
6   Johnson, Williams & Weldon 1977; Mi'kmaq Health Research Group 2007.

people have seen a serious increase in obesity, diabetes mellitus and gallstones. Professor of human ecology Kim Travers cites three causes of nutrient-poor diet among the Mi'kmaq: low income, lack of access to transportation, and reserve land unsuitable for agriculture, fishing or hunting. Travers notes that Mi'kmaq people living on reserve are often limited to eating highly processed protein such as peanut butter, wieners or bologna.

Traditionally, the Mi'kmaq diet was meat-heavy, consisting of beaver, fish, eel, birds, porcupine and sometimes larger animals such as whales, moose or caribou, supplemented by vegetables, roots, nuts and berries. The use of animals as food also figures prominently in our Mi'kmaq legends. Food production is gendered in Mi'kmaq culture. While women were trained in food gathering, cleaning and preparation, hunting was a traditionally male activity connected with the maintenance of virility. The killing of a moose acted as a symbol of a boy's entry into manhood.[7] To reject such practices undercuts methods of male Mi'kmaq identity construction. Yet the context in which this identity develops has changed significantly since the arrival of the European colonialists. Meat, as a symbol of patriarchy shared with colonising forces, arguably binds us with white colonial culture to a greater degree than practices such as veganism, which, although overwhelmingly white itself, is far from hegemonic.

Carol J. Adams argues that the creation of meat as a concept requires the removal from our consciousness of the animal whose dead body we are redefining as food. Adams writes:

> The function of the absent referent is to keep our 'meat' separated from any idea that she or he was once an animal ... to keep some*thing* from being seen as some*one*. Once the existence of meat is disconnected from the existence of an animal who was killed to become that 'meat,' meat becomes unanchored by its original referent (the animal) becoming instead a free-floating image, used often to reflect women's status as well as animals'.[8]

---

7   Wallis & Wallis 1955, p. 255.
8   Adams 1990, pp. 14–15.

While evident in the fur trade, the fishing industry and factory farming, the detachment that Adams describes is not foundational to the Mi'kmaq oral tradition. In our stories, the othering of animal life that makes meat-eating psychologically comfortable is replaced by a model of creation in which animals are portrayed as our siblings. Mi'kmaq legends view humanity and animal life as being on a continuum, spiritually and physically. Animals speak, are able to change into humans, and some humans marry these shapeshifting creatures and raise animal children.[9] Human magicians may take animal form, some people may transform into their *teomul*, or totem animal, and still others are changed into animals against their wishes.[10] An eco-feminist exegesis of Mi'kmaq legends enables us to frame veganism as a spiritual practice that recognises that humans and other animals possess a shared personhood.

Mi'kmaq legends portray human beings as intimately connected with the natural world, not as entities distinct from it. Glooscap is formed from the red clay of the soil and initially lacks mobility, remaining on his back in the dirt.[11] His grandmother was originally a rock, his nephew sea foam and his mother a leaf. In the legend 'Nukumi and Fire', the Creator makes an old woman from a dew-covered rock. Glooscap meets her and she agrees to become his grandmother, providing wisdom for him if he will provide food for her. Nukumi explains that as an old woman meat is necessary for her because she cannot live on plants and berries alone. Glooscap calls to Marten, and asks him to give his life so Glooscap's grandmother may live. Marten

---

9   See, for example, 'The Magical Coat, Shoes and Sword' and 'The History of Usitebulajoo' in Rand 1893/2005a.

10   For the transformation of magicians, see 'Robbery and Murder Revenged', 'Glooscap and Megumoowesoo', 'The Small Baby and The Big Bird', 'The Adventures of Katoogwasees', 'The Adventures of Ababejit, an Indian Chief and Magician of the Micmac Tribe' and 'The Liver-Colored Giants and Magicians' in Rand 1893/2005a and 'Glooscap, Kuhkw, and Coolpujot' in Rand 1893/2005b. For *teomul* transformations, see 'The Magical Dancing Doll', 'The History of Usitebulajoo', 'The Invisible Boy', 'The Adventures of Ababejit, an Indian Chief and Magician of the Micmac Tribe' and 'The Two Weasels' in Rand 1893/2005a. For unwilling transformations, see 'The Boy That Was Transformed into a Horse' and 'Two Weasels' in that same volume.

11   Burke 2005a; Burke 2005b; Burke 2005c; Augustine 2012.

agrees because of his friendship with Glooscap. For this sacrifice, Glooscap makes Marten his brother. Based on this story, Glooscap, the archetype of the human being, would appear to have not been a hunter prior to the arrival of his grandmother. This story also represents, through the characters of Glooscap and Marten, the basic relation of the Mi'kmaq people with the creatures around them. The animals are willing to provide food and clothing, shelter and tools, but always they must be treated with the respect given a brother and friend.

A Mi'kmaq creation story tells of the birth of Glooscap's nephew from sea foam caught in sweetgrass.[12] To celebrate the nephew's arrival, Glooscap and his family have a feast of fish. Glooscap calls upon the salmon of the rivers and seas to come to shore and give up their lives. Although not unproblematic, this dynamic is at least open to the possibility of refusal on the part of the animal. As well, the story undermines the widespread view that humans have an innate right to use animal flesh as food. Glooscap and his family do not want to kill all the animals for their survival, indicating moderation in their fishing practices. The theme is one of dependence, not dominion. Human survival is the justification for the death of Glooscap's animal friends. The animals have independent life, their own purpose and their own relationships with the creator. They are not made for food, but willingly become food as a sacrifice for their friends. This is a far cry from the perspective of the white colonial hunter, in which animals are constructed as requiring population control, turning slaughter into a service performed rather than one received.

An interesting exception to this thread is the Wabanaki story of 'Glooscap and His People', which blames the animals themselves for man's aggression towards them. In this tale Malsum, an evil counterpart to Glooscap, turns the animals against Glooscap. Glooscap announces: 'I made the animals to be man's friends, but they have acted with selfishness and treachery. Hereafter, they shall be your servants and provide you with food and clothing.'[13] The original vision of harmony is lost, and inequality takes its place as the punishment for listening to Malsum. In this way, the story is similar to the Genesis story of the

---

12   Augustine 2012.
13   Hill 1963, p. 24.

expulsion of Adam and Eve from the Garden of Eden. Glooscap shows the men how to make bows, arrows and spears, and shows the women how to scrape hides and make clothing.

'Now you have power over even the largest wild creatures', he said. 'Yet I charge you to use this power gently. If you take more game than you need for food and clothing, or kill for the pleasure of killing, then you will be visited by a pitiless giant named Famine.'[14] Even in this story, which attempts to justify dominion, the proper relation to the animals is only for food and clothing. Exceptions to this principle appear in stories where a malevolent human magician has taken the form of an animal. In these cases, the protagonists often kill the animal without purpose other than defeating their human enemy. These stories characterise animals as independent people with rights, wills and freedom. If animal consent is required to justify their consumption, then it opens the possibility that such consent may be revoked. Overfishing, overhunting and the wholesale destruction of their natural habitat could certainly give the animals cause to rethink the bargain.

Another feature of Mi'kmaq stories is the regret that comes with animal death. In 'The Legend of the Wild Goose', Glooscap is concerned for the safety of the small migrating birds and charges the Canada Goose with their protection. In 'Nukumi and Fire', Glooscap snaps Marten's neck and places him on the ground but immediately regrets his actions. Nukumi speaks to the Creator and Marten comes back to life and returns to his home in the river. On the ground now lays the body of another marten. This story is far from a straightforward tale of why we eat animals. Marten is both dead and alive: dead as a marten available for consumption by the grandmother, but alive as Marten, the friend of Glooscap and his people. 'The Adventures of Katoogwasees' tells how Glooscap's grandmother used magic to obtain unlimited amounts of beaver meat from a single bone, reflecting a wish for abundance disconnected from the need to hunt.[15]

Regret and kinship also feature in the story of 'Muin, The Bear's Child'. In one version of this tale a young boy, Siko, is trapped in a cave

---

14   Hill 1963, p. 24.
15   Rand 1893/2005b, p. 200–211. See also 'Glooscap and the Megumwesoo' and 'The Magical Food, Belt, and Flute', in Rand 1893/2005b.

by his evil stepfather and left to die. The animals hear him crying and attempt to save him, but only the bear is strong enough to move the rocks blocking the cave entrance. Siko is adopted and raised as a bear. Later, Siko's bear family is attacked by hunters and his mother is killed. He addresses the hunters: 'I am a human, like you. Spare the she-cub, my adopted sister.' The amazed hunters put down their weapons and gladly spare the cub. In addition, they are sorry for having killed the bear who had been so good to Siko. Here we see that regret at animal death is contextualised in the kinship relation between humans and animals. At the end of the story Siko declares: 'I shall be called Muin, the bear's son, from this day forwards. And when I am grown, and a hunter, never will I kill a mother bear, or bear children!' And Muin never did.

This regret is also expressed in rituals surrounding the act of hunting. Mi'kmaq Elder Murdena Marshall describes one such ritual, a dance 'to thank the spirit of the animal for giving its life for food. In the dance, one displays hunting abilities and skills through a re-enactment of the hunt. People sing and share stories as the dance is performed.'[16] In contrast to the enlightenment view of humans as distinguished from animals by speech and thought, here animals are not only capable of thought and speech, they can also be said to be persons. The value of the animal lies not in its utility to man but in its very essence as a living being.

Not all Mi'kmaq food traditions centre upon meat. Glooscap's mother was a leaf on a tree given life and human form by the sun.[17] The feast celebrating her birth is entirely vegetarian, consisting of plants, roots, berries, nuts and fruit, and the nephew, whose role is usually that of hunter, becomes the gatherer in this instance. If we recognise that activities traditionally performed by Mi'kmaq women, such as fruit, vegetable and nut gathering, are also fully Aboriginal traditions then we can form Indigenous counternarratives to the promotion of meat.

The values obtained from an eco-feminist exegesis of Mi'kmaq stories can serve as a starting point for an Indigenous veganism. The personhood of animals, their self-determination and our regret at their death all show that choosing not to ask for their sacrifice is a legitimately

---

16   Confederacy of Mainland Mi'kma 2001, p. 80.
17   Augustine 2012.

Aboriginal option. Since the consumption of animals for food, clothing and shelter is no longer necessary, as vegan culture testifies, then the Mi'kmaq tradition, as manifested in our legends, suggests that hunting and killing our animal brothers is no longer authorised.

Because Aboriginal people are the targets of genocide, the cultural practices we adopt or reject are vitally important. Bonita Lawrence notes that daily life practices have historically been used to assess the authenticity of Native identity claims and accord Indian status.[18] Some may argue that the embodiment of Mi'kmaq values into new practices, such as veganism, is not a legitimate development, and may even threaten the ways our treaty rights are assessed by others. Yet those who value only the preservation of an unchanging tradition join with the colonial powers in seeing no place for a contemporary indigeneity. There is more to our culture and to our relationship with the land, particularly as women, than hunting and killing animals.

The modern commercial fishery, often touted as offering economic security for Aboriginal communities, is actually further removed from our Mi'kmaq values than modern-day vegan practices are. The former views fish as objects to be collected for exchange, with economic power taking the place of sustenance, while the latter is rooted in a relationship with the animals based on respect and responsibility. Again, the theme is one of necessity, not pleasure. If women initiated the hunt, as in the story of Glooscap's grandmother, then surely changing circumstances can empower us to end it.

One must also be aware of changing circumstances and needs among the Mi'kmaq population. Few of us can sustain ourselves through traditional hunting, fishing or gathering. As research shows, those Mi'kmaq people living on reserve are usually dependent on store-bought food. In addition, half of Canada's Aboriginal population live in urban areas.[19] When Aboriginality is defined as a primordial lifestyle, it reflects our intentional extinction as a people.

The reinterpretation of tradition and the malleability of ritual enabled our ancestors to survive genocide, famine, disease, forced moves, isolation on reserves, residential schooling and a host of other

18   Lawrence 2004, p. 4.
19   Siggner & Costa 2005, p. 8.

colonial ills. Similarly, we must find ways to adapt to the increasing individuality of urban life. One solution is to embody our traditional values in new rituals. With the adoption of a vegan diet, our meal preparation and consumption can become infused with transcendent significance, as we recall our connection with other animals, our shared connection to the Creator, and prefigure a time when we can live in harmony with the animals, as Glooscap did before the invention of hunting. Shared food practices, values and daily life rituals can create ties between Aboriginal people that help counteract the isolation and individualism of urban life. Veganism offers us a sense of belonging to a moral community whose principles are made concrete through daily practices that are in keeping with the values of our ancestors, even if they may be at odds with their traditional practice.

At stake in the creation of an Aboriginal veganism is the authority of Aboriginal people, especially women, to determine cultural authenticity for ourselves. Dominant white discourse portrays our cultures as embedded in the pre-colonial past. This perspective must be replaced with the recognition that Aboriginal cultures are living traditions, responsive to changing social and environmental circumstances. In retelling our stories, bringing postcolonial and eco-feminist interpretations to them, or in creating new stories, Aboriginal women claim authority over our oral traditions. In doing so, we recognise that our oral culture is not fixed in time and space, but is adaptable to our needs, to the needs of our animal siblings and to the needs of the land itself.

References

Adams, C. J. (1990). *The Sexual Politics of Meat* (10th ed.). New York: Continuum.

Augustine, S. (2012). 'Mi'kmaq Transcript.' *Four Directions Teaching 2006–2012.* http://www.fourdirectionsteachings.com/transcripts/mikmaq.html

Briggs Jr., K. (2010). Veganism is a revolutionary force in the class war. *The Scavenger.* 12 September. http://thescavenger.net/social-justice-sp-24912/animals/461-veganism-is-a-revolutionary-force-in-the-class-war-32867.html

Burke, P. (2005a). Native American Legends: Muin, The Bear's Child. *First People: The Legends.* https://bit.ly/2FSrJ4r

Burke, P. (2005b). Native American Legends: Nukumi and Fire. *First People: The Legends*. https://bit.ly/2FSkJV9

Burke, P. (2005c). Mikmaq Legend of the Wild Goose. *First People: The Legends*. https://bit.ly/2YrrfZx

Confederacy of Mainland Mi'kmaq (2001). *Mikwíte'lmanej Mikmaqu'k: Let Us Remember the Old Mi'kmaq*. Halifax, NS: Nimbus Publishing.

Hill, K. (1963). *Glooscap and His Magic: Legends of the Wabanaki Indians*. New York: Dodd, Mead & Company.

Hunter, R. (1999). *Red Blood: One (Mostly) White Guy's Encounters with the Native World*. Toronto: McClelland & Stewart.

Johnson, J. L., C. N. Williams and K. L. M. Weldon (1977). Nutrient intake and meal patterns of Micmac Indian and Caucasian women in Shubenacadie, NS. *Canadian Medical Association Journal* 116(12), 1356–59.

Lander, C. (2008). *Stuff White People Like: The Definitive Guide to the Unique Taste of Millions*. New York: Random House.

Lawrence, B. (2004). *'Real' Indians and Others: Mixed-blood Urban Native Peoples and Indigenous Nationhood*. Vancouver: University of British Columbia Press.

Mi'kmaq Health Research Group (2007). *The Health of The Nova Scotia Mi'kmaq Population*. Sydney, NS: Union of Nova Scotia Indians.

Rand, S. T. (1893/2005a). *Legends of the Micmacs. Volume I*. West Orange, NJ: Invisible Books.

Rand, S. T. (1893/2005b). *Legends of the Micmacs. Volume II*. West Orange, NJ: Invisible Books.

Siggner, A. J. and R. Costa (2005). *Aboriginal Conditions in Census Metropolitan Areas, 1981–2001* [Statistics Canada Catalogue 89–613-MIE –008]. Ottawa, Ont.: Statistics Canada, 2005.

Taylor, D. H. (2000a). Real Natives don't eat tofu. *Now Magazine*. 13 July. https://nowtoronto.com/news/real-natives-dont-eat-tofu/

Taylor, D. H. (2000b). *Redskins, Tricksters and Puppy Stew* [film]. Toronto: National Film Board of Canada.

Travers, K. D. (1995). Using qualitative research to understand the sociocultural origins of diabetes among Cape Breton Mi'kmaq. *Chronic Diseases in Canada* 16(4).

Wallis, W. D. and R. O. Wallis (1955). *The Micmac Indians of Eastern Canada*. Minneapolis: University of Minnesota Press.

10

Nonhuman animal labour and transformative dialogue: (Re)worlding meat

C. Vail Fletcher and Alexa M. Dare

Many omnivores understand the toll that meat wreaks on the planet, and we can't help but feel the tension between loving animals in the abstract while eating them with abandon on the plate. All of this creates feelings of defensiveness, so when a vegan comes along, their very presence seems like an affront. To an omnivore, every vegan looks like a preachy vegan.[1] This chapter was inspired by the authors' frustration with the often-formulaic ways public discourses and dinner table conversations about meat-eating are characterised by gaslighting and resistance, and our hope for a different kind of dialogue about the meat industry. Vegans and vegetarians are often demonised in everyday conversations, memes, cartoons and punchlines while carnivorism has become the global and dominant status quo. Even the Dalai Lama eats meat, performing a certain type of moral gymnastics around the Buddhist belief that animals should not be killed for food. It is no surprise, then, that the burden has been placed on non-meat-eaters to demonstrate how or why *they* do not eat nonhuman animals rather than the opposite. The typical tropes about the questionable ethics of meat-eating have effectively been scoffed at by most mainstream members of societies, and this diminishes opportunities to engage in

---

1   Manjoo 2019.

difficult debates about nonhuman animal welfare and/or nonhuman animal rights.

So, we (the authors) asked ourselves a question: How might societies and communities create opportunities for more meaningful and hopefully transformative discussions about eating meat and the meat industry without it digressing into name-calling, defensiveness and labels, among other reactions and outcomes? That is, how might societies resist the business as usual in-person and mediated conversations that benefit neither side of the argument (the 'animals being killed and eaten' side, especially), while instead resisting the 'business as usual' cruelty and exploitation germane to the meat industry?

We start this project with a provocation from an Instagram exchange that helps capture the commonly entrenched discourse we find most problematic in an effort to set the stage for the kind of resistance that might best transform both the discourse and, ultimately, the practices around meat-eating and how we think about the meat industry. Here is the exchange (condensed for brevity):

On 15 January 2018, @havstadhatco (Havstad Hat Company, run by Kate Havstad) posted a photo of her squatting over two cow skins laid out on a concrete floor. The caption states:

> two steers chris raised as bottle calves, Wayne and Garth. They were characters, they are animals we invest years of time and resources into, yes we grow fond of them. I cried and said some prayers of thanks the day they were harvested. They will feed 8 families and their extended communities, I'm proud of the life they lived with us and we will do our best to honor them and remember that the food on our plates comes with a much bigger picture attached. This day reminded me, I can not accept any meat raised or harvested in any lesser of a way. This farm continues to shape me in ways I couldn't have expected. It's not easy, but what great story was ever based around an easy journey?

Six months later, the post had 1,511 likes and 103 comments. The overwhelming majority of the comments from her now 25,000-plus followers were positive ('Agreed. If only more people where [sic] doing it that way. Beautiful.'), expressing excitement about the process ('Isn't fleshing a blast?') or speaking of/for the intentions of the cows themselves ('I cannot give thanks enough to the animals that gives itself so selflessly to help us eat and grow. They will never know how sacred they really are. Thank you.'). Then the first author of this chapter (@thecroftfarm) made the first comment that challenged the underlying assumptions of the post: 'Thanks for sharing. This will be unpopular, but you don't have to eat other sentient beings. Their lives matter greatly to them.' What followed will be familiar to most readers who have participated in or overheard a conversation about meat-eating.

The first response to @thecroftfarm's comment came from the original poster (OP) herself: '... @thecroftfarm this could lead to further conversations about what is sentient? Many studies would say plants and fungi are sentient as well, so really all that we consume is sentient.' Another follower chimes in: 'Life feeds on life. Ethically raised meat is far from being a myth. When you die other living forms will consume your remains. The end.' Then the replies begin to become more presumptuous, and the more blatant personal attacks begin: 'No point in asking you to look deeper into what organic actually means as aggressive vegans tend to hold their views like myths on a pedestal.' And then another escalation, again from the OP, Kate:

> @thecroftfarm the righteousness of aggressive vegans to call what we are doing unethical will never cease to amaze me. I knew I could count on at least a few, and I still left comments open out of true curiosity. What highly evolved ethical humans would waltz over here to be ethically rude. Bravo you further perpetrate [*sic*] my experiences with aggressive righteous vegans. Perhaps one day I'll come to your homestead and evaluate your ethics as to where all the food on your shelves come from? Oh are you typing on an iPhone? Let's start there.

Other followers join in along the way, continuing to condemn 'the vegans':

> I find it appalling that vegans will come on here and straight up deliver their OPINIONS as fact and insult a process that clearly was

an emotional experience for you. Not sure what's "ethical" about insulting someone's choice to live THEIR life the way they want.

And another comment concerned with ethics:

If vegans had to take responsibility for all the animals *ethically* raised to feed families around the world, they would quickly realise that you simply cannot keep all the animals as pets. I think this is amazing, and a true vegan would be proud of you.

Then, predictably, name-calling: 'talk about a self-righteous asshole'.

Finally, another presumably non-meat-eater (@kyleroberts) replies to the OP:

… it is the space to publicly post photos of murdered sentients and not expect any non-positive, unsupportive comments about the act and scene though, yes? And it's alright, I've spent a good chunk of my life working cattle and training up horses, I'm not some wonky outsider talking out of my rear. No one doubts you're good people, no one is name calling or being a jerk about it to you, yet the walls went up and accusations came flying. The dogma is so strong here that 'vegans' are being called self-righteous. That is an absurd notion. You kill fellow living beings, you get called out: I don't understand why someone wouldn't feel ashamed of committing such a heinous act and then showing it to 23,000 people like there's something to gain from it. It's gross, standing up for what is morally upright is not bullying.

The exchange ends with @havstadhatco editing the original post so that it starts with

**Vegan trigger warning! Unfollow now if you would describe yourself as a self righteous vegan who just can't help but express your judgements! Really, unfollow, I'm not your person*

This particular back and forth is not unusual in a culture rich with meatsplaining; rather, it is exemplary of similar dialogues online and offline that divide meat-eaters and non-meat-eaters by reinforcing a clear division between the two groups and strive to assert a hierarchy wherein one group is ethically superior to the other. While no single commenter argues that he or she is more ethical than others, the *critiques* repeatedly question the other's ethics. There is, of course, little persuasion happening here; rather, each side follows a script that ultimately entrenches a division between 'us and them'. Our motivation for this chapter, then, is a reaction to this initial provocation by looking for new ways to disrupt the tendency for human discourse to divide the world into 'us and them'.

Inspired by Donna Haraway's work in 'multispecies storytelling',[2] we examine human and nonhuman relations through the lens of labour in an attempt to suggest an alternative view of the world (what Haraway calls 'worlding') where our profound 'entanglement' with nonhumans offers possibilities for an interspecies solidarity. Our goal is to tell a different story about the complicated relations between animals – human and nonhuman – so that we might, as Haraway suggests, 'redo ways of living and dying attuned to still possible finite flourishing, still possible recuperation'.[3] Like Haraway, we are interested in telling stories that are complex and imperfect and that do not resolve easily, and suggest that this messiness can itself be a corrective to the kind of purist or divisive rhetoric perpetuated by the meat industry and evident in many conversations about meat-eating.

The meat industry relies on a well-defined division between humans and nonhumans as a central logic, and this logic infuses public and private conversations about meat. The discursive construction of 'meatsplaining' through industry rhetorical practices has implications for discourse far beyond the bounds of product advertising or lobbying. Indeed, discourse that reifies human–nonhuman divisions (and, more destructively, human exceptionalism) exists in both carnivore and much vegetarian/vegan talk, and this discourse limits possibilities for real change in nonhuman animal welfare and/or nonhuman animal

---

2   Haraway 2016, p. 10.
3   Haraway 2016, p. 10.

rights. You can see this in the Instagram exchange above, and more broadly in the way in which the concept of ethics continues to dominate so much of the talk about meat-eating. A conversation about meat that focuses on which human is more ethical does two things. First, it removes nonhuman agency from the conversation and reinforces the idea that humans, with all of our free will, are the only beings capable of acting to harm or to save nonhuman animals, whose own lives matter, but only to the extent that they might be saved or ended. Second, these ethical choices follow a neoliberal consumer logic. Despite widespread consumer familiarity with the inhumane and ecologically destructive conditions in the meat industry, the massive political and economic power of this industry rarely features in debates between meat-eaters and vegans. Elsewhere, we have shown how opposing sides in a land-use controversy both used human exceptionalism to argue for or against conservation.[4] We see a similar tendency reinforcing human–nonhuman divisions in the discourse about meat. We suggest that one way to resist human exceptionalism is to take seriously the ways in which human and nonhuman lives are deeply (and historically) intertwined, and we use human–dog relationships as a way to leverage widespread human familiarity with (and in many cultural contexts, deep affection for) dogs in the service of a more complex understanding of meat-eating and the meat industry. What if the above Instagram exchange, which occurred in the United States, involved dog skins? It is immediately easy to imagine how different this discussion might look. Our goal is to escape the traps and tropes of a 'vegans vs. carnivores' discourse (one perpetuated by the meat industry) and to imagine and model an alternative story.

Dog meat trade

The dog meat trade (DMT) is prevalent in many Asian countries, including China, Vietnam and South Korea, and while dog meat is dwarfed by cow, pig and chicken slaughter globally, it is a regionally significant part of the meat industry. Millions of dogs are killed for

---

4   Dare & Fletcher 2018.

consumption in Asia each year, even amidst a rising tide of local and international nonhuman animal rights organisations and activists giving widespread attention to the industry, and country-level bans in Singapore, Taiwan, Hong Kong and the Philippines.[5] DMT is in one sense a particularly problematic case to use in our worlding (i.e. multispecies storytelling) since it sits atop pre-existing East–West ethical landmines often linked to cultural practices and notions of difference that are steeped in racism and nationalism. And tropes of the Western gaze do not help the relevant critique rid itself of the obvious hypocrisy of Western animal-eating cultures asking Eastern animal-eating cultures to stop eating a particular animal, and neither do historical and modern legacies of colonialism.[6] There are numerous local and global organisations dedicated to ending the DMT, by focusing on rescuing individual dogs, lobbying for stronger animal cruelty laws and, more nebulously, by attempting to change cultural practices around (dog) meat-eating. Still, we think this is a powerful case for two reasons. At one level, examining the assumptions and practices of the DMT from our position in the West, we see an opportunity for revealing how individuals navigate the meat industry's framing of more common agricultural nonhuman animals (e.g. cows, pigs, chickens). The work of anti-DMT activists also provides a case for examining resistance strategies. We hope to tap into this opportunity to harness the almost sacred status of dogs to many American consumers, while carefully cradling the cultural and racial overtones that often emerge in conversations about this topic.

We are guided by a sense that traditional arguments in support of nonhuman animal welfare/rights are hobbled in their ability to make change by the powerful dual forces of capitalism and human exceptionalism. Millennia of human subjugation of the nonhuman will, alas, will not be undone with a persuasive rhetorical appeal. And yet, examples abound of human action that makes a difference and that powerfully resists the status quo (e.g. the wonderful work chronicled in this volume, such as by Toronto Pig Save, or the work done by groups

---

5 Czajkowski 2014.
6 Yan & Santos 2009.

focused on ending the DMT, such as Change for Animals Foundation or Free Korean Dogs), offering an inspiring vision of resistance. What is striking in much so-called animal activism is how it showcases human–nonhuman solidarity. Mind you, this solidarity is often masked with more human-exceptionalist tendencies such as pity towards the nonhuman and a kind of 'human saviour complex' that overemphasises human agency and neglects nonhuman agency. We believe that these discursive legacies of human exceptionalism, even among those who work tirelessly for change, contribute to an overarching sense that humans can and should make individual choices that may or may not be ethical, and that may or may not make a difference in the lives of nonhuman animals. And, importantly, that these beliefs make it very easy for consumers (and the meat industry) to use a kind of ethical relativism to resist changing their behaviours or changing the system, as with the Instagram commenters above who responded to a critique of animal slaughter with a suggestion that since 'plants are sentient, too' it would be absurd to stop eating meat on the basis of an ethical determination of sentience.

There is ample evidence of unbridled cruelty towards nonhuman animals in both the US meat industry[7] and the DMT. And despite exposés, celebrity campaigns and growing niche markets that support vegan 'lifestyles', cruelty as status quo persists. In our home state of Oregon, an anti-cruelty statute exists, yet, as with many similar statutes, it precludes protection of nonhuman agricultural animals. We see the need for a different kind of intervention, one inspired by Donna Haraway in *Staying with the Trouble*, who muses poetically that

> It matters what matters we use to think other matters with; it matters what stories we tell
> to tell other stories with; it matters what knots knot knots, what thoughts think thoughts,
> what descriptions describe descriptions, what ties tie ties. It matters what stories make
> worlds, what worlds make stories.[8]

---

7   e.g. Adams 2015.
8   Haraway 2016, p. 12.

We are inspired by a new crop of genre-bending (often feminist) writing that draws from art, philosophy, history, science fiction, ecology, biology and even quantum physics to offer different stories about the urgency of our contemporary epoch (variously characterised as the Anthropocene or the Chthulucene or the Capitolocene) and to lay the groundwork for the mass changes needed to counteract violent, degrading and world-destroying 'business as usual' practices: industrial agriculture, fossil fuel extraction and consumption, and ecosystem degradation, among others. Books like *Arts of Living on a Damaged Planet: Ghosts and Monsters of the Anthropocene* (Tsing, Swanson, Gan, Bubant), *Staying with the Trouble: Making Kin in the Chthulucene* (Haraway) and *The Mushroom at the End of the World: On the Possibility of Life in Capitalist Ruins* (Tsing) attempt to tell stories about the world that recognise how humans are deeply interconnected with nonhuman animals and ecosystems. The purpose of this storytelling is not just symbolic. The authors/editors see these more expansive views of biological interconnection as having the potential to resist capitalist/ neoliberal practices in ways that more traditional political or scientific arguments have been unsuccessful. The Instagram provocation above will likely be recognised by readers of this chapter as a familiar genre of social media exchange. Outrage and certainty drown out complexity and contradictions. Our contention is that we need to interrupt this kind of exchange, not with reasoned examples or more righteous conviction, but with a story that entangles and implicates rather than divides and separates.

We suspect that current attempts to transform the meat industry and/or cultures of meat consumption must capture the embodied, affective dimensions of cruelty in order to tell a story that resists existing tropes that excuse meat-eating and that obscure the neoliberal pressures that have shaped the meat industry. Tropes such as the 'angry vegan' and the 'natural carnivore' reinforce a false narrative of individual choice and consequence. And so we turn to our beloved dogs to help us tell a different story about human–nonhuman entanglements. Humans and dogs share ancient histories, and our lives and bodies have been intertwined in shared labour and shared affection for at least tens of thousands of years, perhaps longer. While human–dog affection can be a powerful motivator for empathy towards other nonhuman animals, and most certainly towards ending the DMT, here we turn our attention towards the concept of labour in order to tell a different kind of story of dogs and humans. In part, we were nudged towards labour by Donna Haraway, who suspects that 'we might nurture responsibility with and for other animals better by plumbing the category of labour more than the category of rights'.[9]

Nonhuman animal labour

As workers, dogs (and cows, pigs, chickens and other meat animals) are intelligible to us humans as *collaborators* in ways that pity or outrage discourses might obscure. Jason Hribal helps set the stage for this turn towards thinking about animal labour in his article, 'Animals are part of the working class':

> Since the 17th century, a great many animals have been put to work, they have produced large monetary profits, and they have received little to no compensation or recognition for their efforts. The farms, factories, roads, forests, and mines have been their sites of production. Here, they have manufactured hair, milk, flesh, and power for the farm, factory, and mine owners. And here, they are unwaged. Indeed, we can think of others who operate under similar circumstances: human slaves, children, homeworkers, sex-workers, to name a few. The basic fact is that horses, cows, or chickens have labored, and continue to labor, under the same capitalist system as humans.[10]

Thinking about animal labour helps to reveal our own similar (and different) trajectories within the capitalist system, and to think about how animals are not just victims and humans are not just perpetrators, but that we are intersected in complex webs *and* that we *all* – human and nonhuman – are every day doing the *work* that maintains this particular system, abhorrent and cruel as it is. There are surprisingly

---

9   Haraway 2008, p. 73.
10   Hribal 2003, p. 437.

few academic articles or activist initiatives that make the link between the labour conditions of slaughterhouse workers and the nonhuman animals being slaughtered for food. It seems, instead, that the plight of the workers and the plight of the animals are perceived as separate spheres of concern. There is virtually no discussion (in English) of labour or working conditions in the DMT. And yet, thinking about workers and nonhuman animals as both entwined within and beholden to capitalism offers an alternative narrative to the typical individualist consumer-choice story of meat.

One of the few researchers who examines both workers and animals, Natalie Purcell considers human–animal relations in the slaughterhouse, first through the lens of intimacy and then more broadly as comrades in a capitalist system. She considers and then rejects the idea that greater intimacy between humans and animals might disrupt the alienation of meat-eaters from meat animals. She demonstrates how slaughterhouse workers are indeed deeply intimate with cows and pigs, if intimacy is understood as being in close physical and intense emotional context, and offers example upon example of human cruelty *despite* the intimate conditions. Instead, she argues that the working conditions are related to 'profit-oriented corporate policies, including: the targeting of an economically and socially vulnerable workforce, the failure to train and care for workers adequately, and the imposition of unreasonable speed and productivity expectations'.[11] Her analysis is not meant to excuse human cruelty as much as it is intended to suggest a kind of class consciousness between human and animal labourers.

While a Marxist approach to human–nonhuman relations is tantalising, we find ourselves moved even more by the concept of emotional labour. The original definition of emotional labour focused on the emotional work that employees are required to do as part of their jobs, in terms of performing, regulating or masking certain emotions. Workers in the meat industry, like other 'dirty jobs', do emotional labour to manage the so-called 'taint' of the work.[12] We also see how

---

11   Purcell 2011, p. 72.
12   Researchers have studied taint management in such dirty jobs as the U.S. Border Patrol, prison guards and the butcher trade.

the meat industry, in its advertising and secrecy, lessens the emotional labour of the meat-eater, especially since it might be here that the true alienation created by the consumption of corpses rests. It is no surprise that widespread agricultural gag laws in the United States are a calculated response and acknowledgement of the reality that meat-eaters would not respond well to seeing nonhuman animals slaughtered – in fact, it could shatter the meat industry. The intense emotional labour experienced by slaughterhouse workers is linked to higher turnover rates, depression and interpersonal violence, among other malignant personal outcomes.[13] An employee does not have to be directly killing and/or aiding in the killing of nonhuman animals to experience the trauma and psychological pain associated with dead animals; merely being around their dead bodies necessitates emotional labour. San Diego's Dead Animal Removal Program (DARP) actively rotates and increases compensation for employees when their dead animal removal and disposal shift commences.[14]

There is also the emotional labour of confronting the meat industry, which we see in the Instagram posts that opened this chapter. When we started this chapter, we knew that any anger or yelling on our part would indeed be 'self-righteous' (a critique long attributed to nonhuman animal activists), so we set ourselves to the task of looking for a way to sidestep entrenched critiques by (re)creating 'worlds in the making'[15] – by acknowledging and disrupting 'the speciousness of "the given".[16] Critiquing both exploitative labour conditions and the complexities of emotional labour associated with human–nonhuman relationships (both between meat-eaters and the animal corpses they consume and between humans and dogs) might provide non-meat-eaters with a coping mechanism for the immense emotional labour they must do – something that goes beyond just trying to explain why eating animals is problematic, while also helping push the dialogue beyond the entrenched conversations about the ethics of eating meat that so often emerge when we talk about meat.

---

13 Dillard 2008.
14 Lulka 2013.
15 Goodman 1978, p. ix.
16 Goodman 1978.

Rebecca Solnit (whose 'mansplaining' neologism has spread like wildfire across vast plains of taken-for-granted ways of thinking; this 'meatsplaining' homage is but one of many texts that runs with her idea) tells a story about gender, space, power ... and a pit bull:

> Almost twenty years ago, while taking care of a friend's dog, I took the animal out for a stroll. Along the way, three tall young men came walking directly toward us, a situation in which I always give way, step aside. But I had a pit bull on a short leash. I walked right through those men like Moses parting the Red Sea. I never tried that again, but I never forgot what I learned in that moment: So deeply had I known who owned the sidewalk that I'd always yielded, without even noticing.[17]

She tells a good story, but imagine what it would have sounded like to hear from the pit bull. Here the pit bull is described as a mere catalyst for her own awareness, but it is easy to imagine how we might also acknowledge the labour of that consciousness-raising and sidewalk-clearing pit bull. S/he (Solnit doesn't gender the pit bull) isn't just strolling and isn't just 'being taken out for a stroll' but is labouring with the humans in this story – is moving with and through these bodies in this space. And as Haraway puts it, this is indeed 'communication about relationship [between men, women and dogs], ... and the means of reshaping relationship and so its enacters'.[18]

In another example, Instone and Sweeney adopt a dog perspective to examine human–dog relationships in an urban space. They argue for the need to shift one's 'focus from discourses about the place of dogs, their control, management and breed to thinking about the multiple coexisting dogs, humans and hu/dogs, which are brought into being through the performance of heterogeneous actors in a variety of urban places'.[19] Again, without an explicit focus on communication, these researchers nonetheless push forward an understanding of human–nonhuman interaction that highlights an embodied

---

17 Solnit 2017.
18 Haraway 2008, p. 26.
19 Instone & Sweeney 2014, p. 782.

'coperformance'. What each of these writers opens up is an opportunity for thinking beyond the human and instead considering the contours of a more-than-human world.

Working for and with dogs: Telling the story differently

So, let's try this alternative storytelling, this (re)worlding of how consumers and nonconsumers of meat could begin to share a journey through (re)considering our relationships with the nonhuman animals we eat in the billions each year. It must be said that, at a minimum, what follows is a much-needed improvement from the dialogue exchange with which we began.

This is the fictional story (though based on real events) of an activist and a dog whose lives get tangled up in the international forces of the dog meat trade. The activist is a 29-year-old white woman who holds a US passport. She has travelled to Yulin, China, to protest the annual Dog Meat Festival (a real annual event). She has taken her only two weeks of yearly vacation and, on her own dime, flown to Shanghai, China, to join a group of similar activists and protesters, mainly from Europe, Australia, Canada and the United States.

Upon arrival, they load 100 dog carriers and tons of emergency veterinarian supplies onto a large commercial truck and drive 18 hours across the interior of southern China to the mostly rural town of Yulin where they will 'make camp' for the next 10 days of the festival. They do not stay in Yulin because they do not want to patronise local businesses. Their goal is singular: they hope to intercept the trucks, each carrying up to a thousand dogs, headed to Yulin for the festival and save the dogs from being skinned alive and eaten. If they can properly barricade the country roads and bribe the drivers of the trucks to leave peacefully, they will then offload the dogs to a large fenced warehouse compound, begin emergency treatment for the mostly diseased and gravely ill dogs, and plan the dogs' deportation back to their home countries where eager, though mostly inadequately funded, non-profit animal rescues await.

The dog in this story was raised for meat at a local dog meat breeding farm. The dog is a Golden Retriever, now a very popular dog meat breed in China since they are so easy to manage and large enough to provide lots of meat. The dog is nameless, grossly overweight and has lived his entire life (approximately one year) in a cage infested with fleas and ticks. He lives with five to six other Golden Retrievers from the same litter. The dog's first time leaving his cage was to be loaded on the truck headed to Yulin, which was then stopped and overtaken by the international activists, including the American woman. She takes an immediate liking to the Golden Retriever, and their connection is instantly familiar to her in a place/country where so much is deeply unfamiliar (she speaks no Mandarin, has never left the US and cannot stand that the 'Chinese food here is nothing like at home – yuck'). She is determined to be the 'flight hero' that escorts the Golden dog back to the US.

After two stressful and high-energy weeks during which over half the rescued dogs ultimately die from their pre-existing diseases and conditions, each activist leaves China with up to six dogs travelling with them. The woman and the Golden, however, are stopped at immigration control and told they cannot leave. The Golden does not have the right vaccines and must remain in China for 90 days. A trial to appeal the decision is set for later that day.

In court, the judge asks the woman why she is in China, and the woman timidly explains that she came to rescue dogs from being eaten. When prodded further, she shares that she wants the Golden to have a beautiful life with a US human family, sleeping on their bed, going for walks and eating nutritious canned food. Then the judge turns to the Golden and asks what he would like. The dog, having never seen the world, says that he does not know what he wants, but that he misses his littermates. The woman leaps back in her seat, astonished that the dog can speak. She had never considered that dogs could talk or had ideas about what they wanted for their lives. The judge seems incredulous that the woman is surprised: 'Did you not think the dog had its own thoughts and desires? Or had you merely presumed that dogs love the life that you provide in your country? Had you never considered asking the Golden what he wanted for his one and only life?' The woman, still speechless, slowly shakes her head to indicate 'no'. 'So you came all this way, judging our culture and intervening and disrupting our way of life, and you are not even certain that what you have to offer is what the dog actually wants? That seems presumptuous, no?'

The judge then says that the woman's answer to one question alone would help her decide the ruling of the court: 'Do you eat nonhuman animals?' The woman muttered, 'Yes, but not dogs'. 'What animals do you eat?' the judge inquires. 'Bacon, hamburgers, sushi', the woman replies. 'You mean, pigs, cows and fish. Well then, the Golden stays here, and will immediately be reunited with his littermates. You cannot expect me to believe that you would eat all these other animals but would not indeed eat this dog. Your ethics are no greater than ours, just different. And so I see your actions as less emancipatory and more devious and misguided. You pretend to be something you are not.' Just then, the dog interrupts the judge's ruling. 'Why are you humans always talking about ethics? You talk and act as if you alone have the ability to make choices and affect lives. While I'm grateful that your actions and this trial have delayed – for now – the cruel execution waiting for me in Yulin, nothing will change for my brothers and sisters whether you "save" me by sending me to the US or if I'm sent back to Yulin to die. We have, with and without your help, been escaping this fate for generations; for millennia, even. But we remember our shared history differently than you do. We remember our history of shared labour, of survival forged in a mutual, imperfect give-and-take. And we wonder, why are your memories so bad? How do you so easily forget our shared ancestors, our neighbourliness?

'Listen', says the Golden, 'here is what I see that you, blind to our history, cannot: *All* of our lives, human-animal and nonhuman animal, depend on whether you can start remembering where you came from. You human animals need to stop saving us and start noticing all of the ways that we dogs have been desperately, against the odds, surviving the holocaust of human progress by using our labour, our own kindnesses and ingenuity. In your acts to eat me, you deny my liberty. In your acts to save me, you still deny my liberty.'

Conclusion

Perhaps what is most useful about this worlding, this narrative practice of 'storying' another world, is that it can be merely a forgotten history that disrupts current thinking and doing: *nonhuman animals used to be put on trial.* For hundreds of years, all sorts of agricultural and companion animals were put on trial in courts for crimes committed either alone or alongside a human. In medieval Europe and colonial America, thousands of animals were put on trial for all sorts of crimes including bestiality, eating crops, trespassing, murder and rape.[20] In Bartholomew Chassenee's 16th-century article *De Excommunicatore Animalium Insectorium*, and in other legal monographs, he argued that all animals – wildlife included – should be granted the same rights as humans, including the right to jury and a trial. Have we digressed from this space that nearly set a precedent for all future human–animal relationships! If only we could begin again, to start the story from a different place in history, and give dogs, cows and pigs agency and bodily liberty. While the contemporary justice system is far from a utopian ideal of emancipation, the possibility that we humans once saw ourselves and our institutions as naturally connected with nonhumans is a radical reminder. We have not always been so insistent in our separation from nonhumans. And, small insight as it is, this opens the possibility that this way of seeing the world is one that can be recovered.

We mainly aimed to do three things in this chapter: (1) move away from the common trappings of typical conversations about eating meat found in the exemplary Instagram exchange and find another, more productive, way to talk about nonhuman animals and how and why we eat them; (2) to create an alternative option for coping with the emotional labour needed to confront the reality of our industrial meat industry; and (3) to give a voice to nonhuman animals, even if fictional, to imagine their worlds and lives.

As much as the goal of this worlding project is to decentre humans, in the end we must return to (and appeal to) human agency and human affect as imperfect but inescapable sources of potential change. The material world is *already* a world where humans are entangled with nonhumans, one where who we are is deeply and repeatedly shaped by who we *are with* animals. And yet, these intra-active[21] relationships are more often than not backgrounded so that the decision to eat meat, to work in a slaughterhouse, to adopt a dog or to give water to

---

20   St. Clair 2010.
21   Barad 2003.

a suffering pig on its way to its slaughter is mistaken for a kind of singular or individual *choice*. And yet, dogs and other animals who live and work alongside humans very likely sense that our fates have always been intertwined. For us, labour is a generative concept for rethinking human–nonhuman relations in a more politically powerful way. To the extent that we are able to recognise the kinds of entangled oppressions experienced by both human and nonhuman labourers, whether in industrial agriculture or in other kinds of exploitative industries, we are able to build a foundation for interspecies solidarity.[22] As Haraway puts it, 'accountability, caring for, being affected, and entering into responsibility are not ethical abstractions; these mundane, prosaic things are the result of having truck with each other'.[23] The conditions of animal consumption are heartbreaking, and telling stories that show how we human animals have both historical precedent and capacity for interspecies solidarity offers a means of resisting the desire to turn away from the heartbreak.

We do not suggest that the (singular) 'solution' to unsustainable, unethical and cruel meat-eating is that everyone should tell a new kind of 'worlding' story. This is the work that we, the authors, are paid to do, with our own dogs helping us to see and tell the story in a particular way. But for others who do other kinds of work, there may be other kinds of material and affective ways of recognising our interspecies solidarity. Eating is fraught with complexity, and in humanity's short history, we alone have merged cruelty and consumption in ways that no other species has. And yet we must eat. 'We cannot denounce the world in the name of an ideal world ... Decisions must take place somehow in the presence of those who will bear their consequences.'[24] And so, our conclusion is modest. We humans already know what it is to work alongside and love nonhuman animals. We do not suggest a magical leap from loving a dog to ending industrial agriculture, but we do (sometimes) find hope in remembering that, from a different

---

22 Both 'entangled oppressions' and 'interspecies solidarity' are terms used by
    Coulter 2016, p. 211.
23 Haraway 2008, p. 36.
24 Haraway 2016, p. 12.

angle, we humans can look less like apocalyptic destruction-machines and more like, well, the human-animal we are.

References

Adams, C. J. (2015). *The Sexual Politics of Meat*. Bloomsbury Publishing.

Barad, K. (2003). Posthumanist performativity: Toward an understanding of how matter comes to matter. *Signs* 28(3), 801–831. doi:10.1086/345321

Barad, K. (2012). On touching – the inhuman that therefore I am. *differences* 23(3), 206–223. doi:10.1215/10407391-1892943

Beirne, P. (1999). For a nonspeciesist criminology: Animal abuse as an object of study. *Criminology* 37(1), 117–147.

Coulter, K. (2016). Beyond human to humane: a multispecies analysis of care work, its repression, and its potential. *Studies in Social Justice* 10(2), 199–219.

Czajkowski, C. (2014). Dog meat trade in South Korea: a report on the current state of the trade and efforts to eliminate it. *Animal Law* 21(1), 29–64.

Dare, A. M. and C. V. Fletcher (2019). A bird's eye view of the Malheur Wildlife Refuge occupation: Nonhuman agency and entangled species. *Environmental Communication* 13(3), 1–12. doi:10.1080/17524032.2017.1412998

Dillard, J. (2008). A slaughterhouse nightmare: Psychological harm suffered by slaughterhouse employees and the possibility of redress through legal reform. *Georgetown Journal on Poverty Law & Policy* 15(2), 391–408.

Goodman, N. (1978). *Ways of Worldmaking*. Indianapolis: Hackett Publishing Company.

Greenfieldboyce, N. (2018). Math bee: Honeybees seem to understand the notion of zero. *NPR*. 7 June. https://n.pr/2FR1Die

Haraway, D. J. (2008). *When Species Meet*. Minneapolis: University of Minnesota Press.

Haraway, D. J. (2016). *Staying with the Trouble: Making Kin in the Chthulucene*. Durham: Duke University Press.

Hribal, J. (2003). 'Animals are part of the working class': a challenge to labor history. *Labor History* 44(4), 435–453. doi:10.1080/0023656032000170069

Hribal, J. (2010). *Fear of the Animal Planet: the Hidden History of Animal Resistance*. Petrolia: AK Press.

Instone, L. and J. Sweeney (2014). The trouble with dogs: 'animaling' public space in the Australian city. *Continuum: Journal of Media & Cultural Studies* 28(6), 774–86. doi:10.1080/10304312.2014.966404

Koerth-Baker, M. (2018). Humans are dumb at figuring out how smart animals are. *FiveThirtyEight*. 18 May. https://53eig.ht/2YswDv8

Kolitz, D. (2018). Are plants conscious? *Gizmodo*. 28 May.
    https://gizmodo.com/are-plants-conscious-1826365668
Le Guin, U. K. (1985). She unnames them. *New Yorker*. 21 January.
    https://bit.ly/2EiKD3O
Lulka, D. (2013) The posthuman city: San Diego's dead animal removal program.
    Urban Geography (34)8: 1119–1143. doi:10.1080/02723638.2013.799326
Manjoo, F. (2019). Stop Mocking Vegans. *The New York Times*. 19 August.
Puig de la Bellacasa, M. (2017). *Matters of Care: Speculative Ethics in More than
    Human Worlds*. Minneapolis: University of Minnesota Press.
Purcell, N. (2011). Cruel intimacies and risky relationships: Accounting for
    suffering in industrial livestock production. *Society & Animals* 19(1), 59–81.
    doi:10.1163/156853011X545538
Solnit, R. (2017). Occupied territory. *Harpers*. July.
    https://harpers.org/archive/2017/07/occupied-territory/
St. Clair, J. (2010). Let us now praise infamous animals. In J. Hribal (Ed.), *Fear of
    the Animal Planet: The Hidden History of Animal Resistance*. Petrolia: AK
    Press.
Tsing, A. L. (2015). *The Mushroom at the End of the World: On the Possibility of Life
    in Capitalist Ruins*. Princeton: Princeton University Press.
Tsing, A. L., H. A. Swanson, E. Gan and N. Bubandt (2017). *Arts of Living on a
    Damaged Planet: Ghosts and Monsters of the Anthropocene*. Minneapolis:
    University of Minnesota Press.
Wilde, O. (1910). *The Soul of Man Under Socialism*. Boston: J.W. Luce & Co.
Wohlleben, P. (2016). *The Hidden Life of Trees, What They Feel, How They
    Communicate: Discoveries from a Secret World*. Berkeley: Greystone Books
    Ltd.
Yan, G. and C. Santos (2009). 'China, forever': Tourism discourse and
    self-orientalism. *Annals of Tourism Research* 36(2), 295–315. doi:10.1016/
    j.annals.2009.01.003

11

The Save Movement: Bearing witness to suffering animals worldwide

Anita Krajnc

> When the suffering of another creature causes you to feel pain,
> don't succumb to the initial desire to flee from the suffering one,
> but on the contrary, come closer, as close as you can to him who
> suffers, and try to help him.
> – Leo Tolstoy, *A Calendar of Wisdom*[1]

We all have a duty to not look away when we see someone suffering, but
to come close, as close as we can, and try to help. The Save Movement
began in Toronto as a project of collectively and regularly bearing
witness at a downtown pig slaughterhouse. Toronto Pig Save formed
in December 2010 after I adopted Mr Bean, a Beagle/Whippet mix,
from Animal Alliance of Canada's Project Jessie. On our morning walks
along Lake Shore, we'd witness sad and scared pigs looking out of
portholes of transport trucks in rush-hour traffic.

After holding monthly, vegan potluck meetings to build up our
base, Toronto Pig Save started holding three vigils per week in July
2011. Twice per week we held early-morning vigils in rush-hour traffic
near Quality Meat Packers at Lake Shore and Strachan, a busy
intersection about a kilometre away from the slaughterhouse, to bear
witness up close to the pigs when the transport trucks stopped at the

---

1   Tolstoy 1997, p. 64.

traffic lights. Our weekly presence gave visibility to the pigs. Thousands of people could see us during the peak traffic times. We would ask drivers and passers-by to look at the pigs in the trucks, take vegan outreach and animal rights literature, and join us. On Sundays, we held our third weekly vigil right in front of the slaughterhouse. We witnessed the pigs being unloaded at a distance of 50 metres. The pigs screamed as the drivers stuck their electric prods in the portholes, sometimes hitting the pigs in the face with these instruments of torture. Across the street there is a dog park and pool and residential houses, so the slaughterhouse was very accessible.

Toronto Pig Save's goal was to develop a model of resistance *against* the meat industry and their propaganda by witnessing and putting out stories of the individuality of the animals. The encounters with pigs, cows, chickens, ducks, pigeons, sheep, goats, rabbits, fish and horses at slaughterhouses and live markets brings people face to face with the victims of the meat, dairy and egg industries. Bearing witness as a strategy counters the mass disconnect produced by the secrecy in the slaughterhouse industry and the distancing effect of corporate globalisation. Distancing is defined as 'the severing of ecological and social feedback as decision points along the chain are increasingly separated along the dimensions of geography, culture, agency, and power'.[2]

Also, the objective for the movement was to spread worldwide and have vigils at every slaughterhouse. Toronto Pig Save began with the main strategies of bearing witness, vegan outreach and using a love-based community organising approach. Bearing witness means being present for the suffering animals and trying to help them. By being present in front of slaughterhouses, activists are able to put faces on the nameless numbers. At vigils, you connect with the animals in a very personal way and an emotional sense. You see the animals' souls and feel you and everyone should do everything possible to free them from this gross injustice and suffering. You realise it could be your dog or you in that truck. Bearing witness is such a powerful experience, people often stop eating animals and animal products after seeing the sad and terrified animals. Given the power of bearing witness and its

2   Princen, Maniates & Conca 2002, p. 16.

potential to be a life-changing experience, it is imperative to get the whole world to bear witness.

Facing the animal victims also creates new and more motivated activists. Using a love-based community organising approach enabled Save groups to attract more people. The approach draws on the principles of Leo Tolstoy, Mahatma Gandhi, Cesar Chavez, Lois Gibbs, Saul Alinsky and other advocates of nonviolence and community organising. From the start, the objectives for Save vigils attendees was to expand veganism and foster new and more determined activists and organisers to build the animal rights movement.

The sense of urgency also arises from the multiple issues resulting from animal agriculture such as catastrophic climate change, social justice issues, world hunger and threats to public health. As a result, Toronto Pig Save also set up a Climate Vegan campaign and these multiple issues were addressed in the Pig Trial (2015–2017) when I was charged with criminal mischief for giving thirsty pigs water. Subsequently, in 2018, the Save Movement formed three branches: Animal Save Movement, Climate Save Movement and Health Save Movement.

Animal Save Movement

The Animal Save Movement is a global movement of people bearing witness to animal victims at slaughterhouses that stemmed from Toronto Pig Save's initial campaign. Save groups around the world follow the same strategies of bearing witness, vegan outreach and love-based community organising. The overall movement is decentralised and non-hierarchical. The aim is to create vigils at every slaughterhouse and make bearing witness a way of life. For bearing witness to become a new society norm, everyone must refuse to look away when they see someone suffering, but instead come close, as close as they can, and try to help, to paraphrase the ethical realist writer Leo Tolstoy. We have a duty to bear witness, but we also have a duty to organise.

In the US, there are more than 6,000 large slaughterhouse facilities inspected by the Food Safety Inspection Service (FSIS).[3] There are many

---

3   Wasley 2018.

small slaughterhouse facilities as well such as live markets, for example, in New York City. The UK slaughterhouse map lists 300 large killing facilities. There are likely millions of slaughterhouses around the world if you count the live markets, smaller killing facilities and the fishing industry. At just over 900 Save groups as of April 2020, the movement is just beginning.

The first Save groups to emerge outside Toronto were in Burlington, Melbourne and New York. Between 2011 and 2015, the Animal Save Movement spread across Canada, Australia and the US. Once the Pig Trial began, the number of Save groups grew exponentially. In 2016, the movement doubled in size from 50 to 100 groups; in 2017, it tripled to almost 300 groups; and in 2018, it doubled to 600 chapters. In February 2016, Manchester Pig Save, the United Kingdom's first of many Save groups, held its first vigil at Tulip Meats. In June, they were followed by Liverpool and Essex Pig Save. Two years later there were 65 groups in the United Kingdom. In 2017 in Europe, 11 countries were added: Belgium, Croatia, France, Germany, Ireland, New Zealand, Norway, Portugal, Spain, Switzerland and The Netherlands. VegFests (explained below) and organising tours helped start a number of new groups.

In 2017, Save groups started in two new continents – Asia and Latin America – and 25 new countries. In Asia, Hong Kong Pig Save was holding regular vigils at Tsuen Wan and groups in Japan and Sri Lanka formed. In March 2017, Save Movement Lima and Save Movement Bogota, the first Save groups in Latin America, held their first vigils. At Lima's first vigil, activists gave water to cows, and in Bogota, a slaughterhouse worker threw blood at peaceful vigil goers. By the end of 2017, Save groups had started in 11 countries in Latin America: Argentina, Chile, Colombia, Costa Rica, Honduras, Mexico, Nicaragua, Panama, Paraguay, Peru and Uruguay.

By 2020 there were over 900 groups in 72 countries on six continents. If trends continue, there will be potentially thousands of groups in five years' time. The number of US groups grew from 24 at the start of 2016 to over 100 by 2020. Australia and New Zealand have over 40 groups. The Animal Save Movement in Europe grew from 2015 to 2020 in particular with over half the Save groups in mainland Europe. In March and April 2018, five groups formed in

Denmark. The first vigil on 27 March was a three-group joint vigil held by Randers, Odense and Horsens Animal Saves at Danish Crown, a large pig slaughterhouse. Germany and Spain also grew at a rapid rate, with 32 and 30 groups respectively, following Save organising tours. In Asia, new Save groups emerged in 2018 in Seoul, South Korea, Metro Manila in the Philippines, and Kolkata, Pune and Lucknow in India. On 14 April, the first vigil in the Philippines was held at Kayang Meat and Slaughterhouse by Metro Manila Animal Save. In the same month, Kolkata Animal Save held India's first Save vigil. They bore witness to an open market where chickens were being dismembered within view of other chickens. Activists provided water for dehydrated chickens.

The growth of the movement occurred as vigil attendees from other regions attended vigils while travelling and subsequently were inspired to start groups in their home region. Others started groups after watching powerful social media posts and viral videos, a testament to the power of bearing witness to suffering animals as an igniter of activist communities. In addition, the media attention from the Pig Trial (2015–2017) contributed to bolstering the movement. But the Animal Save Movement also developed a conscious organising tour strategy. Drawing on the experiences of labour unions and community organising, it developed organising drives by attending VegFests and music festival tours and by sending teams of organisers across continents to start new chapters.

In order to challenge the mass disconnection encouraged by the animal exploitation industry, the Animal Save Movement's aim to hold vigils at every slaughterhouse requires millions of activists and organisers in most countries engaging in strategic campaigns with escalating tactics, if we are to follow the 3.5 per cent rule Erica Chenoweth discovered in studying the number of people mobilised in successful rebellions worldwide. Consider that the civil rights movement in the US had hundreds of professional organisers, tens of thousands of organisers and hundreds of thousands of activists.[4]

Here are ten strategies for building the Animal Save Movement.

---

4   Chenoweth & Stephan 2011; Mann 2011.

1. Regular vigils

The strategy of holding regular activist events is used by a number of global movements: in September 2018, Greta Thunberg and her student colleagues started holding daily school strikes in front of the Swedish Parliament before the national election for three weeks. Then they continued weekly school strikes every Friday, called Fridays For Future, which subsequently spread globally. In the same vein, Toronto Pig Save started with three vigils a week in July 2011 until Quality Meat Packers went bankrupt in April 2014. Now the three vigils a week occur in the Toronto area but spread out to new locations including Fearmans Pork, Inc. in Burlington and weekly vigils in Toronto for cows and chickens. Frequent, regular vigils helped build the organisation and also spread the movement. Attendance at Toronto area vigils has increased to about 30 or so people at each of the weekly vigils and over a hundred at special, all-day vigils.

We have a duty to seek out the slaughterhouses in our communities. These killing facilities are often very accessible in city centres or close by in the outskirts. More and more people are likely to join the vigils if they are held frequently and regularly. Melbourne Pig Save started out with a few individuals in 2012 and now has 50 to 60 or more people at their rallies and vigils. IJsselstein Pig Save in The Netherlands had their first vigil on 28 February 2018, and a few months later, on 2 May, they had a record attendance of 62 activists. Los Angeles Animal Save holds the largest weekly vigils with 150 people on average attending the pig vigils at Farmer John slaughterhouse. When the group first formed in December 2016, organiser Amy Jean Davis says around 50 people attended. By March 2017, there were 80 to 100 coming, by October 2017, 125 to 150. At a May 2018 vigil, when their megaphone ran out of battery, the police stepped in and let social media influencer 'Earthling Ed' use the PA system in the police car, in a testament to the success of the love-based organising.

In addition, what helps boost attendance is being able to bear witness for a significant amount of time. It is very difficult to bear witness and connect with the animals unless the trucks stop for a few minutes. In Toronto, activists initially had to stop the trucks at the cow and chicken slaughterhouses by standing at the entrance. By 2015,

Toronto Chicken Save negotiated with the plant manager at Maple Leaf Poultry for each transport truck to stop for five minutes at their weekly vigils. Other Save groups have achieved Safety Agreements. LA Animal Save works with the Vernon Police Department to stop each truck for a couple of minutes at Farmer John pig slaughterhouse. LA Animal Save organiser Amy Jean Davis says:

> We are fortunate to work with the amazing Vernon Police Department ... The way it works is we have people who will stand in front of the gate on the sidewalk when a truck is approaching. This is what stops the trucks ... Some guidelines: Always approach the trucks slowly, calmly, and with a gentle voice. Water is the priority, photos and videos are secondary. Work with a buddy if you can, one giving water and one documenting. IMPORTANT: LOOK FOR SNOUTS. Do NOT start spraying or pouring water into the trucks. Find a snout. If there is no snout near you, just offer love. We need to be very careful not to stress the pigs out more than they already are. If the truck rolls up and the pigs are sleeping, do not wake them up. Offer water to a snout near you very gently.

In The Netherlands, Boxtel Pig Save established an unusual agreement with the slaughterhouse whereby activists are issued passes which they have to show to enter a designated area to stand on the slaughterhouse property. The slaughterhouse provides bottles and a big blue bin of water where activists can refill their bottle. In England, Essex Pig Save organiser Lauren Hollas says: 'In England a love-based approach works best.' The group developed a positive police relationship in which officers stop the trucks. It hasn't always been that way. The activists have proven their approach is love-based and all they want to do is peacefully bear witness. They keep the police in the loop and notify the police of the upcoming vigil a couple of weeks in advance. In Australia, Perth Pig Save have reached a voluntary agreement with the Linley Valley Pork – Craig Mauston Group slaughterhouse. The trucks stop for two minutes. The slaughterhouse calls the truckers beforehand, so they know there is a vigil. Jen Regan, an organiser with Perth Pig Save, says: 'Ever since [social media influencer] Joey Carbstrong turned up at a vigil, the attendance doubled. At Christmas [in 2017] it tripled.' That is when they rescued a sow whom they named Carol.

Vigils also take place at ports to protest the live export of animals to slaughter. Setubal Animal Save holds vigils against live exports at Setabul, a coastal city near Lisbon, Portugal. There ships load live animals destined for Israel, Egypt and Jordan. The group's vigils, a petition drive, viral social media and mass media coverage are helping to raise awareness of the live export trade where cows and sheep are transported on a large ship to Israel and can take up to 12 days to reach their destination, with not all the animals making the journey and being thrown overboard. Activists often witness bleeding injured animals being loaded onto the ship. Other Stop Live Export Save groups were set up in port cities in Slovenia, Croatia and France. Organisers Alice and Noelle say more people are coming into contact with the animals as a result of the port vigils and the group is receiving more media attention, including prime-time television coverage. 'Now people are awakening and speaking about it. The police are friendly. Our group works with dock workers and is talking to locals. Hopefully they will be on our side because it's the right side.'

In time, the vigils worldwide began to cover more animals: rabbits, sheep, goats, horses, fish and furred animals. In Spain, Granollers Rabbit Save held their first vigil in April 2018. Castellon Animal Save, also in Spain, bears witness to rabbits as well. It is a shocking sight to see innocent rabbits bunched in crates in a huge transport truck. The scared rabbits are packed tightly like the hens we witnessed at Stockton Animal Save's all-day vigil during the May 2018 Animal Liberation Conference in Berkeley, California.

In 2017, Fish Save groups appeared beginning with Toronto Fish Save's launch on World Day for the End of Fishing on 25 March 2017. There are now more than a dozen Fish Save groups including in Boston and Berkeley (US), Playa del Carmen (Mexico), Valencia (Spain), and Gothenburg and Helsingborg (Sweden). The Fish Saves mission is to help people realise that marine animals are individuals who create close bonds with others, much in the same way as other animals do, and deserve to live just as we do. Yet we destroy their habitats, separate their families and kill 2.7 trillion marine creatures every single year. Marine biologists estimate that the world's oceans could be virtually lifeless by 2048.

2. All-day vigils and special vigils

From 2011 to 2013, Toronto Pig Save held annual Labour Day 'Veggie dog giveaways' across the street from the pig slaughterhouse, invited local residents to enjoy live music, free veggie dogs, face painting, chalk art and information tables and videos. Toronto Pig Save held its first all-day (12-hour) vigil in 2012 and a 30-hour Toronto Cow Save vigil in 2013. All-day vigils are held throughout the year, but especially in the warmer months when the attendance is much higher. Some all-day vigils are held at multiple slaughterhouses: usually the vigil starts with the Fearmans pig slaughterhouse in Burlington about 40 minutes from Toronto; next the destination is Toronto at the two adjacent cow slaughterhouses; and in the evening it ends up at the Maple Leaf Foods chicken slaughterhouse a few blocks away. There is vegan outreach in front of Fearmans at a major intersection at Harvester Road and Appleby Line. In Toronto, the slaughterhouses are on industrial roads in the north-west part of the city, so vegan outreach teams also go to the nearby main intersection at St. Claire and Keele and ask people to join them. There have been door-to-door invitations to some of the special events. In England, Andrew Garner went door to door before a Manchester Pig Save special vigil and distributed 600 leaflets inviting community members to the vigil. Ten locals came out.

Other special vigils include five-day vigils and hunger strikes, vigils for truck rollovers and memorial vigils at barn fires. In Australia, Animal Liberation Victoria organised a five-day vigil and fast in 2017. This was replicated by London Chicken Save in Ontario with a former chicken slaughterhouse worker and another activist joining the fast. They slept in cars and tents. In the second week of June 2018, Dusseldorf Animal Save held a five-day vigil, called Animal Justice Camp, in front of Europe's biggest pig slaughterhouse called Tönnies in Rheda-Wiedenbrück in North Rhine Westphalia, Germany. They kill 25,000 pigs per day and 20.6 million per year. Barcelona Animal Save held a five-day vigil and hunger strike in August 2018 and 2019. Toronto Chicken Save joined in August 2019 for the first time.

3. Love-based community organising

> When you do a good deed be grateful that you have had the chance to do it.
> – John Ruskin cited in Leo Tolstoy, *A Calendar of Wisdom*

Linda started De Hoef Animal Save near Amsterdam in The Netherlands. During her initiation call on 19 January 2018, she said, 'I felt I couldn't be happy unless I was active.' She says the slaughterhouse kills sheep and cows and specialises in halal. The owner is very proud to open the doors of the slaughterhouse and show people around. She wants people to look into the eyes of the animals: 'Veganism is the answer to so many problems.'

The foundations of Animal Save Movement are love-based community organising. The philosophy and practice of love and nonviolence are drawn from Tolstoy (*The Kingdom of God Is Within You*) and Gandhi (*Autobiography: My Experiments with Truth*). Community organising involves inspiring people to take action at a particular site of injustice where they live. The site of community organising may be a specific neighbourhood where 'doors line the streets' at the location like a slaughterhouse or live market, mobile sites like transport routes of slaughterhouse trucks and ports where ships engage in live transport. The grassroots organising approach is a model being turned to again and again because it is seen as more effective than impersonal, top-down approaches. In Saul Alinsky's pioneering work, he says: 'Power just goes to two poles – to those who've got money, and those who've got people. You haven't got money, so your own people are your only source of strength.'[5]

Power lies in numbers, but, more specifically, it is derived from organising ordinary people to counter the financial resources and power of corporations or governments. By mobilising large numbers of individuals and groups at a community or neighbourhood level, community organisers can build powerful organisations and demonstrate the strength of numbers, also known as people power. Faced with issues of injustice, community organising is necessary

---

5   Sanders & Alinsky 1970, p. 33.

because, as Lois Gibbs explains, 'no one will do it for us'.[6] There are two essential objectives of community organising in the Alinksy model: successfully meeting your campaign goals and developing a powerful community organisation so that the group has the capacity to ensure victories have lasting effects and can take on other issues. Community organising is inclusive and encourages the idea that everyone is a leader. Continuous training and acquiring of new skills are essential.

There are two approaches to recruitment drives. First, building a new organisation from scratch involves recruiting new individual members, either through direct contact or face to face such as door-to-door canvassing, and then setting up a meeting. In addition, Alinsky's 'organization of organizations' involves focusing on existing groups as the building blocks of a coalition. As Alinsky explains:

> In July 1939, the first such People's Organizations arose in Chicago's notorious stockyard section, Back of the Yards. On that day a people's congress met and gave birth to an organization uniting all of the institutions, agencies, power blocs, and interest groups which made up the life of that community. This People's Organization bridged all of the economic, social, religious, and political cleavages previously existing between these groups.[7]

Alinsky's model involves professional organisers entering a particular neighbourhood and building a coalition in a community. The organisers' first task is to identify pre-existing networks and Indigenous leadership in community groups and also to involve business leaders. Their task would be to further develop local leadership by broadening their perspective through helping expand their view on their obligations to society.

North Carolina Farmed Animal Save engages in both types of recruitment. North Carolina has the most pigs raised for slaughter, after Iowa. The Smithfield slaughterhouse in Tar Heel is the largest pig slaughterhouse in the world. It has three Butina gas chambers running simultaneously, killing 33,000 pigs a day. The group's monthly vigils

---

6   Gibbs 1997, p. 146.
7   Alinsky 1946, p. 73.

started in October 2016 and have gained a steady following. Organiser Roxanne says: 'North Carolina has a large vegan community but not a lot of activists. Still the vigils are popular. People will travel a long distance to attend to stand outside a corrugated building. Duplin County is rural but within two hours of two big cities.' Duplin County is where environmental justice groups have been fighting spray-fields – factory farms spray pig shit in the air which enters people's homes. NCFAS has partnered with local women's groups, such as Women Organizing for Wilmington and Grandmothers for Peace and two environmental organisations, Cape Fear River Watch and Clean Cape Fear. The protests educate people in eastern North Carolina about the many issues regarding Concentrated Animal Feeding Operations (CAFOs). Their first CAFO protest in early 2018 drew more than 70 people. Duplin and Sampson Counties, just upriver from Wilmington, North Carolina, are the most heavily factory-farmed places on the planet, with an unprecedented number of pig, chicken and turkey CAFOs in close proximity to one another. Downstream from these areas, are two rivers – the Neuse and the Cape Fear – which have been named in the top-ten list of most endangered rivers in the United States, in large part due to factory farming. NCFAS started holding '5 Day Save' events in June 2018 during which they and coalition partners organised another CAFO protest.

Kate Bronfenbrenner highlights the success of bottom-up, comprehensive campaigns in her work for the US labour movement. Her model serves as a useful template for other movement organisations to follow.[8] No single tactic is a silver bullet; rather, combined tactics prove most effective. Comprehensive campaigns include at least five tactics involving rank-and-file member mobilisation. Strategic and tactical choices do matter in winning campaigns. Bottom-up approaches produce significantly higher win rates for organising drives than traditional union strategies comprised of impersonal, top-down, low-intensity campaigns launched from union headquarters. Comprehensive campaigns also contribute to movement building through the development of rank-and-file leadership and mass participation.

---

8   Bronfenbrenner, Friedmann, Hurd, Oswald & Seeber 1998.

Comprehensive, bottom-up campaigns involve:

- a representative organising committee
- house calls
- small-group meetings
- staging frequent direct actions, such as solidarity days, rallies and job actions
- media campaigns
- corporate campaigns (targeting corporate leaders and interfering with employers' relations with lenders, clients, shareholders and consumers)
- community–labour coalitions
- surveys of members of the unit on a one-on-one basis about the contract
- a focus on dignity, fairness and justice as key issues

Comprehensive campaigns are mainly bottom-up campaigns with a representative organising committee and small-group meetings; frequent direct actions; a focus on dignity, fairness and justice; and a culture of organising. 'By fully involving rank-and-file members ... the potential exists to create an army of experienced and committed rank-and-file organisers.'[9] Comprehensive campaigns also have top-down elements, such as media campaigns and strategic corporate campaigns. The use of personal approaches like small-group meetings as well as a large set of bold and disruptive grassroots tactics such as direct action, community–labour coalitions and media and corporate campaigns are highly effective even in a highly globalised context.

Successful tactics possess certain characteristics related to their numbers, quality and intensity. First, deploying 'as many as possible' tactics in comprehensive campaigns, if properly done, leads to greater success. In her work, Bronfenbrenner found that the likelihood of the union winning the election grew by 10 per cent for each extra rank-and-file-intensive tactic used. Individual tactics were not necessarily important in and of themselves and were rarely sufficient as there is no silver bullet. Instead, combined tactics produced results.[10]

---

9   Bronfenbrenner et al. 1998.
10   Bronfenbrenner et al. 1998, p. 32.

Secondly, the quality of tactics matters. Bronfenbrenner found that simply going door to door and dropping off literature in a weekend blitz is 'much less effective than a campaign in which the union sets up small-group meetings with two or three workers at workers' homes, in community centres, or in the workplace and workers have an opportunity to express their concerns and to be inoculated against the employers' campaign, to mobilise for solidarity actions, and, most important, to develop leaders for the long haul to come'.[11] Thirdly, the intensity of tactics refers to how many unions are employing comprehensive campaigns. In the animal rights context, if there are many strong street activist groups in a city, such as Anonymous for the Voiceless, Animal Save, Direct Action Everywhere and other groups, each is more likely to have an impact, with the multiple platforms of activism reinforcing each other.

4. The duty to rescue animals

Animal rescues occur during regular vigils as a result of relationships developed with the slaughterhouse workers and managers. Activists' requests for animals have spared many animal lives in Toronto, Bolton, UK, and live markets in Philadelphia, New York City and Orange County. Alicia Santuro, an organiser with Stockton Animal Save near San Francisco, says her group has rescued dozens of chickens through an arrangement with New Stockton Poultry that allows them to save lives every time they host a vigil there: 'The slaughterhouse agreed to release a chicken to us after every vigil if Save only hosts monthly vigils that last an hour.' In December 2017, Perth Pig Save asked the slaughterhouse owners to spare a life before Christmas. Carol, the rescued sow, is now living happily at a sanctuary.

> [An activist] approached the general manager at Linley Valley Pork in Wooroloo to ask if in the spirit of Christmas, he would consider surrendering a sow, a mother pig who was due to be slaughtered, to the sanctuary for her to live out the rest of her life. He came

---

11   Bronfenbrenner et al. 1998, p. 34.

back within half an hour and agreed, and organised Carol (she was named in the spirit of Christmas) to be dropped off at Greener Pastures animal sanctuary within the following few weeks.[12]

Carol experienced confinement all her life and didn't know how to eat a watermelon.

> When Carol arrived at the sanctuary, she had pink spray paint on her back, marking her to be slaughtered. Her muscles were weak from being confined for most of her life to a sow stall, she was given fruit to eat but didn't know what to do with it, having never seen fruit in her life. But that same day, after a little warming up, she got excited and started running and dancing around the paddock happily. She also had her very first mud bath. Now, a few months on, Carol has settled well into her new sanctuary life. She was introduced to the other pig residents, has established herself within the pecking order, and has seemingly even adopted a son, Iggle Piggle, a younger pig. The two are inseparable and are often found cuddling together. We like to think of Iggle Piggle as the son she never got to keep, having had between 80–120 piglets taken from her in her 4–5 year lifespan.

Carol is now thriving at Greener Pastures Animal Sanctuary with her new family. Perth Pig Save raised $1500 for the sanctuary.

Save activists, simply by their presence at slaughterhouses, have rescued many animals who escape from transport trucks while the animals are being unloaded. In April 2018, the fourth year in a row that Newmarket Meat Packers agreed to spare lives of sheep at Easter/ Passover, a baby lamb escaped off a transport truck while activists were there picking up two mother sheep and their two babies. The driver told his child that the lambs always come back to the group (and then will be slaughtered too), but this lamb ran to the forests. Hours later activists found him (they named him James) and took him to Dog Tales Rescue and Sanctuary to join the other sheep. A couple of weeks later, on 22 April, Las Vegas Animal Save organiser Giselle witnessed a duck escape.

---

12   Perth Pig Save 2018.

As she picked up the duck, a slaughterhouse worker ran to her, grabbed her hair and violently pulled the duck's wing. Giselle refused to let go and was able to rescue the duck.

A calf was born on a slaughterhouse truck outside the gates of the slaughterhouse during a Buenos Aires Animal Save vigil on 16 December 2017. Save activists asked for mercy after witnessing the birth. The calf, named Save, was released after hard negotiations to a sanctuary called Santuario Equidad in Cordoba, Argentina. The following day an emergency vigil was called demanding the release of Save's mother at the slaughterhouse. Liz Solari, a social media influencer, encouraged her Instagram followers to attend the vigil. After an hour of negotiations, the slaughterhouse owner said the mother had been killed. Heartbroken activists then held a symbolic ceremony of love and grief. The story received major mainstream media coverage.

There have been many attempts to rescue animals from truck rollovers. On 7 December 2017, just before Christmas, Katie Harkins from Thames Market Animal Save was with Ed and Luna from East London Chicken Save on their way to a university as part of the Big Vegan Activism Van tour and found out about a transport truck carrying hundreds of turkeys on their way to slaughter overturned in a motorway accident in Worcestershire, England. They rushed to the scene and pleaded with the police, officials and the farmer to allow them to take the injured birds to a sanctuary. Katie clung onto one turkey for at least an hour, refusing to move from the bird's side. 'The farmer eventually gave in and agreed for them to take the turkey to a sanctuary, with him being given the name "Asha", meaning hope, where he lives with other rescue farm animals.'[13]

5. Social media portraits of individual animals

Our daily social media shows the individuality of the animals in the slaughter trucks and their extreme exploitation and unimaginable suffering. Through its regular vigils worldwide, the Animal Save Movement has put these profound animal images and stories into the

---

13   Hollas 2018; Horton 2017.

public realm. The documentation lets the animals tell their stories. Activists are encouraged to bring a camera to the vigils and to use their mobile phones to take photographs and videos, and share, use hashtags and tag on social media. The footage taken at the vigils by so many activists resonates within each of their networks of friends.

The most viral footage of the Animal Save Movement, with 5–20 million views on 'Best Video You Will Ever See' on Facebook, is of activists giving water to thirsty pigs. Toronto Pig Save and Los Angeles Animal Save's pig vigils have produced videos that are fraught with palpable emotions of the activists and pigs. Viewers feel as though they are present as tearful activists try to help the desperate pigs by passing water bottles through the metal walls of the truck.

Federico Callegari, an organiser with Buenos Aires Animal Save and a co-ordinator with the Save Graphics Working Group, proposed a renaming of the organisation from the Save Movement to the Animal Save Movement in the spring of 2018. Towards the end of that year, the Animal Save Movement created two new branches: Climate Save Movement and Health Save Movement. Also, the graphics team created a social media campaign encouraging people to bear witness and participate in vigils and additional animal activism. He says: 'We all feel ugly when we look away. We have to have the courage to look.' Memes that say 'Like, comment, share and save' will help images go viral and awaken consciousness and increase public participation on social media. Multiple-choice billboards asking the viewer to choose between 'Empathy' or 'Apathy' or 'Look' or 'Turn away' and featuring poignant images of pigs, cows and chickens on slaughter trucks raise critical consciousness and generate public empathy through a message that invites reflection and forces the public to take a side on questions of speciesism, animal exploitation and suffering, and activism. The campaign promotes the idea that we all share a duty to bear witness and to become activists.

6. Mass media attention

The Animal Save Movement Media Facebook page was created in early 2018 to collate the mass media coverage Save groups are garnering around the world. The Save guidebook contains a template for a media plan for a group's first vigil. The media often cover a group's initial vigil. Special vigils such as events organised during a heatwave or cold spell, all-day vigils, truck rollovers and barn fires often get mainstream coverage. Creative nonviolent direct actions at vigils also draw media interest. For example, on 28 January 2018 Buenos Aires Animal Save activists performed a symbolic hug around a transport truck full of cows waiting to be unloaded at the slaughterhouse. The cows initially were nervous, but the energy of the hug was contagious and calmed the cows. The livestream went viral with over a million views on Facebook, and several mass media outlets covered the action. LA Animal Save received exemplary front-page coverage in the *LA Times* in 2019.[14]

The Pig Trial in 2015–2017 generated worldwide attention for Toronto Pig Save and the Animal Save Movement. My two vegan defence lawyers, James Silver and Gary Grill, along with Save groups around the world, PETA, Animal Justice and other groups, provided support on the ground and on social media. Both the pre-trial and the five-day trial had surprisingly large media scrums at the courthouse.[15] Towards the end of the trial, the courthouse was so packed with supporters that journalists were asked to sit in the prisoners' box. The Pig Trial brought animal interests before the courts. Senior criminal attorneys Silver and Grill and their assistant, Ali Pester, were able to put animal agriculture on trial by focusing on the ethics, animal suffering, environment and health aspects of animal agriculture. Although I was acquitted for giving water to thirsty pigs and the ethical precept of the Golden Rule ('When I was thirsty, you gave me water') remained intact, it was only a partial victory. Judge Harris continued to speak of pigs as property under the law and not persons. The battle for the personhood of pigs and other animals continues on the streets as animal rights groups bear witness at slaughterhouses and also 'Meat the Victims' in animal farms.

---

14 Arellano 2019.
15 Krajnc 2017.

7. Celebrity activism

> It's the most powerful activism I've ever experienced. It took
> activism to the next level. It shapes how I speak, how much more
> motivated I am, how much more perspective I have.
>   – Joey Carbstrong[16]
> Everyone should be forced to bear witness. Unless people see
> the truth, things won't change.
>   – Marc Ching at an all-day vigil in Toronto in 2016

Vegan celebrity activists and social media influencers, mainstream
celebrities, reporters, representatives from large organisations and
politicians can help inform their followers of the power of bearing
witness and draw a big turn-out when they attend vigils. Well-known
YouTube vegan activists such as Bite Size Vegan, Vegan Gains, Earthling
Ed, James Aspey, Joey Carbstrong, High Carbs Hannah, This Little
Vegan and Seb Alex have played an important part in helping raise
awareness of bearing witness and joining many vigils around the world.
For example, on 24 September 2015, Bite Size Vegan, Kris Giovanetti
(Sentient Beast), Amy Jean Davis, Liz Marshall and Vegan Gains joined
Toronto Pig Save for a 24-hour all-day vigil. Close to 400 people came
out, making it one of the biggest vigils. More than half of the attendees
were new to bearing witness. Travelling vegan celebrities Joey
Carbstrong, Earthling Ed and James Aspey attended an Essex Pig Save
vigil on 17 July 2017 and drew over 90 activists, making it the largest
Essex Pig Save vigil to date. Jen Regan, an organiser with Perth Pig Save,
says: 'Ever since Joey Carbstrong turned up at a vigil, the attendance
doubled.' Joey has also made waves in the UK in early 2018 when he
appeared on a BBC radio interview with 7 million people listening.

LA Animal Save regularly draws mainstream celebrities to its
weekly vigils including Joaquin Phoenix, Rooney Mara, Moby (his first
vigil was on 15 October 2017), Kat Von D, Mena Suvari, Craig
Robinson, Damien Mander, Toby Morse and Nimai Delgado. Organiser
Amy Jean Davis says: 'I don't think anything super sparked it, but I
know that with Shaun and Joaquin coming it drew some people in. But

---

16   Carbstrong 2018.

honestly I think it's mostly the ability to give water that gets people there!' In Toronto, Miss Tina Louise was the largest celebrity attending a Toronto Pig Save all-day vigil on 8 May 2018. She shared a poignant Instagram posts with her two million followers.

It's also important to invite community leaders, including vegan politicians, to vigils. Esther Ouwehand, a Member of Parliament for Partj voor de Dieren (Party for the Animals), attended a Boxtel Pig Save vigil on 9 April 2018 and made a poignant video about her experience, which she said she would share with parliamentary members.

8. Climate Save and Health Save co-benefits

> We are close to the tipping point where global warming becomes irreversible. Trump's action could push the Earth over the brink, to become like Venus, with a temperature of 250 degrees, and raining sulphuric acid.
> – Stephen Hawking, *Democracy Now!* 30 March 2018

Global warming is the greatest threat to life on Earth. The Earth is heading for catastrophic climate change unless we see radical shifts in ending consumption of fossil fuels and a move away from animal agriculture towards a plant-based food system. Already, some tipping points are being crossed. Animal agriculture is responsible for at least 14 per cent of worldwide greenhouse gas emissions, more than the exhaust fumes from all transportation combined, according to conservative estimates by the Food and Agriculture Organization (FAO). World Bank experts Robert Goodland and Jeff Anhang have estimated animal agriculture is responsible for 51 per cent of greenhouse gas emissions using a full life-cycle analysis.

Toronto Pig Save launched a Climate Vegan campaign in 2016. Activists organised a series of teach-ins, attended climate change marches and rallies, and developed a subway ad campaign entitled 'We are eating the planet to death'. In 2018, the Animal Save Movement launched the Climate Save Movement and Health Save branches. Governments, corporations, the media and communities must acknowledge the devastation caused by animal agriculture and the leading role it plays in climate chaos and ecological breakdown. The mission of the Climate Save branch is to pressure governments, corporations and other institutions to phase out fossil fuels by 2025 (following Extinction Rebellion), end animal agriculture and fishing, transition to a just vegan food system and reforest the Earth. Our mission is to promote and make accessible a plant-based diet to solve the epidemic of preventable diseases and improve the quality of life in our community.

The three branches work together on solutions that involve individual change and system change. Our demands focus on vegan diet change, activism and #FoodSystemChangeNow! The Animal Save Movement places a focus on the individuality of the animals. Animals are persons, not property. The focus is brought back to individual animals through animal vigils while the climate and health campaigns highlight the need to transition to plant-based food systems.

9. Save organising drives

The Civil Rights Movement launched Freedom Summer in 1962 in Mississippi to register African American voters, the US labour movement created Union Summer in the 1990s for students to help with organising drives and the Service Employees International Union (SEIU), the biggest and fastest-growing union in the US, spent a quarter of its resources on organising. Similarly, the grassroots animal rights movements need to invest major resources in organising drives. The Animal Save Movement has sped up the movement-building process and expanded the worldwide network of chapters by arranging multiple organising drives. In 2017–2018, teams of organisers were sent to North America, Latin America and Europe to set up new groups in new countries. These organising drives have inspired and mobilised many vegans, helping them become activists and to bear witness in their community.

After the Pig Trial, Toronto Pig Save received more support. Increased funding enabled local Saves around the world to receive start-up and vigil grants, and globally the movement was able to launch a series of organising drives. We began with a VegFest program in Canada, the US and Latin America and Veggie World in Europe.

Besides tabling, organisers held vigils after the VegFests to start new groups. This had a major impact on extending the Animal Save Movement in the US, Latin America and Europe.

In the 2017, Save organisers participated in Summer Warp Musical Tour, the longest-running music tour in the United States. Ananda Elora (Niagara Farm Animal Save), Mariah Noelle (Brampton Chicken Save) and Jocelyn Cole (Portland Animal Save) joined the tour in 21 cities. With many of the touring bands interested in animal rights and the festival's audience being mainly young and progressive, it was a great place to table and raise awareness. Slaughterhouse vigils were held in each city and new Save groups were started along the way in Salem, Okachobee, Tampa and Hartford. Sam from Neck Deep, one of the headlining bands, wore a Save Movement t-shirt on stage. Jocelyn Cole says: 'Along the tour, chickens were liberated at vigils in both Florida and Texas and taken to sanctuary to live out the rest of their lives surrounded by love.'

VegFests tours are resource intensive involving flights to events and accommodation costs. More efficient and effective multi-city and multi-country Save organising tours began as a way of limiting travel costs and expanding the movement at a quickened pace. Teams of organisers go town to town and country to country in extended tours lasting anywhere from one month to over a year, often with the organisers staying at activists' homes. The mission of the organisers is to build a vegan and animal activist community, identifying and recruiting leaders and organising groups to hold regular animal activism. Oftentimes the tour organisers are heading into areas not only where there is little to no street animal activism, but also where veganism is very new. The tour organisers hold animal activist workshops to explain and train participants in a variety of activist approaches.

The first #SaveLatino tour in 2017 in Central and South America saw huge successes in holding vigils, starting new Saves, developing strong activist communities and, in some cases, even liberating animals and gaining access to slaughterhouses. Karol Marocho, Alex Bez and Taty Melo went to 11 countries in Latin America beginning in Sao Paolo, Brazil, then Asuncion, Paraguay; Curitiba, Brazil; Montevideo, Uruguay; Panama City; Costa Rica; Nicaragua; Honduras; Guatemala; Buenos Aires, Argentina; and the Dominican Republic.

In Panama they went to a slaughterhouse vigil at 4 am and saw a couple of trucks. The chicken slaughterhouse receives ten trucks a night. The neighbours complain about the smell. They say the slaughterhouse sprays the area with a scent! Activist Bruce Motto carpooled and provided food at the vigils. Bruce's family owns the largest airline in Latin America and also a huge ranch. He's chosen a different path. At the vigil in Costa Rica, on 20 October 2017, activists asked for a chicken. The slaughterhouse manager asked for money. Taty says they refused to pay but pleaded for a small or sick animal. The manager relented and gave them Pepita Rosario, a chicken they named after her. In Guatemala, there was difficulty in following up and organising regular vigils after a coup took place, prohibiting any criticism of the government.[17] In Managua, Nicaragua, the cow slaughterhouse in the semi-residential area was so big it covered a whole block. The slaughterhouse's slogan was 'Your friendly slaughterhouse'.

In Honduras, the taxi driver came and bore witness with the activists. Outside the slaughterhouse, there was a short man with a shotgun slung around his shoulder. Taty says they smiled at him and he relaxed and smiled too. They told him: 'We want to spend time with the animals. We love animals.' He agreed to let the activists bear witness beside the truck. The activists then ventured inside the slaughterhouse. What they next witnessed was the worst thing Taty ever saw. In the slaughterhouse, an instructor and groups of students were artificially inseminating 'dairy' cows on the kill floor pen. The instructor asked the veterinary student trainees why the observers were there. Trembling, they replied they were simply interested in animals. Since the state-run slaughterhouse was not trying to protect a brand, the instructor was less concerned about the curious onlookers and continued the demonstration. The last cow kicked and screamed and tried to get away. The instructor's attitude changed when the mother cow started to fight back. He began to insult her: 'If you want to resist, soon you'll be gone! You'll be turned into soup and hamburger. You'll be sent to China to make

---

17 This group is not able to be active due to political instability in the country.

leather bags.' Finally, the instructor decided: 'She was already used. Go to the next one. Let her go.' The saddest part, Taty says, was that when they untied her legs and head, the young mother cow simply collapsed on the floor motionless and looked straight ahead. 'She just had a blank stare. She had left herself, just like a human would.' Taty jumped into action and asked the one woman among the students to 'put yourself in that position'. Later that women took a selfie with the cows, so it was unclear what impact the intervention had. When the cows were slaughtered, Taty said at least then their suffering ended. The next day, the activists went back and saw students arriving again for more practice on the mother cows in the slaughterhouse kill pen.

In Buenos Aires, Karol and her team met with Voicot organisers to start the Animal Save Movement in Argentina (Voicot stands for Boycott). Buenos Aires Animal Save (BAAS) has become one of the strongest groups worldwide. It holds vigils every two weeks. In a December 2017 vigil, as noted above, activists observed a calf, subsequently named Save, being born on the truck. Fede says: 'The rescue highlighted how pregnant mothers are sent to slaughter.' The next day, at an emergency vigil, BAAS organiser Milena went into the slaughterhouse to negotiate the release of Save's mother, but sadly she had been slaughtered. At the next scheduled meeting, the slaughterhouse agreed to release any babies and also to stop every truck. That's how they got to do the hug around the truck. The group has received a lot of media coverage of Save and his mother, the hug and the vigils. The movement is growing quickly in Argentina with 21 Animal Save chapters, 7 Climate Save organisations, and 11 Health Save groups by September 2019. Another very active group, Mar De Plata Animal Save is 400 kilometres from Buenos Aires. Maria Paula, an organiser, says the coastal city offers great opportunities for vegan outreach as a major tourism destination.[18]

In November 2017, Alex and Karol continued with the European leg of the tour. There, Alex started doing two-hour talks on bearing

---

18   Karol and Taty embarked on their second Latin American tour in April 2018, hoping to reach countries with no Saves, such as Ecuador, revisit countries where Saves are building momentum and start additional groups there, and to shore up groups in Colombia with new organisers.

witness to help people understand why bearing witness is important and to connect people in advance of attending a vigil. In Barcelona, they booked an old cinema the night before the vigil. Thirty people showed up. Alex Bex says: 'People are not used to slaughterhouse vigils so it's important to familiarise them first. The next day 60 people came to Barcelona's first Save vigil.' At the vigil, activists rescued seven chickens. Lena, who later became a Save organiser in Austria and Germany, kept going into the slaughterhouse and taking more chickens. Meanwhile, a police officer was negotiating the release of additional chickens. A year before, a vigil had been organised by Cathy Clemenceau and this same officer was called. She was there again, and they recognised each other. The officer said: 'I know this woman. I helped this woman get a chicken because she was so peaceful and love-based.' The officer's partner, another female officer, helped stop the transport truck. She walked by as activists engaged in open rescues. 'She saw these and chose to ignore them', says Alex. The tour extended to Alicante and Mureia, Spain, with the biggest vigils in the south of Spain.

In Budapest, Hungary, Alex, Karol and Boro, a local organiser who scoped out the area, visited a cow slaughterhouse. The cows walked down the road to the slaughterhouse and then waited outside on a grassy patch. 'The cows licked our hands', says Karol. 'We spent an hour with the cows, feeding them grass.' They were given full access to this slaughterhouse.

Overall, the tour resulted in holding vigils at each of the cities and starting over a dozen new Save groups. Activists went inside six slaughterhouses, entering three kill floors and three slaughterhouse pens, and were even allowed to record. Using the love-based approach opened doors in unexpected ways. Communicating in a kind way with employees made the difference in their ability to negotiate 15 rescues during their tour, including chickens, horses, geese and a calf. The organisers' conclusion is: 'Be bold! You can get into slaughterhouses and witness the animals inside the pens and even the kill floor.' Angie, a local organiser for the Honduras Save, said, 'I had never been to a slaughterhouse until Taty, Karol and Alex came.'

Julie O'Neill presented a workshop on Animal Save Movement in Bombay at the Federation of Indian Animal Protection Organizations (FIAPO) Boot Camp on 20 December 2017 and was able to recruit activists to start new Saves in Kolkata, Pune, Lucknow and Mumbai. Julie is a Toronto resident but travels each year to India to volunteer for Animal Aid Unlimited. Bearing witness in the Indian context may be difficult. There are concerns that vigils may be interpreted as political or religious; there is a danger bearing witness to cow or goat slaughter could be mistaken for religious Hindu protests and inflame religious hatred. Kolkata Animal Save decided to target chicken meat shops around the city, where chickens are killed in the open, since these animals are also widely eaten by Hindus. The chickens are often transported on bicycles with five or ten chickens tied upside down on each handlebar. Organisers Pragya and Darshana Muza reported: 'It's very distressing to see them hung upside down. How do you make people actually look at the animals?' The challenge is to sensitise the public, used to seeing chickens slaughtered, to view chickens as sentient beings.

In March 2018, Shivonne Kaspara Egen and Ruth Leysner launched a year-long, 20-plus-country Northern and Eastern Europe tour. Shivonne is from Norway and turned vegan in 2015 and became an activist in 2017 when she was in England and joined Ed Winters and Luna at the Surge Animal Rights March. A year later she asked to start a tour across Northern and Eastern Europe after she met Save organiser Karol Marocho at the Luxembourg International Animal Rights Conference. Shivonne started by holding workshops in The Netherlands to encourage various forms of activism, drawing on the workshops that Paul and Asal held for Anonymous for the Voiceless. 'What people need is encouragement and support,' she says. Then she helped set up new groups in Norway. Ruth became vegan around the same time as Shivonne and in 2017 decided to quit her job and live with her mother so she could do full-time animal activism.

Before they travel to a location, they find slaughterhouses and locate local activists through social media groups. Once they arrive, they hold workshops to empower groups and activists to do street activism. The workshops cover 'a talk about the Animal Save Movement, Direct Action Everywhere (DxE), Anonymous for the Voiceless (AV), Challenge 22 and some other types of basic street activism'. Their objective is to 'create a more solid activist scene in Eastern Europe … and organise at least two events in every city'. At each stop, after they hold the animal activism workshop, they organise slaughterhouse vigils and one or more Cubes of Truth, disruptions and vegan outreach events.

> If there is no activist scene we will help create one. If there already is either a Save group, Cube of Truth or DxE chapter we will contact them and try to work together to create a stronger local activist scene. We will hold workshops about activism in every city to inspire people to do more in their area and to learn more about street activism. We try to find organisers for future vigils, Cubes and disruptions and ask other activists for help with permission [or permits] and to reach out to the local media.

The tour's mission is to show people how they can do activism in so many ways and start new Save, AV and DxE chapters where there is interest. Their plan was to start 40 Save groups. They were able to start dozens of Save, AV and DxE groups and help existing groups grow. Each of these grassroots groups complement each other by doing different forms of activism.

Activism, or at least street activism, is new or in its infancy stage in many places on the tours. For example, in Slovenia, there was little or no street animal activism before Shivonne and Ruth's activist van arrived. Now local organisers have a platform and are speaking out against local slaughterhouses. Shivonne explains what drives her: 'To see the change within people when they go from vegans to vegan activists and how they grow together as a community in a very short time and being able to help motivated activists to become organisers and start up in their local area.' Ruth says she likes to help 'make them feel proud of what they are doing ... to see this movement growing, is truly a gift'.

This is their summary after the first month of the tour:

> We have met many great activists from different cities and seen new vegan families being born ... We do see that a lot of people are very sceptical towards vigils and DxE, but after the workshop this changes in most people and we see that the people who join the workshops are also joining the vigil afterwards even if they were sceptical to begin with.

… We try to always do a workshop and a Cube before the other events so people already are connecting a bit and feel stronger when we are outside slaughterhouses, and this seems to be working quite well. So far, we have been having many great experiences and are very happy that we can open up for people who have been wanting to organise for a while but didn't know how to. We have gotten a lot of feedback from people saying that they really needed us to come and start this up and most people are very grateful and want to start doing things in their area. It is not always that we manage to find new organisers for all events, but there have always been new organisers for at least one of the events. We try to keep contact with some people so when someone is interested in organising we will help them get in touch with the right organisation. We are still learning a lot about how we can do it better and be more effective and we see that it is already going better now than in the beginning.

Lena and Alex's tour began in Spain: Tenerife and Mallorca. The tour also included Switzerland, Denmark and Sweden and ended in Austria with a new group in Salzburg. Both Alex and Lena are very love-based and showed activists the effects of being friendly to slaughterhouse workers. Using this approach, Lena has managed to have slaughterhouse workers in Vienna bring her and other activists to the kill floor. She says: 'We are there for the animals. We ask the slaughterhouse workers if they can stop the trucks so we can be safe.' Lena sends a friendly email to the slaughterhouse. In his first European tour, Alex's friendly chat with a slaughterhouse guard resulted in the man coming to his talk that evening in Barcelona.

On the third European tour (March–May 2018), Alex and Lena went on a six-country tour to start new Save groups, with an emphasis on Germany. With a human population of over 84 million and thousands of slaughterhouses, there remains a lot of room for growth.[19] Their tour included a ten-city German tour with new groups started in Munich, Freiburg, Stuttgart, Frankfurt, Halle-Leipzig, Hanover, Hamburg, Dresden and Nuremberg, and the group in Berlin was

---

19   A specific Climate Save tour had begun in Germany in the fall of 2019.

renewed following Lena and Alex's Save organising tour.[20] Their approach was often to contact the AV organisers in the cities they visited since AV already has more than 60 groups in Germany.

Gerion is active with the local Albert Schweitzer Centre chapter. He has lived next to a slaughterhouse his whole life. When he was a student, his school was near a slaughterhouse. Their new group, Kiel Animal Save, is near Hamburg, part of Schleswig-Holstein, where there are 15 slaughterhouses in a state dominated by the farming industry. Toennies is the biggest slaughterhouse with 80 trucks. His co-organiser Dilara lived close to a slaughterhouse in Lupig. She passed it every day on her way to school but never had any contact with the animals and only saw them at a distance. Now she's decided to face the animals and do more. She says being vegan is not enough: 'It bothers me how little people know. I have friends who are good people. If they knew, they would never do this. I feel responsible to open their eyes. Organising vigils is a good way to do this.'[21] Gerion's mother founded the Green party in the town they come from. She initiated a movement of local residents against the expansion of the slaughterhouse.

10. Ongoing mass training

In the animal rights movement, the DxE Forum, now Animal Liberation Conference, the convergences and the various Animal Justice Boot Camps in Europe have all played a great role in training activists in skills development and nonviolent direct action. We need permanent mass trainings to help build the movement further, using skilled and knowledgeable activists and organisers. Save started a Save Trainings working group in 2018. Save organisers have started offering training in community organising, strategic corporate research, campaign planning, momentum-driven organising and nonviolent direct action. Our strategic corporate research trainings on Cargill (a slaughterhouse and animal feed company that has been called 'the worst company in the world' by the Washington-based environmental campaign

---

20   Hollas 2018.
21   Interview, 13 March 2018.

organisation Mighty Earth) and Maple Leaf Foods (a protein company that is investing in both new plant-based and slaughter facilities) has helped us develop campaigns with escalating tactics. Our eight-week training series on momentum-driven organising included reading and discussing the book *This is an Uprising* and watching the accompanying webinar series on the Ayni Institute website. Save has set up a team of country and regional liaisons and climate campaigners who are also starting reading circles to study momentum organising. Seventeen Save organisers also took a four-day training course on Kingian nonviolence in Ohio with lead trainer David Jehnsen, who worked with Martin Luther King in the 1960s. Those on Save tours can further spread the trainings by offering training workshops across the world.

Conclusions

The Animal Save Movement emphasises that everyone has a choice when confronted with suffering animals: to look away or to come close and try to help. Everyone knows it is wrong to look away and do nothing in the face of suffering and injustice. Our goal is to hold vigils at every slaughterhouse, auction house and animal agriculture farm and have everyone bear witness in a more complete way. We need to create opportunities for people to bear witness regularly, to hold more and larger vigils, including all-day vigils with vegan food, vegan celebrities and workshops, and to unify the animal rights movement and build animal and social justice coalitions and alliances. We also need to move beyond single tactics to a campaign focus with escalating tactics. Save trainings in strategic corporate campaigns, campaign planning and nonviolence have already helped us in developing campaigns and targeted actions against specific slaughterhouse companies and animal feed companies.

References

Alinsky, S. (1946). *Reveille for Radicals*. Chicago: University of Chicago Press.

Arellano, G. (2019). As pigs await slaughter at Farmer John, strangers offer water, love and comfort to the doomed. *Los Angeles Times*. 5 March. https://lat.ms/2FKvBUU

Bronfenbrenner, K., S. Friedman, R. W. Hurd, R. A. Oswald and R. L. Seeber (Eds.) (1998). *Organizing to Win*. Ithaca: Cornell University Press.

Carbstrong, J. (2018). Telephone interview with author. 14 February.

Chenoweth, E. and M. J. Stephan (2011). *Why Civil Resistance Works: the Strategic Logic of Nonviolent Conflict*. New York: Columbia University Press.

Engler, M. and P. Engler (2016). *This is an Uprising*. New York: Nation Books.

Gibbs, L. (1997). *Dying from Dioxin: A Citizen's Guide to Reclaiming our Health and Rebuilding Democracy*. Montreal: Black Rose Books.

Goodland, Robert (2010). *'Livestock and Climate Change': Critical Comments and Responses*. Washington: World Watch Institute.

Hollas, L (2018). The Save Movement UK and Europe Highlights.

Horton, H. (2017). Christmas turkeys make a break for it after trailer overturns – and one is saved by vegan activist. *The Telegraph*. 8 December. https://bit.ly/2YtcrcV

Krajnc, A. (2017). Bearing witness: Is giving thirsty pigs water criminal mischief or a duty? *Animal Law Review* 23(2).

Mann, E. (2011). *Playbook for Progressives*. Boston: Beacon Press.

Perth Pig Save (2018). Perth Pig Save highlights and future plans.

Princen, T., M. Maniates and K. Conca (Eds.) (2002). *Confronting Consumption*. Cambridge: The MIT Press.

Sanders, M. K. and S. Alinsky (1970). *The Professional Radical: Conversations with Saul Alinsky*. Evanston and London: Harper and Row.

Tolstoy, L. (1997). *A Calendar of Wisdom* (P. Sekirin, Trans.). New York: Scribner.

Wasley, A. (2018). 'Dirty meat': Shocking hygiene failings discovered in US pig and chicken plants. *The Guardian*. 21 February. https://bit.ly/2YsnumA

12

Afterword: Meatsplaining in the Pyrocene

Jason Hannan

On 20 August 2019, just as this collection was being finalised, the cyberworlds of Twitter, Facebook and Instagram were set alight by the hashtag #prayforamazonia, a desperate and haunting cry for help in response to the tens of thousands of fires eating away at one of the great wonders of the natural world: the iconic and internationally revered Amazon rainforest.[1] The sense of alarm over the destruction of the Amazon was most pronounced on Twitter, where hundreds of users posted disturbing images of burning forests, pleading with the world to pay attention to an unfolding ecological catastrophe. Commonly known as 'the lungs of the Earth', the Amazon is widely understood to be a vital ecosystem, serving not just as a natural carbon sink but also as a biodiversity hotspot to millions of plant and animal species. The Amazon is also home to hundreds of Indigenous communities, who have lived in a state of genuine harmony with the surrounding environment for millennia. News of the Amazon going up in flames therefore understandably sparked widespread fears across social media. As one Twitter user put it: '#ICantSleepBecause The Amazon has been burning for 3 weeks, and I'm just now finding out because of the lack of media coverage. THIS IS ONE OF THE MOST IMPORTANT ECOSYSTEMS ON EARTH. SPREAD

---

1   Madani 2019.

AWARENESS #PrayforAmazonia.'[2] Some users posted disturbing video footage of Sao Paulo with a daytime sky so thoroughly blackened by smoke that it appears to be the dead of night, thereby adding to the sense of apocalyptic horror.[3]

The deforestation of the Amazon was the entirely predictable outcome of the election of Brazilian President Jair Bolsonaro, a man aptly dubbed 'the Trump of the tropics'.[4] A former military officer with a long history of complicity in state violence, Bolsonaro is regarded as a real-life monster by human rights groups, environmental organisations and NGOs. As an authoritarian strongman with fascist impulses, he sees women, the poor, Indigenous communities and environmental activists as so many irritating and recalcitrant obstacles to Brazil's march towards political and economic glory. Bolsonaro has long viewed the industrial development of the Amazon as the key to this glory. He therefore exhibits a sociopathic contempt for human rights and the environment.[5]

In response to climate scientists who have warned that further deforestation of the Amazon will exponentially exacerbate climate change, Bolsonaro's foreign minister, Ernesto Araújo, declared climate change a 'hoax' perpetrated by 'cultural Marxists'.[6] For rapacious ranchers, loggers and miners hungry for fast and easy money, the election of Bolsonaro in 2018 was the green light for which they had long been waiting. Now they were finally free to clear the Amazon without fear of repercussion.[7] Since Bolsonaro's election, deforestation of the Amazon has skyrocketed, reaching a horrifying rate of two football fields per minute. In 2019 alone, almost 10,000 square kilometres were lost to logging and deliberate forest fires.[8] Brazil's National Institute for Space Research recorded more then 80,000 fires in 2019.[9] Amazon forest fires are part of a larger problem of

2   Johnson 2019.
3   Jackson 2019a.
4   Phillips 2018.
5   Lopes & Bostford 2019.
6   Watts 2018.
7   Londoño & Casado 2019.
8   Watts 2019.
9   Phillips 2019.

anthropogenic wildfires, which have inspired environmental historian Stephen Pyne to declare our age the Pyrocene.[10] We now live in a world of calamitous wildfires raging across the globe.

The burning of the Amazon has become a powerful wake-up call for the international community. Horrific aerial images of vast swaths of primeval rainforest razed to the ground have prompted inquiries into the primary drivers of deforestation. According to Yale's School of Forestry and Environmental Studies, cattle ranching is responsible for a staggering 80 per cent of deforestation rates in the Amazon. Some 200 million cattle now inhabit what used to be old-growth rainforest, making up one quarter of the international beef market. Because Brazilian cattle are fed a diet partly of soy, the dual production of both cattle and soy drives ranchers ever deeper into the Amazon. With the introduction of new roads, transportation, electricity, meat processing plants and other key pieces of development infrastructure, cattle ranching has become easier and more lucrative than ever. Shockingly, the production of beef requires five times as much land as poultry and ten times as much land as grain. The total amount of land devoted to beef production in Brazil is five times that devoted to crop production, making it by far one of the most land- and resource-intensive forms of agriculture in the world.[11] Although fire has long been used as a method for maintaining healthy soil, it has also become a cheap and easy technique for ranchers to clear the land of old-growth forest and make room for more cattle. Ranchers eager to raise cattle on new land have no hesitation setting fire to the forest and no concern about the consequences for the planet.

The revelations about the role of the meat industry in the destruction of the Amazon have rightly unleashed a flood of alarming headlines: 'Revealed: rampant deforestation of Amazon driven by global greed for meat', 'The Amazon is burning because the world eats so much meat', 'How beef demand is accelerating the Amazon's deforestation and climate peril', 'As Amazon continues to burn, fingers point to beef industry as driving force behind fires', 'Brazil is the world's largest beef exporter – here's why eating meat is linked to the Amazon

---

10   Pyne 2015; Pyne 2019, p. 195.
11   Global Forest Atlas n.d.

fires', 'Cows are killing the Amazon' and 'Every meat-eater on the planet is helping to fuel the Amazon forest fires – here's how'.[12] On social media, stories like these have gone viral, along with memes making much the same point, but in simpler and more memorable form. One of the most powerful and dramatic of these memes depicts a gigantic fork picking up a neatly cut morsel of rainforest land, its soil-covered roots having been violently torn from the earth. The morsel is covered with trees. But beneath the trees are the blood-red sinews of rare steak. The message could not be clearer: every bite of beef contributes to the destruction of the Amazon.[13]

How, then, has the beef industry responded to this unprecedented negative publicity? One response has been flat-out denial. This is the approach, for example, of BEEF Magazine, a major industry publication that actively denies the link between beef production and climate change by featuring blogs and videos of industry representatives citing, referencing and interviewing other industry representatives.[14] The half-hearted and transparent propaganda of industry representatives citing their own kind establishes a clear disregard for the planet, but also indicates a lack of seriousness in their own talking points.

A far more dangerous response, however, comes from proponents of so-called humanely farmed grass-fed meat. Pitting themselves against factory farming, this segment of the meat industry stakes its reputation on the supposed sustainability of grass-fed meat. Incredibly, many proponents of grass-fed meat claim they hold the key to tackling our environmental crisis. Unlike their industrial counterparts, who simply deny the link between cattle and climate change, proponents of grass-fed meat insist the problem lies specifically with the industrial model of cattle farming. By contrast, they claim the grass-fed model is not just environmentally friendly; rather, it actually holds the power to fight climate change.

Consider, for example, an article in *Civil Eats*, a news and opinion outlet for the slow food movement, entitled, 'A livestock farmer's

---

12 Phillips, Wasley & Heal 2019; Mackintosh 2019; Ingraham 2019; Jackson 2019a; Hyde 2019; Lockwood 2019.
13 PETA 2019.
14 Radke 2019.

response to the Amazon fires'. The author, Carrie Wasser, acknowledges the problem of rampant forest fires and deforestation in the Amazon. She rightly attributes this problem to animal agriculture. Yet, in contrast to those calling for an indefinite moratorium on meat production and consumption, Wasser asks, 'Does local, humanely raised meat have a role to play in preventing more destruction of the Amazon?' As a livestock farmer, Wasser takes pride in producing 'humane' and 'grass-finished' meat. As she puts it, 'I've chosen only humanely raised meat for the past 10 years because animal welfare is my number one priority'. Wasser says she only buys grass-fed beef, because a diet of grass is healthier for cows and because 'some of those animals are grazed on pastures that are sustainably managed to improve the soil and sequester carbon'. Wasser suggests that by buying local, grass-fed meat, North American consumers will reduce the market for imported Brazilian beef. She therefore affirms the role of grass-fed meat in combatting Amazon deforestation. The deforestation of the Amazon thus serves as an inadvertent marketing opportunity for the grass-fed beef industry.[15]

What, according to Wasser, makes grass-fed beef so special? She concedes that much of the beef produced in Brazil is technically grass-fed. Yet, she insists, not all grass-fed beef is alike. Some grass-fed farming methods enable 'farmers to raise livestock in a manner that does not destroy the world's most vital ecosystems'. Wasser takes her inspiration from organisations such as Regeneration International, the Inga Foundation, the Rodale Institute and the Savory Institute. These organisations, she says, 'teach farmers how to manage grasslands so that they remain healthy and productive and capture carbon from the atmosphere'. Through their supposedly revolutionary farming methods, these organisations hold that not only can we mitigate the effects of climate change, we can also *reverse* climate change altogether. As an adherent of this thinking, Wasser believes that grass-fed meat is an environmental miracle.[16]

Wasser's position is part of a powerful and rapidly growing movement in the Western world that invests enormous hope and faith

---

15   Wasser 2019.
16   Wasser 2019.

in humane and organic animal farming. In addition to the organisations mentioned above, other prominent organisations in this movement include Carbon Farmers of America, Carbon Farmers of Australia, the Pasture Fed Livestock Association, Soil Carbon Coalition, Land Steward Project and Sustainable Food Trust. This movement disseminates its message through books, documentaries and countless YouTube videos.[17] Their media universe is an example of what Todd Gitlin calls a public 'sphericule': a limited and self-contained space for public communication that exists alongside countless other such spaces.[18]

What, exactly, does the humane meat movement believe? As a baseline, it sees an almost supernatural power in ruminants – herbivorous mammals that extract nutrients from plants through a complex, multi-chamber stomach that breaks down tough plant material through a process of fermentation. The humane meat movement regards ruminants as a kind of all-purpose wonder of nature. Ruminant dung, the argument goes, replenishes the soil with vital minerals and nutrients. When the animals trample the ground, they help mix that dung into the soil. By enriching the soil, they help regenerate the land, thereby making different forms of crop farming possible. Ruminants therefore play a critical and indispensable role in a sustainable food system.

But the belief in the power of ruminants does not stop there. A more extreme argument maintains that ruminants hold the power to combat climate change. This view focuses very narrowly on greenhouse gas emissions, and only one greenhouse gas at that: carbon. According to this extreme view, by grazing on grasslands, replenishing the soil and regenerating the land, ruminants not only prevent the release of stored carbon from the ground, they also enable carbon sequestration through the soil. This view downplays the significance of other potent greenhouse gases, such as methane and nitrogen. It maintains that biogenic methane produced by domesticated ruminants is no different and no worse than that historically produced by wild ruminants (i.e. buffalo) before their eradication by European settlers. Therefore,

---

17 Influential books include Niman 2014; Schwartz 2013; Brown 2018.
18 Gitlin 1998.

domesticated ruminants reared through holistic management do not, in the aggregate, contribute to climate change. This extreme view also maintains that because the atmospheric lifespan of methane is much shorter than that of carbon, it is misguided to obsess over methane at all. Instead, we should focus exclusively on carbon.

Perhaps the most influential spokesperson for this extreme view is Allan Savory, best known for his TED Talk, 'How to Green the World's Deserts and Reverse Climate Change'. Savory is a Zimbabwean ecologist and animal farmer. He is the president of the Savory Institute and the founder of the holistic management model of animal agriculture, which he pioneered in the 1960s. The basic premise of Savory's holistic management model is that animal farming that 'mimics nature' and operates in a symbiotic relationship with every element of the surrounding environment can contribute to ecological sustainability. Holistic management, Savory argues, can mitigate and even reverse the effects of anthropogenic environmental change, such as desertification and global warming. Savory claims that holistic management holds truly incredible potential for carbon sequestration. In his TED Talk, Savory makes the following unbelievable claim:

> we can take enough carbon out of the atmosphere and safely store it in the grassland soils for thousands of years, and if we just do that on about half the world's grasslands that I've shown you, *we can take us back to pre-industrial levels* while feeding people. I can think of almost nothing that offers more hope for our planet, for your children, for their children, and all of humanity.[19]

This is more than a mere empirical claim. It's magical thinking – the full-blown promise of ecological and humanitarian salvation, presented in quasi-religious language by a charismatic figure who has achieved cult status in the humane animal farming movement. At the time of this writing, Savory's TED Talk has been viewed nearly four million times on YouTube. It is therefore worth asking: is there any evidence to support his bold claim about the power of holistic management in reversing climate change?

---

19   TED 2013.

A 2016 review by Swedish researcher Maria Nordberg concluded that the claims about reversing desertification and climate change lacked any empirical basis.[20] Nordberg found that the Savory Institute relied on only a handful of peer-reviewed studies. Of these studies, only six actually use quantitative analyses, while five are based on qualitative research in the form of surveys and interviews. Moreover, none of the studies offers any conclusive evidence in support of the climate change reversal thesis. Nordberg also found no study demonstrating the superiority of the holistic management model over conventional farming practices. Rather, the 'claimed benefits of the method thus appear to be exaggerated and/or lack broad scientific support'. Nordberg further found some of the claims 'directly at odds with scientific knowledge'. She points out that the rate of carbon sequestration through holistic grazing is at best seven times lower than that claimed by the Savory Institute to support its central thesis concerning climate change reversal. Nordberg therefore concludes that the holistic management model 'can thus not reverse climate change'.[21]

Other studies support this negative conclusion about holistic management and the alleged magic of livestock grazing. A 2008 study published in the *Journal of Arid Environments* compared the effects of wild ungulates (large mammals with hooves) versus livestock on soil organic carbon. It found that areas in which livestock grazed the land had half the soil organic carbon as those traversed by wild ungulates.[22] A 2010 study in *Agricultural Systems* compared three different models of beef production, and found that grass-fed beef had the highest impact in terms of energy use, greenhouse gas emissions and eutrophication.[23] Contrary to Savory's claim that livestock grazing holds the power to sequester carbon, a 2013 study in *Agriculture, Ecosystems & Environment* found that livestock grazing drastically reduced the amount of organic carbon in the soil, while keeping the land free of grazing resulted in a higher concentration of carbon.[24] A

---

20 Nordberg 2016.
21 Nordberg 2016, p. 32.
22 Fernandez, Neff & Reynods 2008.
23 Pelletier, Pirog & Rasmussen 2010.
24 Daryanto, Eldridge & Throop 2013.

2014 article in the *International Journal of Biodiversity* found that the 'use of HM in an attempt to capture atmospheric greenhouse gases and incorporate them into soils and plant communities, thereby reducing climate change effects, is demonstrably impossible'.[25] A 2017 report by Oxford University's Food Climate Research Network analysing livestock grazing systems concluded that such systems produce more greenhouse gas emissions than they sequester. It further concluded that livestock grazing systems cannot meet either current or future demands for meat and milk, and that expanding the current systems in a misguided attempt to meet such demand 'would cause catastrophic land-use change and other environmental damage'.[26] A 2018 article in *Environmental Research Letters* found that a nationwide switch in the US to grass-fed beef would require increasing the total number of cattle from 77 million to 100 million, resulting in a far higher environmental impact.[27] Contrary to what the humane animal farming movement claims, then, study after study indicates that the holistic, grass-fed model is a detriment to the environment.

Yet, despite the deafening lack of evidence, the humane animal farming movement nonetheless persists in making wildly extravagant claims – some of them misleading, many of them outright false – about the environmental promise of the holistic management model and grass-fed meat. How, then, to explain this dogmatic persistence? How do we account for the obstinate disregard for scientific evidence, the belief in the absurd, the desperate clinging to a demonstrable falsehood? Is this belief part of a deeper current of irrationalist, anti-modernist thinking? I would like to suggest the rapid growth of the worldwide humane meat movement is a case of what Andrew Potter calls 'neoprimitivism'.[28]

Potter sees the paleo diet, the 'ancestral health' movement and the anti-vaccine movement as symptoms of the phenomenon of neoprimitivism. He observes that a frighteningly large segment of contemporary society now looks upon 'the main tributaries of

25   Carter, Jones, O'Brien, Ratner & Wuerthner 2014.
26   Garnett et al. 2017, p. 124.
27   Hayek & Garrett 2018.
28   Potter 2015.

modernity' with unapologetic scepticism and hostility. But instead of actually rejecting modernity, they have merely swapped one part of it for another, thereby living in the fantasy that they have somehow escaped it altogether. Potter calls this desire to escape modernity the 'quest for authenticity'. As he puts it, 'This is the search for meaning in a world that is alienating, spiritually disenchanted, socially flattened, technologically obsessed, and thoroughly commercialised.' And, we might add, environmentally ravaged by a modern industrial food system. In the face of a disenchanting and alienating world, the idea of authenticity acquires a certain powerful and irresistible allure.[29]

Yet, Potter observes, the turn to authenticity as a way to find meaning in a meaningless world has two very dangerous consequences. The first is that the quest for authenticity becomes a form of competition, 'exacerbating many of the very problems it was designed to solve'. The second is that the perfectly valid concern with certain negative aspects of modernity can easily slide into a dangerous kind of anti-scientific thinking. One form of such thinking is the irrational romanticisation of the past, even a past that never existed. As Potter puts it:

Modernity, as a civilisation, sits at the confluence of secularism, liberalism, and capitalism, and it is not everyone's cup of coffee. The promise of the authentic is that it will help us carve out a space where true community can flourish outside of the cash nexus and in a way that treads lightly upon the Earth. More often than not, this manifests itself through nostalgia, for a misremembered time when the air was cleaner, the water purer, and communities more nurturing.[30]

But, Potter argues, this craving for authenticity, for grapes that we can never grasp, is really a craving for status. He invokes Thorsten Veblen's concept of conspicuous consumption to make this point. To take a few familiar examples, organic food, yoga, bone broth and kombucha are just as much a matter of public style as they are of private taste. They

29 Potter 2015.
30 Potter 2015.

define personal identity and interpersonal difference. They demarcate the self from the other, us from them, and communicate status within a social hierarchy.

Yet, the lines of demarcation are never stable. Once the objects of conspicuous consumption become common, they are no longer conspicuous. They leave the consumer craving more of whatever unattainable quality it was that set them apart. The consumer therefore desires a return to a lost status in the status hierarchy. As Potter puts it, 'The problem is you can only be authentic as long as most of the people around you are not, which has its own built-in radicalizing dynamic.' This in turns leads to the problem of extremism. It is a short step, for example, from eschewing the many unnecessary and harmful products of the pharmaceutical industry to rejecting vaccines. The quest for authenticity can easily devolve into 'a thoroughgoing rejection of science, technology, and reason itself'. Hence, the implacable hostility of the anti-vaccine movement to the science of immunology, regardless of how much evidence is adduced in defence of vaccines.[31]

I want to suggest that the grass-fed meat movement is an example of the neoprimitivist quest for authenticity. The legitimate disgust with modern industrial animal farming – the confinement of animals, the unnatural animal feeds, the administration of hormones and antibiotics – gives the idea of 'organic', 'free-range' and 'grass-fed' meat a certain seductive appeal. Yet, the more common grass-fed beef becomes, the more watered down its appeal. This in part explains the rise in pointless and unnecessary hunting among many women who now see wild game as the most natural and authentic kind of meat.[32] This also explains the quest for purity among grass-fed beef enthusiasts, who feel the need to distinguish better from worse grass-fed meat. Most importantly, it explains the fanaticism with which so many cling to the myths of grass-fed meat and the hostility towards scientific scrutiny of those cherished myths. Fantasy is more comforting and nourishing than reality.

But worse, it is precisely this irrational faith in grass-fed meat that, I want to suggest, accounts for the bizarre idea that grass-fed

---

31   Potter 2015.
32   Mitchell 2014.

meat is not only the answer to world hunger but also the solution to our ecological crisis. It appears that having invested so much hope and optimism in grass-fed meat, it is not much of a leap to turn to cows for outright salvation. This twisted idolatry is perfectly in keeping with the magical, anti-scientific thinking of neoprimitivism. If there is one lesson, it is that meatsplaining in the Pyrocene is more than mere industry propaganda. When sincere faith in miracles becomes the premise of a movement, its rhetoric becomes all the more seductive, potent, durable and resilient. The true believer will tenaciously cling to belief in miracles and faith in the absurd, even as the world burns, perhaps precisely *because* the world burns. Arguing with a true believer in the age of the Pyrocene therefore only risks adding further fuel to the fire – literally and metaphorically.

Even as this volume was being put together, new patterns have emerged in meat industry rhetoric. In response to declining sales, the dairy industry has launched a campaign against plant-based milks and the beef industry has launched a similar campaign against popular new plant-based products like the Beyond Meat™ burger and the Impossible™ burger.[33] The meat industry has further sought to police language and prohibit the use of terms like *milk, butter,* cheese and *burger* in the labelling of plant-based food products.[34] While contempt and hostility towards vegans is nothing new, trolling vegans has become a new marketing gimmick.[35] And as the Amazon burns, humane animal farmers have rushed to distinguish grass-fed beef as ecologically sustainable. Thus, even in the short time it took to put this volume together, the terms and terrain of meat industry rhetoric have evolved and expanded, and will very likely continue to evolve and expand for the foreseeable future. This collection was designed to start a necessary and urgent conversation about the phenomenon of meatsplaining – to make it explicit, to propose a basic typology and to offer several initial analyses of meatsplaining in practice. This collection is just the start of a much larger and ongoing collective project of bringing one of the most powerful and ubiquitous forms of industry rhetoric under systematic

---

33   Atkin 2018; Rothman 2018; Purdy 2019.
34   O'Conner 2017; Selyukh 2019; Shanker & Mulvany 2019; Szklarski 2019.
35   Kateman 2019.

critical scrutiny. The hope is that it will provide students, scholars and activists with new terminology and a new conceptual framework for making sense of meat industry rhetoric, for deconstructing and dismantling the industry's ever-expanding list of talking points, and for challenging the manipulation of public opinion. If our ecological crisis has taught us anything, it is that the dual project of critique and resistance is, to borrow a phrase from Alasdair MacIntyre, 'not a right, but a duty'.[36]

References

Atkin, E. (2018). The war on soy milk. *The New Republic.* 20 July. https://newrepublic.com/article/150006/war-soy-milk

Brown, G. (2018). *Dirt to Soil: One Family's Journey into Regenerative Agriculture.* Vermont: Chelsea Green Publishing.

Carter, J., A. Jones, M. O'Brien, J. Ratner and G. Wuerthner (2014). Holistic management: Misinformation on the science of grazed ecosystems. *International Journal of Biodiversity, 2014:* 1–10.

Daryanto, S., D. J. Eldridge and H. Throop (2013). Managing semi-arid woodlands for carbon storage: Grazing and shrub effects on above- and below-ground carbon. *Agriculture, Ecosystems & Environment* 169, 1–11.

Fernandez, D. P., J. Neff, R. L. Reynods (2008). Biogeochemical and ecological impacts of livestock grazing in semi-arid south-eastern Utah, USA. *Journal of Arid Environments* 72(5), 777–791.

Garnett, T., C. Godde, A. Muller, E. Röös, P. Smith, I. de Boer, ... H. van Zanten (2017). Grazed and confused? Ruminating on cattle, grazing systems, methane, nitrous oxide, the soil carbon sequestration question – and what it all means for greenhouse gas emissions. Oxford: Food Climate Research Network.

Gitlin, T. (1998). Public sphere or public sphericules. In. T. Liebes and J. Curren (Eds.), *Media, Ritual, and Identity* (pp. 168–174). London, UK: Routledge.

Global Forest Atlas (n.d.). Cattle ranching in the Amazon region. *Yale School of Forestry and Environmental Studies.* https://globalforestatlas.yale.edu/amazon/land-use/cattle-ranching

Hayek, M. N. and R. D. Garrett (2018). Nationwide shift to grass-fed beef requires larger cattle population. *Environmental Research Letters* 13, 1–8.

---

36   MacIntyre 1968.

Hyde, J. (2019). Cows are killing the Amazon. Pledges from Walmart and Nike didn't help save it. *Los Angeles Times*. 4 October. https://lat.ms/3lkchyn

Ingraham, C. (2019). How beef demand is accelerating the Amazon's deforestation and climate peril. *Washington Post*. 27 August. https://wapo.st/34tCgNQ

Jackson, H. (2019a). Sao Paulo shrouded in darkness as Amazon rainforest continues to burn. *Global News*. 21 August. https://globalnews.ca/news/5789726/sao-paulo-darkness-amazon-wildfires/

Jackson, H. (2019b). As Amazon continues to burn, fingers point to beef industry as driving force behind fires. *Global News*. 27 August. https://bit.ly/34mVrJ0

Johnson, J. (2019). #PrayForAmazonia goes viral as Twitter users call attention to 'International Emergency' of fires devastating Brazil's rainforest. *Common Dreams*. 20 August. https://bit.ly/2YKaVTV

Kateman, B. (2019). Arby's is unknowingly trolling many of its own customers with its 'carrot' made of meat. *Entrepreneur*. 9 July. https://www.entrepreneur.com/article/336200

Lockwood, A. (2019). Every meat-eater on the planet is helping to fuel the Amazon forest fires – here's how. *The Independent*. 23 August. https://bit.ly/3lcxUQZ

Londoño, E. and L. Casado (2019). Amazon deforestation in Brazil rose sharply on Bolsonaro's watch. *New York Times*. 18 November. https://nyti.ms/34tiG4g

Lopes, M. and J. Botsford (2019). 'We see destruction.' Bolsonaro wants to develop the Amazon. The Munduruku fear the end of their way of life. *Washington Post*. 21 August. https://wapo.st/2Yp4qFG

MacIntyre, A. 1968. 'Le Rouge et le Noir.' *New Statesman*. 22 November. In P. Blackledge and N. Davidson (Eds.), *Alasdair MacIntyre's Engagement with Marxism: Selected Writings 1953–1974* (p. xlvii). Chicago, IL: Haymarket Books.

Mackintosh, E. (2019). The Amazon is burning because the world eats so much meat. *CNN*. 23 August. https://cnn.it/3j4XXrt

Madani, D. and Associated Press (2019). Raging rainforest fires darken skies in Brazil, inspire #prayforamazonia. *NBC News*. 21 August. https://nbcnews.to/34qnPd4

Mitchell, A. (2014). Why more women are taking up hunting. *The Globe & Mail*. 22 August. https://tgam.ca/3lfSkss

Niman, N. H. (2014). *Defending Beef: The Case for Sustainable Meat Production*. Vermont: Chelsea Green Publishing.

Nordberg, M. (2016). *Holistic Management – A Critical Review of Allan Savory's Grazing Method*. Sweden: Swedish University of Agricultural Sciences.

O'Connor, A. (2017). Got almond milk? Dairy farms protest milk label on nondairy farms. *New York Times*. 13 February. https://nyti.ms/3ld0u4Q

Pelletier, N., R. Pirog, and R. Rasmussen (2010). Comparative life cycle environmental impacts of three beef production strategies in the Upper Midwestern United States. *Agricultural Systems* 103(6), 380–389.

PETA (2019, 21 September). So powerful! When you take a bite of meat, you're also taking a bite out of the #AmazonRainforest [Twitter post]. https://twitter.com/peta/status/1168238353474576391?lang=de

Phillips, D., A. Wasley, and A. Heal (2019). Revealed: Rampant deforestation of Amazon driven by global greed for meat. *The Guardian*. 2 July. https://bit.ly/32nTlWw

Phillips, T. (2018). Trump of the tropics: The 'dangerous' candidate leading Brazil's presidential race. *The Guardian*. 19 April. https://bit.ly/3j8Oj7g

Phillips, T. (2019). 'Worst of wildfires still to come' despite Brazil claiming crisis is under control. *The Guardian*. 28 August. https://bit.ly/2EiMdCM

Potter, A. (2015). Authenticity, anti-vaxxers, and the rise of neoprimitivism. *Ottawa Citizen*. 21 February. https://bit.ly/3jbl3ge

Purdy, C. (2019). Congress' beef with plant-based companies using the word 'meat'. *Quartz*. 28 October. https://bit.ly/34t8iZZ

Pyne, S. (2015). The fire age. *Aeon*. 5 May. https://bit.ly/3jl17aP

Pyne, S. (2019). *Fire: a Brief History* (2nd ed.). Seattle: University of Washington Press.

Radke, A. (2019). 5 resources to combat the cattle & climate change link. *BEEF Magazine*. September 30. https://bit.ly/2YupH0O

Rothman, L. (2018). The meat lobby's bill to ban the phrase 'fake meat' shows the real threat of plant-based alternatives. *Vice*. 24 May. https://bit.ly/3ldn79a

Schwartz, J. (2013). *Cows save the planet: And other improbable ways of restoring soil to heal the earth*. White River Junction, VT: Chelsea Green Publishing.

Selyukh, A. (2019). What gets to be a 'burger'? States restrict labels on plant-based meat. *NPR*, July 23. https://n.pr/3j9hTt4

Shanker, D. and L. Mulvany (2019). Big dairy battling vegan industry in butter-labeling war. *Fortune*. June 17. https://bit.ly/3jl1bHB

Szklarski, C. (2019). Battle over vegan cheese label is a freedom of expression issue, lawyers say. *CTV News*, July 31. https://bit.ly/32kCqnN

TED (2013). How to green the world's deserts and reverse climate change | Allan Savory [video]. 4 March 2013. https://youtu.be/vpTHi7O66pI

Wasser, C. (2019). A livestock farmer's response to the Amazon fires. *Civil Eats*. September 4. https://bit.ly/2FHNZxF

Watts, J. (2018). Brazil's new foreign minister believes climate change is a Marxist plot. *The Guardian*. 15 November. https://bit.ly/34r6QYd

Watts, J. (2019). Amazon deforestation 'at highest level in a decade'. *The Guardian*. November 18. https://bit.ly/3j9HP8c

About the Contributors

Núria Almiron is Associate Professor at Universitat Pompeu Fabra (UPF) in Barcelona, Spain. Dr Almiron's main research areas are critical animal and media studies, the ethics and political economy of communication, interest groups and advocacy regarding the climate emergency and nonhuman animals' oppression. She has published more than 50 peer-reviewed articles and is an author, co-author or editor of 30 volumes, including the co-edited books *Critical Animal and Media Studies* (Routledge, 2016) and *Public Relations and Climate Change Denial* (Routledge, 2020). She is the co-director of the UPF-Centre for Animal Ethics, the director of THINKClima Research Project and the director of the MA in International Studies in Media, Power and Difference.

Lisa Barca is Senior Lecturer in the honors college at Arizona State University, where she teaches humanities seminars and courses on animal ethics. Her research critiques journalistic representations of veganism and of nonhuman animals, exposing how the media normalize speciesist violence and omit truthful representations of exploited animals and those committed to protecting their interests. She is also the singer, writer, and guitarist for the all-vegan punk band Scarlet Rescue.

Alexa Dare is Associate Professor of Communication at the University of Portland, where she also directs the Social Justice minor. She works and teaches at the intersection(s) of Cultural Studies and Environmental Communication and is guided by an overarching interest in materiality and embodiment, especially in the context of protest and activism. Much of her recent research examines questions related to interspecies solidarity and human-nonhuman relations. She is the co-editor (with Vail Fletcher) of the forthcoming book, *Intimate Relations: Communicating (in) the Anthropocene.*

Vail Fletcher is Associate Professor in the Department of Communication at the University of Portland and Co-Director of the Gender and Women's Studies program. Dr Fletcher currently teaches courses related to Ecofeminsim, Poverty and Development, and Conflict and the Environment. Her research broadly focuses on the intersections of culture, conflict, and environmental communication. She has recently published three edited volumes: *Intimate Relations: Communicating (in) the Anthropocene* (Lexington, 2020), *Natural Disasters and Risk Communication: Implications of the Cascadia Subduction Zone Megaquake* (Lexington, 2018), and *Understanding Occupy from Wall Street to Portland: Applied Studies in Communication Theory* (Lexington, 2015). She lives on a farm that practices interspecies collaboration on Sauvie Island, Oregon (on unceded Chinook land).

Daniel Lees Fryer is Associate Professor of English at Østfold University College, Norway. His research interests include systemic functional theory, social semiotics, and discourse analysis, especially as applied to scientific/medical research, social movements, and human-nonhuman animal relations.

Jason Hannan is Associate Professor in the Department of Rhetoric, Writing, and Communications at the University of Winnipeg. He is the author of *Ethics Under Capital: MacIntyre, Communication, and the Culture Wars* (Bloomsbury, 2020) and editor of *Truth in the Public Sphere* (Lexington, 2016) and *Philosophical Profiles in the Theory of Communication* (Peter Lang, 2012). His current book project is *Trolling*

Ourselves to Death: Democracy in the Age of Social Media (under contract with Oxford University Press).

Anita Krajnc is co-founder of Toronto Pig Save and the global Animal Save Movement. The groups bear witness to animals at slaughterhouses using love-based community organizing. In 2019, Animal Save Movement expanded to include Youth Climate Save, Climate Save and Health Save movements, moving the group's focus beyond vigils to strategic and intersectional campaigns. Dr Krajnc has taught university courses on social movement strategies and is a follower of Leo Tolstoy and Gandhi's philosophy of love and nonviolence.

Saara Kupsala completed her PhD at the University of Eastern Finland. Her research concerns human–animal relations from a sociological perspective. Her PhD thesis examined Finnish attitudes and perceptions regarding animals used in food production. Her postdoctoral research at the University of Helsinki has concerned institutional catering, climate sustainability, and plant-based foods. She has also studied the marketing strategies of the Finnish meat industry. Dr. Kupsala's articles have appeared in journals such as *Food, Culture & Society*, *Society & Animals* and *Journal of Agricultural and Environmental Ethics*.

Margaret Robinson is a Tier 2 Canada Research Chair in Reconciliation, Gender, and Identity. She is is Assistant Professor at Dalhousie University, cross-appointed to the Departments of English and of Sociology and Social Anthropology. She holds a PhD from the University of Toronto. Dr Robinson is a feminist scholar from Eskikewa'kik, Nova Scotia and a member of Lennox Island First Nation. She leads community-based research work on sexual and gender minority health, substance use, and is passionate about Indigenous and queer cultural supports for wellness. Dr Robinson is an Affiliate Scientist at the Centre for Addiction & Mental Health in Toronto, where she conducted her postdoctoral training, supervised by Dr Lori Ross and Dr Janet Smylie.

Norie Ross Singer is Professor in the Department of Communication at Saginaw Valley State University. Singer has previously published essays on the discourses surrounding food and agriculture system transformation, environmental movements, nonhuman animal advocacy, and intersectional justice for the oppressed. Dr Singer's interest in these issues partly stems from his upbringing on an intergenerational family farm in the American Midwest. He is the lead author of *Rooted Resistance: Agrarian Myth in Modern America* (University of Arkansas Press, forthcoming).

Kelsey Speakman is a PhD candidate in Communication and Culture at York University. Her research interests include: political ecologies of food provisioning and marketing, the ethics and social practices of shopping and food consumption, and human-nonhuman interactions in consumer culture. Her recent work includes publications and presentations on meat marketing, alternative proteins, and new trends in grocery shopping. Her current research explores communication practices surrounding beef in contemporary Canadian supermarkets.

Gonzalo Villanueva is an academic and professional historian. He received his PhD in history at the University of Melbourne. He is the author of *A Transnational History of the Australian Animal Movement, 1970–2015* (Palgrave, 2018). He has published peer-reviewed articles in *Sophia: International Journal of Philosophy and Traditions, History Australia,* and *Australian Journal of Politics & History.*

Eliza Waters completed a Bachelor of Arts with Honours in Politics & International Studies and French at the University of Melbourne in 2015. She is currently a Juris Doctor candidate at the University of Melbourne and is working as a research assistant. In 2019, she was Animal Issues in the Law Officer within the Melbourne University Law Students' Society Environment Portfolio.

Barb Willard is Associate Professor in the College of Communication at DePaul University. Her research focuses on environmental communication with an emphasis on agricultural rhetoric that informs and shapes US cultural eating practices that have a significant impact on sustainability. She explores the conceptual and symbolic tension between meat-based and plant-based diets. She has published in a variety of journals including *Environmental Communication, Rhetoric Society Quarterly, and the Journal of Popular Culture.*

Index

abattoirs *see* slaughterhouse
absent referent 231, 239
Academy of Nutrition and Dietetics 209
activism 99, 228–230, 253, 254, 260, 268, 270–275, 280–294; *see also* Animal Save Movement
  as a duty 280–282
  celebrities and 285
  community organising and 276–280
  criminalisation of 80
  mass media coverage and 283
  social media portraits of animals as 282
  undercover investigations as 80, 97
  vigils as a form of 272–275
Adams, Carol J. 33, 125, 231–232, 239
advertising 39, 62, 80, 87, 190, 229, 258
  campaigns 147
AFA Foods 34
agrofuels 106
Alberta Beef Producers 110
Alexis, Nekeisha Alayna 66
Alinsky, Saul 269, 276–277

Amazon rainforest 299, 310
American Farm Bureau Federation 45
American Meat Institute (AMI) *see* North American Meat Institute
ammonia 46–48
ammonium hydroxide 34, 47
Anhang, Jeff 165, 286
animal abuse 60, 66, 138, 220
  and confinement 219, 274, 281, 309
  and mass slaughter 46, 84, 86–87, 93, 97, 220, 227, 252, 257, 281, 283; *see also* slaughterhouse
  and reproduction 220, 223
animal agriculture industry 4–5, 15, 19–24, 166
  climate change and the
  environmental impact of the 22, 135, 148–153, 198
  industry standards of the 4, 80
  international competition and the 82
  marketing/public relations of the xiii, 2, 18, 23, 32, 35, 49–51, 168, 232
  media access to the 80
Animal Liberation Conference 274, 295

Animal Liberation Victoria 275
animal rights 11–14, 21–24, 60, 62, 64,
   81, 144, 166, 213, 215, 227, 248,
   251–253, 268–269, 280, 284,
   287–288, 292, 295
   de-individualisation and 84–86, 92,
      98
   objectification and 84, 85, 98
Animal Save Movement 269–292, 296;
   see also activism
animal welfare 62–64, 71, 73, 80
animal-industrial complex (AIC) *see*
   animal agriculture industry
animals as property/labour 10, 27, 65,
   256
Anonymous for the Voiceless 280, 292
anthropocene 187–188, 255
anthropocentric perspectives 98, 115
antibiotics 43, 218, 309
Araújo, Ernesto 300
Aspey, James 285
astroturfing 23, 37–38, 39, 42, 45,
   48–49
Atria 87, 91–91, 95, 96, 97
Atwater, Wilbur 140
Aune, James Arnt 50
Australia 26, 187–203, 260, 270, 273,
   275
Australia in the Asian Century white
   paper 194
Australian Live Exporters' Council 200

Backus, Susan 156
Baker, Susan 203
Baldwin, Andrew 114
Bauman, Zygmunt 85
BEEF Magazine 302
Beef Products Incorporated (BPI) 32,
   33, 35, 39, 40, 41, 44, 47, 50
BeefFacts 40

beef xiv, 8, 23–25, 31–35, 39–52, 70, 95,
   103–126, 136, 143–147, 151, 188,
   195, 198, 200, 212, 301–303,
   306–307, 309–310
   Kobe beef 52
Belcourt, Billy-Ray 191
Bez, Alex 288
biodiversity 16, 148, 149, 149, 158, 203,
   299
biomedical 11, 17, 18
bison 116, 125–126
Bite Size Vegan 285
blogging 88, 90, 95
Bolsonaro, Jair 300
bolt gun 2–3
Booren, Betsy 155
bovine spongiform encephalopathy
   (BSE) 32, 32, 52, 106, 110
Brandt, Paul 118
Brazil 8, 150, 154, 188, 288, 300–303;
   see also Amazon rainforest
Briggs Jr, Konju 238
Broad, Garrett M. 35
Brody, Jane 215–217
Bronfenbrenner, Kate 278
Brophy, Brigid 12
   The rights of animals 12
Brown, Wendy 38
Bsumek, Peter K. 36
Bull, John 70
Burwell, Sylvia 153–154, 156

Callegari, Frederico 283
Calvo, Erika 190
Cameron, Laura 114
Campbell, T. Colin 17–18
Canada xiv, 3, 103–126, 215, 222, 242,
   244, 260, 267, 270, 287
   Alberta 107, 110, 125
   Banff National Park 125

Index

law 4
Saskatchewan 103, 125
Canada Beef 24, 103–105, 108–126
  'Canadian Beef Advantage' 104
Canada–Korea Free Trade Agreement
  (CKFTA) 108
Canada's Seasonal Agricultural
  Workers Program (CSAWP) 119
Canadian Roundtable for Sustainable
  Beef (CRSB) 107
cancer 17–18, 224
  carcinogens 107, 176, 177
capitalism 5–10, 26–26, 82, 105, 192,
  201, 210, 253, 257, 308
carbon emissions 16, 203
Carbstrong, Joey 273, 285
Cargill 35, 39, 41, 50, 295
Cattlemen's Beef Board 40
Center for Consumer Freedom 23, 39,
  42
Change for Animals Foundation 254
Chassenee, Bartholomew 263
cheese 16, 310
Chenoweth, Erica 271
Chicken Run 66
chickens 16, 67, 69, 73–74, 81, 84,
  87–98, 217, 219, 229, 252–253, 256,
  268, 271–283, 288–292
  beak trimming 89
  broiler 24, 73, 80–81, 84, 87, 90–98
  free-range 64, 71, 309
  meat from 292
China 17, 71, 187, 196, 198, 252,
  260–261, 289
  Yulin 260–262
'China Study' 17
Chinese Academy of Preventive
  Medicine 17
Ching, Marc 285
circus animals 13

class consciousness 257
Clemenceau, Cathy 291
Cleveland Clinic, Ohio 17
climate change 14–16, 19, 25, 135, 137,
  142, 150, 156, 157, 163–168, 170,
  173–179, 269, 286, 300–307
Climate Save Movement 269, 283, 286
CLITRAVI (Liaison Centre for the
  Meat Processing Industry in the
  European Union) 168–178
Cole, Jocelyn 288
Cole, Matthew 191, 212
colonialism 26
  postcolonialism 26, 237, 245
  settler 26, 105, 111, 113–114, 117,
    121–122
commodity fetishism 7–9
Comprehensive Economic and Trade
  Agreement (CETA) 108
Concentrated Animal Feeding
  Operations (CAFO) 278
concentration camps 65
conspicuous consumption 26, 196,
  308–309
Cooren, Francois 36
COP21 Paris 166
Cornell University 17
coronary artery disease (CAD) 18; *see
  also* heart disease
corporate responsibility 80
corporate transparency 82–83
corporate ventriloquism 23, 36, 49–52
Couldry, Nick 38
Council of Ethics in Advertising, The
  (Finland) 88
Country of Origin Labelling (COOL)
  108
cowboys 110, 117–120, 125

cows xiii, 45, 81, 114, 219, 229,
248–249, 252–253, 256–257,
262–263, 268–276, 284, 289–292
dairy 13, 15, 59, 71, 79, 81, 109,
138–149, 153, 156–158, 169, 178,
193, 195, 212, 219, 238, 268, 289,
310
feeding of 115, 291
forced impregnation 220
meat from *see* beef
milking of 220
mad cow disease *see* bovine
spongiform encephalopathy (BSE)
ranching of xiii, xiv, 24, 103–104,
114–126, 126, 289, 300–301, 301
Cox, J. Robert 38
Creutzfeldt-Jakob disease (CJD) *see*
bovine spongiform encephalopathy
(BSE)
Cross, Russell 40
CTV (Canada) 4

Dalai Lama 247
Dalziell, Jacqueline 201
Davis, Amy Jean 272–273, 285
Davis, Garth 18
Davis, Karen 213
Dead Animal Removal Program 258
deforestation 16, 106, 165, 192, 203,
300–303; *see* land clearing
denialism 19
developing nations 189, 192
development theory 201
diabetes 17, 140–141, 217, 224, 239
Direct Action Everywhere (DxE)
292–295
'diseases of affluence' 141
division 173, 251–252
human vs non-human animal 212
vegan vs non-vegan 226

Dog Tales Rescue and Sanctuary 281
dogs 209, 230, 252–264, 275
trade in meat from 252–254
Yulin Dog Meat Festival 260
DuPuis, Melanie 43

Earls (restaurant chain) 107
economy 5, 43, 126, 138, 166, 190
global 14, 106
local 2
Edmonds, Michael 196
Egen, Shivonne Kaspara 292
eggs xiii, 9–11, 13, 23, 23, 59, 62–65,
69–71, 73, 141, 143, 145, 216, 219,
220, 223, 268
electric prod 2, 4, 268
elitism xiii, 171
Elliott, Charlene 109
Ellis, Colter 115, 120
Elora, Ananda 288
emotional labour 257–258, 263
Escobar, Arturo 193
Esselstyn, Caldwell 17
ethical behaviour 4, 24, 63–67, 82, 200,
209–211, 215–221, 228–229, 252,
254
legally conferred
ethical consumerism 24, 62–64
European Commission 171–173
European Free Trade Association
(EFTA) 169
European Union 151, 171
Common Agricultural Policy (CAP)
169, 179
Transparency Register 169–171
Extinction Rebellion 287

Facebook *see* social media
farming 1–2, 5, 9, 11, 16, 24, 63, 66, 72,
79–84, 91–92, 96, 110, 136, 227, 240,

278, 295, 302–309; *see also* animal
  agriculture industry
and farmers 10, 24, 62–68, 72, 81–82,
  87, 89, 91–92, 96, 115–121, 123,
  282, 303–305, 310
  depictions 118, 120
fast food xiv, 5–6, 31, 34
Fearmans Pork Inc. 272, 275
Federation of Indian Animal
  Protection Organizations 291
feminism 19, 95, 105, 255
  eco-feminism 26, 237, 240, 243, 245
Fiddes, Nick 189, 202
film 14, 60, 62–74, 217, 219
Finland 24, 80–81, 87–88, 95
Finney, Wray 141
Finucan, Michael 197
fishing 27, 164, 239–242, 244, 270, 274,
  287
Fitzgerald, Amy J. 190
food groups
  Basic Four 141, 144
  Food Guide Pyramid 144–147
food hygiene 198
food security 136, 149–158, 177, 199
Forks over knives 18
fossil fuel industry 15, 18
fox hunting 12
Franklin, Adrian 191
Free Korean Dogs 254
free market rhetoric 45
Freeman, Carrie P. 213
Friendship, Robert 4
fur industry 10, 13, 71, 240

Gandhi, Mahatma 269, 276
Garner, Andrew 275
gaslighting 247
gender dynamic 21

Germany 150, 154, 196, 270–271, 291,
  294
Gibbs, Lois 269, 277
Gitlin, Todd 304
Glenn, Cathy B. 35, 39
globalisation 46, 109, 268
Godlovitch, Stanley and Roslind 12
  Animals, men and morals 13
Goodland, Robert 286
Gore, Al 167
  An Inconvenient Sequel 167
Gorsevski, Ellen W. 35, 39, 50
Greene, Joel L. 34
Greener Pastures Animal Sanctuary
  281
greenhouse gas emissions 15, 106, 148,
  163–165, 198, 286, 304–307
greenwashing 23, 37–39, 44–50, 96,
  179, 191, 197, 203
Greger, Michael 18
Greig, Edvard 23, 59, 70
Grill, Gary 284
Guthman, Julie 43

hamburgers xiv, 6, 8, 34, 45–46, 262
Harari, Yuval Noah 188
Haraway, Donna 27, 251, 254, 256, 259,
  264
Harkins, Katie 282
Harrison, Ruth 12
  Animal machines 191
Hauter, Wenonah 51
heart disease 17–18, 142–143, 146, 224;
  see also coronary artery disease
  (CAD)
Helvarg, David 45
holistic management model (of
  agriculture) 305–307
Hollas, Lauren 273
Honduras 289

hormones 43, 309
hotdogs 8
Hribal, Jason 9–10, 65, 256
Hughes, David 199
human exceptionalism 251–254
Hunt Saboteurs Association 12
Hunter, Robert 237
hunting 12, 27, 232, 239–245, 309

Ibsen, Henrik 71
India 187–188, 199, 271, 292
Indigenous peoples xiii, 116–117, 121,
    125; see also Mi'kmaq First Nations
    people
Indonesia 200
industrialisation 67, 197–198
Instagram 88, 91, 248, 252, 254, 255,
    258, 263, 282, 286, 299
Instone, L. 259
Ivey, Adrienne 103, 125

Jehnsen, David 296
journalism 26, 32, 33, 157, 179, 213,
    215, 228, 233
Joy, Melanie 18

Kafka, Franz 4
Kenny, Jeannie 146
Klein, Naomi 166
Knöbl, Wolfgang 194
Ko, Aph and Syl 66
Kobayashi, Audrey 114

labour 6–10, 86, 119–119, 251,
    255–265, 271, 275, 278–279, 287; see
    also animals as property/labour
lamb 151, 188, 198, 200, 281
land clearing 192; see also deforestation
Lander, Christian 237
lateral appropriation 23, 37–39, 45, 49

Lawrence, Bonita 238
laws 4, 12, 27, 32–36, 108, 116, 178,
    253, 258, 284
    ag-gag laws 14, 32
    food libel laws 32
lean finely textured beef (LFTB) 31–32,
    34–52
leather 9, 10, 13, 290
legislation 81, 171
    Federal Meat Inspection Act 12
    Pure Food Act 12
Lemke, Jay L. 60
Lerner, Daniel 192
Leysner, Ruth 292
LFTB see lean finely textured beef
    (LFTB)
Linley Valley Pork – Craig Mauston
    Group 273, 280
live exports 201, 274
Livestock's Long Shadow report 16, 148,
    163, 168, 173
lobby groups 19, 170
Louise, Miss Tina 286

MacIntyre, Alasdair 311
mad cow disease see bovine
    spongiform encephalopathy (BSE)
Madigan, Edward 145
Manitoba Pork 1, 5
mansplaining 19, 21, 105, 259
Maple Leaf Poultry 273
market-based society 6–7
Marocho, Karol 288, 290–292
Marshall, Murdena 243
Marx, Karl 5–11
Marxism 5, 11, 257, 300
masculinity and meat consumption xiv,
    22, 26, 190, 224, 232
mass extinction 16
McCready, Wayne 109

Index

McGovern, George 141
  Dietary Goals for the United States
    142–143
meat, as a concept removed from the
  animal 231, 239
Meat & Livestock Australia (MLA) 195
  Red Obsession 197
media coverage 26, 163, 231, 274, 282,
  290, 299
  bias 26, 234
Melo, Taty 288
Mercy for Animals 2, 13
middle classes 195–196, 202
Middle East, the 26, 188, 192, 194–197,
  200, 202
migration xiii, 12, 24, 88, 119, 126
Mi'kmaq First Nations people 26; *see
  also* Indigenous peoples
Mills, Milton 18
modernisation 26, 189, 192–204
Monk, Ray 16
Moor, Liz 109
moral distancing 84
moral-market 38–39, 41, 43, 46, 49–50
Morgan, Karen 212
Motto, Bruce 289
Mozart, Wolfgang Amadeus 72
multiculturalism 122, 124
Muza, Pragya and Darshana 292
mystery meat 31

National Cattlemen's Beef Association
  (US) 40, 45, 136, 141, 143, 146
National Farmers' Federation
  (Australia) 199
National Milk Producers Federation
  (US) 145–146
nationalism 24–24, 61, 110, 117, 253
  nation branding 109–110
Nazis 65

Nemecek, Thomas 158
neoconservatism 38, 43, 45
neoliberalism 37–38, 43, 47
  free trade 37, 108, 151, 169
neoprimitivism 307, 310
Nestle, Marion 137
Newkirk, Ingrid 13
Newmarket Meat Packers 281
Nibert, David 211
Noelle, Mariah 288
Non Government Organisations
  (NGOs) 167, 300
Nordberg, Maria 306
North American Meat Institute 39, 136,
  145, 155
  MeatSafety.org 41, 44
Norton, Ann 38
Norway 62, 70–71, 270, 292

Oikeutta Eläimille 81
Oliver, Jamie 31
Olmsted, Larry 52
O'Neill, Julie 291
oppression xiii–xv, 6, 11, 66–67, 96,
  124, 211–212, 216, 238, 264
organic 23, 59, 63–64, 69, 71, 93, 106,
  249, 304, 306, 308, 309
Ouwehand, Esther 286
Oxford University 17, 307

Paris climate agreement 14
patriarchy 190, 239
Paula, Maria 290
Peeples, Jennifer 36
People for the Ethical Treatment of
  Animals (PETA) 13, 66, 166, 284
Pester, Ali 284
Phoenix, Joaquin 285
Pig Save *see* Animal Save Movement;
  see also Toronto Pig Save

pigs xiii–xiv, 2–5, 8, 27, 252–253, 256–257, 262–264, 267–287
  castration 2–3
  euthanising of 4
  gestation crates and 2–3
  meat of *see* pork
  tail removal from 2
'pink slime' *see* lean finely textured beef (LFTB)
political economics 5, 11, 32, 104–105
Pollan, Michael 13, 157
Poore, Joseph 158–158
Popkin, Barry M. 193
pork xiv, 1, 5, 8–9, 151, 154, 155, 188
Potter, Andrew 307–309
Potts, Annie 33, 67, 190
poverty 199–199, 238
Prestige, John 12
privatisation/private sector 37, 44, 45, 200
protest 38, 145, 151, 189, 215, 227–231, 260, 274, 278
Purcell, Natalie 257
Pyne, Stephen 301
pyrocene 301, 310

Quality Meat Packers 267, 272

racism xiii, 119, 253
Rampton, Sheldon 46
Red Meat Advisory Council (Australia) 199
Regan, Jen 273, 285
Rifkin, Jeremy 202
Riley, Janet M. 39
Rist, Gilbert 193
Rome Declaration on Nutrition 149
Roosevelt, Theodore 12
Rostow, Walt 192
Roth, Eldon 42

Ruskin, John 276
Ryder, Richard 12

Sachs, Wolfgang 193
Saha, Jonathan 192
salmonella 67, 70
Santuro, Alicia 280
sausage making 8
Savory, Allan 305–306
Schneider, Jen 36–37, 49, 50
school lunches 31, 34, 46
Schwarze, Steve 36
sheep 188, 190, 268, 274, 276, 281
  exports 188, 274
  meat from 196, 276; *see also* lamb
Silver, James 284
Sinclair, Upton 12
  The Jungle 12
Singer, Peter 13
  Animal Liberation 13
slaughterhouse xiii–xv, 21, 24, 80–81, 84–87, 90–97, 169, 191, 223, 257–258, 267–296
slavery
  of animals 65, 219
  of people 9, 65, 256
social hieroglyphic 7
social media 13, 24, 27, 60, 73, 79, 87–88, 95, 97–98, 123, 255, 271–274, 282–285, 292, 299, 302
  blogging/bloggers 24, 80, 83–98, 156, 302
  Facebook 23, 62, 70–73, 88, 91, 231, 283–284, 299
  sponsored posts 74
  trolling 21, 70, 310
  Twitter 103, 231, 299
Solari, Liz 282
Solnit, Rebecca 19, 259
soy 301

speciesism xiii, 11, 12, 26, 209,
212–215, 227, 230, 283
spirituality 238, 240, 308
stance 50, 60, 96, 177
Stauber, John C. 46
steroids 43
strawman arguments 219
Stuart, Tristram 70
Sullivan, Louis W. 144
superexploited commodities 10
sustainable diets 149–152, 155
Sustainable Diets and Biodiversity 149
Sweden 150, 274, 294
Swedish Food Agency 151
Sweeney, J. 259

Taylor, Drew Hayden 237
Taylor, Nik 190
Thunberg, Greta 272
tobacco 25, 168, 174, 179
Todd, Anne Marie 50
Tolstoy, Leo 267, 269, 276
Tönnies slaughterhouse 275
Toronto Pig Save 253, 267–269, 272,
275, 283–287; *see also* Animal Save
Movement
The Pig Trial 269–271, 284, 287
Torres, Bob 5–6, 9, 10, 65
Transatlantic Trade and Investment
Partnership (TTIP) 170
Travers, Kim 239
'trope of uncertainty' 143
tropical diseases 14
Trump, Donald 158, 286
Tuck, Eve 126
Twine, Richard 104, 111, 190
Twitter *see* social media

UECBV (European Livestock and Meat
Trades Union) 168–174, 178

United Nations 14–15, 148, 153, 163,
166
Environmental Program (UNEP) 153
Food and Agriculture Organization
(FAO) 16, 148–149, 153, 154, 163,
168, 173–175, 286; *see also*
Livestock's Long Shadow report
Framework Convention on Climate
Change (UNFCCC) 166
Intergovernmental Panel on Climate
Change (IPCC) 14–15, 142, 165
United States 21, 31, 52, 108, 139, 157,
252, 258, 260, 278, 288
2015 Dietary Guidelines 136–138
Department of Agriculture (USDA)
31, 34, 46, 136, 140–141, 143–144,
146–148, 152–157
Department of Health and Human
Services 143, 147
Dietary Guidelines Advisory
Committee (DGAC) 136, 151–156
Duplin County 278
Environmental Protection Agency
158
National School Lunch Program 137
trading with the 108
Women, Infants, and Children
Program 137
urbanisation 195, 202

value 1, 3, 6–14, 35–46, 49, 61, 65,
95–96, 105–106, 109–113, 118, 120,
122, 126, 189, 191, 194–196,
209–210, 232, 243–245
exchange 6–9
of animals
surplus 9–9
use 6, 9
Veblen, Thorsten 308

veganism 14–18, 21–23, 26–26, 68–70,
    177–178, 209–221, 227, 230,
    233–234, 237–245
  Indigenous 26, 243
  negative depictions of 23, 210, 223
  philosophy of 210, 233
vegetarianism 16, 177, 219–221
VegFests 270–271, 288
Vilsack, Tom 136, 153–156
vivisection 13, 25, 168, 174, 176–179
Voicot 290

Wadiwel, Dinesh 201
Wasser, Carrie 303
Weis, Tony 193

'western diet' 17, 135, 193, 203, 238
What the Health documentry 216–219
Wilson, Gary 146
Winfrey, Oprah 32, 51
Winnipeg 1
working class 9–10, 65, 256
World Health Organization (WHO)
    107, 149, 171

Yang, K. Wayne 126
Yoquinto, Luke 44

Zaraska, Marta 219–225
Zontek, Ken 125